SOUTHERN WHITE MINISTERS
AND THE CIVIL RIGHTS MOVEMENT

SOUTHERN WHITE MINISTERS

AND THE

CIVIL RIGHTS MOVEMENT

Elaine Allen Lechtreck

University Press of Mississippi / Jackson

www.upress.state.ms.us

The University Press of Mississippi is a member of
the Association of University Presses.

First printing 2018

∞

Library of Congress Cataloging-in-Publication Data

Names: Lechtreck, Elaine Allen, author.
Title: Southern white ministers and the civil rights movement / Elaine Allen
Lechtreck.
Description: Jackson : University Press of Mississippi, [2018] | Includes
bibliographical references and index. |
Identifiers: LCCN 2017054274 (print) | LCCN 2018002201 (ebook) | ISBN
9781496817549 (epub single) | ISBN 9781496817556 (epub institutional) |
ISBN 9781496817563 (pdf single) | ISBN 9781496817570 (pdf institutional)
| ISBN 9781496817525 (hardcover : alk. paper) | ISBN 9781496817532 (pbk. :
alk. paper)
Subjects: LCSH: Clergy—Attitudes. | Race relations—Religious
aspects—Christianity. | Church and social problems. | Church work with
African Americans. | Clergy—Political activity—United States—20th
century. | Civil rights—Religious aspects—Christianity—History—20th
century. | African Americans—Civil rights—History—20th century. | Civil
rights movements—United States—History—20th century. | Civil rights
movements—Southern States—Religious aspects—History. | United
States—History—20th century.
Classification: LCC E185.61 (ebook) | LCC E185.61 .L469 2018 (print) | DDC
261.7—dc23
LC record available at https://lccn.loc.gov/2017054274

British Library Cataloging-in-Publication Data available

CONTENTS

ACKNOWLEDGMENTS

I am not a southerner but I came to love the South, the warmth of its people, the slower pace of life, the live oak trees, the lush pine and hickory forests, the underground springs and caves, the stately old mansions with colonnaded porches—I longed to be part of the habitat. In 1991 I moved to Alabama when I married Roy Lechtreck, a professor at the University of Montevallo. I then began doctoral studies in US history at the Union Institute of Cincinnati, Ohio; an internship at the Department of Archives and Manuscripts at the Birmingham Public Library; and a search for a research topic. I consulted Marvin Yeomans Whiting, head of the Department of Archives and supervisor of my internship. I told him of my interest in finding stories of southern ministers who preached for racial justice during the 1950s and 1960s. I asked him if he knew of any of these ministers. He replied, "I am one." He told me his story, and I knew my life's work had begun.

Whiting (1934–2010), a Georgia native, was assigned to two small Methodist churches in rural southwest Georgia after his graduation from the Candler School of Theology at Emory University in 1959. When the wife of one of his parishioners claimed that a black man approached her with sexual advances, the husband and his friends responded by tying the accused to the end of a pickup truck and dragging him across the countryside until he was "a bloody mess" and died. As part of a sermon, Whiting condemned the lynching, but nothing was done to apprehend the murderers. Instead, Whiting was suddenly called before the officers of the church and asked to resign with the approval of the bishop: "In the South there was a culture of silence before and after the Civil War, especially within the churches. It was forbidden to speak of racial crimes."[1]

Whiting then decided that he was better suited to an academic career. He left the ministry and continued his education, earning a master's degree, cum laude, in history from Emory University; a PhD in American religious history from Columbia University; and another master's degree in librarianship from Emory University. He then embarked on a long career as director of Archives for the Birmingham Public Library, curator of the Birmingham/Jefferson County History Museum, professor of American history at Birmingham Southern University, and author of many books and scholarly articles.[2]

During the late 1970s, while serving on the board of the Birmingham Historical Society, he worked to establish the Birmingham Civil Rights Institute and became one of its founding fathers. He commented, "I am proud of what is there and what it says as a voice for Birmingham."[3] At last Whiting was able to do something for racial justice. He is commemorated by a plaque at the institute's entrance. Whiting led me to many of the ministers whose stories are included in this book.

Another person to whom I am indebted is Arkansas poet and professor emeritus of English at the University of Arkansas, Miller Williams. When Williams told me about his father, Rev. E. B. Williams (1894–1968) of the Northeast Arkansas Methodist Conference, I knew I had another story that needed to be told. Rev. Williams began his civil rights activism during the 1930s when he established a branch of the fledgling and short-lived Southern Tenant Farmers' Union (STFU) in the basement of his church in Hoxie, Arkansas. The STFU was interracial and constantly under attack as a subversive Communist organization in defiance of local laws. The local authorities could not see that the meeting was being held because there were no windows in the basement of the church. If they could see what was going on, Rev. Williams and all involved would have been arrested.[4]

During the 1940s, long before the civil rights movement, E. B. Williams insisted on open seating in his churches; he established interracial youth groups, preached for the equality of women, and taught his children never to use the "n" word. On one occasion in Fort Smith, he was called out of his house in the middle of the night by a man with a rifle. As Miller Williams relates, "My father went out because he thought the man was calling for help. When my mother realized he was in trouble, she joined him. The man with the rifle forced both of them to lie face down on the front porch and threatened to kill them. Gradually, my father managed to establish a dialogue with the man. As the man began to sober up, he backed off and disappeared. . . . My father probably told him there were different ways of looking at situations." Miller Williams commented, "People at those critical times feared that their way of life was disappearing. . . . They became members of the Nightriders, the Ku Klux Klan, and later the White Citizens' Councils and White America, Inc., because they feared change."[5]

In 1957 E. B. Williams, age sixty-three, then pastor of Gardner Memorial Methodist Church in North Little Rock, protested the action of Governor Orval Faubus when the governor ordered a barricade to keep nine black students from entering Central High School in Little Rock. E. B. Williams preached, "If God is for us, who can be against us?" He urged his people to forget striking out against black neighbors and to go forth and proclaim the good words of the Bible, "You shall love your neighbor as yourself." The sermon was reported in major media around the country by a popular news commentator, Drew Pearson.[6]

Miller Williams added, "People were always leaving my father's churches," and the family of six children was forced to move again and again, but Williams hoped that his father would be remembered with love and gratitude: "There were many ministers and laypeople who did more and braver work than will ever be known." E. B. Williams may have regretted that he could not do more to bring about a peaceful transition to school desegregation in Little Rock, but he left a mindful imperative for his children:

> We, your parents, have lived our lives and mistakes we have made, so we pass our deepest desires on to you, namely that you work for the elimination of injustice and needless suffering for all peoples everywhere. If you will do this, we know the satisfaction that will be yours will be ample reward, and as you pass this passion on to your children, none of us will have lived in vain.[7]

E. B. Williams was able to make incremental changes within southern society in a quiet, modest way and within the structure of his church. I am grateful to his son for sharing his father's story. Over the years Miller Williams has encouraged me to find more such stories and never to give up in my search.

◆ ◆ ◆

I acknowledge the help I have received from the ministers and members of their families who have shared with me their hearts, emotions, and inner thoughts. I am especially grateful to Bishop H. George Anderson, Dallas and Glenda Blanchard, Helen Brabham, Bettie Jones Bradford, Lauren Brubaker, G. McLeod Bryan, Thomas Butts, Will Campbell, Donald E. Collins, Raymond and Rachel Davis, George and Jean Edwards, Joseph Ellwanger, Floyd Enfinger, W. W. and Mary Lib Finlator, W. W. Finlator Jr., William Kirk Floyd, Robert Graetz, Ruth and Bishop Duncan Montgomery Gray, Powell Hall, C. G. Haugabook, Dorise Turner Haynes, Robert L. Hock, Edgar Homrighausen, Larry Jackson, Rhett and Betty Jackson, Edwin King, John Lyles, Howard and Barbara McClain, Margy McClain, Nate McMillan, Frank McRae, Robert D. Miller, Thomas Moffett, David and Judy Moose, John and Wright Morris, Ralph and Jane Murray, Denson and Jean Napier, Dunbar Ogden III, Alvin Price, Brooks Ramsey, Fred and Dorothy Reese, Joseph Rice, Sherrard Rice, Joseph Sanderson, Gilbert Schroerlucke, Roberta and W. B. Selah Jr., Ennis Sellers, Robert Seymour, James H. and Elizabeth Smylie, Eben Taylor, Randolph and Arline Taylor, Keith Tonkel, Grayson Tucker, Andrew Spencer Turnipseed, Arnold Voigt, Al

Webster, Charles Webster, Marvin Whiting, Matthew Whiting, Patterson Cousins Wolfe, H. Davis Yeuell, and others who have helped me locate ministers and their relatives: Paula Crosson, Stephen M. Fox, Tom Gholson, Will B. Graveley, Flynn T. Harrell, Ed and Normanda Huffman, Darwin Keichline, Elizabeth Motherwell, Dale and Deborah Pauls, James Pitts, Sylvia Smith, Lot Therrio, Mary Thies, Gavin Wright, and Richard O. Ziehr.

Special thanks to Rev. James H. Smylie, professor emeritus of church history at the Union Theological Seminary in Richmond, Virginia, who mentored me through version after version of my manuscript and appreciated everything I ever wrote. I also have special gratitude to the late Dallas Blanchard, member of the Alabama–West Florida Methodist Conference, professor emeritus at the University of West Florida, polite radical, pastor, sociologist, teacher *extraordinaire*, who inserted many corrections and made me laugh and smile at his vibrant southern humor: "Armadillos sleep in the middle of the road in Alabama with their feet in the air"; "Fire ants in Alabama consider your flesh a picnic"; and "Anthropological studies analyzing DNA samples from groups surrounding the globe have determined that no single person on earth is no more distantly related to anyone else on earth than 32nd cousin. . . . The State of Alabama had a law (which may still be on the books) that any person in Alabama with 1/32 Negroid ancestry was legally black; *ergo, every individual in the State of Alabama should have been defined as black.*"

Academic advisers Stanford J. Searl Jr., Susan D. Amussen, and the late Marjory Bell Chambers of the Union Institute were always encouraging, helpful, and patient. I have special thanks to James Baggett of the Department of Archives and Manuscripts at the Birmingham Public Library in Alabama, where I served as an intern.

I thank all the archivists who helped: Jeri Abbot and Amanda Moore of Koinonia Farm, Americus, Georgia; Yvonne Arnold and Toby Graham of the McCain Library at the University of Southern Mississippi, Hattiesburg; Lauren Auttonberry of the Diocese of Mississippi; Robert L. Beamer of the Washington Street United Methodist Church, Columbia, South Carolina; Kathy Bennett of the Nashville Public Library, Nashville, Tennessee; William Bynum and Ginny Daley of the Presbyterian Archives, Montreat, North Carolina; Megan Crummitt of the South Carolina Christian Action Council, Columbia, South Carolina; Tricia Gesner of the Associated Press, New York City; Nicholas Graham, Jason Tomberline, and Matthew Turi of the North Carolina Collection at the University of North Carolina, Chapel Hill; Christian Higgins, Steve Lucht, and Christopher Ann Paton of the Episcopal Archives, Austin, Texas; T. Raleigh Mann of the Mercer University Archives, Macon, Georgia; Deborah McIntosh of the Millsaps College Archives, Jackson, Mississippi; Harry Miller of the Wisconsin Historical Society, Madison; Charlene

Peacock and Natalie Shilstut of the Presbyterian Historical Society, Philadelphia, Pennsylvania; Sally Polhemus of the Knoxville Library, Knoxville, Tennessee; Kristina Polizzi of the McCall Library, Mobile, Alabama; Edwena Seals of Toulminville–Warren Street United Methodist Church, Toulminville, Alabama; David Spence of the Warren County Memorial Library, Warrenton, North Carolina; Sharon Tucker of Huntingdon College, Montgomery, Alabama; and others who are not named.

I am ever grateful to Craig Gill, director of the University Press of Mississippi, who always appreciated my work; to the anonymous reviewers who gave valuable criticism; and to my late husband, Roy Lechtreck, professor emeritus at the University of Montevallo in Alabama, who spent long hours and many years driving me throughout the South for interviews and archival research. Without his help the book could never have been written.

SOUTHERN WHITE MINISTERS AND THE CIVIL RIGHTS MOVEMENT

INTRODUCTION

In every city, small town, and hamlet, and on every country road across the South, there may be as many as two dozen churches representing different Christian denominations and sects. Some buildings are no larger than a cottage; some are grand with tall steeples; some are African American; and some represent small, independent evangelical communities. A few congregations are integrated. In every church, ministers are preaching from the Bible, but not all the preachments are the same, and they were not the same during the civil rights movement, although in some instances ministers who supported segregation and those who opposed segregation chose the same Bible verses.

At that time some ministers preached that "the cross of Christ has nothing to do with social movements or realities beyond the church; it's a matter of individual salvation."[1] Others said: "Jesus never intended the mixing of races; his message was for his own people, the Jews; the disciples were told emphatically, 'Go nowhere among the Gentiles, and enter no town of the Samaritans, but go rather to the lost sheep of the house of Israel'";[2] or "God has never set aside His decree concerning the three sons of Noah and their descendants, but has taught that segregation of the races was and is His desire and plan;"[3] or "Segregation of the races is a divine law and must be obeyed, or we suffer, as the many mongrelized nations are proving today."[4] One prominent clergyman maintained that the verse "God made from one every nation of men to live on all the face of the earth, having determined allotted periods and the boundaries of their habitation," to be a direct decree for segregation.[5] This minister feared that tampering with that order would destroy the purity of each race. A more moderate minister gave another interpretation: "Do not fear mongrelization. We must teach our young people how to intermingle without thinking of marriage.... Purity of the race is a principle of great importance to the Negro as well as to the whites."[6] Segregationists believed that separation had nothing to do with love. They could love their black neighbors as long as their black neighbors remained in "their place." They could give poor black people their old textbooks, their old clothes, their old automobiles, their left-over food, as long as blacks did not agitate for improved educational opportunities, open public facilities, voting rights, or better jobs and wages.

The ministers who opposed segregation preached from the prophet Isaiah that all people who held fast to God's covenant would be accepted at his altar,

and from the prophet Amos, "Let justice roll on like a river and righteousness like a never failing stream";[7] or "Segregation is immoral because it violates
each of the Ten Commandments."[8] Another minister advised that white people must sound a trumpet against oppression as did the prophets of old when
they denounced policies that were unrighteous, as Jeremiah did before many
kings, "as Samuel did before Saul, as Nathan before David, as Elijah before
Ahab, as John the Baptist before Herod . . . and . . . Martin Niemoeller before
Hitler. . . . The church is never more true to its nature," he proclaimed, "than
when it tries to make the voice of the Eternal heard in all the affairs of men."[9]
Some preached on verses from the Letter of Paul to the Galatians: "There is
neither Jew nor Greek, slave nor free, male nor female; for you are all one in
Christ Jesus; For the whole law is fulfilled in a single command, 'Love your
neighbor as yourself.' But if you bite and devour one another take heed that
you are not consumed by one another,"[10] and 1 John: "He who hates his brother
is in the darkness and walks in the darkness."[11] "No one has ever seen God; but
if we love one another, God lives in us and his love is made complete in us."[12]
Some preached from Paul's Letter to the Hebrews, "Let us run with perseverance the race that is set before us, looking to Jesus the pioneer and perfecter
of our faith," and, most sacred of all, Jesus's message to the Pharisees: "You
shall love the Lord your God with all your heart, and with all your soul, and
with all your mind. This is the great and first commandment. And a second is
like it. You shall love your neighbor as yourself. On these two commandments
depend all the law and the prophets."[13]

These courageous ministers came from the states of the "Old Confederacy": Alabama, Arkansas, Georgia, Kentucky, Mississippi, North Carolina,
South Carolina, and Tennessee, where the cultural milieu was to keep African American people separated from the rest of the society. Reduced generally to menial and servile positions, African Americans were on their own to
fend for themselves and make the best of life in their restricted environment.
All aspects of society were segregated, from public transportation and waiting rooms to schools, libraries, churches, hospitals, restaurants, hotels, water
fountains, movie theaters, parks, swimming pools, public lavatories, drinking
fountains, sports teams, luncheon counters, sidewalks, taxicabs, Laundromats,
and even graveyards. This was the world into which these southern white ministers were born.

The use of the term "minister" must be explained. The term refers to any
individual who has been duly authorized or licensed by a church to preach
the gospel and administer the sacraments. A pastor is a minister who has
been assigned to lead a congregation. Some ordained ministers in this narrative were pastors for only brief periods of time and some not at all, but their
ordinations were for life. The ministers mentioned in this study were almost

all men, but times were changing in the Protestant world. In 1965 the Reverend Rachel Henderlite became the first woman ordained in the Presbyterian Church in the United States (PCUS), the southern church. Although she was ordained, she never became a pastor, but continued her role as a professor and director of curriculum development for the PCUS Board of Christian Education in Richmond, Virginia. In 1967 Henderlite left her post to teach at an all-black Presbyterian seminary. She will be mentioned for her participation in the Selma to Montgomery march in 1965.[14]

In the aftermath of World War II, the United States had become the most prosperous nation in the world, but its intense rivalry with the Soviet Union, the expansion of Communism in the Eastern Hemisphere, and the proliferation of nuclear weapons led to a paranoia unparalleled in US history. Civil rights activists were considered to be part of a Communist plot to overtake the world. White southern ministers (and northern ones) who supported desegregation were caught in a web of suspicion that prompted twenty-eight young Methodist ministers in Mississippi to declare publicly: "The basic commitment of a Methodist minister is to Jesus Christ as Lord and Savior. This sets him in permanent opposition to communism. He cannot be a Christian and a *communist*."[15] At the same time, as Americans became more prosperous, they left behind huge pockets of poverty, especially in the South and northern urban centers. Voices from the margins of society cried out for equality and a share of the abundance. These ministers were deeply moved by the struggle of African Americans for educational opportunities, desegregation of public facilities, and opportunities to improve their living standards. They looked for ways to help their neighbors.

Their stories present a picture of the South during those years that is alarming yet hopeful: alarming because of the intensity of the opposition, yet hopeful because the ministers were not alone in their efforts to help African Americans. Other white southerners were in their camp. As this book shows, the South is not monolithic. In spite of setbacks and difficulties, the South *can* change its racial patterns.

Chapter 1 focuses on local episodes of the school desegregation crises. The *Brown v. Board of Education of Topeka* decision in 1954 gave hope and vigor to African Americans that perhaps apartheid might come to an end. Many southern white ministers and their denominations also saw in the decision opportunities to affirm their belief that enforced segregation was out of harmony with Christian principles and teachings. The chapter shows that the South was not yet ready for desegregation, especially of the schools; nevertheless, many southern white ministers signed proclamations in support of the *Brown* decision, and some became so personally involved that they put their careers in jeopardy. Chapter 2 traces their involvement in the explosive episodes of the civil rights movement: boycotts, sit-ins, Freedom Rides, and massive demonstrations. The narrative shows a slackening in the number of ministers who ventured into direct action. Perhaps the majority of the ministers compromised for the sake of their families. The narrative indicates that they marched and protested when it was fairly safe to do so, although there are several who were jailed and one who was tortured. Chapter 3 indicates that church visitations, or kneel-ins as they were sometimes called, also became part of the movement. African Americans who participated in these episodes believed that church people would treat them with compassion and welcome them as fellow Christians into their segregated churches, but only rarely did this happen. The visitations, however, gave many southern white ministers opportunities to welcome black people, but often those who did suffered harassment and termination of their ministries. Chapter 4 traces the activities of southern white ministers as the movement continued. The March on Washington was something of a reprieve from the violence and the nervous strain caused by the boycotts, sit-ins, Freedom Rides, mass demonstrations, and protests. The march presented an opportunity for sympathetic white people, northern and southern, to participate in a demonstration that was national, neither northern nor southern, and well removed from danger. Hundreds of white clergy participated, but those from the South did so in peril. The stories of these courageous few are contained in the chapter. The chapter also shows how differently the movement played out in the Upper South (North Carolina and Kentucky) than in the Deep South, namely Selma, Alabama, where violence and even death resulted. Chapter 5 narrates the rise of the Black Power movement and its effect on the nonviolent civil rights movement and the white ministers. Included are the responses of the white southern ministers to Black Power and also to the assassination of Martin Luther King Jr. The death of King was not a happy event for the nonviolent civil rights movement or the integrationist southern white ministers, and many expressed deep sorrow. Chapter 6 recognizes brave ministers who continued their support of civil rights during the years of Black Power, even in eastern Arkansas. These stories tell of courage and persistence.

The ministers represented seven different denominations, all with a sizable presence in the South during the 1950s and 1960s. Chapter 7 relates the efforts of the denominations and ministers within their ranks to work for change. At the end of the chapter, I address the decline of these denominations that were once the lifeblood of religion in the South and in the United States. I also include a brief story of the ecumenical Delta Ministry in Mississippi, a story that reveals how difficult it was for denominations, northern and southern, to work together for change. Chapter 7 can also be read as an overall summary and analysis.

I make every effort to connect all stories throughout the book to events in the civil rights movement and beyond. In many cases, I have come to understand southern history through the experiences of these southern white ministers. At the close of each chapter, I try to answer the question: Did their efforts produce results? In the conclusion, I look for more answers: Does a minister remain silent in the face of injustice? What happened to important ministerial concepts such as "freedom of the pulpit"? How could a minister balance the prophetic with pastoral duties? Does a pastor ignore the inclusive message of the Christian Church for fear of losing a pulpit? Can a minister safely be involved in social action? How much can he or she actually achieve? Has the minister's prophetic role in society diminished, or even disappeared? Did their efforts help change race relations in the South, and, an even larger question: Is religious faith relevant in a troubled society? In my search for answers, I examine the statements of the ministers and those factors that influenced their actions.

Giving these ministers labels has been difficult. Recent historians have called them moderates, progressives, and the "last hurrah" of the early twentieth century Social Gospel movement. Segregationists called them Communists, troublemakers, traitors, heretics, atheists, and some unmentionable names. David Chappell argues that segregationists in the 1950s and 1960s "tended to identify their own white southern churches as their enemy." In answer to a questionnaire, "How would you describe your personal theology?," twenty-two answered "liberal," seven answered "neo-orthodox," one answered, "evangelical liberal," two called themselves "progressives," one said he was an "open conservative," and one said, "I don't like labels and I don't care about theology." The term "liberal" has two connotations. It can mean liberal in theology or liberal on racial issues. Southern white activist and editor Anne Braden indicated that in the South during the 1950s and 1960s, the term was used to "describe a person who opposed, although in varying degrees, the whole system of segregation."[16] In that sense, all ministers who fought for racial justice would be considered "liberal," but they were not all liberal in their theology.

In a memoir, Presbyterian E. T. Thompson (chapter 7) defined himself as an "evangelical liberal," "someone with an open heart who attempted to find truth in all theological viewpoints." According to his biographer, Rev. Peter Hairston Hobbie, "One of Thompson's heroes was Dwight Moody, the popular nineteenth century evangelist who knew no dogma only the person of Christ. 'Keep sweet' or change hearts 'only with love' was Moody's legacy to Thompson." Critics of modernistic liberalism objected to the liberal belief in basic human goodness, the liberal tendency to make Jesus an ethical model rather than a savior, and liberalism's "proclivity to emphasize external progress over internal change." In Hobby's view, an evangelical liberal does not want to lose a belief in the power of God to change people's hearts, while at the same time finding truth in all theological viewpoints.[17] In many ways these ministers can be considered twentieth-century heirs to the nineteenth-century evangelical ministers who fought against slavery.

The biographer Kenneth Kesselus describes presiding bishop of the Episcopal Church John Hines (chapter 5) as a liberal evangelical: "His theology centered on the Cross—the symbol of God's unconditional, saving grace for humanity and of the responsibility for all Christians to take up their crosses, following Jesus in the way of sacrifice."[18]

Lutheran Joseph Ellwanger (chapter 2) defined himself as an "open conservative," which he explains as accepting the doctrines of Jesus as "fully human and fully divine, as dying on the cross and rising again for our salvation," but, he added, "I am open to non-literal interpretations of Scripture and contextual and symbolic interpretations."[19] Ellwanger's definition of an "open conservative" comes very close to the definition of an "evangelical liberal." Methodist Rhett Jackson (chapter 7) defined himself as a "progressive Christian." In an article for the *Zion Herald*, he wrote, "As progressives, we believe (1) that Jesus authentically revealed the very nature and will of God and provided the basis of an ethical system that is forever valid; (2) that the Bible is a record of historic faith and practice that informs the life of the Christian community in every age."[20] Jackson expressed his hope that a way could be found for conservatives and liberals to "live together with integrity."

At times I refer to these ministers as "progressive," in the sense that they favored reform, or as "moderate," in the sense that they supported a gradual approach to desegregation. Several considered themselves "neo-orthodox," a term that connotes a new kind of biblical realism that combines old and new orthodoxy. I often refer to them as "integrationist" or "desegregationist," for that was their political position at this time in history, and some considered themselves "radical," willing to go all the way to apply the radical teachings of Jesus to society.

In his book *Baptized in Blood: The Religion of the Lost Cause, 1865–1920*, Charles Reagan Wilson writes, "On the racial question . . . the Southern historical experience as embodied in the Lost Cause provided the model for segregation that the Southern churches accepted." Many of the ministers represented in this book claimed slave owners and Confederate soldiers in their ancestry, yet they went against "the model for segregation," and could also be termed "dissident."[21] Some were more direct in their protest than others, but even the "quietist" ministers achieved a breakthrough in the massive wall of separation.

In *Stride toward Freedom*, published in 1958 after the Montgomery Bus Boycott, Martin Luther King Jr. wrote, "Many [ministers] who believe segregation to be directly opposed to the will of God and the spirit of Christ are faced with the painful alternative of taking a vocal stand and being fired or staying quiet in order to remain in the situation and do some good. . . . They feel that restraint is the best way to serve the cause of Christ in the South. In quiet unpublicized ways, many of these ministers are making for a better day and helpfully molding the minds of young people. These men should not be criticized."[22] Of course, such an endorsement by Martin Luther King Jr. could not help the reputation of these ministers with segregationists. King and these ministers were all considered to be Communist sympathizers by rabid segregationists.

The great divide between pulpit and pew, cited by many scholars, accentuates the difficulties of those who served as pastors of white churches. They were liberal ministers in conservative churches. If they were confrontational, they lost their pulpits; if they were not confrontational enough, they were criticized by African American activists and northern white activists who traveled south to join demonstrations; and no matter what they did, they were harassed, threatened, and called n____r lovers. Their careers intersected with one of the most dramatic social movements in US history. They were forced to choose their actions, remain silent, or speak out against segregation. It is impossible to know how many southern white ministers actually spoke for an end to segregation. I am sure I have made some valuable omissions, but I am grateful for the privilege of sharing the following stories with the readers of this book. I have been accused of giving these ministers stature as heroes. I readily confess to my guilt. I consider their actions brave and heroic. As the sociologists Ernest Campbell and Thomas Pettigrew wrote in their study of Little Rock's ministry during the school desegregation crisis of 1957, "When all of the ministerial protests are considered together they become of crucial significance."[23] They become a mighty chorus of angels singing in the southern sky.

═ 1 ═

SCHOOL DESEGREGATION
Trouble Ahead

To separate them from others of similar age and qualifications solely because of their race generates a feeling of inferiority as to their status in the community that may affect their hearts and minds in a way unlikely ever to be undone.
—*BROWN. V. BOARD OF EDUCATION OF TOPEKA*, Supreme Court, May 17, 1954

◆ ◆ ◆

The church must strive to keep apace of its Master or become bereft of His spirit.
—STATEMENT OF THE PRESBYTERIAN CHURCH IN THE UNITED STATES (SOUTHERN), 1954

The US Supreme Court decision to end school segregation in 1954 reflected the unflinching persistence of lawyers from Howard University and the National Association for the Advancement of Colored People (NAACP). Robert L. Carter (1917–2012), lawyer for the NAACP, the main architect of *Brown*, stated, "It was clear . . . all we wanted was an engagement. . . . Segregation had to be destroyed. School integration was the only way to do it." Will Campbell (1924–2014), southern white Baptist minister working on school desegregation for the National Council of Churches (NCC), commented, "Without *Brown*, Jim Crow would still prevail in the South." Arguments began in December 1952 and were not resolved until May 1954. No mention was made of how and when the decision would be implemented. One year later the court handed down a second decision, known as *Brown II*. School systems in southern states were ordered to desegregate "with all deliberate speed." Compliance would be the responsibility of a three-judge tribunal within each federal district. If state

11

officials were disobedient to the court order, they would be subject to contempt proceedings. The Court reasoned that "all deliberate speed" would give the South time to adjust to the change, but contrary to expectations, the white South made use of the time to organize campaigns of massive resistance.[1]

In his book *Silent Covenants*, Derrick Bell (1930–2011), another NAACP lawyer working on school desegregation, wrote that soon after the decision, highway billboards appeared across the South stating, "Impeach Chief Justice Earl Warren," and candidates were elected to office with "little more than shouting, 'Never.'" According to the historian Numan V. Bartley, the most virulent "massive resistance" came from the Deep South states of Alabama, Georgia, Louisiana, Mississippi, and South Carolina, where large populations of African Americans resided. In Georgia, candidate Marvin Griffin, running for governor in 1954, vowed to prevent "meddlers . . . race baiters and communists" from destroying every vestige of states' rights. He won the election. Education was, after all, in the domain of the states and not to be tampered with by the federal government. The Baptist minister Will Campbell maintained, "It was acceptable in the South for white people at that time to damn the Supreme Court." In the year separating the two *Brown* decisions, Bartley describes a deeper sinking into hysterical reaction: NAACP activities were banned; pupil-placement plans were put into effect, giving local administrators the right to assign students arbitrarily to segregated schools; some states even allowed for the abolishment of all or part of their public school systems and made it a criminal offense to comply with the *Brown* decision. Bartley called it "legislative hysteria" and "racial fanaticism," but in the midst of hysteria, the major denominations in the United States, all with constituents in the South, issued statements and resolutions in support of the *Brown* decision.[2]

Meeting from May 27 to June 1, 1954, the General Assembly of the Presbyterian Church in the United States (PCUS) Southern became the first to "affirm that enforced segregation of the races is discrimination which is out of harmony with Christian theology and ethics." Meeting from June 2 to 5, 1954, the Southern Baptist Convention (SBC) followed with a similar recommendation: "This Supreme Court decision is in harmony with the constitutional guarantee of equal freedom to all . . . and with the Christian principles of equal justice and love for all men." That same year the Methodist House of Bishops affirmed that the decision was in keeping with all official pronouncements of the Methodist Church, including the Social Creed. In 1955 the General Convention of the Episcopal Church recommended to all clergy and members "that they accept and support the ruling." In 1956 the United Lutheran Church of America affirmed, "The public school system . . . must be upheld and strengthened." In 1957 the Christian Church (Disciples of Christ) declared its position to be in agreement with the World Council of Churches and the NCC: "A non-segregated Church in a non-segregated Society is the Christian ideal."[3]

By 1958 all denominations in the United States endorsed the decision, but did their constituents living in the segregated South pay heed? Not many did. Writing about Little Rock's ministry, Ernest Campbell and Thomas Pettigrew noted that many church-attending southerners thought of the statements "as pious declarations made for the national press and not for us down here [in the South]." Governor Hugh White of Mississippi, a Presbyterian elder, vowed, "If the Supreme Court decision is observed in my church, I will be forced to find some other place to worship." Two elders at the First Baptist Church of Jackson, Mississippi, owners of the *Jackson Daily News*, published an editorial calling the SBC resolution "deplorable" and "not binding." As the historian Randy Sparks noted, "Methodist churches [across the state] passed resolutions condemning their Council of Bishops," and the First Methodist Church of Clarksdale announced that it was "irrevocably opposed to integration of the negro and white races in the public schools.'" A member of a Disciples of Christ church in Kentucky wrote in a personal letter, "The Methodist Church is a very corrupt organization. No sound minister or layman can stay in it and work with it. What is said of the Methodist Church is true of the others. The Sunday school literature of my church is full of rotten teaching and replete with pictures of negroes and whites mixed together. . . . It is saddening to see the churches turning from the Gospel of Christ to sociology, community justice, economics, etc. Our Supreme Court is utterly insane."[4] Mass hysteria took hold of church congregations as they allowed fear of race mixing, miscegenation, and destruction of the white school system to govern their thoughts and actions.

White Citizens' Councils, called "the Klan in business suits" by white Baptist minister and professor at Wake Forest University G. McLeod Bryan (1920–2010), began to organize all over the South, vigorously opposing school desegregation and mainly targeting the churches. In addition, White America, Inc., National Citizens Protective Association, National Association for the Advancement of White People, Pro-America, vigilante groups, the Ku Klux Klan (KKK), White Nights, white educational associations, telephone relays, White Citizens' Councils, Mothers Against School Integration, neo-Nazis, and John Birch Societies all began campaigns to inform southerners of the evils of integration. "What could southern white ministers do if they believed in following denominational statements and the dictates of their consciences?" This was the question asked by Colbert S. Cartwright, pastor of Pulaski Heights Christian Church in Little Rock, Arkansas, in an article written for the *Christian Century* magazine. An answer came from a minister in Virginia: "Suppose I do tell my people our schools should be integrated? I would get fired immediately. . . . I could go to a better church in the north . . . but what would I have accomplished? My people would still be just as they are. . . . Their next minister would be someone they could depend on not to disturb them." This minister decided to remain silent and stay in his church, but Rev. John H. Knibb Jr.

told another story. Knibb was forced to leave his Disciples of Christ church in Virginia in 1956 simply because he wrote a letter to a newspaper expressing support for school desegregation. From his new church in Mackinaw, Illinois, he wrote to the *Southern Patriot*, journal of the Southern Conference Educational Fund, "No minister who is conscientious about his work and who takes his responsibilities seriously can remain forever silent about the evils he sees around him and keep a clear conscience before God. Wherever I go, I may never be a popular preacher, but by the help of God, I'll be an honest one, or none." Knibb's story was all too familiar throughout the South at the time, but so was the answer coming from the anonymous minister. In his article, Cartwright suggested that in the midst of violence, ministers could call for "calm and rational discussion" and appeal to the community "to abide by Christian principles of love and brotherhood."[5] The ministers whose stories are contained in this chapter followed Cartwright's advice, but the results were not always favorable. Like Rev. Knibb, most were forced to leave their churches.

Scholars have argued that school desegregation might have been accomplished more peacefully if white ministers had been more united in support, but many declared their opposition. A minister in Missionary Baptist Church in Hoxie, Arkansas, preached, "God will condone violence if it is necessary to preserve the purity of the white race." A minister in a Presbyterian church in Meridian, Mississippi, preached, "Segregation is God's will. . . . The recent Supreme Court decision is in violation and contradiction to Scripture teachings."[6]

Campbell and Pettigrew blamed much of the trouble in Little Rock on the ministers of the small-sect independent churches, most of which were in the Central High School district. Some were members of the Missionary Baptist Association (not affiliated with the SBC). According to Campbell and Pettigrew, these ministers remained isolated from the larger community and refused to take part in ministerial associations or interdenominational endeavors; many admitted being present in the vicious crowd surrounding Central High on September 4, 1957. Most supported segregation based on scripture and attacked ministers who supported integration. A number asked their congregations to vote on whether they wanted segregation or integration. They reported unanimous votes for segregation. Campbell and Pettigrew observed that when the uptown ministers organized Columbus Day prayer meetings for the peaceful desegregation of the schools, the small-sect ministers organized prayer meetings for the continuation of segregation.[7] As Bartley, Campbell and Pettigrew, Martin Luther King Jr., and others have argued, there was too much "silence" in the middle of extremes.

The stories contained in this chapter are of an outspoken minority who supported denominational resolutions and school desegregation. They became involved in crisis situations in Tennessee, Arkansas, Mississippi, and Alabama. These ministers tried to convince white parents that school desegregation did not mean the destruction of the white race and the entire southern way of life. They tried to convince segregationists that integration was the Christian way, that the "sky would not fall down" if some black children entered white schools.[8] In South Carolina, where resistance was fierce, some ministers tried to approach the issue in a moderate, gentle way, yet they suffered. All these stories reveal the difficulties southern white ministers endured, but also their dedication to racial justice.

Tennessee

Considered the Upper South, Tennessee displayed a moderate attitude toward the *Brown* decision. Bartley recorded that repressive measures were vetoed in 1954 by Governor Frank G. Clement, but in Clinton, a quiet mill town in Anderson County, in the Cumberland foothills of East Tennessee, there was trouble and violence. A reporter from *Time* magazine described Clinton as an improbable place for racial crisis, "since its descendants fought for the North during the Civil War," and out of "3,700 law-abiding citizens, only about 300 were rabid segregationists." There were forty-eight African American families living in a town of about 3,000 people; most of these families owned their own homes and were accepted as solid, sober members of the "Baptist-dry" community.[9]

As early as 1950 the African American families had petitioned the courts for admission to the white schools because no high school for African Americans existed in the county. The petition was denied, and many black parents could not afford the cost of transporting their children twenty-five miles to a black school in Knoxville, even with some remuneration from the county. These children received no high school education. In the fall of 1956 federal judge Robert Taylor ordered the integration of Clinton High School. Desegregation might have proceeded peacefully if not for the presence of outside agitators. On the weekend before school was to open, John Kasper, a native of New Jersey, graduate of Columbia University, and owner of a Washington, DC, bookstore, arrived in town preaching that Communists were behind the Supreme Court decision, that the white race would ultimately be destroyed— "mongrelized," he called it, as he handed out leaflets with a picture of a white woman being held and kissed by African Americans. It was actually an artificial picture made from photographs of African American GIs in Europe during World War II, but the townspeople did not know that.[10]

On August 25 local authorities arrested Kasper "for inspiring to riot." The next day school opened as twelve African American children made their way through jeers and shouts. No sooner had Kasper been arrested than he was released with a restraining order, but an even more aggressive agitator arrived, Asa Carter from Alabama, crying, "We're Anglo-Saxons, the superior race. . . .

I came here because I want to help you start a white citizens' campaign." Some 150 people paid $3 each and joined the White Citizens' Council. By the end of the first week of school, Clinton was under siege by agitators, including Ku Klux Klan members who began holding mass meetings outside the town and burning crosses on vacant lots. Loudspeakers amplified their voices so the town's residents could hear them. The Klan incited child against child, neighbor against neighbor, so effectively that the African American children began to fear for their lives. Their parents kept them home. On the evening of December 3, 1956, the pastor of the First Baptist Church, Paul Turner (1923–1980), born in Jonesboro, Arkansas, the oldest of eight children of Pastor John Henry Turner and Ida Goodrich Turner, told the children that if they wanted to return to school, he would walk with them.[11]

On December 4 a local election was to be held for mayor and three seats on the Board of Aldermen with candidates backed by the White Citizens' Council hoping for victory. That morning Rev. Turner, joined by two townspeople, escorted six African American children to Clinton High School, delivering them to classrooms. On the return to his church, the unthinkable happened. The reporter from *Time*, on the scene, described the attack: "Suddenly three husky men blocked his way. One grabbed him. He twisted, ran headlong into another, broke away, dodged across the street and was caught again. Under a storm of fists, he was beaten. Turner fell back against a car that was soon smeared with his blood. Then he went all the way down." Many others in the crowd joined in, kicking and clawing the fallen pastor. A man and a woman from a nearby insurance office tried to help Turner. The man was driven back and pelted with eggs; the woman was pushed against a storefront by another woman. Arriving belatedly, police broke up the riot and arrested fifteen of the troublemakers, among them an itinerant backwoods preacher who "frequently harangued crowds on what he called the 'evils' of integration." Sneered one of Turner's assailants while being led away, "That'll teach yuh, Reverend."[12]

Almost immediately, Wilma Dykeman and James Stokely, an activist husband and wife writing team, rushed to Clinton to interview Turner. They described him as a friendly, six-foot, blue-eyed parson with a swollen face who told them, "Someone had to step out—and I guess I was elected." To African American students, Turner was a hero: "He just kept saying to us, 'Don't be afraid. I won't let them hurt you.'" One girl's mother added, "He knows courage all right, but I think he must have something else too. Mr. Turner must know love."[13]

Newspapers across the country, including the South, headlined their outrage. The *Nashville Tennessean* carried the picture of the automobile, spattered with blood, and within minutes the people of Clinton went to the election polls in large numbers to reject the candidates of the White Citizens' Council and elect as mayor "fair-minded" Judge T. Lawrence Seeber. The segregationists

were defeated. The people of Clinton were praised for accepting school desegregation, although some in the community did not welcome it. On the following Sunday, Turner told his congregation, "There is no color line at the
cross. . . . Truth and love are sterile concepts unless they are incarnated in life
actions and attitudes. . . . By identifying with those in need I have preached a
sermon to my world about Christ far beyond any homiletical masterpiece I
may deliver to you in words." He later told a reporter for the *Nashville Banner*,
"I felt that at a crucial moment I had made a Christian decision. . . . I offered to
walk with the Negro children as a witness of Christianity."[14]

Turner was hailed by reporters throughout the nation as a courageous
white minister who gave new meaning to the old African American spiritual
"Just a Closer Walk with Thee," but his story did not end happily. The family moved to Nashville, where Turner became pastor of Brook Hollow Baptist Church. Kasper soon arrived in Nashville and began again his rhetoric of
hate. As told by Turner's sister, Dorise, "Turner and his wife feared that Kasper
would harm them or their children and follow them wherever they went." Will
Campbell, who was in Nashville at the time, described Kasper as a professional hate peddler. "No one ever knew exactly what his game was, but he was
a dynamic speaker and persuader and knew how to organize the people."[15]

Turner resigned his pastorate and returned to his alma mater, the Southern Baptist Theological Seminary in Louisville, for recuperation, recovery, and
perhaps a new beginning. He earned a doctorate in sacred theology and in
1972 joined the faculty of the Golden Gate Baptist Theological Seminary in
Mill Valley, California, but apparently continued to be despondent. In 1981 he
was found dead in his home from a self-inflicted gunshot wound. Turner's
body was flown to Nashville. His wife and three children followed for a service at Woodlawn Memorial Cemetery. A large group, stunned by the news,
came from First Baptist of Clinton, some 175 miles away. A loyal friend, Rev.
Ralph Murray, conducted the service: "Paul was a gifted preacher with a warm
heart. . . . We shall miss him and mourn for him." His wife said, "He was just
worn out. People never really knew what a wonderful person he was." C. R.
Daley, editor of the *Western Baptist Recorder*, wrote afterward, "Many of our
hearts were saddened by a tragic case of ministerial burnout. Paul Turner, one
of the most gifted and committed servants of God among Southern Baptists,
took his own life after suffering an extended period of depression. . . . A minister is especially susceptible to burnout. Almost all his time is spent in ministering to others and rarely does anyone minister to him. . . . We could have helped
him, but we did not." "Burnout," it has been said, "hits hardest at achievers."[16]

His sister, Dorise Turner Haynes, maintained that the family was haunted
by their experience in Clinton. "He could never understand the attitude of the
segregationists. His action followed him throughout his career. He was ignored

and ostracized by the state Baptist associations. His friends deserted him and ministerial colleagues told him, 'Desegregation was government action. You should have stayed out of it.'" As his sister reflected, "The years of the Civil Rights Movement were hard years for ministers. Integration was hard. The criticism he heard countless times was that he should have kept out of it."[17]

The attack on Turner was probably the worst of its kind against a southern clergyperson during those early days of the civil rights movement. The *Nashville Banner* called it "a near lynching." It is to be noted that the two townspeople accompanying Turner were unscathed, but Rev. Turner left a legacy: he "willingly shed his blood" for innocent victims of racial prejudice.[18]

Turner's carefully written dissertation, "A Study of Selected Graduates of the Southern Baptist Theological Seminary, 1950–1970," roughly the years of the civil rights movement, is also a legacy. Based on questionnaires sent to 438 graduates who were pastors or associate pastors of Baptist churches across the nation (322 responded), Turner found that more than 95 percent of the respondents believed that it was a minister's responsibility to address social, economic, and political issues. Nine out of ten also agreed that "churches had been woefully inadequate in facing up to civil rights issues and seminaries needed to do a better job in preparing ministers for future service." Thirty-four percent admitted they "had seriously considered secular work," and "twenty-seven percent said they would leave the local church ministry if they were given a reasonable opportunity." Turner's own experience demonstrates the difficulties of ministry in times of political and racial crises, but he never regretted his life as a minister. "In spite of the existence of serious chronic stress, a minister's life can be very satisfying. There is joy in helping people in their times of need and in leading them to the ethic of Christian love."[19]

In the town of Clinton, Turner's witness and sacrifice had an influence above and beyond that of agitators John Kasper and Asa Carter. The town's people defeated the candidates of the White Citizens' Council, and the school successfully integrated, with Bobby Cain becoming the first African American to graduate from a desegregated southern high school. Unfortunately, the militant segregationists did not disappear. The twelve students and their families were constantly harassed and intimidated, and the school was dynamited and almost destroyed on Sunday, October 5, 1958. Fortunately, the school was empty, and the desegregated high school continued in a vacant elementary school nearby until the building could be rebuilt.[20] Turner's life story is heroic. He ultimately became a martyr for the cause of racial justice.

As Eric Snider, the current principal of Clinton High School, has stated, "The great people of Clinton came together and lifted up twelve African American students. Many individuals, pastors, and community members, as well as the National Guard supported these twelve students, protected them, and made history." At the Green McAdoo Cultural Center in Clinton on the site of the former segregated elementary school (now listed on the National Register of Historic Places) can be seen life-size statues of the "Clinton Twelve" and photographs depicting the story of Rev. Turner.[21]

Arkansas

In Arkansas, pupil-placement laws and restrictions on activities of the NAACP were enforced, but Arkansas had not gone as far as other states in nullifying the *Brown* decision. The responsibility for solving desegregation problems was left to local school boards, and several in western Arkansas desegregated their schools with ease.[22]

Little Rock, the state capital, centrally located, a progressive city of over 100,000 people, where buses, parks, and hospitals had quietly desegregated, was another community where school integration should have progressed peacefully but did not. The opposition to the integration of Little Rock's Central High School that began on the morning of September 4, 1957, made headlines across America and eventually the world. Photographs taken by local newspaper reporter Will Counts revealed snarling white citizens carrying Confederate flags; placards with the word "CROSS" (Committee to Retain Our Segregated Schools) written on a cross; caravans of cars with the lead banner, "Education Without Mixing," "Race Mixing Is Communism"; a black newspaper reporter being kicked and beaten to the ground; and at the end of September, paratroopers from the 101st Airborne Division, rifles with bayonets in their hands, escorting nine African American children into Central High.[23] Again, there were ministers who believed they were called by God to help ease the burden for black children,

In 1957 Rev. Marion A. Boggs (1894–1983), born in Liberty, South Carolina, pastor of the Second Presbyterian Church (PCUS) and considered the dean of Protestant ministers in Little Rock, was called before a special state senate committee on school segregation. Boggs made several points: "Compliance with the Supreme Court's decision is the right course of action"; "Efforts to nullify and defeat the decision will only prolong agony, increase tension, and prove ineffectual in the end"; and "Segregation by law is alien to the spirit of American democracy and is out of harmony with Christian brotherhood, theology, and ethics." He made his appeal: "We in the South have reconciled to a new way of life before and we can do it again. . . . Our Negro leaders trust us. . . . Let's give them their rights without being forced to do it by the strong arm of the law." Boggs said he approved of the gradual approach to solving the southern problem and believed it would work, but as opposition seemed to be mounting, he spoke more forcefully to his congregation, "If the Church remains silent when great problems of moral and ethical import are being debated and being decided, it would, in my judgment, amount to cowardice and a neglect of urgent duty. . . . According to the law of Christian love, we are to do unto others as we would have them do unto us."[24]

As events unfolded, Boggs's hopes for a peaceful integration were crushed when Governor Orval Faubus dispatched the Arkansas National Guard to prevent the integration of Central High School. Soon Boggs signed a ministerial petition along with fifteen other local ministers in Little Rock. They protested to the mayor that the National Guard should be called to *enforce* the law, not to *defy* it. Harassing letters and obscene telephone calls became the daily routine for the ministers. When Faubus closed all the high schools in Little Rock the following year rather than comply with the federal order, Boggs signed another proclamation, which Faubus hastily rejected, stating publicly that he knew a large number of ministers in the Presbyterian Church who "had been effectively brainwashed by left-wingers and communists." The ministers asked for an apology. It was never received. In 1962 Boggs, who had been condemned by many churchpeople in other parts of the South, resigned from Second Church, claiming that his age, sixty-eight, prevented him from continuing in a pastorate he had served for twenty-three years.[25]

◆ ◆ ◆

The gradual approach was the plan of Virgil T. Blossom, who became superintendent of schools of Little Rock shortly after the *Brown* decision. The city's three high schools were to be desegregated in 1957, with elementary schools to follow in 1960, but as the historian John Kirk pointed out, when the 1955 Supreme Court implementation order set no timetable for integration (using the indefinite phrase "all deliberate speed"), Blossom altered his plan to please the white citizens. He allowed white students to transfer out of Horace Mann High School to the newly built Hall High in a white affluent neighborhood, but he did not give black students the same right, thus leaving Horace Mann all-black and all-white Central High as the school to be desegregated. White parents living in Central High's district resented the fact that their high school was the only one to be desegregated.[26]

During the summer of 1957, segregationists began to organize: a white Mothers' League of Central High formed to keep the black children out of the school; the Capital White Citizens' Council invited Governor Marvin Griffin of Georgia to speak at a meeting in the heart of the city. Griffin told Arkansians to copy the system in Georgia whereby tax funds would not be used to operate mixed-race schools, and grants would be made to white parents to educate their children at home. Superintendent of Schools Blossom blamed much of the agitation on Rev. James Wesley Pruden (1908–1979), president of the White Citizens' Council and pastor of Broadmoor Baptist Church. Pruden attended local school board meetings asking inflammatory questions like, "If you integrate Little Rock Central High . . . will the Negro boys and girls be permitted to attend the school sponsored dances?" "Would the Negro boys be permitted to solicit the white girls for dances?" "Because of the high venereal disease rate among Negroes, the public is wondering if the white children will be forced to use the same rest rooms and toilet facilities with Negroes?" Pruden later mailed the questions to Superintendent Blossom, whose answers were printed in the local newspaper. Blossom tried to alleviate the parents' fears with such answers as: "Certain social functions of our schools which have been desirable in the past may have to be eliminated," and "Board of Education policy requires the immediate exclusions from school of any pupil having an infectious or contagious disease." But the parents were not satisfied. Blossom noted that the weekend before the ordered integration, an eight-foot-high cross was burned in front of the home of the state president of the NAACP, and a sign found nearby said, "Go back to Africa—KKK."[27]

On the testimony of the Mothers' League of Central High School that gangs with guns and knives were forming near the school, Governor Faubus obtained a temporary injunction preventing nine black children from entering the school. On September 2, 1957, Faubus made his announcement on television that the Arkansas National Guard would barricade the school in order to "maintain order and protect the lives and property of citizens." The next day federal judge Ronald N. Davies ordered the Board of Education to disregard the troops and begin immediate integration. The night of September 3, 1957, Daisy Bates, field secretary for the NAACP, supervisor, comforter, and counselor for the nine students, believed that perhaps the presence of white ministers might have a calming effect and enable the integration to take place peacefully. Although she did not know him, she called Rev. Dunbar Ogden Jr. (1903–1978), pastor of Central Presbyterian Church in the vicinity of Central High School and president of the newly established interracial Ministerial Association. She explained the situation and asked if he could get some ministers to accompany the children. Rev. Ogden, fifty-five-years old, born in Columbus, Mississippi, descendant of one of the state's largest slave-holding families, and, like Rev. Boggs, trained at the Union Theological Seminary in Richmond, Virginia, struggled with the decision.[28]

As told by his son Dunbar Ogden III, Rev. Ogden replied to Bates, "'Do you think this is the business of the church? Do you think it is part of the work of religion to participate in a movement that might be thought of as more political and social than of a churchly nature? Don't you think it's possible it will be said of ministers that they've gotten a little too dramatic, going out there and walking with the Negro children? Aren't there better ways they could help?" She disagreed firmly. Rev. Ogden talked it over with his wife, and together they prayed. In a short while, he returned the call, promising Bates to contact as many ministers as he could. He said he would meet with the students, but he did not know whether he would actually walk with them. The next morning, able to find only one local minister who might join him, he was still undecided, but his second son, twenty-one-year-old David, who stood six-feet-one-inch tall, offered to go with him and "be his bodyguard." Ogden III related, "David was making a kind of joke, but he went out there with them." Together they drove to the meeting place designated by Daisy Bates. The families of all nine children had been notified, with the exception of Elizabeth Eckford, whose family had no telephone.[29]

The day began quietly in front of Central High with about 100 troops of the Arkansas National Guard surrounding the school. At 8:35 a.m. the people standing in front of the school suddenly exploded into a mob. Relman Marin of the Louisville (Kentucky) *Courier Journal* wrote, "It was savagery, chain-reacting from person to person, fusing into a white-hot mass." As Elizabeth Eckford made her way toward the school from a different direction, she was followed by a delirious crowd, screaming, "A n____r is coming. Don't let her in. Go back where you came from. . . . Get her, lynch her. Go home you black bitch." Turned away by the troopers, Eckford retreated slowly, tears streaming down her face. She sat down on a bus stop bench, with Benjamin Fine of the *New York Times* beside her. "Don't let them see you cry," he told her. Finally, the bus came and she escaped to safety. Terrence Roberts, an honors student from Horace Mann High School, another one of the nine, came with a shiny yellow pencil behind his ear and attempted to enter. He was also turned back. "Keep away from our school, you burr head," the crowd roared.[30]

As Ogden III related, Rev. Ogden led the way, with seven of the nine children "straggling along with David [Ogden] behind them." They were met at the front of the school by Lt. Col. Marion Johnson, commander of the troops. Ogden III continued, "My father spoke in his resonant pulpit voice, 'Are you here to see to it that these children enter this school or to prevent them from entering?' He wanted all to hear. He wanted witnesses." As he pointed his nightstick toward the children, Johnson replied, "The school is off-limits to these people." Rev. Ogden tried but did not succeed in gaining entrance for the children. Others helped him get them back through the mob to safety.[31]

The story of Dunbar H. Ogden Jr. is one of inner struggle, strength, triumph, and tragedy. Before the Little Rock crisis, he told an interviewer from the *Southern Patriot*, he thought in terms of "separate but equal": "I was incapable of a real relationship with Negro friends because I was still condescending in my attitude and then came Little Rock. . . . I saw the National Guard with its guns . . . the demonstrating mob with the hate-filled faces . . . all to keep nine young people out of a school with 2,000 youngsters. . . . I had to make a decision, a choice between right and wrong. For me, there could be no answer except integration with the association and sharing it would bring." His son Dunbar commented that the children had given his father courage and a new purpose to his ministry. "He believed it was God's plan that he should help the black children of Little Rock." After the episode, he and Daisy Bates became the initiators of an integrated weekly prayer and discussion group: "People said there was no communication between whites and blacks in Little Rock. It just wasn't so. . . . We became true friends. . . . Racial barriers fell away." The *Arkansas Gazette* published one of his sermons: "We must give to all people not half justice, but whole justice, not half truth, but complete truth, not half love, but love in the fullest measure."[32]

On September 20 Governor Faubus was enjoined by Judge Davies from any further interference with the desegregation of Central High. On Monday, September 23, the Little Rock Nine, as they came to be called, slipped quietly into a side entrance of Central High School while the angry crowd shouted obscenities. By noon, the Nine were removed from the school by Assistant Police Chief Gene Smith "for their own safety." Finally, on Wednesday, September 25, upon orders from President Dwight D. Eisenhower, troops of the 101st Airborne Division of the US Army, bayonets fixed on their M-1 rifles, kept order while the nine black children entered Central High School. Campbell and Pettigrew cited Rev. Ogden as the only civic leader to publicly praise the move. They noted, "Many of his close ministerial friends let him go it alone."[33]

Rev. Ogden did everything he could to support the desegregation of Central High School. His sermons became prophetic. He spoke of Jesus as one who did many kind deeds for others. He quoted Amos: "Let justice roll down like a river and righteousness like a never-failing stream." He preached that to be a Christian is to take action. As keynote speaker at the Dubose Episcopal Conference Center in Monteagle, Tennessee, he told an interracial and interdenominational group of youth leaders, some from Central Presbyterian Church, "As to integration—other churchmen said, 'It is the law of the land.' I say, 'It is the law of the Lord.'"[34]

In May 1958 Martin Luther King Jr. arrived in Little Rock to address the graduating class at all-black Arkansas Agricultural, Mechanical, and Normal College. In addition, he was eager to attend the graduation of Ernest Green, the only senior of the Little Rock Nine. The ceremony was closed to black people except for Green's relatives. Daisy Bates could not get a ticket for King and called her friend, Rev. Ogden. He secured two tickets by asking his church members for unused tickets, and he personally took King to the graduation. For an unknown reason, the guard at the gate let them in. After the ceremony, Ogden attended a party for King at the home of Daisy Bates, where he graciously introduced King to Ernest Green's family. Later, he chauffeured King to the airport, where he was spotted by a member of his church.[35]

What was to be Rev. Ogden's fate in his church after his courageous action? Beginning in the fall of 1957, the Ogden family began to receive hate mail. Mrs. Ogden was shunned by church members. Sunday morning attendance dropped from about 200 to 80. Contributions fell to about one-third. Members told him, "We do not want our pastor meddling in other people's affairs." "You mix into too many things that are not the affair of the church." One of his longtime family friends admonished, "You, Dunbar, have betrayed a race." In July the deacons informed him that his salary would be reduced from $6,200 to $4,000 a year. Rev. Ogden knew that he was being forced to resign. Several days later a vote was taken to ask him to leave as soon as he could find another church. Before he left to become an associate pastor in Huntington, West Virginia, he went to see Bates. "I'm sorry I got you into this," she said. "Don't feel sorry," he replied. "If I had to do it all over again, I would. I believe I'm a better Christian for having been privileged to participate in such a worthy cause." Ogden's son David, his self-appointed body guard, remained in Little Rock for several years until he could no longer bear the insults and harassment. One day tragedy happened. David committed suicide. In later years, Rev. Ogden would often say to his oldest son, "When I look back at my life, I regret nothing. I have no regrets." His son wrote, "Then, his strong voice would soften and crack, 'except for the death of David—except for the death of David.'"[36]

◆ ◆ ◆

Colbert Cartwright (1924–2001), pastor of Pulaski Heights Christian Church (Disciples of Christ), was another white minister in Little Rock who supported school integration. Born in St. Louis, Cartwright grew up in Chattanooga, Tennessee, where his father was pastor of First Christian Church. He attended Yale Divinity School, training ground for many Disciples ministers, where he came in contact with progressive theologians who, no doubt, influenced his decision to become the "public conscience in the South," writing articles, attending political meetings, lobbying at the state legislature for the Arkansas Educational Association, and generally speaking out in an effort to make Christian faith relevant to the world in which he lived.[37]

Arriving in Little Rock in 1954 from First Christian Church in Lynchburg, Virginia, he immediately founded and served as president of the Arkansas Council on Human Relations, a group dedicated to improving cooperation between white and black people. At first, Cartwright was optimistic about what southern white ministers could do to advance school desegregation. In his article for the *Christian Century*, almost ten months before the Little Rock crisis, he cited stories of ministers who were successful in preventing violence when black children entered all-white schools, but, like Rev. Boggs, his hopes were shattered on September 4 at Central High School. On the evening before, he visited the home of Elizabeth Eckford, and the next morning he appeared at the children's side, mainly to observe. In an interview with Eleanor Humes Haney, he repeated the emotional sermon he preached to his congregation the following Sunday: "The thing I want us to remember is that these nine [children] are human beings. We shall be in danger of losing our own souls if in the midst of great impersonal issues we lose sight of some very bright children of high moral character who want an education." He praised the spiritual strength of Elizabeth Eckford, "a girl who quietly read her Bible one night, and then the next morning found that the Bible was true: 'The Lord is my light . . . whom shall I fear?'" In Cartwright's words, the reaction of some church members to his sermon was "violent." Petitions were circulated to silence him and make him retract his statements. Eventually thirty-one persons left the church, but Cartwright refused to be silent and continued to speak out, expressing anger and outrage when Faubus decided to close all the public schools. In 1960 Cartwright was asked to be the chief speaker at a conference on community unity. He urged the city's factions—the African American group, the NAACP, the city authorities, and the white community—to forget their differences and work together to reopen the schools on "moral and religious" grounds. His call for unity was not well received by the segregationists.[38]

Since his antagonists had already left the church, Cartwright did not anticipate strong opposition, but another disapproving reaction surprised him. Some in his membership felt he had gone too far, but a small group within the church seemed to agree with Cartwright's understanding of Christ's message and the church's mission. In 1963 Cartwright, exhausted, left Little Rock and accepted an assignment at South Hills Christian Church in Youngstown, Ohio.[39]

◆ ◆ ◆

During the crisis, Will D. Campbell (1924–2013) arrived in Little Rock as a minister-observer for the NCC. Born on a farm in Amite County, Mississippi, Campbell learned at an early age from grandparents to respect black people. While playing at their grandfather's farm, he and his large group of cousins taunted a black man passing by and called him "n____r." His grandfather scolded, "Don't call that man 'n____r.' He's a colored man and there are millions of people just like him all over the world." His grandmother added, "Be kind to the black neighbors. They may be angels. Skin color don't make folks trash." Campbell heeded the advice of his grandparents, but some of the cousins went on to become members of the Klan and the White Citizens' Councils.

There were always other factors of influence. Educated at Yale Divinity School shortly after Cartwright in 1952 when the Supreme Court was considering the *Brown* decision, Campbell recalled, "Some of us southern boys would get together and debate the fact that we knew the court would rule as it did, but we worried that the battle might begin before we could get back home."[40] Campbell got home in time.

He traveled to Little Rock by way of Nashville and a painful experience at the University of Mississippi (popularly known as "Ole Miss") located in Oxford, which he described in his memoir, *Brother to a Dragonfly*. After serving for two years as chaplain, Campbell decided to disturb the campus by inviting Alvin Kershaw, an Episcopal priest from Ohio, whom he knew to be sympathetic to integration, to speak during Religious Emphasis Week. According to Campbell, it was "a major campus affair and everyone at the university understood that race was not to be discussed." Kershaw, an expert on the subject of jazz, won $32,000 as a contestant on a popular television show, *The Sixty-Four Thousand Dollar Question*. The invitation was sent, and the university was looking forward to having a television celebrity on campus. At the same time, Kershaw decided to leave the game and donate the money to the Southern Regional Council and the NAACP Legal Education and Defense Fund, both considered subversive organizations by Ole Miss, and the invitation was rescinded. When the other out-of-town speakers heard about the "blatant suppression of free speech," they all withdrew. The university chancellor decided to replace them with local ministers, none of whom accepted the invitation. As a protest for rescinding the invitation, Campbell went to the auditorium each day, "pulled the curtain shut upon the stage, leaving two vacant chairs exposed, a spotlight shining on each one," and every morning during Religious Emphasis Week several hundred students, faculty, and townspeople joined him in the "silent hour."[41]

Campbell's troubles continued. At a party arranged by Campbell for new students, someone added a cup of human feces to a large bowl of punch, sprinkled lightly with what appeared to be powdered sugar. Shortly thereafter, he played Ping-Pong with a black minister friend from Oxford on campus. The next day his wife found several dozen Ping-Pong balls spread across their front lawn, "all neatly painted, half-white, half-black." When called to the dean's office, Campbell told him, with characteristic irony, that it was really quite within the southern pattern. "We used separate but equal paddles, the ball was white, and there was a net drawn tightly between us." Campbell infuriated the university's ultraconservative administration, and soon his funds as campus chaplain were cut off. His older brother suggested he leave Ole Miss as soon as possible. He took his brother's advice and left, but with a sense of satisfaction that he had dramatized a truth he considered important in a university setting.[42]

His willingness to speak out on issues at the University of Mississippi attracted the attention of the NCC, a New York–based ecumenical organization, and in 1956 Campbell was appointed director of their newly formed Southern Project. He related, "They really didn't know what to tell me to do, and I had no idea what I was going to do, but I knew one would not be idle working in race relations." They told him he could put his office anywhere in the South. He chose Nashville, Tennessee, because of its central location, and when the crisis came in Little Rock, he went and served as an observer as the children tried to enter the school.[43] Campbell would be heard from again in many movement episodes.

◆ ◆ ◆

The Reverends Boggs, Cartwright, Ogden, and Campbell left Little Rock with some sense of accomplishment. Boggs felt satisfaction for his church's efforts in reopening the schools. Cartwright continued writing articles and telling the story of the Little Rock crisis as a moral lesson for all to know. Ogden felt a sense of victory when Ernest Green graduated from Central High. In an interview, Campbell described himself as inspired by Ogden: "We were in awe of him. He was a prophet for us. . . . I used his Bible passages. I was under his spell."[44]

Dunbar Ogden III remembers the fortieth anniversary of the Little Rock crisis. Rufus King Young, pastor of Bethel African Methodist Episcopal (AME) Church in Little Rock, was chosen to deliver the homily. He included the name of Dunbar Ogden among the most revered civil rights leaders: "Throughout history, God has descended in the human form of Mahatma Gandhi . . . Mother Teresa . . . Nelson Mandela . . . in the personalities of . . . Thurgood Marshall, Martin Luther King, Rosa Parks, Daisy Bates, Dunbar Ogden . . . and a whole lot of others to deliver a people from the evil clutches of racial segregation and discrimination."[45]

Mississippi

In Mississippi in 1954 a newly ordained Episcopal minister, Duncan Montgomery Gray Jr. (1926–2016), born in Canton, Mississippi, and rector of St. Peter's Episcopal Church in Oxford, wrote a pamphlet for the Diocese of Mississippi Department of Christian Social Relations, expressing the hope that the *Brown* decision would initiate a new era in race relations both for his state and his diocese: "Whatever may be said for the doctrine of 'separate but equal' in theory, we must all admit that in practice facilities have always been separate but almost never equal. . . . We in the South have had the opportunity for greatness thrust upon us; we did not ask for it; we may not like it; but we can be thankful for the God-given opportunity to make a significant contribution to the history of our state.... God grant that we may have the vision and the faith to accept this opportunity as consecrated communicants of Christ's Church and to make of it that which God intends it to be." Will Campbell related that the publisher would not permit Gray's name to appear on the document.[46]

Gray sent copies to news media, the governor, and all elected officials of the state, but the responses were negative and angry. It was virtually impossible to desegregate the schools in Mississippi. According to James W. Silver, a fifty-six-year-old professor of history at Ole Miss and a friend of Rev. Gray, "It was a closed society ... inflexible and stubborn ... letting no scruple, legal or ethical, stand in the way of the enforcement of the orthodoxy." The orthodoxy referred to by Silver held fast to the doctrine of white supremacy and segregation. A challenge came on September 30, 1962, when James Meredith, an African American, entered the University of Mississippi by court order after many aborted attempts and eight years after the *Brown* decision. Early that evening, Gray was at Silver's house watching President Kennedy's television appeal to students not to interfere with the admission of Meredith when a sudden interruption announced that rioting had begun. The historian Charles Eagles reported that well before Meredith's actual arrival on campus, segregationist forces mobilized to prevent his entrance, many coming from outside the state. Large groups of US marshals were also arriving to protect Meredith and were lining up at the east side of the Lyceum (the administration building). By 6:00 p.m. the number of raging segregationists, by Eagles's estimate, approached 1,000, but the "marshals stood steadfast." Kenneth L. Dixon of the *Meridian Star* lamented that "not one respected school official" had "made an effort to control the riotous crowd," who threw obscene insults, rocks, bottles, and eggs at the marshals. A few minutes after 6:00 p.m. Meredith arrived from Memphis, escorted by members of the Justice Department, who took him to his campus room through a western entrance. Meredith saw little of the hostile crowd. "We want Meredith." "Get the n_____r out," they cried.[47]

When the rioting began, Gray with others quickly made their way to the center of trouble. He could hardly believe what was happening: bricks were thrown at close range, smashing the windshields and windows of army vehicles loaded with marshals, and a steady stream of nonresident automobiles with Confederate flags moved into the campus. Gray and Rev. Wofford Smith, chaplain to Episcopal students, moved through the mob, grabbing weapons from the students (bricks, pipes, bottles, and anything the students could hurl at the marshals) in an attempt to quell the violence. Many in the mob cursed the ministers and refused to relinquish their weapons.[48]

As Gray moved about, he seemed to be followed by a tall stranger who turned out to be retired general Edwin A. Walker. At one point Walker asked, "Just who the hell are you, anyway, and what are you doing here?" "My name is Duncan Gray," the rector answered. "This is my home, and I am deeply hurt to see what is happening to the university and the state. I am here to do anything I can to stop the rioting and keep more people from getting hurt or killed." Walker turned on him, "You're the kind of minister that makes me ashamed to be an Episcopalian." Gray replied, "I have a proper concern and interest in keeping law and order. You, sir, are a Texan and have no business here." Gray reminded Walker that in 1957 he commanded the soldiers of the 101st Airborne Division as they accompanied nine African American children into all-white Central High School in Little Rock, but Walker responded, "I was on the wrong side that time, but this time I'm on the right side."⁴⁹ Gray and Walker, both Episcopalians, were in direct contrast to each other.

Walker stood on the pedestal of the Confederate monument at the center of the campus crying, "Protest, protest, keep it up. . . . These troops don't have any business here. They ought to be in Cuba." Gray climbed on the pedestal and pleaded with Walker to urge the crowd to stop the violence and go home, but Walker refused. Then as Gray stood on the pedestal, attempting to calm the mob, he could hear the insults, "Oh, he's that white n____r from down at St. Peter's. . . . I'll bet he belongs to the National Council of Churches! . . . Kill him! Kill him! . . . Traitor!" Finally, they turned on Gray and knocked him to the ground. A sheriff and a supportive group of students came to his aid and led him to safety. Fortunately, he was not hurt. Marshals were finally forced to use tear gas to disperse the mob. Eagles related the gunshots and "bullets from unknown sources hit dozens of marshals." Not until 6:15 Monday morning was the campus declared to be free of violence. During the riot, two men were killed, and fifty persons were treated for various injuries. According to Eagles, "Nearly 40% of the more than 500 marshals were injured.⁵⁰

Weeks before the rioting, Gray had urged the members of his congregation to do three things: ensure no acts of violence take place; obey and uphold the law as interpreted by the courts; and accept and treat the first African American student at Ole Miss as a person. Gray believed that "there can be no possible justification or excuse from a Christian standpoint for violence," but Gray's efforts were in vain. On the Sunday after the riot, Gray told his congregation that the blame for the rioting lay not with the US marshals but with every white Mississippian: "The students who rioted were ten years old at the time of the Supreme Court's *Brown* decision and had been steeped in the propaganda of defiance: censored textbooks, mandatory essay contests on white supremacy, and massive propaganda campaigns against the federal courts. . . . There was the cruelty of silence and the cruelty of lies and apathy. . . . True repentance means more than just remorse. Not just grieving but turning, knowing, living the truth of the Gospel. . . . Mississippians must accept the fact that the color of a person's skin can no longer be a barrier to his admission to the University of Mississippi."[51]

Newsmen outside of Mississippi hailed Gray as a person of great courage, but local newspapers not only avoided writing about the attack but also did their best to make him look like a fool. Later that year, when he was invited by seminary friends to preach at Washington Cathedral on the same day as the March on Washington, the local press made it appear that Gray had delivered a sermon at the Washington Monument instead of at the Washington Cathedral. A three-page letter sent by the vestry of Trinity Church, Natchez, to Gray's father, the bishop of Mississippi, suggested that the younger Gray "should seek a more hospitable climate in which to express his opinions." According to Will Campbell, the harassment of Gray never subsided, although much of it was done politely. As Campbell commented, "The elder Gray took no action." It might be thought that his father (bishop of Mississippi from 1943 until 1966) may have been protecting him, but according to Gray, his father always remained in the background. Gray suggested, "Certainly, there were times when I might hesitate to say or do something that might cause him difficulty, rather than myself, but this didn't happen all that often." Gray admits that his father was quite supportive of what he was trying to do: "His only real concern was that I might suffer as a result of my activism." At the time, Gray explained, "The diocese elected and consecrated a Bishop Coadjutor [an assistant bishop with the right of succession], and my father would sometimes refer to him issues or problems that might come about because of my actions, so that there would not be the question of a father-son bias."[52]

Early in 1962 some friends from prestigious St. Paul's Church in Meridian invited Gray to become their rector. Gray related, "I declined because I thought it would be irresponsible of me to leave St. Peter's when the admission of Mr. Meredith seemed imminent." Ruth, his wife, expressed the same feeling: "Duncan and I were never believers that God directs us to the best parking place . . . but after taking serious counsel together on that occasion we had no doubt that the Lord wanted us to remain in Oxford." The invitation came again three years later after the birth of their fourth child. At that time, Gray and his wife decided that perhaps God was calling them this time. After serving in Oxford for eight years, Gray and his family moved to Meridian. "I was never forced to leave," Gray stated, but "I felt that by 1965 it was really time for me to move. St. Peter's Church had experienced a loss of membership and serious financial problems as a result of my words and actions."[53]

Gray was elected bishop of Mississippi in 1974, after nine ballots, an adjournment, and a second election council meeting. "There may have been some politicking on my behalf," he admits, "but by 1974, times in Mississippi had changed and many of the changes I hoped for had taken place."[54] The life of Bishop Duncan Montgomery Gray Jr. bears witness to faith, perseverance, trust, commitment, and the grace to do God's will as he understands it. Gray is an Episcopalian priest who is unafraid to speak the truth as he understands it.

• • •

Mississippians were just as reluctant to desegregate their public elementary and high schools as they were to desegregate Ole Miss. As long as schools remained segregated, state officials did not close them. During the 1950s, Tom Dent, a public information director for the NAACP Legal Defense Fund, reported that of a black population constituting 45 percent of the state's population, only 3 percent had completed high school. Dent asserted that Mississippi spent $122.93 per pupil per year for the education of whites as opposed to $32.55 for blacks at the elementary level. The average yearly salary for white teachers in 1948 was more than double the figure for black teachers. In 1955 famed Oxford author Mississippian William Faulkner, in letters to the *Memphis Commercial Appeal*, the largest city newspaper in the area, wrote that "Mississippi schools were not even good for white people. . . . Why did they imagine they could afford two school systems good enough for whites and Negroes?" For his comments, he was shunned and criticized in his own state.[55]

On January 2, 1963, nine years after the *Brown* decision and fifteen months after the Ole Miss riot, twenty-eight young Methodist ministers issued a statement simply called "Born of Conviction." They wrote in the foreword that they were responding to the massive resistance against school desegregation and the "racial discord within our state." As one of the signatories, Powell Hall, commented, "We also felt it was necessary to counter the threat of the Mississippi legislature to close the public schools." The statement was issued to the *Mississippi Methodist Advocate* and began with another foreword by moderate editor Sam Ashmore, who claimed that it represented the vast majority of conference clerical feeling, although it was signed by only 28 from among 286 members of the Mississippi Methodist Conference who were under the age of forty-five.[56]

The ministers took part of their statement directly out of the 1960 *Methodist Discipline*: "Our Lord Jesus Christ teaches that all men are brothers. He permits no discrimination because of race, color, or creed. . . . In Christ Jesus you are all sons of God, through faith." They opposed unalterably the "closing of public schools on any level and the diversion of tax funds to support private or sectarian schools." Because of accusations of Communist affiliation made against the Methodist Church, the ministers included this statement: "We believe in the Fatherhood of God, the Brotherhood of Man, the public school system, and we are not communists. We publicly concur in the Methodist Council of Bishops' statement of November 16, 1962: 'The basic commitment of a Methodist minister is to Jesus Christ as Lord and Savior.' This sets him in permanent opposition to communism. He cannot be a Christian and a *communist*." When Marvin A. Franklin, bishop of the Mississippi Conference, was asked by the Associated Press to make a statement about the ministers' statement, he responded, "No comment."[57]

Almost immediately, the Mississippi Association of Methodist Ministers and Laymen (MAMML) issued its own "Methodist Declaration of Conscience on Racial Segregation." Although MAMML affirmed a minister's freedom to speak, it maintained that a minister who offends the consciences of his (or her) congregation must be ready to accept the consequences. MAMML believed that the teachings of Paul prescribed segregation by sex or position; therefore, segregation by race was proper and should be maintained: "If Paul's restrictions on women and on servants did not violate the spirit of oneness in Christ, then certainly our Southern system of race relations—with its demonstrated benefits—does not." MAMML maintained no official ties to the Methodist Church, but existed as the primary outlet for prosegregation sentiment among Mississippi Methodists. As the historian Joseph Crespino wrote, "MAMML brought together conservative Mississippi Methodists who strongly considered the possibility of local churches breaking away from what they saw as the liberal national church." Campbell commented that the Methodists were behaving more like members of churches that had no hierarchy (Baptists and Congregationalists) than like Methodists.[58]

What was to be the fate of the signatories? According to the historian Ellis Ray Branch, seven transferred to conferences out of the state. Others moved to "less demanding urban pulpits" within Mississippi. "Two reported cross burnings by the Ku Klux Klan in their front yards. All were harassed by telephone calls and boycotts conducted by members of their congregations." Bill Lampton was forced to leave Pisgah Methodist Church (near McComb) after the district superintendent and Pisgah officials expressed fear that their church would be vandalized if Lampton remained. Two of Lampton's automobile tires were slashed. James Rush was forced to resign two rural churches near Philadelphia, Mississippi, although, as Branch argued, "the action of the two churches violated Methodist practice." James B. Nicholson (1923–2009), born in Lauderdale, Mississippi, serving a church in Byram, had been asked to leave earlier because of his outspoken views on the Meredith incident, but when he signed the statement, his board forced him to leave. In a farewell letter to his congregation, Nicholson wrote, "I would like to share with you not my trials and tribulation . . . but . . . the great joy that comes to us in Christ Jesus. . . . For a time it seemed that all the doors in the world were closing and I came to see that God opens doors that man can never close. I do not know what the future holds, but I am most sure that God will be with me in whatever it brings." Rev. Nicholson went on to serve churches in the Iowa Methodist Conference.[59]

According to Joseph T. Reiff, "There was little support from Conference leaders. Within eighteen months . . . eighteen left the Mississippi Conference and two others departed in the next few years."[60] Some, however, remained to endure the storms against them.

Denson C. Napier (1928–2010), born in Covington County, Mississippi, was one of the signers who remained in Mississippi. A graduate of Candler School of Theology at Emory University in 1954, he served several small churches in the Delta region and for a time as director of the Methodist Campus Ministry at the University of Southern Mississippi. In 1962 he was serving a church in the tiny community of Richton when he helped organize the group that developed what came to be known as the "Statement of the Twenty-Eight." After the statement was released, Napier was told by a member of his church, "Well, you have joined the blacks now, so I guess you are happy." Members of his church suggested that he leave the state, but Napier responded, "When I finished seminary, I made the choice to stay in Mississippi, and I plan to stay here until I die. Nobody is going to run me out. I'm not going to leave." In 1970, when the municipal schools in Jackson were finally desegregated, Napier worked for the Emergency School Assistance Program, a federally funded agency. If there was any problem in any of the schools, or if the principal was having a problem with any of the students, Napier went in and tried to straighten things out. He worked in that capacity for six years until the funding stopped.[61]

Powell Hall (1929–2008), born in Jackson, Mississippi, was serving a church in Scooba when he signed the document. He was moved at the end of the year to an isolated white church in Kingston, where black churches were being burned to the ground all around his church. When Hall condemned the burnings, his salary was withheld, and the family survived on corn bread and beans. A crew of Quaker volunteers came to rebuild the burned-out churches, and with them came a Methodist minister from New Jersey who attended Hall's church and commented that he liked Hall's sermon. Several weeks later Hall received an invitation to be pastor of a church in Point Pleasant, New Jersey, but Hall decided to remain in Mississippi because he believed the church and society were going through an upheaval and that his parishioners, no matter what their views, needed help and guidance. At the end of the next year he was transferred to Sandy Hook, where he taught in the public school and became active in the Mississippi Council on Human Relations. Belonging to such a group made him a victim of the Klan, and a cross was burned on his church property. He was moved again to Vaughan in 1968 and remained there at the time when the Supreme Court finally ruled in 1969 that Mississippi's laws of massive resistance were unconstitutional (*Alexander v. Holmes County Board of Education*). When people in his congregation asked to open a private white academy inside the church, Hall refused: "If you want to use church property for a school, that's all right, but you cannot have a racial bar in the United Methodist Church. You have to let anyone come in who wants to." The school was not established in the church building but elsewhere in Vaughan. Shortly afterward, Hall was transferred to Satartia, a remote region where he had to drive 50 to 100 miles a day to take his children to a public school. Hall and his family finally decided to move to New Jersey: "We felt we had stuck it out long enough in Mississippi. We wanted to be in a place where the children could get an education in an orderly, settled way before they got too old."[62]

For Rev. Keith Tonkel (1936–2017), the only signer not born in Mississippi, but born in New Orleans, signing the document represented his commitment to remain in Mississippi no matter what happened. He was serving a small church in Gulfport at the time and managed to survive for seven years because people along the Gulf Coast were more open-minded than those in interior Mississippi. In 1969, when times were beginning to change, he was assigned to Wells Church in North Jackson, where, under his leadership, the church grew from about eleven people to several hundred. Recovering addicts, interracial couples, and others, uncomfortable elsewhere, could find love and acceptance in its sanctuary. Tonkel was greatly attracted to this type of ministry. He has remained at Wells Church until the present day, ministering to the needs of his large, diverse congregation: "Our church marches each year in the Martin Luther King Day parade, and we probably have the lightest complexion of any group, but we're glad to participate."[63]

The sociologist Donald Cunnigen suggested, and other scholars agreed, that the majority of white Mississippians were unprepared for the social changes forced upon them by "young African Americans and white civil rights activists," but for Duncan Gray and other like-minded citizens, the changes "provided hope for a brighter and better future in the race relations of the South and in Mississippi." The Reverends Napier and Tonkel were among eight who did not leave the Mississippi Methodist Conference after signing the "Born of Conviction" statement. Rev. Hall did his best to follow his convictions, but he finally succumbed to pressure. Joseph T. Reiff and other scholars suggested that "Born of Conviction caused a crack in the Closed Society's united front and caused some crucial doubt on the belief that all white Mississippi Christians supported the maintenance of the white supremacist system."[64]

Alabama

Like Mississippi, Alabama fought to prevent school desegregation through: a pupil-placement law that gave local school boards authority to assign pupils to designated schools; a variety of state amendments allowing private white schools to be funded from the sale, lease, or donation of public property; and a fiercely segregationist governor. Like Orval Faubus, Governor George Corley Wallace of Alabama had once been a "liberal," but that image vanished after his overwhelming defeat in the Democratic primary for governor in 1958. After losing to John Patterson, who ran as a segregationist, Wallace, portrayed as ruthlessly ambitious by Dan T. Carter (although repentant in later years after his near assassination and resulting paralysis), vowed never to be "out-segged" again. In 1959 he began a vigorous segregationist campaign promising to disobey any federal court order to integrate Alabama's schools. Winning a landslide victory in 1962, he told the exuberant audience at his inaugural address, "In the name of the greatest people that ever trod this earth, I draw the line in the dust and toss the gauntlet before the feet of tyranny . . . and I say . . . segregation now . . . segregation tomorrow . . . segregation forever." When African Americans James Hood and Vivian Malone tried to enroll in the University of Alabama in 1963, Wallace promised to prevent their entrance, "even to the point of standing at the schoolhouse door."[65]

The majority of southern white ministers in the states of Mississippi and Alabama remained silent on the incendiary issue, but not Rev. Raymond Davis, white pastor of all-white Our Redeemer Lutheran Church in Montgomery. Davis (1929–2010), born in Orangeburg, South Carolina, was scheduled to deliver inspirational messages on local television. In response to Wallace's inaugural address, Davis dared to speak from his heart and announced before his audience, "Governor Wallace, you should be kneeling in prayer and asking for forgiveness instead of shouting, 'Segregation now, segregation tomorrow, segregation forever.'"[66]

Davis, a recent graduate of the University of South Carolina and the Lutheran Theological Seminary in Columbia, South Carolina, had become liberal toward race early in his ministerial career. Originally planning to serve in the Liberian (African) mission of the Lutheran Church of America, Davis and his wife, Rachel, prepared for such a call at the Kennedy School of Missions in Hartford, Connecticut, where they became friendly with Byron Traub, a black Lutheran minister from Liberia. It was only natural, as devotees to missionary work, to invite their friend home to South Carolina for the Christmas holidays. Traveling on the train, they got as far as Washington, DC, where they would have to change for the southern-bound train. As they walked along the cars looking for three seats, the conductor announced that the black man could not remain with them but would have to sit in another car in the back. Immediately they objected, "This man is our guest, and if he can't sit with us then we will go where he is going," and they went to sit with Rev. Traub in the "black section" of the train. According to Rachel Davis, the conductor tried to make Raymond feel horrible for letting his wife ride in the Jim Crow car filled with black soldiers sitting on wooden benches, returning to their homes for the holidays, but Raymond told him, "I don't think I can make her do anything else." Rachel Davis told the conductor, "No, sir, I won't move. This man is our guest and we will sit with him." At home in Columbia, South Carolina, Rachel and Raymond stayed with Rachel's parents, and Rev. Traub stayed with Raymond's parents. Their church, all-white Mount Tabor Lutheran in Columbia, also welcomed Traub, but he was not allowed to speak from the pulpit, only from the side lectern. Raymond Davis commented, "Thankfully, Rev. Traub never realized that he was slighted."[67] The whole episode fortified and strengthened Davis's resolve to work for racial justice.

Raymond and Rachel Davis and their two children arrived in Montgomery in 1957, just after the Montgomery Bus Boycott. Although sympathetic to the burgeoning civil rights movement, Davis's immediate attention focused on building church programs. It was a new congregation with most members, not southerners, employed at nearby Maxwell Air Force Base, who would stay as briefly as three months or as long as three years. "They knew we were liberals, but they seemed receptive to everything we tried to do," stated Rachel Davis. The previous minister, who had served for only a few months, told Rev. Davis, "You will have opportunities in the community well beyond the congregation, which means you will be part of the Ministers' Association. You will be on radio and television, and you will enhance the name of Lutherans in the city." Rev. Davis accepted his predecessor's charge and became president of the Ministers' Association. Wallace's inaugural statement so infuriated him that he decided to make his television statement, but affirmed that his bold statement was made individually and apart from his congregation. Shortly thereafter, word must have reached Lutheran headquarters. He was called away from Our Redeemer and sent to church headquarters in Philadelphia, Pennsylvania, to serve as director of Vacation and Weekday Church Schools. For one year, he traveled throughout the diverse synods of the United Lutheran Church of America (ULCA) training educational leaders and embracing the northern heterogeneity of the ULCA— African American, Native American, Asian American, and Mexican American—and becoming more diversity conscious himself. Much to his surprise and amazement, late in 1963 he received a call from Montgomery. "Our pastor has left. Would you even think about coming back?" Davis declared, "I thought about it, I prayed, and I went back."[68] Upon his return, Davis became more active and forceful in the cause of racial justice when he attempted to begin a black nursery school within the church building, thus incurring the wrath of some in the congregation, which led again to his dismissal.

◆ ◆ ◆

In spite of Governor Wallace's schoolhouse stand, Vivian Malone and James Hood entered the University of Alabama on June 11, 1963, with the help of federal marshals and without violence. When confronted by Deputy Attorney General of the United States Nicholas Katzenbach, Wallace retreated from his staged position, but immediately began a concerted effort to prevent the integration of the public elementary and high schools.[69]

During the summer of 1963, four Alabama school systems were ordered by the federal judiciary to desegregate: Macon County, Birmingham, Mobile, and Huntsville. According to journalist Claude Sitton, violence and white boycotts were expected in all three locations except Huntsville, which is located in the more liberal region of northern Alabama. Also anticipated was opposition from Governor Wallace. Tuskegee High School in Tuskegee, Macon County, was to be the first test case. The county contained the largest percentage of African Americans in the nation, 85 percent, and the school board, wanting to avoid trouble from the large African American population, was willing to comply with the court order.[70]

On the outskirts of Tuskegee stands Tuskegee Institute (where George Wallace once served as a trustee), pioneer in the education of African Americans, with its dignified student-built brick buildings; its student-built Victorian manse, home to the institute's first president, Booker T. Washington; and its lush fields of okra, beans, and tomatoes, once cared for by the dexterous hands of George Washington Carver. The famous and controversial bust of Booker T. Washington, removing a blanket of ignorance from the eyes of a young kneeling African American, still proudly surveys the domain. The Veterans Administration hospital, once only for African Americans, is near the institute.[71]

Tuskegee was divided into two groups of people: the powerful white group, descendants of the former plantation owners whose mansions lined downtown streets, and the African American group, whose ancestors labored endlessly in the fields and mansions. Within each group were further divisions: conservative whites holding on to the comfortable past and progressive whites ready for change; and docile blacks accepting their "place" in the social order, living in the downtown limits, and progressive blacks, educators and doctors, living within the environs of Tuskegee Institute and the Veterans Administration Hospital, willing and eager to challenge the status quo.[72]

The town became famous during the Supreme Court case *Gomillion v. Lightfoot* (1960). City officials had changed the boundaries from the shape of a square to what famous black attorney from Alabama Fred Gray called "a 28-sided sea dragon," in order to prevent 400 African Americans from voting in municipal elections. Under the leadership of African American C. G. Gomillion of Tuskegee Institute and Gray as attorney, the lawsuit to reestablish the old residential boundary lines was lost at the state level but won at the Supreme Court level. At the same time, Detroit Lee, an employee of the Veterans Administration Hospital and founder of the local NAACP chapter, petitioned the Tuskegee Civic Association (TCA) to support a desegregation suit against the Macon County Board of Education. In 1956 Lee's request on behalf of his oldest son was turned down, with Gomillion explaining that the gerrymandering issue was the organization's top priority. Once the gerrymandering issue was settled, TCA agreed to finance the legal expense for a suit. Fred Gray was retained as attorney. Anthony Lee and eleven other African American students were selected to enter the high school the first Monday in September 1963.[73]

Among a group of white liberal-minded people in Tuskegee was Ennis G. Sellers, born in 1929 in Union Springs, Alabama, and pastor of the First Methodist Church. Sellers grew up in the small town of Georgiana, where everybody knew everybody, including black folks. He was taught to be respectful to all persons regardless of color and say to them, "Yes, sir," and "Yes, ma'am." When he was fifteen, his older brother died of polio, and Sellers began to think more deeply about life and its purposes. Six years later he was licensed to preach in the Methodist Church. Sellers is proud of his Methodist heritage. His great-grandfather was one of the original trustees of the Georgiana Methodist Church, and another ancestor had been licensed to preach during the 1700s by Bishop Francis Asbury. As a young person, Sellers was active in all phases of the Georgiana Methodist Church, including prayer meetings. After briefly serving in the US Air Force, he attended Troy University, where he played football as tackle and was active in religious activities. While attending Candler School of Theology at Emory University, he served five rural churches in southeast Alabama, commuting 500 miles each weekend to and from his churches. After graduation in 1954, he served two more churches until he was appointed to the First Methodist Church of Tuskegee. He was thirty-one years old; strong in body, mind, and spirit; and committed to change.[74]

During his first three years, First Methodist Church, the oldest church in Tuskegee, prospered. Support for all charities quadrupled; 121 new members were received; the sanctuary was renovated and redecorated; and all buildings were repaired. Indebtedness was amortized. Sellers commented, "If a minister intends to provide guidance on controversial issues, he must do his best as a pastor. I was involved with nearly eighty-five percent of the families through some sort of crisis experience. I knew the church building needed improvement, and I went about doing that. I am completely convinced that these factors made it possible for me to say many things during the school crisis that would have not been possible otherwise. The three prominent wealthy men, who pretty well controlled the church board before I came, discovered they could not control me."[75]

In the spring of 1963, when it became apparent that Tuskegee High School was going to be ordered to desegregate, Sellers, with two sons in elementary school, became president of the Parent Teachers' Association (PTA) of the Tuskegee Unified Public School System. The mayor, the county school superintendent, and the high school principal were all members of his church. He spent the summer trying to convince local parents to accept the court order peacefully.[76]

Three days before the impending event, Sellers, as president of the PTA, arranged for an open meeting with parents to allow them, as he suggested, to "blow off steam." Four hundred whites crowded into the auditorium of Tuskegee High to hear the principal, the school board president, the superintendent, and a local lawyer explain how the desegregation order had evolved and how it could be achieved. Tempers flared: "Why don't we postpone the opening of school for a week to see whether the integration can be stopped?" "Governor Wallace offered to provide transportation for white students to attend other schools [pupil-placement law]," and "Call a special session of the legislature to have Macon County's public schools closed." It was apparent to Sellers that "there were members of the KKK, White Citizens' Council, and representatives of Governor Wallace present," but Sellers only allowed parents of children who would be affected by school integration to speak.[77]

Segregationists crushed any attempt by Sellers and other liberals and moderates to avoid the inevitable. At 6:30 a.m. on September 2, 1963, Wallace's state troopers arrived and completely barricaded the school and surrounding streets, reminiscent of Governor Faubus's action in Arkansas in 1957. Sellers told his wife, "I'm going to take the boys and enter the elementary school." (Both schools were across the street from the parsonage on the same campus.) "You will NOT," she said, "we will all go." She carried their two-year-old daughter, and he took the two boys, ages five and seven, by the hand. Slowly, they made their way to the elementary school. Troopers, photographers, newsmen, and spectators were everywhere. When time came for the school to open, all students, teachers, and the principal were turned away. His wife was ordered by the troopers to take the children home, and Sellers, who stood six-feet three-inches tall and weighed 220 pounds, was grabbed by two of the largest troopers and hustled over to Al Lingo, director of the Department of Public Safety for the state of Alabama. Sellers boldly told him that no mention was made of closing the elementary school, and he intended to enter his children. "It doesn't matter," Lingo responded, "both schools are closed. Just leave, you have no reason to be here." Interviewed by a newsman on local television later that day, Sellers expressed his disgust with the governor's action and his complete support for opening Tuskegee High School and the elementary school.[78]

The Board of Education rejected Wallace's blockade and declared, "All schools of Macon County are open as originally scheduled." As Sitton commented, the board's statement was "little more than symbolic defiance" as troopers remained at their stations.[79]

The next day, as Sellers related, rabid segregationists conducted an intensive telephone campaign to convince people to boycott the public schools: "Townspeople received dozens of calls with insinuations that unless they kept their children out of the public school, they were 'n____r-lovers' and did not love their own children." Sellers related that the town changed overnight as a result of the telephone campaign. The liberals seemed to disappear: "While the troopers were resented on Monday and refused even cold water, by Thursday, people were setting up picnic tables and furnishing them with food, drink, and easy chairs." On the Sunday following the blockade, he told his congregation, "Un-Christian comments have been made about the integration. . . . What has happened is a tragedy not only for our individual families but for the whole nation."[80]

Eight days later President Kennedy ordered the Alabama National Guard to enforce the integration. In what was called "an unprecedented procedure," all five federal district judges of Alabama issued an order restraining Wallace from further interference with schools, but, as Sellers observed, the segregationists won the battle: "Some white students attended classes with the black students, but pressure on parents mounted and finally most dropped out. A private white school opened in October in an old two-story house, one block from the school with all kinds of 'begging cans' placed in various stores to raise money."[81]

Conditions in Tuskegee deteriorated. Tuskegee High was reduced to six African American students. The elementary school remained open but segregated. Vandals stole band instruments and athletic and science laboratory equipment from the high school. A group of white boys confessed to the thefts, claiming they were doing it for the private school. They were never apprehended. Pressure was exerted on Sellers to allow the private school to use the church facilities, but Sellers was firm: "I openly state that as minister of the church, I do not give my consent." Sellers's action had repercussions. His church became completely divided into those who supported the private school, those who supported the public school, and those who, through pressure, had placed their children in the private school but still supported Sellers's position. The school superintendent and the principal of Tuskegee High stopped attending the church because of "cold-shoulder" treatment from the pro-private-school group. Harassing phone calls plagued Sellers, the superintendent, and the principal. Many of the members withheld contributions, "presumably giving the money to the private school." The church found itself in financial difficulty, and, according to Sellers, his name was placed on a list of undesirable pastors by the Methodist Layman's Union, a group opposed to integration.[82]

All that year Sellers received insulting telephone calls, silences at the other end, poison pen letters, and threats of violence from the Klan. Sellers related how one of his parishioners, a campaign manager for Governor Wallace, came into his office one day and said, "The Klan is going to burn a cross in the school yard and on your front lawn, two crosses." Sellers asked, "Can you give me the names of Klan members who might come into Poor Richard's Café each morning (the place where Sellers had his coffee)?" Reluctantly, his parishioner gave Sellers their names, and for the next few mornings Sellers appeared at the café joining in the conversation about barn burnings and cross burnings. One morning Sellers said in a loud voice, "I'd surely take a dim view if I ever saw anyone in the middle of the night around my house with fire." Someone replied, "You can't do anything—you're a preacher," but Sellers said, "Listen, feller, I'm a man. I have a wife and three small children. I've already got my shotgun with the plug out and I have five #1 buck shots in it. If I see anyone around my house at night with fire, I'm going to shoot first and ask questions later." "You mean, you would do that? You're a preacher." Sellers replied, "I certainly will. I will defend my family and not have any qualms about it. There's no court anywhere that would convict me for defending my family." Sellers related that the Klan was in such a hurry when they came to burn the cross in front of the school that they didn't get it in the ground. They set it on fire, but it fell over and put itself out, and they never did get across the street to the parsonage.[83] They absolutely believed what Sellers had said.

What was to be Sellers's fate after staunchly upholding the integration of Tuskegee High School? After serving First Methodist Church for four years, his district superintendent attempted to transfer him to another difficult situation, but Bishop Paul Hardin, newly appointed to the Alabama–West Florida Methodist Conference, intervened and appointed Sellers to a good, medium-size church in Mobile, where he stayed for five years.[84]

In 1965 Sellers and a group from the Alabama–West Florida Methodist Conference traveled to Boston University, the Union Theological Seminary (New York City), Drew University (Madison, New Jersey), and Yale Divinity School to explain what southern white ministers with consciences were doing to fight racism. Sellers expressed his sentiments clearly: "We are doing the best we can without completely alienating the people whom it is our lot to serve in the name of Jesus Christ."[85] Sellers was able to combine his prophetic role with pastoral duties, but during the crisis, the segregationist forces seemed to win out.

South Carolina

The foes of school desegregation were just as powerful in South Carolina as in Alabama, Mississippi, and Little Rock, perhaps more so. They were able to maintain a segregated society in a way that avoided violence and did not tarnish, they believed, the sacred name of South Carolina. In 1951 the lawsuit

Briggs v. Elliott, coming from Clarendon County, South Carolina, became the first legal challenge to school segregation in the twentieth century. As the historian Walter Edgar noted, there were 2,375 white children and 6,531 black children in rural Clarendon County's public school system. There were no school buses for the black children, who would often have to walk nine miles to get to a school that had no indoor plumbing or electricity. It was hardly in compliance with the *Plessy v. Ferguson* "separate but equal" doctrine of 1896. In 1950 Harry Briggs, a World War II navy veteran, and twenty-four other Clarendon County black residents filed a suit in the federal district court in Charleston appealing for school buses and equality in their schools. The court ruled two-to-one against the plaintiffs, but the appeal continued to the US Supreme Court.[86] *Briggs v. Elliott* became one of the feeder cases for the *Brown* decision, which unanimously outlawed segregated schools.

In defiance of the Supreme Court decision, the General Assembly of South Carolina passed a statute withholding state funds to any integrated public school. White Citizens' Councils appeared everywhere, busily convincing people it was their duty as southerners to oppose school integration. A "committee of fifty-two" leading white businessmen, clergy, and politicians declared the "necessity of separate schools to preserve public education and domestic tranquility."[87]

It was also from South Carolina that the united southern defiance of *Brown*, the "Southern Manifesto," originated, signed by nineteen out of twenty-two southern senators and 82 of 106 southern representatives. The Southern Manifesto justified any action of disobedience against any order of the Supreme Court. Governors of South Carolina adhered rigidly to the manifesto. George Bell Timmerman Jr. (governor, 1955–1959) even forced Billy Graham to move a crusade from the state capitol grounds to Fort Jackson military base because Graham allowed blacks to participate in his rallies. Timmerman also pressured the administration of South Carolina State College to fire faculty who supported desegregation.[88] This was the atmosphere, political and social, when three young pastors, John B. Morris, Ralph E. Cousins, and John S. Lyles, began preparing a booklet called *South Carolinians Speak*, believing there might be some support for moderation in South Carolina.

Rev. Morris (1930–2010), born in Brunswick, Georgia, and rector of St. Barnabas Church (Episcopal) in Dillon, contacted his friend Rev. Cousins (1929–1970), born in Wilkes-Barre, Pennsylvania, but reared in Elberton, Georgia, and rector of the Church of the Advent (Episcopal) in Marion, suggesting, "It is evident that a great deal of literature is being circulated among southerners upholding traditional views on segregation. . . . There is nothing in print, which I have seen, that can really challenge the conservatism of the average middle-class South Carolinian. Church tracts opposing segregation have little impact on church members." Cousins joined Morris as compiler along with his neighbor, Rev. Lyles (1926–2015), born in Great Falls, South Carolina, and pastor of the Marion Presbyterian Church. They called themselves "Concerned South Carolinians."[89]

Before it was published, the booklet was denounced by Governor Timmerman. According to Lyles, "Someone we contacted had given a copy of the prospectus to Governor Timmerman who relayed the information to newspaper reporters." On July 3, 1957, the newspapers revealed that a booklet on moderation and reason was being authored by a group of "concerned South Carolinians." Timmerman immediately blasted the booklet: "All South Carolinians, not just those self-appointed few, are 'concerned South Carolinians.'" As a new minister, Lyles was unprepared for the effect Timmerman's attack would have on his congregation. A short time later, while Lyles was away at a youth conference, his elders decided that, for the good of the church, he should leave. At the next session meeting (governing body of the church), Lyles agreed to seek another pastorate, but he refused to relinquish his involvement with the booklet.[90]

Some fifty ministers and 150 laypeople throughout the state were contacted for support and possible essays. Two nearby ministers quickly answered the call, Rev. Joseph R. Horn III, rector of St. John's Episcopal Church in Florence, who was told by his senior warden to do the right thing, and Rev. Larry A. Jackson, born in 1925 in Florence and minister of counseling at Central Methodist Church in Florence, who was convinced that segregation was immoral. Horn and Jackson became compilers of the booklet along with Morris, Cousins, and Lyles. Only twelve laypeople from various churches could be persuaded to write essays.[91]

Jackson recalls that, for him, the best part of *South Carolinians Speak* was the introduction. "We spent hours seated around a breakfast table trying to decide just exactly what words we would use to express our convictions. Finally we wrote: 'As Christian pastors of various denominations, we believe that our commitment to Jesus Christ calls us to minister to the sickness of society as well as to the ills of the individual.'"[92]

According to Morris, the booklet was intended to plant seeds of conversion in the hearts and minds of segregationists and give courage to moderates to express their views. The first essay, written by a conservative lawyer in Columbia, questioned the logic of allowing white children to attend schools with blacks whose lives, the author wrote, were intimately involved with "crime, venereal disease, and illegitimacy." The second essay, written by a medical doctor from Clinton, added another conservative viewpoint: "In emulating the white man, many Negroes have succeeded in the professional fields, in the arts, in business, in sports, and in the entertainment world. We do believe, however, that forced integration in the near future would retard advancement of the Negro and would certainly result in increased interracial tension. It would not only be unwise but rather dangerous to forcibly change the customs of a land overnight to appease a few malcontents." Another view expressed the fact that in South Carolina, "most people with moderate ideas on this subject are afraid to even talk about the problem along constructive lines." This businessman from Dillon supported the Supreme Court decision: "To be honest with ourselves, we must admit that under the doctrine of 'separate but equal' we have not given Negroes equal or fair citizenship opportunities in education and in other areas." A woman from Gaffney, a representative of upper-class white South Carolina society, began her essay, "As a follower of Christ, I believe that God is my Father and that all men are my brothers." She supported a gradualist approach to desegregation accomplished by starting with the first grade: "Children are not born with prejudice. A six-year-old, except when he comes from a home where prejudice is loud, vocal, and demonstrated, will normally disregard outward appearance. If adults could only learn from children their ability to judge character and worth without regard to externals, our task would be immeasurably lighter."[93]

Those opposing segregation paid a heavy price for their opinions. The businessman from Dillon was called a Communist and his business declined. The woman from Gaffney received numerous hate messages. Members of the Klan dynamited her home. Fortunately, the family escaped injury, but members of the Klan were never apprehended.[94]

Ten days before the booklet circulated, Rev. Lyles, a World War II veteran, a graduate of the Union Theological Seminary in Virginia, and a Fulbright Scholar at the University of Aberdeen, Scotland, delivered the first of two sermons on race relations, entitled "Amos Diagnoses Our Southern Sickness." He told the congregation about Amos, a rugged shepherd who demanded change in the presence of an entrenched status quo, "a man who carried God's word to a nation sick unto death." Later in the sermon he declared, "Christianity means social justice for all people, white and black. Do you remember those terrifying words of Jesus? 'Depart from me . . . into the eternal fire prepared for the devil and his angels; for I was hungry and you gave me no food, I was thirsty and you gave me no drink, I was a stranger and you did not welcome me, naked and you did not clothe me, sick and in prison, and you did not visit me' (Matthew 25: 41–43). . . . May God give all of us humility to accept His healing and strength to follow His will."[95]

After hearing the sermon, his session asked that he not preach the second sermon, and he agreed. They did not want to challenge his freedom in the pulpit, but made it abundantly clear that they did not approve of his sermon. Lyles regretted that they would not hear the second sermon about the prophet Hosea and the cure for the "Southern Sickness," which would have left them more encouraged.[96]

A few weeks later, after *South Carolinians Speak* was published, his church elders decided that for the good of the church, he should leave. Lyles left Marion in late December 1957, deeply distressed. "It was a painful and anxious moment for a young couple with a baby to be forced out of a pastorate that had been happy until July of 1957," but, as he further explained, "During segregation, it was difficult for any kind of communication to exist. It was impossible to have a town meeting. The school board would call for black and white parents to discuss the problem, but none would attend. If anybody suggested that we could possibly integrate even one grade at a time, they would instantly be silenced because South Carolina was massively resisting."[97]

In spite of the booklet's open discussion on the issue of school desegregation, the compilers suffered, and, except for Joseph Horn, not one remained in South Carolina. Morris went to Atlanta, where he established the Episcopal Society for Cultural and Racial Unity, dedicated to opposing southern segregation in schools, business establishments, and public facilities. Lyles continued his ministry in West Virginia, where the school desegregation problem had been solved, and he could welcome black members into his church. Jackson accepted a position as pastor of the Union Church in Santiago, Chile, but returned in 1973 to become president of Lander College in Greenwood, where he officiated its desegregation program and remained until 1992. Ralph Cousins moved to a church in the Episcopal Diocese of Ohio and died of a heart attack at the age of forty-one.[98]

◆ ◆ ◆

With forces for massive resistance firmly entrenched in the state, African Americans in South Carolina accepted school segregation, but in 1960 African American Harvey Gantt, a native of Charleston, decided to challenge the system by applying for admission to segregated Clemson University's School of Architecture. He sought the aid of Matthew Perry, a young and dynamic civil rights attorney and an NAACP activist. After the denial of three mailed-in applications, Perry advised Gantt to request an interview. It was then that Gantt, a Baptist, found a friend in the white director of Baptist students on the campus, Rev. Charles A. Webster, born in 1934 in Wilson, North Carolina.[99]

Webster first heard of Gantt's trouble through the South Carolina Human Relations Council, of which he was an active member. Webster also met with the Gantt family and assured them that he would do everything he could to help. He then called upon the two Baptist administrators at Clemson, Registrar Kenneth N. Vickery and Dean Walter Cox. Cox was a deacon at the Clemson Baptist Church, where Webster was assistant pastor. He tried to convince them to accept Gantt, but they were definitely not interested. Webster continued his efforts. He accompanied Gantt to the office of registrar to request a personal interview. It took the Board of Deacons at Clemson Baptist Church only a few days to arrange for Webster's departure. On December 27, 1962, with Webster out-of-town visiting family for the Christmas holiday, the vote was taken for his dismissal. According to Webster, no charges were lodged against his "theology, program, or personal life," but in Webster's estimation, "the deacons wished that he would disappear." Webster later learned that the chairman of the Board of Deacons, without his knowledge, met with Robert Edwards, president of the college, who complained that Webster had been interfering in the evening study habits of Clemson students by preaching integration. Actually, Webster had been counseling students to prepare them for the possible entrance of Gantt to the university.[100]

Webster was moved to write an account of his dismissal for the *Baptist Biblical Recorder*, the journal of the North Carolina Baptist State Convention. In it he contended that anyone associated with the South Carolina Human Relations Council, like himself, would be subject to investigation and castigation. The *Biblical Recorder* never published his eight-page letter, which contained genuine evidence that Edwards and the Clemson administration tried to prevent the integration of the university.[101]

Upon court order and without any violence, Gantt was admitted to Clemson University on January 27, 1963, and Edwards performed an "about face." Any violence like that accompanying James Meredith at Ole Miss was to be strictly avoided in South Carolina, but the damage to Webster's ministerial career had been achieved. He was never appointed again to serve in a Baptist church. He left Clemson just as Gantt entered. He had done everything in his power to prepare students for the peaceful acceptance of Gantt, and for that he had no regrets. Webster accepted a scholarship to study in the field of Christianity and culture at the Theology School at Duke University and continued his campus ministry at North Carolina State University.[102]

In 1963 Webster became a leader in a summer-long voter education project in segregated Warrenton, North Carolina, sponsored by the American Friends Service Committee. The group of fourteen college students and three leaders presented workshops on voter registration and voting procedures at rural churches in a county where few African Americans were registered to vote. They were the first interracial group to live together in Warren County and, as such, experienced extreme harassment. They were shunned and verbally abused by white residents, and the Klan desecrated their posters, but they persisted. In eight weeks they conducted thirty workshops; attended NAACP meetings; taught Bible school; helped in farm work; participated in clean-up days at churches, cemeteries, and the African American community center; and talked with hundreds of African Americans about their experiences and fears of registering. According to Gavin Wright of Stanford University, who was also part of the group, "It was a position for which Webster was extremely well suited."[103]

Webster never relinquished his passion for racial justice. One summer day in 1965 in North Carolina, his son, Al, remembers peering out the window of their old Chevrolet, parked at the side of a road, to watch his dad grab a cross wrapped in burlap from a group of men dressed in white robes and hoods. "Just move over a little," his dad told him, "so we can fit the cross into the car and take it home, out of reach of those mean people."[104]

The battle raged for many years as South Carolina Baptists sought legislation to allow their children to attend private white academies at state expense. In 1983 the Supreme Court rejected tax exemption for private religious schools that discriminated on the basis of race (*Bob Jones University v. United States*), but in South Carolina, the Baptists persisted. In 1996 their petitions were finally officially denied.[105]

◆ ◆ ◆

Had the people of the South been ready for this first phase of desegregation, the destruction of Jim Crow might have progressed smoothly and without violence and bloodshed, as most African Americans earnestly hoped, but southern politicians, elected by the majority of southerners, devised incredible methods for resisting change. These politicians also pointed to the de facto segregation (by personal choice) existing in northern schools. "Why should southerners alone be forced to change?"

In spite of difficulties, the *Southern School News* reported that, by 1963, school districts in the Upper South had begun desegregating, but none had done so in Mississippi, South Carolina, or eastern Arkansas, and serious problems still existed in Virginia. This was nine years after the *Brown* decision. At the same time that public schools were being desegregated, all-white private school academies were exploding across the South.[106] The problems of school desegregation were far from over.

The Supreme Court continued its efforts to desegregate southern schools. In 1964 the Court decided that the time for "all deliberate speed" had run out. The Court ruled that the closure of the public schools in Prince Edward County, Virginia, must end (*Griffin v. Prince Edward County Board of Education*). Virginia finally reopened its public schools in Prince Edward County. That same year, Title IV of the Civil Rights Act of 1964 prohibited discrimination in programs and activities, including schools receiving federal financial assistance. This measure encouraged many school districts to desegregate. In 1968 school districts that had discriminated in the past were required to

achieve racial balance in all areas: facilities, staff, faculty, extracurricular activities, and transportation (*Green v. County School Board of New Kent County,
Virginia*). In 1969, with some southern states still resisting, the Court ruled that
Mississippi could no longer operate two separate school systems through its
pupil-placement and freedom-of-choice laws (*Alexander v. Holmes County*).
In 1971 court-ordered busing became a legitimate means of achieving racial
balance (*Swann v. Charlotte-Mecklenburg Board of Education*), but several
years later, in consideration of the widespread objections to busing, the court
began to rescind court-ordered busing from most suburbs (*Millikin v. Bradley*
[1974] and *Dayton Board of Education v. Brinkman* [1977]).[107]

For more than a decade after that, a conservative Court refused to hear
cases that involved court-ordered desegregation and during the 1990s backed
away from enforcing school integration altogether. In 1991 the court ruled that
"desegregation decrees [were] not intended to operate in perpetuity" (*Board of
Education of Oklahoma City v. Dowell*). In 1992, on remand from the Court of
Appeals, the US District Court for the Northern District of Georgia withdrew
its control over four areas in desegregation cases (*Freeman v. Pitts*). In 1995 the
Court returned schools to local control (*Missouri v. Jenkins*). As the historian
Raymond Wolters noted, "School districts were prohibited from practicing
racial discrimination, but they were no longer required to achieve integration." In 2001 white parents in Charlotte, North Carolina, successfully ended
the desegregation process and a bar to the use of race in pupil assignments. In
2002 a report from the Harvard University Civil Rights Project concluded that
America's schools were resegregating.[108]

Although many African Americans have benefited from attending schools
with white students, to call school desegregation a complete success would be in
error. Attorney Derrick Bell, who worked for the NAACP Legal Defense Fund
from 1960 to 1965, concluded in his book *Silent Covenants* that the Supreme
Court was unable to enforce the decision and that "many black and Hispanic
children are [now] enrolled in schools as separate and probably more unequal
than those their parents and grandparents attended under the era of 'separate
but equal.'" Bell is disturbed by the poverty in inner cities, lack of good schools,
high dropout rates, high crime, and illegitimacy. He suggests that independent
black schools, charter schools, vouchers, and sectarian schools may be better
alternatives for parents who want good education for their children.[109]

The economist Gavin Wright, who worked with Rev. Charles Webster on
a voting education project in Warrenton, North Carolina, in 1963, argues in
his book *Sharing the Prize* that despite all the setbacks and disappointments,
a larger historical accomplishment stands out: "Desegregation of southern
public schools facilitated a major upward step in the educational attainment
and economic status of African Americans. By the first decade of twenty-first

century, relative black test scores were higher in the South than in most other regions of the country. These gains did not come at the expense of southern whites whose test scores also improved." He indicates that black dropout rates continue a downward trend and that the gap between scores of black and white students on national achievement tests has decreased. He also describes the phenomenon known as "reverse white flight," whereby white enrollment in public schools has increased. Wright believes that the continuing long-term improvement may be the result of greater investment in minority neighborhoods by municipal governments after desegregation plans ended, an upgrading of the income level and occupational status of African Americans, the relocation of middle-class blacks to suburbs, and greater black participation in school and school district policies. Wright sees this improvement as "a legacy of the Civil Rights revolution," as many scholars will agree.[110]

The historian Elizabeth Jacoway of Little Rock, Arkansas, believes that "in the absence of *Brown*, the Little Rock School Board would most assuredly not have adopted a plan for gradual integration as early as 1955.... *Brown* opened the way to fairness and decency and initiated a dialogue in Little Rock that was long overdue,"[111] and in the absence of *Brown*, some southern white ministers may have missed the opportunity to witness to the Christian message of love and brotherhood.

As for the white ministers who spoke out and risked their careers and well-being, were the results worth their efforts? In Mississippi where Rev. Duncan Montgomery Gray was knocked off the pedestal for trying to calm a violent crowd and eighteen of twenty-eight young Methodist ministers lost their churches for supporting school desegregation, the results are varied. At the college and university level great progress has been made. African Americans freely attend Mississippi's colleges and universities. In a recent statement, James Higgins, a professor at the Natchez campus of Copiah-Lincoln Community College, provides an estimate that is probably true for many regions of the South:

Although the Natchez/Adams County Public Schools are well over ninety percent black, there are some white students and faculty there. There are three Kindergarten-through-twelfth-grade private schools in the county, each much smaller than the public system, each with a religious affiliation, one Catholic, one Episcopal, one non-denominational. They are all predominantly white, but each is racially integrated. The Catholic School has been integrated as long as I have lived in Natchez (now thirty-five years). The other two schools began accepting black students only in the last decade or so. My impression is that the non-denominational school is probably less than ten percent black, but that the Episcopal school is about twenty-five percent black.... On a more positive note, I will point out that my school, the Natchez campus of Copiah-Lincoln Community College, is one of the most racially integrated institutions of any sort in the area. Almost half of our students and almost half of our faculty are black.[112]

As to the schools the ministers helped desegregate, although Clinton High School in Tennessee is only 5 percent black, its success story is impressive. There is an entire wall in the cafeteria containing life-size portraits of the Clinton Twelve as well as many plaques throughout the school. The low percentage of African American students reflects the departure of many African American (and white) families from Clinton due to difficult socioeconomic conditions (lack of employment opportunities and so forth). According to Eric Snider, who has been principal of Clinton High School since 2009, "At the time of the desegregation crisis, the African American population was about thirty percent in the city limits of Clinton. Today it is closer to fifteen percent in the city limits, but the African American students who attend Clinton High School do remarkably well. As a whole, they have a higher graduation rate than our majority and have far fewer disciplinary referrals than our Caucasian population (i.e. majority) and have a higher retention rate than our majority."[113]

On December 4, 2015, five African American students were interviewed about their feelings and experiences at Clinton High School. Senior Sierra Cotham takes vocational classes and early childhood education classes. She hopes to attend college to become a teacher. Although she lives in nearby Oliver Springs, she represents Clinton High School for the local school board and praises the close relationship between the school and community. Cierra Davis, another senior, is an honors student in advanced English and information technology, and early enrollment sociology through Lincoln Memorial University located in Harrogate, Tennessee. She also lives in Oliver Springs and relates how nervous she was when she first entered Clinton High School four years ago. "I came here from a small middle school, but I adjusted very quickly. Although I don't live here, the people are very friendly and welcoming. They have open arms to diversity. The teachers seem to care a lot about the students and I appreciate that." Cotham and Davis could have attended a high school in Oliver Springs that has much fewer African American students, but they chose to attend Clinton, a high school with a high record of achievement. According to Snider, "Out of the five southern school systems that I have worked for throughout my career, Clinton High School has the least amount of drug abuse, least amount of criminal activity, and our students have been accepted and are going to more Ivy League schools than any other school where I have worked."[114]

Junior DeMarea Whitt, another honors student, takes honors English and US history and advanced calculus. He came to the school one year ago from nearby Oak Ridge High School when his family moved to Clinton. "Everyone has welcomed me," he happily states. He participates in football and basketball during the winter and track in the spring. Another junior, J'Quan Thomas, aspires to be on the honor roll. He studies English, algebra, and personal finances. He enthusiastically states, "It's special to see all the different types of people coming together here at the school. There isn't really any bias here. The school is not segregated. I love it here." Freshman Kristopher Morrow has lived in Clinton since elementary school. His family used to live in nearby rural Claxton, where he claims a lot of prejudice existed. "There isn't that kind of blatant racism here in Clinton," he states. "Clinton is a rural community, the seat of Anderson County, but when my grandparents first moved here many years ago, they got hate mail. Groups of white people would walk up and down our road, trying to get us to move, but it isn't that bad now." Kristopher believes his is the only African American family in his neighborhood, but he says, "Clinton is very open to the African American community, and they really try to give us opportunities—to play sports and to go to college. We like it here and pretty much keep to ourselves."[115]

Rev. Paul Turner, who gave up a ministry career and almost his life to help African American children desegregate Clinton High School; Bobby Cain, the first African American to graduate from Clinton High School or any white high school in the South, and now a successful social worker with the state of Tennessee Department of Human Services; and Jerry Shattuck, a white student at the school in 1956, captain of the football team, and a friend and helper to the Clinton Twelve, who is now a Clinton town councilman,[116] would all be proud of these five youngsters.

What about Central High School in Little Rock, Arkansas, where so much agitation took place? Little Rock is the capital and an urban center in Arkansas, with almost twenty times the population of Clinton. In an article written in 2014, Debbie Elliott of National Public Radio reported, "Central High School remains a symbol of the ongoing struggle to achieve integration." Litigation for integration has continued for many years, but Max Brantley, senior editor of the *Arkansas Times*, says for all of the pessimism about racial inequities that remain, there has been a measure of progress at Little Rock when compared to other cities: "Little Rock is sixty-six percent black in its public school enrollment. I don't think there's an urban city in the South that has retained as many white students as the Little Rock school system has retained." Central High School is 55 percent black.[117]

Elliott has recorded the thoughts of several African American students at Central High. Alicia Waits, a student in an African American history class that, except for one Hispanic student, is comprised of black students, notes that the school is far from integrated: "I walked in the cafeteria today, I looked on the left side, I saw only white people sitting at the table. . . . I looked on the right side; I saw only black people." Senior Darius Porch says, "This school is integrated, but I don't feel like we are as one."[118]

After school, civics teacher George West conducts oral history interviews with small groups of students who have a lot to say about the effects of discrimination. Junior Malik Marshall says, "The school is certainly desegregated, and has been since 1957. We're desegregated, but we're not integrated because integration comes from the heart of the people that go here." Marshall takes advanced placement courses and says he's usually one of just a few African American faces in mostly white classrooms. So his friends tend to be white. "It's this barrier between me and the other black people just because they know I like to hang out with white people. To the white people I hang out with, I physically look different. . . . I'm very singled out in that group, but these are the people I know. So it makes me feel like I don't belong anywhere." Senior Micah Booker says, "I get called an Oreo sometimes, which is, you're black on the outside and white on the inside, because of how I talk and other things. So it can be hard." Having such a frank discussion is something that might not have been possible in 1957, and the students here are proud of what Central High School has achieved. It produces more National Merit scholars than any other school in Arkansas. Malik Marshall concludes, "This is my school, I love it here."[119]

◆ ◆ ◆

The ministers mentioned in this chapter were a committed minority who sincerely believed they could do something constructive to advance school desegregation. Often their children were the only white students in the desegregated schools. These ministers believed that helping young African Americans enter white schools was the proper Christian choice. Rev. Paul Turner expressed it to journalists Wilma Dykeman and James Stokely: "As things developed during the week and the Negro children were intimidated out of school, I began to think what could I do. First, of course, I could preach to my congregation about it on Sunday. Then on Monday, I could act, and that's what I did." Rev. Dunbar Ogden Jr. admitted to his son that since early childhood he felt a sense of guilt and shame for what he considered the "sins of the white people," but he never did anything about it until that day standing on a street corner with the African American children in the midst of an angry mob. He told his son, "I looked into their eyes and noticed no fear." He said they were like the young people in his church, like the young people in his home, and all fear drained from him. He knew at that moment that this was the will of God for him, that he must act on their behalf.[120]

Although school desegregation has a mixed record of success, not one of these ministers regretted his actions. Rev. Marion Boggs, in an address to students at Columbia Theological Seminary in Decatur, Georgia, in 1960, stated, "I would not have had respect for myself as a man and a minister if I had not lifted my voice and used my influence for a course that I consider Christian." He also told the students, "We must not expect in our lifetime to find the complete solution to the race question or any other problem so complex and deeply rooted, but we can, with God's help, take a few steps in the right direction."[121] That exactly describes the actions of these ministers. These men were not radical activists but were dedicated ministers who were practicing Christianity as they understood it. Will D. Campbell would call them "Christian radicals," as he would call himself.[122] Many scholars would call them prophets.

⸻ 2 ⸻

THE HEART OF THE MOVEMENT

Boycotts, Sit-Ins, Freedom Rides, Mass Demonstrations

Every time I left the house to go downtown or headed to the airport or drove to another town to carry on my ministry, I knew I was leaving my refuge to go into enemy territory. Each time I said good-bye to Jeannie and the children, I knew that this could be the last time in this world that I would see them.

—ROBERT GRAETZ, white pastor, all-black Trinity Church, Montgomery, Alabama, 1957

Because of the difficulties and defeats encountered during the school desegregation crises, African Americans began to organize boycotts, sit-ins, freedom rides, and mass demonstrations in order to break down the whole system of segregation. A boycott involved picketing and a refusal to have dealings with business organizations or establishments that discriminated against African Americans. Civil rights activists at first engaged in boycotts of bus companies that forced African Americans to be seated only in back rows or in no seats if white people had to stand. Boycotts later spread to business establishments that refused to serve African Americans at lunch counters or in eating booths, and in some cases to clothing and shoe stores that refused to allow African Americans to try on merchandise. Sit-ins or sit-downs (as they were first called) involved the seating of individuals at lunch counters, in drugstores, in variety stores, and in department stores that refused to serve African Americans. Freedom Riders called upon integrated groups of people to ride Trailways and Greyhound buses throughout the South in order to test court-ordered desegregation of terminal waiting rooms, lunch counters, and lavatories. Mass demonstrations involved hundreds of people who would engage in street marches, picketing, boycotts, and sit-ins. Some southern white ministers might be sympathetic to boycotts, sign petitions, offer nonviolent training classes, give emotional support, and make bold statements, but few would become involved in front-line civil disobedience. The few who did were not pastors of all-white churches, for that would have meant immediate dismissal. Two were pastors of black churches; two were seminary students; one worked as a professor at an all-black college; another directed the Episcopal Society for Cultural and Racial Unity (ESCRU); and several in Albany, Georgia, were from the North. These minister activists were disobeying local laws and helping others to disobey local laws considered to be in violation of God's commandment to love one's neighbor as oneself. They considered involvement in the civil rights movement as a demonstration of their love for African American neighbors and were ready to suffer the consequences.

Boycotts

In Montgomery, Alabama, during the 1950s, 75 percent of bus riders were African American. Four days after the *Brown* decision, Jo Ann Robinson, faculty member at Alabama State University in Montgomery and founder of the Women's Political Council, a large group of black women in Montgomery, wrote to the mayor asking for better treatment for blacks on the city buses, but absolutely nothing was done. One year later Rosa Parks, returning home from her job as a department store seamstress, refused to relinquish her seat to a white man. She was arrested. The Women's Political Council distributed meeting notices to black people throughout the town asking them to boycott Montgomery's buses. E. D. Nixon, president of the local chapter of the National Association for the Advancement of Colored People (NAACP) and an officer in the local branch of the Brotherhood of Sleeping Car Porters, organized the Montgomery Improvement Association (MIA) and invited a newly arrived young black minister, Martin Luther King Jr., to be their leader. African American Ralph D. Abernathy, pastor of First Baptist Church, helped King enlist the cooperation of every African American in Montgomery and the few whites who would help them.[1]

The boycott lasted 381 days. Upon advice from attorney Fred Gray, who represented Parks, the leaders of the boycott demanded three small actions: all drivers should display more courtesy toward the "colored" riders; the seating should be arranged on a first-come first-serve basis; and the company should hire "colored" bus drivers on buses running into areas heavily populated by "colored" people.[2]

Donald E. Collins, born in Montgomery, Alabama, in 1931, a white Methodist minister who left Alabama in 1969 worn out and disillusioned after being transferred many times because of his pro-integration stance, asserted in his memoir that if the fourteen white Methodist churches, one-sixth of the white churches in Montgomery, had unanimously supported the boycott, an early resolution might have resulted, but Methodist ministers in Montgomery were fearfully divided and influenced by Rev. G. Stanley Frazer, minister of prestigious St. James Methodist Church. At the end of a long and illustrious pastoral career, Frazer would not tolerate any change, gradual or otherwise, to the status quo of segregation. In 1955 he helped organize a branch of the Methodist Ministers and Laymen's Union (MAMML) with the purpose of developing strategies to maintain segregation. MAMML existed throughout six different Methodist Conferences, with most of its members in Alabama. (In 1963 the Mississippi group, with the most prominent segregationists as members, actively opposed the twenty-eight Methodist ministers who signed a petition in support of school desegregation.) Frazer contended, "The job of the minister is to lead the souls of men to God, not to bring about confusion by getting tangled up in transitory social problems." According to Collins, the Alabama–West Florida Conference of the Methodist Church was a virtual "wall of resistance against impending change: For the next decade and a half, this struggle divided families, congregations, ministers, and the church. No one would remain untouched." If a Methodist minister openly supported the boycott, he could expect harassment from his congregation and reassignment from his bishop. Rev. Ray E. Whatley of St. Mark's Methodist Church in Montgomery and president of the interracial Montgomery chapter of the Alabama Council on Human Relations was transferred to Linden, Alabama, backwoods, hard-core Klan country, when he tried to organize an open discussion on the boycott.[3]

Rev. Floyd Enfinger (1927–2017), born on a farm in Dothan, Alabama, and pastor of Chisholm Methodist Church in Montgomery, typified a minister who remained neutral concerning the boycott. He was shocked out of his complacency when the blast of a bomb thrown in front of Rev. Abernathy's church spread to his windowpanes and caused his young son to say, "Well, Dad, what are you going to do about it?" Enfinger then told his church that he wanted to support King and the bus boycott. It appeared that the congregation respected his wish, or at least Enfinger thought so. He attended planning sessions with King, Abernathy, and a black Methodist minister from Atlanta, Joseph Lowery, who sometimes came to the sessions. Members of the White Citizens' Council, many of whom belonged to Enfinger's church, learned of his attendance at the meetings through his license plate. Crosses were burned on his lawn, and obscene telephone calls plagued his family. He turned aside from the planning sessions and directed his attention to organizing a group of progressive white ministers from the Alabama–West Florida Methodist Conference into a secret group known as the "Core," who worked to change the direction of the conference. As chair of the Board of Social Concerns, his resolutions for an end to segregated Methodist Conferences were constantly defeated. Enfinger was moved by his bishop to a church in Shalimar, Florida, in 1960, where he stayed out of trouble.[4]

Enfinger tried in his limited way to bring about change in the city of Montgomery, but obstacles were present. The extremely active White Citizens' Council planted cells in all the churches and were successful in intimidation campaigns and in forcing pro-integration ministers out of the city, or in silencing them. For Enfinger, his relationship with Martin Luther King Jr., although of short duration, was the high point of his time in Montgomery: "I was impressed with his unselfishness, his prayer life and deep convictions. . . . I learned many things from Dr. King, the most valuable to me was his statement: 'You can accomplish what you want in life if you don't care who gets the credit.' That was the essence of what King practiced."[5]

Gardiner Shattuck, a northern Episcopal minister, included in his study of Episcopalians and race the story of Thomas Thrasher (1909–2003), born in Corinth, Mississippi, rector of the Episcopal Church of the Ascension in Montgomery, and one of only two white members of the Montgomery chapter of the Council on Human Relations. Thrasher, who tried to negotiate a settlement between the mayor (a member of his church) and leaders of the boycott, was forced to leave the prestigious Church of the Ascension when he began to speak of brotherhood in his sermons and suggested church members open their doors and hearts to African Americans.[6] As these stories illustrate, it was almost impossible for progressive white ministers to make any kind of progress in Montgomery.

Unlike the ministers of the white churches, white Rev. Robert Graetz, born in 1928 in Clarksburg, West Virginia, participated fully in the Montgomery Bus Boycott and was able to do so for two reasons: all of the members of his congregation were black and supported him, and he had the encouragement of Rosa Parks, his friend and neighbor. Graetz arrived in Montgomery in 1955, a few months after King, and had much in common with him. Both were recent graduates of theology schools; both were serving their first congregations, King at the Dexter Avenue Baptist Church and Graetz at Trinity Lutheran. Both congregations were African American. King was twenty-six years old; Graetz was twenty-seven years old. Both were married with young children, and both were dedicated to the nonviolent ideals of Jesus, Gandhi, and Thoreau: "Love your enemies, bless them that curse you, do good to them that hate you and pray for them which despitefully use you and persecute you."[7]

Graetz and his wife, Jeannie, fell in love with the members of Trinity Church. "They accepted us totally in spite of the race difference," exclaimed Graetz. In his memoir, Graetz described how he taxied black people, sometimes forty or fifty a day, to and from their places of employment. He was arrested for driving without a taxi permit; his house was dynamited two times, and his family narrowly escaped death. Vandals placed sugar in his gasoline tank (which would destroy the engine) and slashed his tires with knives. The family was constantly threatened, and he was lynched in effigy from a tree in downtown Montgomery.[8]

His efforts extended beyond Montgomery and beyond the car pool. Belonging to two ministerial associations, one black and one white, he organized secret interracial meetings of ministers. He was engaged in fund-raising in Ohio, Illinois, and Indiana, with Rosa Parks; Rev. Solomon Seay, a black activist; and another white pastor, Rev. Howard Vines, of all-white Capital Memorial Church of God. Graetz admitted that he lived in constant fear and knew the time might come when he would have to leave Montgomery, but he and his wife believed that the Lord wanted them to remain as long as they could. When an invitation came to be minister of St. Philip's, an African American Church in Columbus, Ohio, he politely refused. Several months later, he received a visit from Ken Priebe, president of the Ohio district of the American Lutheran Church. "You listen to me," Priebe told Graetz. "Whose church is this, yours or the Lord's?" "The Lord's," Graetz answered. "And who calls his men to be where he wants them to be?" "The Lord," Graetz answered. With five children, three born in Montgomery, the family moved to Columbus in 1958. After they were settled, friends from Trinity visited and told them, "None of us wanted you to move, but we knew if you stayed you would be killed." Graetz retired from active ministry in 1995 and continued a personal ministry to people in rural Appalachia in southeastern Ohio. To civil rights activists in and near Montgomery, he remains a beloved hero.[9]

Many authors have cited Graetz's dedication to the Montgomery Bus Boycott. Attorney Fred Gray commented, "There appeared to be more hostility toward him—if it was possible—than toward Dr. King at that point. It was thought that this was because Graetz, a white, had allied himself with the black cause, which infuriated the most virulent of Montgomery's white supremacists." Graetz, admittedly, attempted to identify himself as an African American, and, not having to convince his black congregation that the cause was just, he could follow his conscience completely. Graetz's efforts during the boycott became known in every state in the country, and other countries as well. Although his denominational superiors encouraged him to leave Montgomery for his own safety and that of his family, they recognized his outstanding contribution to the cause of racial justice. The Board of American Missions of the American Lutheran Church officially commended him "for the calm and deliberate way" in which he applied the Gospel and carried on his ministry in the "unpredicted and unexpected situations that arose."[10]

The Montgomery Bus Boycott succeeded through a combined effort of many people—clergymen, lawyers, and the everyday struggling black workers of Montgomery. As Fred Gray indicated, "Little did they realize that this was the opening event of the modern Civil Rights Movement," and little did they know that they "had set in motion a force that would ripple through Alabama, the South, the nation, and even the world."[11]

◆ ◆ ◆

Inspired by the court action declaring invalid Alabama's state law on bus segregation and by the Montgomery Bus Boycott, thirty-six African American ministers petitioned the Mobile City Commission to repeal an ordinance requiring blacks to occupy seats in the rear of city buses. The ministers pledged to maintain peaceful relations and to avoid the violence and agitation that resulted in Montgomery. At the same time, thirty-one white ministers, some from Mobile's most prestigious churches, presented a supporting statement. The white ministers explained that they were acting independently and individually and commended the Christian spirit with which the African American pastors presented their petition. They asserted that every "intelligent means" should be applied to achieve the goal of peace and harmony. The *Mobile Press Register* identified the names of seventeen white Methodist ministers: Carl Adkins, Chester Bolton Jr., Thomas Lane Butts, Henry Frank Chunn, L. H. Garrison Jr., Joseph E. Hastings, James N. Love, H. E. McCrary, John T. Parker, Eugene Peacock, Lester Spencer, H. E. Whatley, David R. White, Hugh E. Wilson Jr., Comer Woodall, James A. Zellner, and Andrew S. Turnipseed, superintendent for the Mobile Methodist District; six white Presbyterian ministers: John M. Crowell, D. H. Edington, John C. Frist Jr., W. D. Hart, R. L. Kell, and John H. Thompson; five white Episcopalian ministers: Leighton P. Arsnault, Yates Calvert Green, D. Holmes Irving, Benjamin B. Smith, and Francis P. Wakefield Jr.; two white Baptist ministers: Robert W. Clark and Howard M. Reeves; and one white Disciples of Christ minister: A. F. Morrill, president of the Mobile Council of Churches. Six of the seventeen Methodist ministers were transferred to remote regions. Three of the Episcopalian ministers were retired, and the two others were transferred out of their churches. The six Presbyterian ministers appear to have survived at their churches, but the fate of the two Baptist ministers and the one Disciples of Christ minister is unknown.[12]

With their names appearing in the *Mobile Press Register*, their constituents knew immediately who they were, and retaliation was swift. Crosses were burned at four of the Methodist churches, and there were calls for the removal of three of the Methodist ministers. Ministers in the Methodist system are appointed or dismissed by the bishop; therefore, church boards did not have the authority to perform such action, but the boards could withhold the pastor's salary, and that is exactly what happened to James Love, pastor of Satsuma Methodist Church. His board refused to pay his salary, but Rev. Andrew S. Turnipseed (1911–2002), born in Camden, Alabama, and the district superintendent who joined the pastors in signing the statement, continued to pay Love's salary. Immediately, a group of about 100 Methodist laypeople applied to the bishop for Turnipseed's removal. His son, Rev. A. Spencer Turnipseed, related that his father had always been a social justice activist. During the 1930s and 1940s, Andrew Turnipseed fought for the right of labor to organize, traveling throughout Alabama with Hank Williams, famous country singer, helping to organize lumber workers and loggers. Williams would sing, and Turnipseed would give the invocation and a brief speech. During the 1940s, Turnipseed attended integrated church meetings by using codes as to where and when they would convene. He and others would change cars during trips to confuse their opponents.[13]

Turnipseed did his best in his quiet way to bring a concern for social justice into the life of his native state. As district superintendent for Mobile, the largest Methodist district in the Alabama–West Florida Conference, he cautioned his ministers to avoid confrontation until a time when he could be elected to the General Conference, the denomination's quadrennial national gathering, and bring in some outside Methodists to help. When the "Core" (progressive Methodist ministers) boldly decided to support the black ministers of Mobile, Turnipseed joined them. Opposition against Turnipseed mounted. The bishop informed him that he could not guarantee his appointment beyond another year. In 1959 he left Alabama to serve churches in Rochester, New York City, Niagara Falls, and Brooklyn. In all places, Turnipseed became active in local civil rights issues. After the tragic death of his daughter Marti and her infant daughter in an automobile accident in 1972, the grieving Turnipseed family returned to Alabama. With two Doctor of Divinity degrees, Turnipseed began teaching at Huntingdon College in Montgomery, making the best of his situation. As his son commented, "My father was able to maintain a position of leadership in the Alabama–West Florida Conference for twenty-five years, while treading on tight wires, until he came to the aid of the beleaguered supporters of the Mobile Bus Petition."[14]

Among the young Methodist ministers who signed the Mobile Bus Petition was Thomas Lane Butts, born in 1930 in Conecuh County, southeast Alabama, where, he claimed, two-thirds of the bed sheets had eyeholes cut in them. A sharecropper's son, he grew up, he said, "in a racist family, a racist society, and a church that supported racism," but he never forgot the first time he questioned the humanity of the system. He was in the sixth grade and waited with his brothers and sisters for the school bus: "We would get up at five a.m., do chores, have breakfast and then sit on the front porch and wait for the bus."

While they were waiting, Butts remembered a group of black children walking past their house. When he saw them, he knew that they had already been walking for an hour and that they would still be walking long after he and his brothers and sisters arrived at their school. Butts conjectured that the black children would have to leave their school about two or three o'clock in the afternoon in order to get home before dark, which left them only about two or three hours in the classroom. Time for homework was seemingly out of the question. Butts's little sister asked, "Why can't they ride to school with us?," but Butts and his siblings were never able to give her a satisfactory answer.[15]

Butts related that he went through twelve years of public education, four years of college, three years of graduate school at Emory University, and two years of graduate school at Northwestern University, but did not have one African American classmate until his last year at Northwestern. "I am the poorer for that," he remonstrated.[16]

His first pastorate was at Michigan Avenue Methodist Church in Mobile. He called the membership "the rednecks": "I can say that because I, too, am a 'redneck.'" They were from the mud-flats of Mississippi and from south Alabama, whose families came into Mobile during World War II to work in the shipyards and paper mills and stayed. Butts did not choose to become an activist during his first year as a pastor, but when he heard about the petition to end segregated seating on Mobile's city buses, he could not remain silent: "You do not choose the occasion. The occasion chooses you and you either become involved or you forever say 'no' to it." He thought it was a wonderful idea and would be well received by his congregation, but the response was negative. Crosses were burned in front of his parsonage and church. A mass meeting was organized for his removal, but he told them, "The bishop sent me, and you are stuck with me until June, and I am stuck with you. Whether we like it or not, we'd better learn to live together before annual Conference when I could possibly be moved."[17]

Members of his church began withholding contributions, and the Methodist Conference threatened to cut his salary to one dollar and sell the parsonage from under him. Discouraged, he considered leaving the ministry when an unknown white woman appeared at his office one afternoon and handed him an envelope. "I would like to make a donation," she said. "To whom shall I give credit?" Butts asked, but the woman said it was anonymous and walked away. When Butts opened the envelope, he found two $100 bills. Butts had never seen a $100 bill in his life: "It was a lot of money in those days. Even a twenty dollar bill was put under the mattress back then." Butts rushed to the parsonage to tell Hilda, his wife. "But how are you going to get it into the system?" she asked. "You can't drop hundred dollar bills into the plate. They'll know something is wrong." Butts and Hilda devised a scheme. They knew a banker in Brewton, about sixty miles north of Mobile, and went to get those $100 bills broken down into twenties. When the collection plate was passed, with every eye closed and every head bowed, Butts quietly dropped $20 bills into the plate. The woman came every Friday bringing anywhere from $200 to $500 in $100 bills, and Butts and Hilda kept going to Brewton every week to get the bills broken down into twenties, and the offerings started going up.[18]

Although eager to know the woman's identity, Butts and his wife decided that if she wished to remain anonymous, they had no right to invade her privacy. "To this day," he stated, "I don't know who she is, but I always refer to her as my 'good angel' on Michigan Avenue. I probably would have left the ministry had she not come." With the collection increasing, the church did not cut Butts's salary. The unknown woman was the first of Butts's "good angels," and he remained at Michigan Avenue for five years, but his troubles were not over. According to Butts, the police and the Klan were always nearby, ready with intimidation, beatings, cross burnings, and insinuations: "They could make people stop coming to your church. They would call up members of a congregation and tell them you were an integrationist, a n____r lover, and 'Communist inspired.' These were the worst things you could be in the eyes of most of the members."[19]

In spite of his pro-integration activities (Butts had also been a member of the NAACP in Alabama until it was permanently outlawed by a series of state court orders in 1961), Butts survived and gained in stature. A gifted preacher and counselor, in 1976 he was awarded an honorary doctorate from Huntingdon College and was appointed to the prestigious First Methodist Church of Montgomery. "I had a great ministry," he recalled. "We were on the radio at 8:30 Sunday morning and on television at 11.00 a.m." He seemed well on his way to becoming a bishop, but in 1982 his enemies struck. "They were never far away," he confessed. He was accused of heresy, womanizing, drinking alcoholic beverages, and undermining the ministry of an associate. The court of the Alabama–West Florida Methodist Conference declared him guilty of the last offense only. He was suspended for two years, and denied a congregation, salary, living accommodations, and all personal and family benefits. Butts believed he was found guilty of undermining the ministry of an associate because "members of the jury had to find me guilty of something." In an interview after the trial, Butts stated, "I've always considered myself a friend to the oppressed and downtrodden, but I've never been a friend to them like I'm going to be after this, because I know how they feel. Now I know how it feels to be humiliated." He appealed to the Southeastern Jurisdiction United Methodist Court of Appeals in Atlanta. After a review that lasted six months, he was completely exonerated, but his legal fees and loss of income totaled $142,000. Over 500 supporters ("good angels") sustained him. He exclaimed, "I would have perished if not for wealthy friends who supplied me with a place to live, an automobile, a salary, and funds for my children's college expenses. The main support came from Red Blount, multi-millionaire businessman from Montgomery, but once my name was besmirched, it didn't really matter that I was cleared. The goal of my enemies was achieved. I would never become a bishop of the Church."[20]

He told Joanna Bosko, a member of the church and one of his supporters, that his first trial took place eight or nine months after he admitted the first black to membership at First Methodist since 1860. An old state senator told him, "I'll get you for taking a n____r into this church." After the scandal, the presiding bishop offered to find him "a nice church up North," but Butts refused. "No," he said, "I'll not leave Alabama. If you send me to a circuit church, I will still stay here. I will not leave the South." Butts went from a church of 2,700 members to a church of 400 members, but he readily accepted the change: "When you grow up the son of a sharecropper, you have to be pushed really hard to get to a level below where you started, so I was doing all right. I had a house to live in and even air conditioning."[21]

If his signature had not appeared on that bus petition in Mobile in 1958, Butts's dream of becoming a bishop might have come true, but he might not have become the renowned preacher that he is and beloved by many in and out of his native state. In 1993 an eighty-two-year-old woman was influential in bringing Butts to serve his last five years of ministry in the church where she had been a member for more than sixty years, the First Methodist Church of Monroeville, Alabama. Ten years later, Butts introduced the woman, Alice Finch Lee, as she received the Maude McClure Kelly Award given by the Alabama Bar Association for her outstanding legal service to her community and state: "This dignified ninety-one-year-old woman has been on her way to her office every day since 1944.... She is a rare curiosity in Monroeville—a woman lawyer."[22]

Butts retired in 1998 and was made minister emeritus of the Monroeville church with a permanent residence at the parsonage. Butts claims as his benefactor Alice Finch Lee, who is the older sister of Harper Lee, author of *To Kill a Mockingbird*, also a member of the church and dear friend to Thomas and Hilda Butts. Like Graetz, Butts attributes his blessings to God working through his "good angels."[23]

Sit-Ins

The South began to explode during the 1960s as young African Americans demanded the right to sit in any seat on city buses; to order a cup of coffee and a hamburger at a lunch counter; to use facilities at bus and railroad terminals; to picnic, walk, or swim in city parks; to ride merry-go-rounds, roller coasters, and Ferris wheels at amusement parks; to go to beaches; to use libraries; to use clean public lavatories; to attend all-white churches; to live as free and equal citizens in a free society. At the same time, the forces opposing them became louder, stronger, and more vicious: the Klan, the Circuit Riders, the American Nazi Party, the White Citizens' Councils of America (WCC) in eleven southern states (headquartered in Greenwood, Mississippi), the States Rights' Councils, the Association for the Preservation of Southern Traditions, the North Carolina Patriots, the Methodist Laymen's Leagues, the Presbyterian Laymen, the Tennessee Society to Maintain Segregation, the National Association for the Advancement of White People (NAAWP), White America, Inc., Segregationists Stand United (STAND), and the local police. As Rev. R. Edwin (Ed) King lamented (borrowing the phrase from Virginia Durr of Montgomery, Alabama), "There was very little good white people seemed to be able to do," but there was something "good" white southern people did not do. They did not join the Klan, the American Nazi Party, the White Citizens' Councils, the States Rights Leagues, and all the groups in support of segregation. Instead, they organized the Fellowship of Southern Churchmen, the Southern Regional Council, the Councils on Human Relations, Race Relations Sunday, the Methodist Committees for Social Concerns, the Presbyterian Fellowship of Concern, the Methodist Merger Committees, the Episcopal Society for Cultural and Racial Unity, the Lutheran Human Relations Association, the North Carolina Good Neighbor Council, the South Carolina Christian Action Council, Concerned White Citizens of Alabama, and the American Civil Liberties Union; some joined black organizations: the NAACP, the Southern Christian Leadership Conference (SCLC), the Student Nonviolent Coordinating Conference (SNCC), the Congress of Racial Equality (CORE); and some spoke quietly from the places God gave them in this world. White Rev. Robert Seymour, pastor emeritus of Binkley Memorial Baptist Church, Chapel Hill, North Carolina, referred to a scattered church, white people from all walks of life, behind counters, at desks, in kitchens, in schools, in church buildings, and *in pulpits* who were willing to speak on behalf of racial justice: "Those who had been scattered preached the word wherever they went."[24]

◆ ◆ ◆

The historian John Hope Franklin selected the Greensboro, North Carolina, sit-ins of 1960 as the initiator of what he called the "Black Revolution" when on February 1, four well-dressed freshmen—Ezell Blair Jr., Joseph McNeil, Franklin McCain, and David Richmond, from all-black North Carolina Agricultural and Technical College (A&T)—entered Woolworth's Variety Store, made several purchases, and sat down at the lunch counter to order coffee. When told they would not be served, they remained seated at the counter all day until the store closed. McNeil and others claimed that the bravery of the Little Rock Nine gave them courage and inspiration.[25]

The movement expanded until nearly 1,600 students jammed Woolworth's, S. H. Kress's, and lunch counters throughout the city. By the end of March they agreed to stop demonstrating if an agreement could be reached, but the white power structure refused, and sit-ins resumed. On April 21, 1960, forty-five students were arrested on trespass charges, provoking the African American community in Greensboro to stage a massive boycott against targeted stores. Eventually, the white power structure, influenced by business interests, relented, and African Americans were able to purchase a cup of coffee at variety stores.[26] The pattern repeated itself many times throughout southern cities.

Almost immediately white Rev. John B. Morris (1930–2010), who left South Carolina and returned to his native state of Georgia to organize the unofficial and integration-minded Episcopal Society for Cultural and Racial Unity (ESCRU), issued a public statement commending "those citizens who express their love by passive disobedience to unjust laws and mores."[27] Another white minister, Methodist Glen Smiley (1910–1993), born in Loraine, Texas, working for the New York–based Fellowship of Reconciliation, distributed guidelines to civil rights organizations throughout the South, emphasizing Gandhi's teachings. It is apparent that most nonviolent demonstrators attempted to follow these guidelines:

- Investigate. Get the facts. . . . If you are sure that an injustice has been done, be equally sure who is to blame for it.
- Negotiate. Go to your opponent and put the case to him. Maybe a solution can be worked out at this point. . . . Let him know that you are always ready to negotiate further.
- Educate. Keep your group well informed of the issues, and spread the word to the public. . . . Always stick to the facts, avoid exaggeration, be brief and show good will.
- Demonstrate. Picketing, poster-walking, mass meetings, and the handing out of leaflets on the streets . . . All of these must be conducted in an orderly manner. The people who are demonstrating should be neat, well informed and calm, able to endure possible heckling and to withstand possible violence without panic, and without resorting to violence in return. . . .
- Nonviolent resistance is the final step . . . as a last resort. This means a boycott, a strike, the defiance of an unjust law, or other forms of civil disobedience.[28]

The Nashville, Tennessee, sit-ins began twelve days after the Greensboro occurrence in a city considered progressive, where buses and schools were integrated. James Lawson, the second black student admitted to Vanderbilt Divinity School (in Nashville), with the help of Will Campbell, began to conduct nonviolent workshops following closely the Gandhian methods. Lawson proposed, "You don't want to blow up Nashville downtown, you simply want to open it up so that everybody has a chance to participate." Equally committed to nonviolent passive resistance, Campbell stressed "disobedience to law if such law is patently contrary to the will of God."[29]

Campbell, who had become the southern representative for the National Council of Churches in 1956 after his humiliating and disheartening experience at Ole Miss, began anew to assist in changing the almost impenetrable order of southern society. Never in the front line but never far away, Campbell's presence in Nashville was immediately felt by the African American community. The First Baptist Church, formerly the First Colored Baptist Church of Nashville, became his home sanctuary, and fellow Baptist Rev. Kelly Miller Smith became his pastor. As the journalist David Halberstam mentioned, Campbell also joined the local NAACP, put his money in the city's only black bank, hired a black secretary for his office (who later married James Lawson), became a loyal friend to Lawson and Smith, and advocated for the eight student demonstrators who would begin the Nashville sit-ins and become leaders in the civil rights movement.[30]

The sit-ins gained momentum. On Saturday, February 27, 1960, when 100 students prepared to go downtown, Campbell warned that a group of white segregationists was waiting to attack and that the students would probably be arrested; the group went anyway, and the attack came. Some young white men started pulling and beating, primarily the young women, putting lit cigarettes down their backs and into their hair. Police arrested all of the black demonstrators but not a single member of the white group. Campbell, along with C. T. Vivian, a black minister and editor at a black publishing house, helped convince the mayor and businessmen to end segregated lunch counters. Except for the expulsion of James Lawson from Vanderbilt Divinity School, Nashville's sit-in demonstrations were successful eighty-seven days after they began.[31]

Other sit-ins began peacefully, but violence became a constant companion. Between 1960 and 1963 the *New York Times* reported at least fifteen occurrences of violence a week, leading to the arrest of many and the injury of some. Public debates were common during this time between those who believed that sit-ins were ethically justifiable and those who disagreed. In March 1960 the National Council of the Protestant Episcopal Church of the United States issued an advisory to the effect that civil disobedience should be supported in certain circumstances. The advisory suggested, in much the same language as that of Will Campbell, that profound issues of Christian ethical behavior were involved in sit-ins, and although sit-ins defied local law, Christianity always taught that civil disobedience is justified for grave moral reasons.[32]

In objection, the bishop of Alabama, Rt. Rev. Charles C. J. Carpenter, urged Alabama Episcopalians to ignore the 7,000-word advisory on the grounds that "if carried to its ultimate conclusion, it would condone lawlessness." In strong words, white Episcopalian minister John Morris called Bishop Carpenter's request "unfortunate." In Morris's opinion, the advisory of the national Church was "a most worthwhile document . . . of value to Christians of all churches." Morris feared that divisions between clergy ready to implement Christian teaching on race and those "choosing to remain chaplains to the dying order of the Confederacy" were undermining the Church.[33]

The debate reached the Presbyterian Church when Rev. Eugene Carson Blake (1906–1985), a northern moderator who himself would become a demonstrator, made a clear declaration in support of sit-ins while his southern counterpart, Rev. Ernest Trice Thompson (1894–1985), was cautious in his defense. Thompson emphasized that white students from the Presbyterian seminary in the South who joined blacks in sit-ins at Thalheimers in Richmond, Virginia, were doing so as individuals "on the basis of conscience" and not as representatives of the southern Presbyterian Church. Thompson expressed sympathy for the aims of the sit-ins, but doubt as to their value: "Gains can probably be made in better ways than by breaking laws," but Thompson defended his Church, pointing out that Southern Presbyterians did not segregate blacks into separate governing bodies and the Church's four seminaries in the South had been open to African Americans for "perhaps twenty years." He suggested that southern Presbyterian ministers were awakening the conscience of the people toward realizing that the laws must be modified—"some quietly, some outspokenly."[34] Thompson was going through his own struggle as the leader of his southern Church. Later he would become more approving of demonstrations and himself a participant in the March on Washington and the Selma to Montgomery march in 1965.

◆ ◆ ◆

A southern white minister might express approval and offer advice and encouragement, but who would actually take a seat alongside black students at a whites-only lunch counter? Dallas A. Blanchard (1933–2008), born in Mobile, Alabama, and studying for the Methodist ministry at Vanderbilt Divinity School during the time of the sit-ins, decided he could do nothing better than to sit beside a demonstrator. Born to a family firmly opposed to integration (his father once served as a river boat captain along the Mississippi River), Blanchard completely rejected his family's racist sentiments. During the Nashville sit-ins, he became a "spotter" to warn demonstrators that attackers were approaching and joined the demonstrators at counters to show his support. Fortunately for him, he was not arrested. As editor of the divinity school newspaper, he supported the dean and twelve divinity professors who resigned when his African American classmate, James Lawson, was expelled for organizing the Nashville sit-ins. Later, as an ordained Methodist minister, he attempted to maintain a church in Toulminville, Alabama, a section of Mobile rapidly changing from a white to black. To solve the dilemma of a declining membership in a church with a $100,000 mortgage, Blanchard arranged for a group from the all-black Warren Street Methodist Church in the inner city to unite with the Toulminville church and insisted that both church groups be included in all district-wide meetings and activities, like all other Methodist churches. He established youth activities and preached sermons of hope and encouragement, but white members continued leaving, even leaving the Methodist denomination. Blanchard recalled, "One former member sat in his car and just observed every Sunday as the congregation filed in and out of services." His old Sunday school teacher reportedly said, "I don't know what happened to Dallas. He was such a nice little boy." After many years, harassed by segregationists and threatened by the Klan, Blanchard became frustrated and decided to attend graduate school and pursue the study of the sociology of religion at Boston University. He became an author of sociological monographs and an esteemed professor at the University of West Florida in spite of the fact that an official at the University of South Alabama reportedly told his colleagues, "Dallas Blanchard will never be hired by this university in any capacity, even to sweep the floors." Meantime, Blanchard remained an ordained minister of the Alabama–West Florida Methodist Conference and struggled to free the conference of its racist sentiments. He continued activism as a member of the Committee of Southern Churchmen (1963–1965) and the Alabama Advisory Committee on Civil Rights (1967–1969, 1970–1972). Nor did members of the Toulminville–Warren Street United Methodist Church ever forget the pastor they considered their founding father. Blanchard was honored after his death at their Homecoming Celebration, September 3–4, 2011, as a "major player in the drama of the Invisible Merger."[35]

Born in 1936 in Vicksburg, Mississippi, R. Edwin King, while studying for the Methodist ministry at the School of Theology of Boston University, was sent by the Fellowship of Reconciliation to assist the Montgomery, Alabama, sit-in campaign with behind-the-scenes interracial communication. He did not intend to be a sit-in demonstrator, but he became involved in an unexpected way when he joined white student activists from MacMurray College in Jacksonville, Illinois, listening to black student activists from Alabama State College and members of Martin Luther King Jr.'s SCLC tell of their experiences during the Montgomery Bus Boycott. They met at the black-owned Regal Café in Montgomery. Local police considered the meeting an infraction of segregation laws and arrested the entire group. Attorney Fred Gray described the ridiculous dimensions of the case: "It was an African American restaurant in an African American community with an African American owner who was perfectly willing to provide food service for the integrated group. The group was orderly, and there was no disturbance whatsoever. The police somehow learned of the luncheon, came in, and arrested all present," including Ed King.[36]

For Ed King, the experience in jail was mortifying. Whites were herded into one cell, blacks into another, and all were called intolerable names by jailers, beaten, and denied even minimal conveniences. When the case came before the Montgomery County Circuit Court, the white group was exonerated, but the black group, represented by attorney Gray, was declared guilty (ultimately released on appeal). According to Gray, that kind of injustice demonstrated the lengths to which the "power structure in Montgomery was willing to go for the purpose of maintaining segregation." Ed King noted that arrests were never made for integrating a facility; the arrests were always for disturbing the peace, trespassing, or disorderly conduct.[37]

When Ed King returned to Montgomery from Boston for a hearing, he was arrested again, this time for trespassing in the Jefferson Davis Hotel in downtown Montgomery, where he was a guest. This was a legal scheme developed by the attorneys from the SCLC. "May I have a Methodist minister come have breakfast with me and put it on my bill as a paying guest in your hotel?" asked Ed King. "Certainly," replied the manager. Ed King brought his white friend to breakfast, and the next day asked again, "May I bring a Methodist minister to luncheon and put it on my bill?" The manager quickly consented, wondering why he bothered asking. When Ed King brought African American Rev. Elroy Embry to lunch on June 7, 1960, he and Embry were immediately arrested for trespassing. This time, he and Embry were sentenced to a week of hard labor chopping wood and cutting grass along the roadside. This second experience of incarceration was worse than the first. He was tortured and beaten and told he would be killed during the night. (He was not killed thanks to another white inmate who happened to have a knife and guarded King the entire night.) Fred Gray told him, "They mean it because if you are killed, they won't have a case to take to the Supreme Court." Gray believed it was a case that could easily be won because Ed King was arrested for trespassing in a hotel where he was a paying guest. As a result of the arrest and notoriety, Ed King's parents were forced to leave Mississippi.[38]

These arrests were only the beginning for Ed King, who would become one of the most daring and committed activist white ministers in the South. Like Campbell and Duncan Gray, Ed King grew up in Mississippi, where he witnessed extreme atrocities of racial injustice, and, like Campbell and Duncan Gray, he was determined to do something substantial to bring about social change.

To understand Ed King, it is necessary to recognize his admiration for Medgar Evers. Evers applied to the University of Mississippi Law School shortly after the *Brown* decision, only to be turned away on the grounds that "he failed to submit recommendations from white people in the state." Impressed with Evers's courage, the NAACP appointed him as its first full-time paid employee, state field secretary for the Mississippi NAACP, headquartered in Jackson. Ed King, while an undergraduate student at Millsaps College in Jackson, met Evers in 1955 at an interracial event at Tougaloo College. They belonged to a group called the Intercollegiate Fellowship, an interracial alliance of students and faculty from white colleges, Millsaps and Ole Miss, and black colleges such as Alcorn State College, Jackson State College (now Jackson State University), and Tougaloo College. Evers worked for greater understanding between the groups and wanted white people to understand what it was like to be black in Mississippi. He told them about his father, a stroke victim, who was left to die in the basement of the only white hospital in the state that accepted blacks. In the cold of winter, Evers found his father in a room with "water dribbling from pipes, rats and roaches running around, a line of black people laid out on cots with no doctors or nurses anywhere." Evers never forgot the sight of his father dying without dignity. Evers told of brutal lynchings and white mobs with pistols and rifles on the prowl in black neighborhoods. He told how black people couldn't vote, couldn't pay poll taxes, couldn't enter the town hall to register, and if they signed petitions for school desegregation or even for the improvement of black schools, they would lose their jobs. Evers's presentation convinced King that he must become part of the civil rights movement, as he left Mississippi to pursue his calling to the ministry at Boston University School of Theology, alma mater of Martin Luther King Jr. There he would be a classmate of James Lawson, an old friend who had organized the sit-in movement in Nashville. According to church historian Charles Marsh, the Methodists of Mississippi considered Boston University School of Theology "a hotbed of social gospel teaching and radical political activism," but for Ed King it was precisely the right school.[39]

◆ ◆ ◆

Another white southern minister who helped organize and engage in sit-ins was Presbyterian Merrill Proudfoot (1923–1998), born in Osceola, Iowa, but raised in Texas, who published a diary of his experiences in a sit-in in Knoxville, Tennessee, from June 9, 1960, through July 18, 1960. Unlike Ed King's experience, Proudfoot's sit-in occurred in a town where the mayor, John Duncan, organized a biracial negotiating committee whose aim was to convince downtown merchants to open lunch counters. Proudfoot was twelve years older than Ed

King and already an ordained minister and had learned from some discouraging experiences as a pastor in Texas just how little he could actually accomplish in a white, segregated congregation. In Texas, he campaigned for integrated seating at a public function and attempted to welcome a black Presbyterian family into his congregation, and failed at both efforts. He became a professor of religion and philosophy at Knoxville College, a predominantly black Presbyterian institution, where he believed he could contribute to the emerging civil rights movement. As the Greensboro sit-ins progressed, students at Knoxville became eager to organize a sit-in. Proudfoot became involved when one of his students, Robert Booker, asked for his help. Proudfoot urged Booker to give negotiations a chance, but when he realized that negotiations wouldn't work, fearful as he was of participating, he nevertheless joined Booker at a counter at Rich's Department Store, "trying to look like an ordinary customer." The sit-ins were unsuccessful at first, but with an increase in the number of participants and their persistence, businesspeople gradually gave in. What made these sit-ins different than those in the Deep South or even Nashville was that the police arrested the white hecklers and not the protestors. Demonstrators adhered closely to nonviolent decorum and never retaliated when insulted or beaten. When merchants closed their counters and stores, it hurt them more than it hurt the demonstrators. This ultimately led to desegregation, as businesspeople no longer wanted a loss of income.[40]

The Southern Regional Council released a report on August 7, 1960, stating, "Twenty-seven southern cities and counties have opened their lunch counters to all customers." Some places mentioned were Miami, Florida; Greensboro and Winston-Salem, North Carolina; Frankfort, Kentucky; Knoxville and Nashville, Tennessee; Austin and San Antonio, Texas; Fairfax County, Fredericksburg, Williamsburg, and Richmond, Virginia. The council emphasized that desegregation came about because there was fair-mindedness among white southerners and "good sense and good manners" on the part of African Americans seeking equal rights. The council was optimistic that more desegregation would occur peacefully and lead to greater opportunities for African Americans in the South,[41] but it remained to be seen whether those hopes would be realized.

Freedom Rides

Could any person have anticipated the brutality inflicted on the interracial groups of Freedom Riders (no ministers) as they traveled throughout the South to test court-ordered desegregation of terminal waiting rooms, lunch counters, and lavatories? Sponsored by CORE and the Fellowship of Reconciliation

(FOR), it was relatively peaceful as they traveled the Upper South, but in Alabama, savage assaults began. When a Greyhound bus pulled into Anniston, an angry mob with iron bars and knives slashed the bus's tires, broke its windows, and hurled a bomb inside. The passengers managed to escape, only to be beaten by the mob. One hour later, a Trailways bus arrived. This time, assailants boarded the bus, cursed and beat passengers, and pushed them to the rear. Sixty-one-year-old Walter Bergman, from Wayne State University in Michigan, received head injuries causing him to have a stroke and bringing him close to death. In Birmingham, they were met with iron bars. James Peck, a white rider from New York, was knocked unconscious and left in an alleyway in a pool of blood. When revived, he was taken to the home of an African American Baptist pastor. Photographs of Peck's bandaged head appeared in newspapers all over the world.[42]

Violence resumed as a new group of Freedom Riders with Diane Nash and John Lewis made their way to Montgomery. Lewis related, "In Montgomery . . . people came out of nowhere . . . men, women, and children with baseball bats, clubs and chains," with no police present. Jim Zwerg, a white student from Madison, Wisconsin, got off the bus only to be beaten and damaged for life. John Lewis was smashed in the head and received a brain concussion. Will Campbell arrived in Montgomery the same day as the Freedom Riders, ready to give emotional and spiritual support. John Seigenthaler, Campbell's friend from Nashville, working as an agent of President Kennedy, was attacked and left lying on the street for more than an hour before an ambulance came to get him. As Campbell drove through the streets, he noticed the presence of two white ministers who acted as if nothing was happening. In Jackson, Mississippi, over 300 Freedom Riders were arrested and taken to Parchman State Penitentiary (maximum security), located in the Mississippi Delta. Among them was James Farmer, who related that all the men were herded into one large cellblock with thin straw mattresses: "When their voices rang out with freedom songs, prison officials asked them to stop, lest their exuberances reach other prisoners. If they did not stop, the guards threatened to take their mattresses away. . . . They took the mattresses away and they sang as they never sang before."[43]

Ed King commented, "When you have someone totally in your control, you can use violence and brutality to break their spirit." That was the psychological type of torture used at Parchman and the kind Ed King experienced in Montgomery. Ed King visited prisoners in Parchman along with black ministers, a rabbi, and a white Unitarian minister, but no others. "Visiting Parchman," Ed King stated, "was a dangerous undertaking. Local police and others would record our license tags and later harass and terrorize us."[44]

The Southern Regional Council suggested that most of the resentment came because the groups were from outside the local region. Black people as

well as white questioned their sanity. It seems unreasonable that Rev. William
Sloane Coffin (1925–2006), born in New York City, chaplain at Yale Divinity School, and himself a Freedom Rider arrested in Montgomery, chastised
southern white clergy for not supporting the Freedom Riders. Ed King stated
that he supported the Freedom Riders, but was on a church assignment in
Montana and could not participate with the first group. He also knew his participation would mean danger for his family. Northern ministers like Coffin
were insensitive to the difficulties and problems facing southern white ministers. Coffin was further resented because he came from a northern university
that had no black faculty (at the time) and from New Haven, Connecticut, a
city that had plenty of its own racial problems. Ed King pointed out that integrationists in the South did not know how they could do anything against the
madness of segregation without jeopardizing the safety of their relatives.[45]

There were, however, some southern white ministers who embarked on
Freedom Rides, albeit several months after the horrendous attacks when
most violence had subsided. On the morning of September 12, 1961, an
interracial group of twenty-eight Episcopal clergymen known as the Prayer
Pilgrims left New Orleans on a Trailways bus bound for Detroit and the
triennial general convention of the Episcopal Church. Two white southern ministers were aboard: Rev. John Morris of ESCRU, who organized the
pilgrimage, and Rev. Lee Belford of Mississippi. There were no problems
until they arrived in Jackson. Three black and twelve white clergymen were
arrested and sentenced to four months in jail for attempting to have lunch at
the whites-only terminal restaurant. According to Morris, they were kept in
segregated jail cells for one week and released on bond while the rest of the
group went on to make a witness in Sewanee, Tennessee, at the University
of the South, site of the desegregation crisis of 1952, where the Claremont
Restaurant and the Sewanee Inn still refused to serve and give accommodations to black people. The remaining group arrived late at the convention
but in time to tell of their experience and concern for racial problems. Morris later commented that the stereotypical perception of the sweet and mild
vicar was changing: "In his place came the outspoken activist, picket sign in
hand and ready, if necessary, to be hauled away in the paddy wagon."[46] John
Morris was that new kind of vicar.

Morris attributed his activism for integration to a daguerreotype of his
grandfather with his black wife. Morris's grandfather, an Episcopal missionary
in Africa, married a beautiful native of Sierra Leone who had been educated in
France and taught at a girls' high school in Freetown. His grandfather wished
to bring his bride home to Georgia, but interracial marriage was strictly forbidden. The couple divorced, but the story fueled young Morris's sense of
racial injustice, and the photograph has been a treasured keepsake.[47]

The Prayer Pilgrimage was just a beginning for the activism of Morris and other members of ESCRU. They would picket the segregated Lovett School in Atlanta, where Martin Luther King Jr.'s son was denied admission. They would protest segregated business practices throughout the South and make efforts to integrate all Episcopal parishes. Members were encouraged to engage in local demonstrations and join parishes near their homes that were of a different race and culture than their own. Their work was vigorous and intended to open southern society to black people. In an address to the Michigan Chapter of ESCRU, Morris proclaimed, "Christ might be understood as Lord of even the sit-in and the freedom-ride."[48]

Mass Demonstrations

In 1903 W. E. B. Du Bois described southwest Georgia as a land "luxuriant with forests of pine, oak, ash, hickory and poplar; hot with the sun and damp with the rich black swamp-land," where great plantations of "many thousands of acres used to run," and where "in 1890 lived ten thousand Negroes and two thousand whites." Albany was the center, "two hundred miles south of Atlanta and two hundred miles west of the Atlantic . . . the center of life for ten thousand souls; their point of contact with the outer world . . . of news and gossip, their market for buying and selling, borrowing and lending, their fountain of justice and law." Henry Hampton and Steve Fayer described the Albany of the 1960s as a place where workers from the surrounding fields of cotton and peanuts would come "to conduct business, buy supplies, attend church, and search out entertainment." The population in 1960 included 23,000 black residents and 33,000 white residents, a completely segregated town, but according to local black osteopath Dr. William G. Anderson, "Blacks held no positions in any of the stores downtown as salespersons, clerks, [or] as policemen, and blacks held no political office. . . . You couldn't say that it was a community where you could experience racial harmony." Their goals included establishment of a biracial committee to work out a timetable for desegregation of all places of public accommodation, including buses; recognition by the city that African Americans had the right to protest segregation peacefully under the US Constitution; and a declaration from the city that it would abide by the Interstate Commerce Commission's decision desegregating travel terminals.[49]

On December 12, 1961, eleven Freedom Riders disembarked from a Greyhound bus and entered the terminal. This was still the Deep South, and the group was immediately arrested. Over 276 black people paraded in support of the eleven, knowing that they, too, would be arrested. During the next several days, 700 were arrested for parading without a permit and scattered in jails throughout the county, wherever room could be found. According to Dr. Anderson, "Going to jail was probably the most feared thing in rural Georgia. . . . Many blacks were never heard from again," but as they marched they sang, "We are not afraid; we are not afraid. . . . Oh-oh-oh deep in my heart, I do believe, we shall overcome . . . some day."[50]

"We will never negotiate with outside agitators whose avowed purpose is to create turmoil." Such was the constant cry of Mayor Asa D. Kelley of Albany and his police chief, Laurie Pritchett. Outsiders arrived in Albany during the summer of 1961 in the persons of Charles Sherrod, twenty-two years old, and Cordell Reagon, eighteen years old, members of SNCC and veterans of the Freedom Rides. Joining Dr. Anderson, they quickly decided that a mass movement in Albany might achieve results, but the black ministers of Albany did not want the confrontational tactics used by SNCC and invited Martin Luther King Jr., who they knew would be less confrontational and possibly successful. King, leader of the SCLC, arrived from Atlanta with Rev. Andrew Young and Rev. Ralph Abernathy, and they became the second, third, and fourth outsiders in Albany. King only intended to encourage the people as he spoke from the pulpit of Shiloh Baptist Church, "Go to jail without hating the white folks. . . . Before the victory is won, some must face physical death to free their children from a life of psychological handicaps, but we shall overcome." Two hundred and fifty people marched the next day and were immediately locked up, among them King, Anderson, Abernathy, and Young, "charged with parading without a permit, disturbing the peace, and obstructing the sidewalk." King vowed to stay in jail until the city desegregated.[51]

The movement agreed to call off mass demonstrations in return for concessions by the city fathers. King and most of the prisoners were released from jail on bond. The bus and train stations were desegregated, but the city reneged almost immediately on its promises and became virtually a "police state." Bond loans were canceled. Buses, parks, theaters, and lunch counters remained segregated. King said later, "I didn't understand at the time what was happening. We thought that the victory had been won. When we got out, we discovered it was all a hoax." Demonstrations of any kind were prohibited. Anderson was arrested for walking down the street holding a piece of paper, and four African Americans were arrested in front of all-white First Baptist Church for attempting to enter with a petition for prayer and reconciliation.[52] Peaceful marching did not succeed in Albany.

Rev. Brooks Ramsey, born in 1922 in Memphis, Tennessee, and pastor of the church, related that white ministers were forewarned that such attempts by black people might occur. He met with his deacons the night before and pleaded with them to open the church doors and let the African Americans in, but they refused. He offered a compromise: "Let them sit in the balcony or go

down to the TV room where they can watch the service." Again, they refused.
"At least," he told them, "if you are going to turn them away, will you agree
not to have them arrested?" They agreed; but the next day the chairman of the
deacons informed the police that African Americans would attempt to enter
the church. The police stationed themselves in a strategic place and made the
arrests. Ramsey commented, "The deacons violated the one agreement they had
with me. They placed guards at the door to keep people out. This was a denial of
the Gospel that I believed in." Ramsey recalled that eight groups of demonstrators went to eight different churches that Sunday. They were turned away but
not arrested. He believed the visitors at his church were singled out for arrest as
an affront to him because he was the most moderate minister in town.[53]

After the service, black activist Andrew Young was waiting for Ramsey
and told him how sorry he was about what happened: "We didn't intend to
hurt you because we know that you are our best friend in Albany." A reporter
from the *Atlanta Journal*, Walter Rugaber, approached Ramsey and asked him
if he agreed with his deacons' actions. "I do not," Ramsey responded and made
a statement that was published in newspapers across the country: "*This is
Christ's church and I cannot build any wall around it that He did not build, and
that includes a racial wall.*" After his statement, the deacons held a meeting and
told Ramsey not to preach the following Sunday. He preached anyway, knowing that his days at First Baptist were numbered.[54]

Ramsey admitted that he moved cautiously with his congregation: "I
did not go into the ministry as a crusader, but as someone who could work
for change in a quiet, gentle way, but when confronted with a crisis, I had to
act decisively. The Lord requires that we do not withhold ourselves in such
situations. When Rugaber asked me if I agreed with the church's actions,
I responded, 'I do not agree,' and made my statement." After the incident,
Ramsey continued to stand for racial justice and found a few others in Albany
who shared his convictions. Before King left Albany, a group of eight white
ministers, including Ramsey, attended a meeting in the basement of a black
church to hear King talk of "redemptive suffering," something designated by
Julian Bond as the "spiritual force of social revolution." "All unmerited suffering is redemptive," suggested King. Ramsey added, "I'd like to believe that and
hope that it would be in the plan of God, but I think a lot of suffering is not
rewarded. Perhaps in the overall plan of God, Martin Luther King, Jr., is right. I
hope that all the suffering we have done for righteous causes will in some way
advance those causes."[55]

Within the year, all eight ministers were forced to leave Albany. If the eight
ministers had marched with African Americans in Albany, it would not have
done much good, as they also would have been placed in county jails, as were

the group of seventy-five outside ministers and laity who arrived on August 28, 1962, to conduct a prayer vigil. At city hall and after several moments of silence, Rev. John W. P. Collier of Israel Memorial AME Church of Newark, New Jersey, read from the sixth chapter of Galatians, "For whatsoever a man soweth, that he shall also reap." Chief Pritchett asked several times, "All right Reverends, what's your purpose?" Rev. Norman C. Eddy of East Harlem Protestant Parish in New York City replied, "Our purpose is to offer our prayers to God." Prtichett urged them to leave. When they would not, he gave the command, "Put them in jail," and charged them with "disorderly conduct, creating a disturbance, congregating on the sidewalk, and refusing to obey an officer." Four hundred whites watched and cheered as fifty-five clergy and twenty-five laypeople were herded into the side door of a building, their Bibles and other possessions taken from them. When one prisoner gave his race as white, a policeman was heard to reply, "Well, you may be part white." Among them were members of the Protestant, Roman Catholic, and Jewish faiths, mostly from the North, but a few from the South.[56]

Ramsey lamented, "There was nothing I could do to help." When more outside ministers showed their concern, the hitherto silent white ministers of Albany advised them to remain at home. In a printed resolution, the silent white ministers intimated, with the same attitude as their mayor, that outsiders could add nothing constructive to the racial situation in Albany. Speaking for his group of eight ministers, Ramsey asserted, "We were not a part of that resolution; we could not be, because we were opposed to segregation."[57]

Civil rights leaders deemed the Albany movement a failure. More than 1,200 arrests were made in nine months. Ramsey commented, "Never before had so many arrests been made within the entire nation," but in the eyes of many, the Albany movement revealed remarkable perseverance, hope, endurance, and buoyancy on the part of black people. The wonderful freedom songs energized them. It has been said that Albany, home to singer Ray Charles and the Shiloh Baptist Church a cappella choir, would never have had a civil rights movement without music.[58]

While King vowed to stay in jail, some unknown person paid the bond, and Pritchett told King he had to leave. King did not want to leave, but was released, and on July 21 the city attorney obtained a federal court order enjoining King and other leaders "from further demonstrations." King obeyed, and, like Ramsey, he left within a year. Like King, Ramsey had done his best. Throughout his ministry, he struggled with the problem of being pastoral and prophetic, but at the moment of crisis, he became prophetic.[59]

◆ ◆ ◆

In 1951 Carl Rowan (1925–2000), a young black reporter, described Birmingham as "the world's most race-conscious city . . . where the color line was drawn in every conceivable way . . . where Eugene 'Bull' Connor, white supremacist police commissioner, saw that no man, white or black, crossed the line." Connor, once a member of the Klan, said at the time of the civil rights movement, "The so-called Negro Movement is an attempt to take over our country by the lazy, the indolent, the Beatniks, the ignorant, some misguided religionists, and bleeding hearts." In *Why We Can't Wait*, Martin Luther King Jr. wrote, "In 'Bull' Connor's Birmingham, you would be a resident of a city where a United States senator, visiting to deliver a speech, had been arrested because he walked through a door marked 'Colored.' . . . From the year 1957 through January of 1963, while Birmingham was still claiming that Negroes were 'satisfied,' there were seventeen unsolved bombings of Negro churches and homes of civil-rights leaders."[60]

In his memoir, *Mary and Me*, Rev. John Rutland describes his experiences during the 1950s and 1960s when he served Woodlawn Methodist Church in Birmingham, which "Bull" Connor attended. Rutland describes how Connor once got up from his pew during worship service announcing, "I'm not going to sit here and listen to that n_____r preaching," and outside the church he would say to others loudly so Rutland could overhear, "I'm his police commissioner and he is trying to unseat me, and he's my preacher and I'm trying to get another one." When Rutland first arrived at Woodlawn, Connor and two others were standing in front of the church, arms folded across their chests ready to keep African Americans out of the church. Pastor Rutland told him, "Mr. Connor . . . this is not your church. This is God's church. It is a Methodist church, which belongs to the North Alabama Conference. I am the appointed pastor. I will decide who can and cannot enter this building. Now I am going to my office for five minutes. When I come back if you are still here, I will call Sheriff Bailey and swear out a warrant for your arrest." As he walked away, Rutland could hear him say, "Come on boys, that son of a b____ will do what he says." They left and Rutland doubted if he ever really would have called the sheriff. Rutland served Woodlawn Methodist Church from 1953 to 1962.[61]

After his defeat in Albany, Martin Luther King Jr. was determined to do everything possible to break down Birmingham's segregation barriers. In January 1963 King met at a local church with Ralph Abernathy, Wyatt T. Walker, Fred Shuttlesworth, and about twenty-five other African American pastors of Birmingham to plan strategies for attacking segregation, Project C—"c" for confrontation. One white minister, Rev. Joseph Ellwanger, pastor of all-black St. Paul's Lutheran Church, one of Alabama's many black Lutheran churches, met with them. Born in 1933 in St. Louis, Ellwanger spent part of his childhood in his father's store-front church in the black section of St. Louis and the rest of his childhood in Selma, Alabama, when his father became director of an all-black Lutheran high school and seminary, but Ellwanger was unable to attend the all-black Lutheran high school because the segregation laws of the state of Alabama would not permit him to do so. Both experiences gave him the determination to fight the racial segregation and injustice that existed all around him. His bachelor of divinity thesis at Concordia Lutheran Seminary in St. Louis was entitled "Integration and the Lutheran Church in the South." His master's thesis in sacred theology was entitled "Racism and the Christian World Mission." After his graduation and ordination in 1958, he accepted a call to the black congregation and returned to the South to make a stand for integration. When members of his congregation urged him to join in planning demonstrations, he willingly agreed.[62]

Ellwanger was no stranger to hostility. In 1961 he took two black students, members of his church, to a youth rally at a white Lutheran congregation in Tuscaloosa (at the youth pastor's invitation) and became the victim, along with the parents of the two students, of threatening phone calls. He read three days later in the Birmingham papers that the youth pastor, Vicar James Fackler, had been seized by the KKK and taken to the railroad tracks, where he was beaten and abandoned. On another occasion Ellwanger was threatened because he was seen driving a truck loaded with his church's black youngsters to a youth rally in Selma. He was told that a bomb was going to explode near his house, but when the fire department inspected, it turned out to be a scare tactic. Troubles would come again in 1963, when he joined a demonstration at a downtown department store. The Klan seemed always present to create disturbances, violence, and fear.[63]

King began Project C with small student protests at segregated lunch counters and the singing of the freedom songs "We Shall Overcome" and "Ain't Gonna Let Nobody Turn Me Round." Mimicking Pritchett's tactics, Connor placed all protestors in jail, but on April 7, Palm Sunday, when King's brother, Rev. A. D. King, a pastor at nearby Ensley, led a prayer march through downtown streets, the full force of police action began. Twenty-six black people were arrested, bringing the total to 102 in five days. What might have been a beautiful and calm Palm Sunday became a prelude to police brutality that would shock the nation. The situation grew more intense when, on April 10, an Alabama circuit court judge issued an order prohibiting 133 civil rights leaders, including King, Abernathy, and Shuttlesworth, from participating or encouraging sit-ins, picketing, or other demonstrations. The order was disobeyed on April 12 when King and Abernathy and a huge crowd of marchers, dressed in blue jeans and blue cotton shirts to dramatize their efforts to boycott the buying of Easter finery, marched quietly through the streets of Birmingham. King, Abernathy, and sixty others were arrested, with King placed in solitary confinement, forced to sleep on metal slats without a mattress or linens.[64]

On the day after his arrest, a small item appeared in the *Birmingham News*, signed by a group of local clergymen:

> We are confronted by a series of demonstrations by some of our Negro citizens, directed and led by outsiders. We recognize the natural impatience of people who feel that their hopes are slow in being realized, but we are convinced that these demonstrations are unwise and untimely. . . . We strongly urge our own Negro community to withdraw support from these demonstrations and to unite locally in working peacefully for a better Birmingham. . . . We appeal to both our white and Negro citizenry to observe the principles of law and order and common sense.[65]

The statement—signed by Episcopal bishop Charles C. J. Carpenter; Roman Catholic bishop Joseph A. Durick; Rabbi Milton L. Grafman; Methodist bishop Paul Hardin; Methodist bishop Nolan B. Harmon; Episcopalian bishop coadjutor Rev. George M. Murray; Presbyterian minister Rev. Edward V. Ramage; and Baptist minister Rev. Earl Stallings—was a call for law and order but also an attack on the intrusion of outsiders for the purpose of solving Birmingham's racial problems. The newspaper, smuggled into King's jail cell, evoked a passionate and angry response, which became known as King's "Letter from a Birmingham Jail," written in the margins of the newspaper and on toilet tissue. In the letter, King recognized the contribution and sacrifice of some white ministers and southern whites, but he expressed great disappointment with the white Church in general and its leadership in particular, who, he believed, "remained silent behind the anesthetizing security of stained-glass windows." The letter became a harsh indictment against ministers who were more devoted to "order" than to "justice." King's "Letter from a Birmingham Jail" disturbed many white ministers, and perhaps it was meant to do that. Few could say he was incorrect. Pastor Ellwanger was one who totally agreed with King. "To be silent," Ellwanger observed, "was to approve the *status quo*."[66]

King and Abernathy were released from jail on bond on April 20, and the second phase of Project C was planned, called "The Children's Crusade," inasmuch as adults were reluctant to demonstrate and jeopardize their jobs. It was during this phase of Project C that the whole nation was exposed to the television sight of police dogs and high-pressure fire hoses forcing the retreat of children demonstrators. Hampton and Fayer mentioned that the pressure from the hoses was powerful enough to rip the bark off trees. More than 250 children were arrested, displaying no resistance, but angry adult onlookers began hurling bricks and bottles at the firemen. Demonstrations by adults and children, arrests, and jailing continued until, finally, Burke Marshall, chief of the Justice Department's civil rights division, arrived in Birmingham to persuade white and black leaders to reach a settlement. After a total of five weeks of demonstrations, pledges were made to desegregate facilities in large downtown department and variety stores; to promote qualified black employees; to set a timetable for desegregating the city's schools, parks, and playgrounds; and to hire additional black city employees, including policemen. Immediately, segregationists cried, "sell out," and the Klan and National States Rights Party increased activity, but, according to Claude Sitton, statements by the new mayor-elect, Albert Boutwell, encouraged King to believe that changes would eventually be made.[67]

Ellwanger became involved in the Birmingham demonstrations when he picketed downtown department stores. Although he was not put in jail, he was taken to city hall and questioned as to why he was the only white person on the picket line. Ellwanger explained that the department stores had agreed to hire some black salespeople but reneged on the promise, so he, along with blacks, protested. While at city hall, he was asked if he wanted to confess to anything. Puzzled, Ellwanger responded, "What are you talking about?" A black man in a prison uniform came into the room and accused Ellwanger of attempting to assault him sexually in a bathroom in the city hall while he was cleaning. Ellwanger had not been at the city hall prior to that day for several months and refused to confess to something that was obviously false. The chief told him, "Well, you think it over. If you confess right now, we'll let you off; otherwise, we will have to bring it to a trial." He received another call a few days later, and again they asked if he wanted to confess, telling him, "If you leave town we'll drop the charges." Ellwanger told them he was not about to leave; they could go ahead with a trial, but he wanted to see the charges on paper. Ellwanger commented, "They never did produce the papers, and the whole episode demonstrated how ruthlessly and deceptively the police attempted to control the actions of people." Ellwanger did not exactly know who informed on him, but suspected that it may have been a Klan group that was watching the picketing and were angry about his presence. According to Ellwanger, the Klan was everywhere, always collaborating with the police: "Many policemen were KKK members and 'Bull' Connor was known to be in direct contact with the Klan at all times."[68]

Retaliation against black activists by the Klan and police had become fierce in Alabama as the civil rights movement progressed. Ellwanger had great compassion for black people, whom he felt were defenseless and at the mercy of the white power structure: "Many of the atrocities committed against them were never known, but it was precisely the violence coming from the police and the KKK, the threats and the like that helped to bring pressure on the blacks to finally fight for change."[69] Ellwanger would be present again during the Selma demonstrations, actively participating in the protest movement.

◆ ◆ ◆

The frontline activities of Rev. Ed King during the Jackson, Mississippi, demonstrations of May and June 1963 may have prompted Martin Luther King Jr. to modulate his harsh indictment of southern white clergy. After completing his studies at Boston University School of Theology, family members and white Methodists advised him never to return to Mississippi, but his friend Medgar Evers, state field secretary for the Mississippi NAACP, told him, "You must return." Believing the Church offered the best hope for racial justice, Ed King resolved to return and try again for ordination. One of his good friends at the seminary, African American Woodie White, who would one day become the Methodist bishop of Indiana, told him he was still narrow-minded because he was thinking of the Methodist Church as only a white church. King had forgotten that it was also a black Church, and upon his return to Mississippi, he decided to accept a position as chaplain at predominantly black Tougaloo College, on the outskirts of Jackson. His duties as chaplain began in January 1963; thus Ed King returned to Mississippi and the struggle for black equality. Medgar Evers was delighted to have him back.[70]

In the meantime Evers, John Salter, and Dave Dennis of COFO carefully planned a boycott. As Ed King explained, "By *not* doing something, by *not* buying that new dress or pair of shoes for Christmas or Easter, black people might begin to make a stand against discrimination and eventually they might walk all the way." The intention of the boycott planners was threefold: "to inform local black people that they had a right to demonstrate and that things could be different," "to inform local white people that blacks were not satisfied," and "to show the rest of America and the rest of the world that non-violent protestors were dignified revolutionaries." They began by boycotting downtown merchants who would not allow black people to try on clothes. When those in the first group of demonstrators, six college teachers, were arrested, the boycott collapsed. Evers tried to negotiate, first with the mayor and then with white business leaders, "not to talk about instant integration but to consider what steps might be taken on what issues." All their attempts were ignored.[71]

On May 20, 1963, the Supreme Court handed down a ruling that made it a federal offense to prosecute black people who demonstrated for the right to eat in privately owned business establishments. The news encouraged Evers, Salter, Ed King, and others to try again to penetrate Jackson. In late May they sent three black college students, Anne Moody, Perlina Lewis, and Memphis Norman, to the Woolworth's lunch counter, with Ed King, in clerical attire, planted to observe what was going on and report back to Evers. Several white people left when the students sat down, but one white woman stayed. "I'm sorry," she told the students, "I wish I could stay longer, but I have to leave." She told them that she was glad that demonstrations had started in Mississippi as nothing else was going to bring about change, but she told Ed King that her husband would lose his job if anyone knew she was there, and she had to leave before the reporters could see who she was.[72]

The cautious attempt turned into a nightmare for the three students. The police did not arrest them as Ed King and Evers expected. As Ed King explained, "With the recent Supreme Court ruling, if the police had arrested the demonstrators, we would have had a winning case. . . . Instead, the police allowed a mob of about 400 to form and do their work for them, although many policemen in plain clothes were hidden among the crowd. Memphis Norman was grabbed from the counter, clubbed, beaten, and knocked unconscious. He was left to lie on the floor, blood spurting from his mouth and nostrils. The crowd then went after the two women, pouring mustard, garbage, salt, pepper, and vinegar over them and then dragging them by the hair through the garbage. One white lady brought a bottle of ketchup, which she proceeded to pour over the students and those whom she knew were supporting the students." The avalanche of ketchup was intended to mark the demonstrators as red Communists. The students at the counter, Ed King affirmed, were trained in nonviolence: "They prayed; they sang religious hymns and freedom songs. Had they fought back they probably would have been killed. Three hours later, Woolworth headquarters in New York ordered the store closed." The violence was shown on national television, but, as Ed King remarked, that night the Jackson television stations had "cable trouble" and commercials replaced the scenes of violence: "The local news showed only a picture of empty seats at the lunch counter with a voice explaining that all lunch counters in Jackson had been closed because of demonstrations."[73]

The *New York Times* displayed the photograph of Norman being beaten by Benny G. Oliver, former policeman in plain clothes. (Ed King related that Oliver was wearing tennis shoes when he kicked Norman; had he been wearing his heavy police boots, his victim would surely have died.) Norman later told how attackers threw mustard and thumbtacks at him, threw him from his stool, and stomped him in the face, head, stomach, and back. Ed King went to New York City to speak about Mississippi at a program sponsored by the Broadway Tabernacle Congregational Church. He asserted, "Jackson claims it has the best race relations in the United States." "Perhaps," he added, "second only to Johannesburg, South Africa."[74] Surely, Ed King, Medgar Evers, and Memphis Norman helped to bring the nation's attention to the reality of life in Mississippi for African Americans during the 1960s, but the worst was yet to come for Ed King and Evers.

In the meantime the annual Mississippi Methodist Conference was meeting at Galloway Church in Jackson, where Ed King was to be voted on for membership. He tried appealing to a conservative Methodist minister, a bystander at the Woolworth's sit-in, whom he believed could influence the mob to go home. He was told, "They're your demonstrators, why don't you tell them to leave." Ed King told him, "They can't leave. They'll be killed before they could walk through all those people and get to the front door." "You're a communist on the way to Hell," the minister told him and reported to the conference that Ed King had organized the sit-in at Woolworth's (which was not true).[75]

During ensuing demonstrations, the police no longer remained in the background. On Thursday, May 30, 1963, Ed King and thirteen others, ministers and students, black and white, were arrested while they held a prayer meeting on the steps of the post office, a federal building they thought would be off limits to local police, but they were mistaken. Once in jail, they were mugged, fingerprinted, and thrown into tiny segregated cells, including the ministers.[76]

Evers bailed King out in time for him to attend the white Methodist Conference, but the bishop refused to allow him to speak. A vote was taken, and King's relationship with the white Methodist Conference of Mississippi was terminated. King was undaunted because 85 out of 174 clergy voted on his behalf, although he admitted that 15 of them were ministers who had signed the "Born of Conviction" statement and were leaving the state. The close vote indicated the tense division within the white Methodist Conference over the issue of race. Taylor Branch mentioned that there was weeping as King sadly left the meeting.[77]

The next day Bishop Charles F. Golden of the all-black Methodist jurisdiction telephoned King: "I understand you are without a denomination and without a bishop. I take you now under my authority"; thus King became a member in good standing of the black Methodist Central Jurisdiction, and his activism continued.[78]

On June 1, 1963, 600 black children parading peacefully in pairs carrying freedom banners and American flags were immediately arrested and herded into patrol wagons, canvas-covered trucks, and garbage trucks. They were thrown into a large pen in the Jackson fairgrounds without beds or bathroom facilities, their signs and flags confiscated. Evers called the scene "Nazi Germany." On June 2, 1963, Evers and Roy Wilkins, executive secretary of the NAACP, were arrested as they picketed the F. W. Woolworth Company. Two hours later more than 100 black children were again arrested and taken to the fairgrounds. On June 3 there was some easing of picketing as Mayor Allen Thompson agreed to begin accepting applications for black policemen and school crossing guards (only in black neighborhoods), but Evers continued to demand a biracial committee to discuss all racial problems, segregated lunch counters, voting restrictions, and the like. African American Ralph Bunche, Nobel Prize winner and undersecretary of the United Nations, himself a victim of segregation when denied a room at a hotel in Atlanta in 1962, stated in an address to the graduating class at Colgate University, in Hamilton, New York, "Our standing as a nation, our position of leadership, all suffer grievously and become tarnished as the entire world witnesses the sordid spectacle of Birmingham and Jackson with their revolting use of police dogs, high-pressure hoses, mass arrests and other police brutalities, all directed at peaceable Negro and occasional white demonstrators seeking only to march, sing, and pray."[79]

On June 12, 1963, Evers was making plans to invite Martin Luther King Jr. to Jackson. As he returned home that night, he stepped out of his car and was killed by an assassin's bullet, and Martin Luther King Jr. never marched with the Jackson demonstrations. The nation, outside of Mississippi, was shocked, mortified, and enraged. One hundred and fifty-eight people marching to protest the murder in Jackson were arrested, as white supremacists insisted that "the slaying would not change the patterns of segregation." John Salter, a Native American sociology professor at Tougaloo College, was clubbed and struck on the head and beaten to the ground, where he lay bleeding and seemingly unconscious. Four days later Ed King and Salter were arrested again when they marched with Evers's mourners, singing hymns and freedom songs in civil disobedience to a police order for silence. They were taken to the fairgrounds prison, where they were forced to lean against a wall lined with many prisoners, hands outstretched above their heads, "braced against the wall in an almost straight angle." Whenever anyone would groan or cry and begin to drop their arms or shift the position of their bodies, the armed guards would walk up, curse, and sometimes poke people with their guns or clubs. Ed King protested, "There was absolutely no reason for being forced to stand like that. . . . We had no weapons." After an uncomfortable length of time in 103 degrees of heat, denied even a drink of water, they were taken to the city jail and released the next day.[80]

◆   ◆   ◆

Almost every attempt to challenge segregation in Mississippi failed, stymied by police dogs, arrests, torture, and murder. In 1961 Herbert Lee, a black farmer who drove SNCC worker Bob Moses throughout Amite County to talk to blacks about voter registration, was murdered, "the first martyr of the Mississippi Movement." In 1962 Corporal Roman Ducksworth, riding a Greyhound bus from his post in Fort Ritchie, Maryland, to Taylorsville, Mississippi, to visit his newborn son, was shot and killed by a Taylorsville police officer because he thought Ducksworth was a Freedom Rider. In 1963 James Travis of Jackson, a member of SNCC working on voter registration in Greenwood, was shot and seriously injured. In June 1963 Medgar Evers was assassinated, and two days later, an automobile driven by John Salter, containing Rev. Ed King as a passenger, was forced into a wreck, resulting in almost death for both men and a permanent facial injury for Ed King. During the Freedom Summer voting drive, 1964, the mutilated bodies of Charles Henry Moore and Henry Hezekiah Dee, student demonstrators, were found in the Mississippi River, and the bullet-ridden bodies of James Chaney (Chaney's body was also mutilated), Andrew Goodman, and Michael Schwerner, workers for voting registration, were found "beneath fifteen feet of dirt in a newly completed earthen dam" five miles southwest of Philadelphia, Mississippi. During Freedom Summer, Julian Bond noted that eighty people had been beaten, thirty-five shot at, five murdered, and more than twenty black churches burned to the ground.[81]

Mississippi was truly, as Ed King commented, another South Africa, but he would continue his crusade, in the future, as someone involved in national politics.

Some of the vicious actions encountered by demonstrators during the major episodes of the civil rights movement explain why so few southern white ministers, other white liberals, and even black people dared to participate in front-line civil disobedience. It was, however, these very brutal attacks on nonviolent demonstrators that aroused the sympathy of many across the nation for the plight of African Americans.

Southern white ministers might have asked these questions during the heart of the civil rights movement:

- Should I join a boycott calling for an end to restricted seating on buses?
- Should I sit-in at lunch counters in department stores, drugstores, and waiting rooms?
- Should I ride Greyhound and Trailways buses to test the Interstate Commerce Commission's order to end segregation of passengers in interstate travel and in terminal waiting rooms, rest rooms, and restaurants?
- Should I participate in the mass demonstrations starting in Albany, Georgia, and continuing in Birmingham, Alabama, and Jackson, Mississippi?
- Should I bring about the end to my church appointment?
- Should I endanger my life and the lives of my family?

For most of the ministers, the answer was "no." Southern ministers committed to ending segregation might help conduct nonviolent workshops, encourage activists, join interracial ministerial associations and councils on human relations, sign proclamations, or attempt to change the hearts of segregationists individually, and in those activities they believed they were advancing the cause of racial justice, but engaging in direct confrontation, getting beaten, or being arrested was something they would not do. Why did Will Campbell remain away from the Nashville sit-ins, not far from his office as representative for the National Council of Churches? His answer: "I am not an activist. My approach is as a moderate."[82]

The ministers would not engage in direct action because it was too dangerous—for them and for their families. When Ed King went to Montgomery, he only intended to minister to student activists; he did not expect to be arrested and placed in jail. It took Merrill Proudfoot hours of prayer and soul-searching before he agreed to participate in the Knoxville sit-ins. His diary reveals his struggle and the hesitancy, confusion, and timidity of Knoxville's clergy.[83] Toward the end of his experience, in response to a question posed by his African American student, "Why did you do it?," Proudfoot could finally state, "I am participating in this movement because of my Christian beliefs. . . . Jesus made it very clear that many will come from the East and West and sit down at table in the Kingdom, but the children of privilege may be cast into outer darkness. He taught us that the commandment, 'Thou shalt love thy neighbor as thyself' is 'like unto' the first commandment, 'Thou shalt love the Lord thy God,' and Jesus himself gave us the supreme example of humble, self-less love."[84] For Joseph Ellwanger, there was no other choice. For him, nonparticipation meant approval of the status quo.[85]

Upon his return to Mississippi, Ed King, under the tutelage of Medgar Evers, became a full-fledged, voracious civil rights activist, without hesitancy, fear, confusion, or timidity. The demonstrations in Jackson were proficiently designed and bravely performed, but the costs were immense: the assassination of Medgar Evers, the mindless incarceration of children, the police brutality enacted against demonstrators and those who paid their respects to the slain leader, and the almost assassination of Ed King; but subtly, in the margins, as King and Ann Moody suggested, there were tiny signs that white Mississippi could change.

This section asks the question, "Did the small number of white southern ministers who actually participated in episodes of the civil rights movement contribute anything to end Jim Crow in the South?" The answer, in this author's estimation, is "yes." The effort of Robert Graetz in providing a taxi service for the Montgomery demonstrators helped end segregation on the city's buses; the willingness of seventeen white ministers to sign a petition in favor of integrated buses helped end segregation on Mobile's buses. The willingness of Merrill Proudfoot to sit-in at Knoxville's lunch counters and to keep on sitting-in with his African American friends and students helped to finally end segregated lunch counters in Knoxville. The hardest tasks of all were the attempts Ed King made to break through the massive wall of segregation and discrimination that enveloped Mississippi. It took a long time and tragic events, but eventually Mississippi businessmen decided to end segregation. These few white ministers made black activists aware that white people might help them. Yet, contrarily, it demonstrated to Martin Luther King Jr. and black activists that there were too few white ministers or white people who were willing to march with them, go to jail, or even be killed.

Black people as well as white people considered engaging in the Freedom Rides to be a form of madness and suicide, as events in Alabama seemed to confirm. When the Reverend John Morris embarked on a Freedom Ride with four rabbis and fourteen ministers, the extreme danger seemed to have ended; yet Morris and his group were willing to go to jail. Morris believed the "Prayer Pilgrimage," as he called it, was necessary to demonstrate that segregation was incompatible with the teachings of Christ. The Prayer Pilgrimage made an important statement to the Episcopal Church, and the exceptional courageous acts of those mentioned in this chapter were examples of the bravest expressions of Christian love.

═ 3 ═

CHURCH VISITATIONS
Trouble Outside, Trouble Within

SERVICES

9:00 A.M. & 10:00 A.M.

SUNDAY WORSHIP

ALMOST ALL

ARE WELCOME[1]

Along with boycotts, sit-ins, Freedom Rides, mass demonstrations, and marches came church visitations by small groups of young African Americans, generally college students, sometimes with white Christian ministers and white college students, and sometimes African American parents with children. Attempting to worship at Christian churches, whether all-white or all-black, did not seem unusual to black Christian believers and some white Christian believers, but to avid segregationists, the attempts were anathema. In their view God did not intend the races to mix and especially to mix in church. They considered that each race had their own way of worshipping and that any mixing would lead to fraternization and intermarriage. Besides, all the denominations maintained separate churches for African Americans, so why would they want to enter a white church anyway except to cause a disturbance? Even people of Asian Indian heritage were denied entrance to many white southern churches. Such was the case when white Baptist pastor Clarence Jordan took two Asian Indian exchange students to the Baptist church in Americus, Georgia, where he was a member. The congregation mistook them for black people and told Jordan never again to enter the church.[2]

In Atlanta in 1960, when the campaign for church visitations began, white Rev. Robert Seymour recounted that "blacks were carried out bodily from the First Baptist Church," with one greeter reportedly to have said, "If you were

Christian, you wouldn't be here." According to Seymour, "All over the South, churches resurrected obsolete membership rules requiring prospective members to meet with deacons to ascertain whether their motives for affiliating were pure," and many churches instituted closed-door policies. By 1963 the situation had not changed. According to a survey taken by editors of Southern Baptist newsletters, by that year *no* African American was admitted to membership in a church belonging to the Southern Baptist Convention in the states of Alabama, Mississippi, and Virginia. The historian Carter Dalton Lyon writes about Rev. E. Owen Wright of Houston, Texas, who, in 1963, instructed his ushers to admit all visitors to his all-white Southern Baptist church regardless of race and a membership policy that excluded blacks. When one black visitor asked to become a member, Wright said he was unable to do anything about it because of the exclusionary policy, which the church refused to change; thus, even in Texas, a closed-door policy toward African Americans continued. Lyon also writes, "While it may be true . . . that most white ministers were reluctant to confront the immorality of racial discrimination, one must not lose sight of those who did."[3]

This chapter recounts detailed stories about ten southern white ministers who were willing to "confront the immorality of racial discrimination" in their churches. They were ministers from the Presbyterian (US), Southern Baptist, Methodist, Disciples of Christ, and Churches of Christ denominations. Their stories are significant because they were serving churches in the Deep South: Alabama, Mississippi, and Georgia, where segregationist sentiments were strongest.

H. Davis Yeuell

In 1963 H. Davis Yeuell, born in Tuscaloosa, Alabama, in 1930, and professor and chaplain at African American Stillman College, went with a group to First Presbyterian Church in Tuscaloosa and was denied entrance in spite of the fact that it was his own family's church in the town where he was born.

This was not Yeuell's first attempt to speak out against segregation. In 1947, at the age of seventeen, as a representative from the Alabama Presbyterian Synod, he attended a meeting of the General Assembly Youth Council at the Montreat Conference Center, about twenty miles east of Asheville, North Carolina. The Youth Council, desiring to include a representative from the all-black Snedecor Memorial Synod, also invited a black member to the meeting, who was given a bed in the black servants' quarters behind Assembly Inn. A small group of three whites and the one black decided to have a "Polar Bear Club" and went swimming in scenic Lake Susan on the Montreat grounds.

Immediately, the group was informed by the president of the Montreat Association that they could not engage in interracial bathing in Lake Susan. One can imagine how the young delegate from the Snedecor Synod must have felt. The "Polar Bears" took action and asked their adviser to call the integrated Warren Wilson College in nearby Swannanoa, to see if extra rooms were available. A few hours later the group checked in at the Warren Wilson College. In addition, the Youth Council wrote a letter to the Board of Christian Education for the Presbyterian Church (US) requesting an ending to segregation at Montreat. The group continued to meet every year at the Warren Wilson College until the segregation policies at Montreat finally ended.[4]

In 1954, at his first pastorate at Montevallo Presbyterian Church near the campus of the University of Montevallo in Alabama, Yeuell was invited by a church elder to attend an orientation meeting for the White Citizens' Council. Young and curious, he went. As the only pastor present, he was asked to give the opening prayer. He prayed, "I ask for God's judgment on this meeting. It is contrary to the purposes of the Lord," and he walked out, but Yeuell was not asked to leave his church.[5]

Stillman College in Tuscaloosa was founded in 1874 as "an institute for the training of colored ministry" by Charles A. Stillman, white pastor of the same First Presbyterian Church that Yeuell had attended as a child. In 1958 Samuel Burney Hay, an innovative president, expanded Stillman Institute into a senior liberal arts college and invited Yeuell to become a professor. After serving Montevallo Presbyterian Church for only three years, he did not think he was ready to accept a new position, but Myrtle Williamson, a member of the Stillman faculty, had a vision that Yeuell would teach at Stillman College. Late in September Hay telephoned Yeuell, "Myrtle insists that you are coming to Stillman." Yeuell and his wife prayed for guidance, and the next month they arrived in Tuscaloosa with their two young children.[6] The president of Stillman was white, the faculty was integrated, and the student body was black.

Returning to his childhood home, Yeuell went to see his parents. His father, who grew up in northeastern Alabama and descended from a family of Union sympathizers during the Civil War, was supportive of his son's position at Stillman, but his mother, a segregationist, was deeply distressed.[7]

Two years later an African student came to study at Stillman from a Presbyterian mission in the Congo with financial support from First Presbyterian. Anxious to thank the people for supporting him, he telephoned the pastor for permission to visit the church, only to be told he would not be welcome. He shared his disappointment with his dormitory friends at a time when church visitations were beginning. Ten black students agreed to go with him to try to enter the church for Sunday worship, and Rev. Yeuell joined them. There on the steps to the church's door, the deacons, two of them Yeuell's high school classmates, forcibly kept the group out. Yeuell was dismayed, "Do you mean I cannot enter my own church as long as these students are with me?" The answer, "You cannot enter," was heard by his mother seated in the sanctuary. The incident had an amazing affect upon her. She demanded a meeting with the church's session (the group making rules for the congregation) and told them, "You may segregate schools and public accommodations, but the church of Jesus Christ must be open to all people." Although Yeuell was unsuccessful in gaining entrance for his black students into First Presbyterian Church of Tuscaloosa, Alabama, in 1963, his mother had been transformed.[8]

Tensions in Alabama were rising that year. Yeuell also became active in helping African Americans James Hood and Vivian Malone gain entrance to the University of Alabama. Because of his efforts, he and his family began receiving obscene phone calls, day and night. The life of his daughter, just entering kindergarten, was threatened by the Klan. The family became terrified. "You know," Rev. Yeuell stated, "you can make a decision for yourself but when it comes to the safety of your family, you have to consider their well-being." The family moved from Tuscaloosa to Richmond, Virginia, where Rev. Yeuell became an associate in the Division of Higher Education for the Board of Christian Education of the General Assembly of the Presbyterian Church (US). As they were driving to Richmond on June 5, 1963, the National Guard was on its way to Tuscaloosa to enforce the desegregation of the University of Alabama.[9]

Earl Stallings

On April 15, 1963, two photographs appeared on the front page of the *New York Times*, one of African Americans being turned away from the First Presbyterian Church of Birmingham, Alabama, by three stern-looking ushers, and one of Rev. Earl Stallings (1916–2006), born in Durham, North Carolina, and pastor of the city's First Baptist Church, with hands outstretched as he welcomed three African Americans into the church. As the historian S. Jonathan Bass wrote, "Since 1954, the church maintained an open-door policy for black visitors." The policy, however, had never been tested until Easter Sunday, April 14, 1963, when the first black visitors arrived.[10]

The visitors were civil rights activist Andrew Young and two young women. The ushers seated them near the back of the church, at which point seventy white people walked out. After the service, Stallings greeted the visitors on the steps of the church, shook Young's hand, and received a form letter explaining the demonstrators' motive, which contradicted the supposed motivation: "They came to First Baptist on the Day of Resurrection to seek a new life together with our separated brothers and sisters." Segregationists in the divided church did not accept this explanation. As related by Bass, one woman who had been attending the church for sixty-five years complained, "I think what happened in our church Easter Sunday was the most awful thing that could have happened. . . . The worst part of the day was when Stallings shook the hands of those Negroes." She asked for a letter of transfer so she could go to another church. A Southern Baptist from Georgia wrote, "Any one that can back up that bunch of low down Negroes that are sent down here to the South to cause trouble . . . and call himself a Baptist minister is beyond me. . . . Men like you make me sick."[11]

Bass suggested that the visitation was probably arranged by the Southern Christian Leadership Conference (SCLC) in order to expose discord in local white churches and attract the attention of the national media, but Stallings maintained that the issue was not about whether the visitors had come as agitators, but "whether the church would do the Christian thing." As more African Americans came to worship at First Baptist, Stallings was forced by segregationists to leave. In 1965 he became pastor of First Baptist Church in Marietta, northern Georgia, a church that announced itself as a diverse group of followers of Christ. He was welcomed and accepted.[12]

J. Herbert Gilmore

J. Herbert Gilmore (1929–2007), born in Knoxville, Tennessee, became the pastor of First Baptist in Birmingham in 1968 and continued the policy of welcoming African Americans. In 1970 a crisis developed when Winifred Bryant, an African American, and her twelve-year-old daughter, Twila, who had been part of a tutorial program set up by Gilmore, applied to become the first black members of a congregation that had been exclusively white for all of its ninety-eight-year history. The deacons were willing, but on the very day that Winifred Bryant and Twila were presented to the congregation, a vote was taken to deny them membership. While Gilmore was attending a meeting of the Baptist World Alliance in Tokyo, the congregation planned to dismiss him, but before they could do so, Gilmore resigned, making his statement from the pulpit, "I have said that I would not be the pastor of a racist church. I meant what I said! So, this morning I respectfully request that you accept my resignation, effective November 1, 1970."[13]

That was not the end of the story. By 1970 the group of integrationists within the church had expanded. Calling themselves "The Company of the Committed" (the title of a 1961 book by Quaker Elton Trueblood), they decided to follow their pastor, resign, and establish a new church. They formed the Baptist Church of the Covenant with 306 charter members, 255 from First

Baptist. They became the first multiethnic and multiracial congregation in Birmingham, with Rev. Gilmore as pastor in a new building on land next to the old church. Gilmore wrote in 1972, "The most significant thing in the struggle . . . is not that the segregationist opposition, by the counting of noses, had their way. Rather, it is that two hundred and fifty-five people in Birmingham disavowed such a racist position and committed themselves to build an interracial, intercultural, and international fellowship. This is nothing short of a miracle in a city that only a few years before had earned itself the contempt of the world for its racial tactics." Gilmore remained pastor of Church of the Covenant until 1992, when he had to resign due to ill health.[14]

Joe Patterson, Robert Miller

Troubles for ministers who tried to integrate churches in Alabama were common. In June 1963 Rev. Joe H. Patterson, thirty-three years old, merely recommended that his Baptist church in Linden, Alabama, admit African Americans. "I thought the issue was simple and clear from a Christian standpoint," he told the deacons, but they and a small group from the church strongly disagreed. A cross was burned on his lawn, and rocks smashed the windows of his home. Patterson resigned rather than "tear up the church." Patterson claimed that his resignation made the church face the racial issue for the first time in its existence. At First Presbyterian Church in Tuskegee, Alabama, Robert Miller was forced to resign when he welcomed into his sanctuary two professors from nearby Tuskegee Institute, one white and one black.[15]

Miller, born in 1934 in Washington, DC, but raised in Virginia, probably inherited his social concern tendencies from his famous father, Francis Pickens Miller, professor, war hero, writer, editor, delegate to international Christian conferences, one of the founders of the journal *Christianity and Crisis*, and best remembered as an opponent to the Byrd machine of Virginia. He ran unsuccessfully for the Democratic governorship of Virginia in 1949 and the US Senate in 1952. Son of a Presbyterian minister from Kentucky, Francis Miller firmly believed that "faith without works was dead." The works he set out to accomplish in his lifetime were "making more real the church universal," "turning the tide in America against Hitler," "liberating Europe from Nazi rule," "reviving democracy in Virginia," and "securing justice for the Negro."[16] It was this last objective that greatly influenced his son.

Robert Miller arrived in Tuskegee in 1961, having just received a master's degree in divinity from the Union Theological Seminary of Virginia. First Presbyterian was a small, white clapboard building across the street from the courthouse and included in its congregation some of the fiercest segregationists in Tuskegee. Young and idealistic, Miller believed he would be free to speak his conscience, act on behalf of brotherhood, and change some hearts. He supported the integration of the public schools and fought against the ultraconservative local *News*, which saw everything liberal and progressive as "Communist inspired."[17]

The complete separation of the races in Tuskegee bothered Miller, but he hoped that he would have an open church where black people would be welcome. That was not the case. The session voted not to admit black people, although Miller and one lawyer voted against the ruling. It was Miller's policy that if blacks got into the sanctuary, they were "home free." That was the code language that told him that a black person had entered the sanctuary. Generally black people did not try to enter, but Miller had worked on voter registration at the Tuskegee Institute and made many friends; thus it was not unusual that some might want to visit his church. On July 17, 1964, two professors from Tuskegee Institute walked in and sat down, without guards at the door to keep them out. The sanctuary was small, and Miller could see directly what was happening. Miller's sermon that day was a beautiful expression of the Christian message as he understood it, half discourse and half poetry. He began with lessons from the Old Testament: "God called out the people from Egypt and gave them as their law the Ten Commandments. . . . [But] they built for themselves the golden calf. . . . When God fulfilled his promise to give them land . . . they followed the people of that land and worshiped Baal." He continued with other examples, but, Miller counseled, "God never ceases offering new beginnings." This he said in the form of a lyric poem:

> The end and the beginning. . . . In ceaseless cycle they seem to go.
> The touch of God and the spoil of man.
> The height of creation and the earth laid low. . . .
> Still the inner voice of man cries out "must it be so?"
> Earth and heaven with bated breath await reply
> And the sovereign God responds. . . .
> And so the story goes.
> God makes the move to bring newness-re-creation
> And man brings it to an end. . . .
> From the end that man had made, God created a new beginning:
> "For God so loved the world that he gave his only begotten son
> That whoever believes in him should not perish but have eternal life."[18]

Then he gave the congregation a challenge: "If you intend to lead a new life and are in love and charity with your neighbor, full of sorrow for what you have been, and eager to seek a new beginning, I invite you to the communion table . . . but if you do not intend to change your ways . . . I forbid you to come." It was a bold approach, and as he passed the communion plates to two of the elders, he bowed his head in prayer. When he looked up, he saw one of the elders, Richard Lightfoot, brother to Philip Lightfoot, former mayor and defendant in the famous 1960 gerrymandering case, deliberately refuse to serve communion to the two visitors. When the elders returned the plates, Miller left the communion table, took one of the plates, and served the visitors the bread and wine. It was a dramatic moment in the life of First Presbyterian Church of Tuskegee, and immediately segregationists in the congregation demanded his resignation. Miller did not want to resign but rather hoped that his actions might influence his congregation in the direction of openness, but he came to see that his efforts were in vain. He resigned in 1965. "It was a period of time in my career that I will never forget," Miller commented. "The people respected me but simply did not agree with my views." Elizabeth Lightfoot, wife of Richard Lightfoot, wept when Miller left the church.[19]

Miller and his family relocated to the Lakeview Presbyterian Church in South St. Petersburg, Florida, a large traditional church situated in a middle-class neighborhood that was changing from white to black. About 200 to 300 white members left during the time of transition, but the white members who remained pledged to create a congregation that would be interracial and dedicated to community service. Aware of what had happened to Miller in Tuskegee, they called him to be their pastor, knowing he would probably fit in well. Miller began his ministry with a sermon entitled "Let the Church Be the Church," and, as told by Bill McKee, the church historian, he preached the same sermon many times. The church planned many outreach activities during the Miller years in order to demonstrate love for neighbor. Miller related, "We were able to install a Head Start program, an assistance program of clothing, food, and financial aid for utilities, and, most important of all, we were able to call a second pastor, African American Irvin Elligan."[20]

Miller and Elligan engaged in what became known as an Experimental Ministry, an integrated pastorate in an integrated congregation with the goal of serving the community in all of its needs. The years of the Experimental Ministry, 1966–1972, were turbulent years in Lakeview—continuing black migration and white flight, school integration, strikes by sanitation workers and teachers, demonstrations by Black Power advocates, civil disorders and unrest—but the church assisted where it could and managed to survive. It provided meeting space for striking workers (which infuriated some members) and formed an integrated Boy Scout troop, a summer black culture camp, a coffeehouse, a health center, and a community youth program for at-risk teenagers. Other church groups joined Lakeview Presbyterian in forming "Congregations United for Community Action." Many of the programs still exist.[21]

Rev. Elligan stayed at Lakeview for two-and-one-half years and left to become pastor of New Covenant Presbyterian Church in Miami. Rev. Miller left in 1972 to serve Westminster Presbyterian Church in Montgomery, Alabama, where he was able to establish an open door policy and welcome several black families into the church, but the Miller and Elligan legacy lives on in St. Petersburg. Miller proudly stated, "The ministry at Lakeview provided the opportunity to fulfill some of the hopes and dreams of Christ's church." At Lakeview, Miller was able to accomplish what he could not in Alabama.[22]

Church Visitations in Mississippi

Mississippi was no more hospitable to pastors who welcomed African Americans than Alabama. Church visitations, also referred to as "kneel-ins," came to Jackson, Mississippi, in 1963 and 1964. The historian Carter Dalton Lyon wrote, "Jackson was the only city where groups mounted a sustained campaign to protest segregation by attempting to worship at white churches." Ed King and Medgar Evers organized these demonstrations, reasoning that if blacks and whites could pray together, the "closed society" might open even slightly. The first group of students from Tougaloo College decided that if they were not admitted to a church, they would quietly leave, but if they were going to be beaten, they would submit to arrest.[23]

They first visited Governor Barnett's church, First Baptist, a huge complex opposite the state capitol, the most powerful church in the state, where Rev. William Douglas Hudgins preached a gospel firmly focused on the salvation of individual souls, avoiding any mention of racial problems. According to Ed King, the demonstrators were not beaten, but the experience of being rejected from a Baptist church, their own denomination, was so painful that some of the women wept. The group then went to Galloway Memorial Methodist Church, the most prestigious Methodist church in the state, one block away, where they thought they might be welcomed. As Ed King stated, "By Methodist doctrine, the church was open, but the ushers closed the doors and told the students to leave." On the Sunday after Evers's funeral, as narrated by Tougaloo student Anne Moody, groups of students tried again to worship at Jackson's churches, but each church was prepared for their visit with armed police, police wagons, and dogs.[24]

They tried again the following Sunday, this time with some success, which gave them hope for the future. They first went to the Church of Christ, where the regular ushers offered to give them cab fare to the "Negro" extension of the church. Just as they refused the cab fare and were walking away, an old woman stopped them. "I'll sit with you," she said, and asked the ushers to please let them in, but she was told, "The church has decided what is to be done. A resolution has been passed, and we are to abide by it." According to Moody, the woman was not to be placated by the ushers: "Who are we to decide such a thing? This is a house of God, and God is to make all the decisions. He is the judge of us all." A few blocks away Jeanette King, Ed King's wife, picked up the girls and took them to St. Andrew's Episcopal Church, where, to their amazement, the ushers seated them and asked them to sign the guest list.[25]

William Bryan Selah and William J. Cunningham

That June, when the governing board of Galloway Church passed a resolution barring the entrance of African Americans, the revered and respected pastor of eighteen years, Rev. William Bryan Selah (1897–1985), tried to convince the board that the better thing to do would be to seat blacks and treat them the same as all worshippers. Although he never told anyone, Selah decided that if black people were ever turned away from a worship service, he would leave. In sermons, he stressed brotherhood, Christian love, and equal rights for all, and insisted "forced segregation is wrong."[26]

On Sunday morning, June 9, 1963, as Rev. Selah was going from his study into the sanctuary to deliver his sermon, he noticed a large crowd on the street in front of the church and asked Jerry Furr, his associate, to investigate and tell him what was happening. As the choir was finishing the anthem, Furr sat beside him and whispered that five African Americans had been turned away and went across the park to the Roman Catholic church, where they were welcomed. Selah shortened his sermon with an announcement: "I have been saying for eighteen years that there can be no color bar in a Christian church and that all men, black and white, should be treated not on the basis of color but on the basis of conduct. Now I either have to repudiate my convictions or leave." Selah resigned that day. He was sixty-six years old, and fear of reprisal was not an obstacle. Jerry Furr left with him. Selah became vice-president of Central Methodist College in Fayette, Missouri. Furr went to a church in Las Vegas. Both experienced reductions in salary, but Selah asserted, "The reduction in income did not hurt me. It was vastly overshadowed by the peace which came into my heart because I had done the right and decent thing." Lyon mentioned that people of different faiths and from many places wrote letters of admiration to Selah for his action.[27]

Three months after Selah's resignation, a replacement was found, Rev. William J. Cunningham (1905–1994). Cunningham told the search committee that he did not approve of the closed-door policy, but after several ministers refused to be their pastor, the search committee decided to appoint him anyway. Generally in the Methodist structure, the bishop appoints the minister, but at Galloway, powerful laymen decided who their pastor would be. Cunningham, fifty-nine years old, born in Luca, Mississippi, was a member of the church while a student at Millsaps College in Jackson and remembered happy years. He served as president of the youth organization, sang in the choir, and was president of his Sunday school class. He was in his eighth year at St. John's Methodist Church in Memphis, Tennessee, and quite satisfied, but at the bishop's urging, he accepted the new assignment, hardly suspecting that difficulties would follow. On the first day of his arrival, he found a clipping on his desk from the Jackson *Clarion-Ledger* announcing his appointment with his picture smeared in red. Someone in the church accused him of being a Communist, a Communist sympathizer, or some far-left radical, almost as bad as being a "n____r lover."[28]

For three years the doors remained closed to African Americans, but they kept coming each Sunday in an attempt to open them. Cunningham avoided direct confrontation in his sermons but stated his opposition to the closed-door policy to small groups and individual members. In sermons he used what he termed the "oblique approach," stories of how Jesus attempted to open the hearts of the Jewish people to accept and love outsiders. In one sermon, however, he spoke directly of deplorable conditions in Mississippi: "The American Medical Association has reported that the highest numbers of deaths from tuberculosis in this state are within the Negro race and yet of the 522 beds available for the treatment of that disease, only forty in the state are for African Americans. . . . There are over a million African Americans in this state, but only one African American physician for every 15,000 of them." In another sermon, he spoke about the Babylonian captivity of the Jewish people, who were "surrounded by the allurements of the magnificent civilization" and "the threat of moral decline," but Ezekiel, the prophet, continued to preach the word of God and, in Cunningham's words, became a watchman who blew his trumpet. Cunningham's message soon became obvious. He expected the people in his church to "sound a trumpet" against segregation.[29]

He was never threatened personally or harassed on the telephone. "Those days had passed," he wrote. Instead, his antagonists made critical statements and wrote vicious letters. One woman explained her husband's absence from church with the comment, "Too much sounding the trumpet." In one letter, Cunningham was told in no uncertain terms to resign: "You are not preacher material." "Why can't you preach on something besides race?" People started leaving the church, some because of fear that blacks would be allowed to enter, others because of resentment that Galloway would never allow black people to enter and disturbances would continue forever. Cunningham begged these people to stay.[30]

A decline in membership from 3,500 to 2,900 alarmed the governing board, and pressure on Cunningham to leave began. His health deteriorated and he became emotionally distressed, but his faith helped him maintain serenity: "I knew that I was doing what I thought the Lord wanted me to do. I was standing by the church, its teachings, and I was not compromising my calling." After twenty-seven difficult months, Cunningham, under pressure from the board and his superiors, resigned. Galloway Church finally abandoned its closed-door policy in January 1966, but, according to Cunningham, "It didn't make any big difference. . . . Negroes didn't just pile in. . . . They didn't want to come anyway." Cunningham believed change finally came in Mississippi because of the "amazing patience of a devoted minority," a difference in the political climate, and far-sighted businesspeople "who saw the practical wisdom of accepting the change." He stated, "The church could not change the culture; the culture changed and carried the church along with it."[31]

Roy S. Hulan

Galloway Methodist Church was not the only church in Jackson to initiate closed-door policies. In 1954, after serving several country churches within the Disciples of Christ denomination, Rev. Roy S. Hulan (1910–1991), born in Shelbyville, Tennessee, was appointed to the prestigious First Christian Church. The frontispiece of the church's bulletin in 1956 contained a reproduction of a small gothic cathedral with the following caption: "This is a local congregation of the Disciples of Christ, and was founded in 1838 in Jackson for the purpose of promoting Christian unity. . . . It seeks to share a religious experience that is loyal to the spirit of Jesus, prophetic in its voice in world affairs, friendly in its welcome to all people, and inspiring to all who come within its influence."[32] But in 1954, after the Supreme Court ruled that segregation in public schools was unconstitutional, First Christian Church seemed to abandon its dedicated mission. The governing board required new pastors to answer three questions: Are you a brotherhood man, believing in the cooperative work in all its phases? Do you like the functional pattern of organization of the local congregation? Do you intend to use the pulpit to discuss the race issue? To the first two questions, Hulan's answer was "Yes," but his answer to the third question was evasive: "I was born and reared in the South and am conversant with the general attitudes of this area in race relations. I shall never knowingly use the pulpit as a sounding board for any utterance which I am sure is of such a nature as to divide the church or unduly disturb the spiritual sensitivities of any member; however, I intend to preach the gospel in human relationships as I understand that gospel." Hulan was appointed as new pastor and did his best to avoid controversy for nine years. Church membership increased, and two new congregations were formed from their membership.

Hulan was content and hoped, perhaps, to remain at the church for the rest of his life, but in 1963, on the same day that black people attempted to enter Galloway Church, four African Americans arrived at the front door of First Christian Church and were told by the greeters that the church was for white people and that they should leave and attend their own church. The following Sunday Hulan preached from the letter of Paul to his friend Philemon. Philemon's slave, Onesimus, had escaped and came to Paul while Paul was in prison in Rome. Paul converted Onesimus and loved him as a son. Paul entreated Philemon to receive Onesimus back, not as a slave, but as a dear brother in Christ. Hulan's message to the members of First Christian Church was clear: "In the spirit of Paul's letter to Philemon, I believe that to deny any person . . . on account of race or color access to the House of God—not my house, not your house, not First Christian Church's house, but God's house— is an un-Christian act. This I believe."[33]

For nine years Hulan did not have the courage to speak out, but when faced with the situation of people being turned away from the church, he could no longer remain silent. He was welcomed back in Kentucky, where he had previously served and soon became pastor of Cynthiana Christian Church. The president of the College of the Bible and representatives from Transylvania College, his alma mater, attended his installation. There were no provocative questions asked.[34]

Al Price

Not far away on Capitol Street stood the Church of Christ. In 1964, at the age of twenty-three, Alvin H. Price, known as Al, born in Oakland, Mississippi, and raised in Coffeeville and Water Valley, became the pulpit minister. Price noticed immediately that two men were standing at the door when people entered for worship service. After a few weeks, he asked the elders why they were there and could tell they were a little embarrassed by the question. According to Price, "Many congregations held meetings to discuss what to do should some blacks attempt to attend their service. Most decided to direct them to the nearest black congregation. That way they could feel that they were not actually denying them the opportunity to worship." Price admits that at the time he had not yet come to a full understanding of inclusion, tolerance, and respect for all humanity, but nevertheless he knew that keeping black worshippers or any other people out of the church was wrong and unscriptural. Like many ministers in this narrative, Price tried to change people's hearts through sermons, telling the Good Samaritan story in many ways, how the person helped was of a different religion and different ethnic background, and had been avoided by others. Price was not forced to leave his church as Cunningham was, which speaks well for that particular Church of Christ church, and as a result of his preaching, the elders eventually changed their policy, and the two men did not stand at the door anymore. Price left Jackson in 1967 to study for a graduate degree at the University of Tennessee in Knoxville, but he would return in 1973 to Winona, Mississippi, but that is another story that will be continued in chapter 7.[35]

Thomas J. Holmes

Rev. Thomas J. Holmes (1918–1985), born in Sandersville, Georgia, a large, powerfully built man, wept when he related his story of sorrow and struggle. Holmes had been pastor of the Tattnall Square Baptist Church in Macon, Georgia, on the campus of Mercer University. In 1962 the trustees of Mercer University voted to admit all qualified candidates, regardless of race, color, or national origin, but the Tattnall Square Church and other member churches of the Georgia Baptist Convention were not ready for that decision. When the church denied membership to Sam Oni, a native of Ghana, the first black admitted to the 133-year-old, all-male Baptist university, Holmes and his two assistants tried to convince the congregation that denying Oni admission to the church was to destroy their mission program in Africa where Oni had been converted to Christianity. To deny him membership in the church was, therefore, reprehensible to Holmes and his assistants, Jack Jones, the music director, and Doug Johnson, the youth pastor. Shortly thereafter, the congregation voted, 250 to 89, that the three ministers had to leave. News of the incident made headlines. Oni was seen on national television on October 2, 1966, again attempting to enter the church and being carried away and placed in a police car.[36]

Holmes and other church members believed that the clause in the original deed was reversed when Mercer desegregated its campus and, of course, that Oni would be welcome. The deed was given to the church by the university and stated, "If the facilities ceased to be used for a church, the property would revert to Mercer." Holmes mentioned that a rumor circulated that the pastor's desire to open the doors to blacks was actually a clever ruse to "steal" the church property for Mercer. What was stated in the deed happened. The church membership continued to decline, and in 1980 the church became the property of Mercer University. The beautiful church building is now used as a hall for students engaged in individual religious studies.[37]

In October 1966, when Holmes spoke at his alma mater, Southern Baptist Seminary in Louisville, Kentucky, he was asked, "What hope can you give to young ministers who are preparing to enter the pastorate very soon when we know that if we go and preach the gospel as it is revealed in the New Testament the same fate awaits us which has befallen you?" Holmes expressed the hope that the tide would turn and the day would come when God would work through the witness of faithful pastors and preachers.[38]

Jimmy Carter and Bruce Edwards

A Baptist church in rural southwest Georgia, where civil rights agitation was quickly suppressed by police, became famous and in the news because the thirty-ninth president of the United States, Jimmy Carter, worshipped there. He and his wife, Rosalynn (formerly a Methodist), his parents, his sisters, his brother, his three sons, his cousin Hugh, and Hugh's three children were all baptized at the Plains Baptist Church. Until 1965 African Americans occasionally attended the church without any problems, but when civil rights agitation began, twelve deacons unanimously recommended that the ushers refuse to admit blacks "or any other civil rights agitators" to all worship services. Fifty-four against six in the congregation carried the motion. Among the six opposing were Jimmy Carter and four members of his family.[39]

No African Americans, agitators or otherwise, attempted to enter until November 14, 1976, when Rev. Clennon King, a black activist from Albany, Georgia, asked Bruce Edwards, the pastor, to admit him as a member. On October 31, 1976, Clennon King waited on the church's steps trying to enter while three members of the Klan paraded nearby. He was turned away, and the regular service was canceled. In response, Jimmy Carter called on members to "open the church doors" and allow anyone who worships Christ into the church. The very next day, Rev. Edwards held a press conference and mentioned that the "n" word was used several times by the deacons. Without delay, a deacons' meeting was held, with a unanimous decision to ask for the pastor's resignation. A meeting of the congregation then met to vote on the deacons' proposal. About 200 members were present, among them Jimmy Carter and his mother, Lillian. All this occurred several days before his election. His cousin and lifelong friend, State Senator Hugh Carter, proprietor of the local antique shop, spoke on behalf of Edwards: "I think Bruce Edwards is a fine preacher, and I think most all of us loved him dearly before all this trouble began. . . . He's talked too much to the press. He's used some words in his press conference that I don't think any of us approve of. But I still don't think we have sufficient reason to ask him to resign. . . . . This statement is from my heart—the way we act in our church, at times I wonder if we are really

Christian." The motion to dismiss the pastor failed, at least for the time being. Another motion calling for an open door at Plains Baptist Church passed, and finally the closed-door policy of 1965 was rescinded.[40]

Trouble seemed over, but in February 1977 a special conference was called, ostensibly to pay a sum of money to send some corn to a children's home. One hundred and forty-nine members were present. After the budget decision was made, one of the members stood up and, unexpectedly, presented a motion that Rev. Edwards be dismissed. According to Hugh Carter, those asking for Edwards's dismissal had gathered a large group of people whose names were on the church roll, eligible to vote, but who had not attended the church for years. (President Carter could not be present at the meeting.) Every motion that would have delayed Edwards's dismissal failed. Anticipating his formal dismissal, Edwards presented the following motion: "Because of the future of this church and action here today, I hereby resign, effective April 30, 1977." Hugh Carter was devastated: "I frankly felt that our church had been left in shambles and that Rev. Bruce Edwards had been 'crucified.'" Hugh Carter had been a deacon for thirty-one years, church clerk for twenty-eight years, and song leader for eighteen years, but along with Rev. Edwards, he, too, resigned. He wrote, "As I see it, this whole controversy in the Plains Baptist Church was based on an 'anti-black feeling,' an 'anti-Carter feeling,' and an 'anti Bruce Edwards' feeling, plus a 'longtime feeling of jealousy that has built up between certain families in this community.'" Edwards later told a reporter from the *Los Angeles Times*, "They got my job. What else do they want? It's like rubbing salt in my wounds—and they did it in a cowardly way.... The church did not issue the statement.... The deacons' report said, 'Reverend Edwards, Senator Carter, and several others have been the cause of most of our disagreements by making irresponsible, disruptive, and misleading statements to the press contrary to the best interest of Plains Baptist Church.' I want the world to know that this statement is filled with half-truths and lies."[41]

As told by Hugh Carter, a group of about fifty people met in a vacant building belonging to the Lutheran Church and formed a new congregation, calling it the Bottsford Baptist Mission, later to be known as Maranatha Baptist Church ("*Marantha*" is an Aramaic word meaning "the Lord cometh"). Rev. Edwards and his wife were in attendance. With all the controversy behind them, the group was thankful to worship freely. They sang "What a Friend We Have in Jesus," "Trust and Obey," and "I Gave My Life for Thee." An eighty-seven-year-old woman who had been a member of the Plains Baptist Church for more than fifty years played the piano.[42]

On February 20, 1977, Rev. Bruce Edwards, thirty years old, born in Florida, gave his farewell sermon at the Bottsford Baptist Mission. Rev. Clennon

King was the first person to arrive and asked to be admitted as a member to Bottsford Church.[43]

In August 1977 President Carter was scheduled to return to Plains for a visit. As Hugh Carter related, reporters from newspapers and television stations gathered at both churches to see which one President Carter would attend. Those who waited at the Maranatha Church were pleasantly surprised. Reporters asked if he felt a greater affinity with members of the Maranatha Church than that of his old Plains Baptist Church, to which he responded, "Yes, I do. Most of the members who voted with me on the controversial issue of allowing blacks to attend services moved out of the old church and I feel more compatible with that group." Hugh Carter wrote to evangelist Billy Graham about the incident and received a contribution of $10,000 toward a new building. Jimmy Carter, to this day, teaches Sunday school at Maranatha Church when he is at home in Plains. All visitors are welcome, and many come from around the world to hear a former president of the United States teach Bible classes.[44]

Rev. Edwards, with his wife and two sons—one dark-skinned, half-Hawaiian, and adopted—left for his new assignment at the Makakilo Baptist Church in a working-class neighborhood in Honolulu. In an interview for *People* magazine, he stated, "The new job is a pioneer mission. There are new names to learn—and to pronounce." He visits members in their homes and does family counseling. Speaking about his experience in Plains, Edwards said, "I didn't see myself as a civil rights leader. I'm a minister, and through my understanding of the Scriptures, I believe in civil rights. The preacher has to be the voice of conscience, especially when the congregation is doing something immoral."[45]

◆ ◆ ◆

The *Atlanta Constitution* (morning paper) and the *Atlanta Journal* (afternoon paper), now combined, were edited from 1942 through 1960 by Ralph McGill, who also became the publisher from 1960 until his death in 1969. For his provocative editorials on hate crimes in the South, he was awarded a Pulitzer Prize in 1959. McGill became more aggressive in his attacks on segregation as the civil rights movement progressed, inspiring its defenders to malign him as a traitor to his race. McGill also covered visitations to churches by blacks, harassment of white integrationist ministers, church conferences, and church statements probably more than most other newspapers in the nation. In his book *The South and the Southerner* (1963), McGill quoted a letter to the editor from a white woman in Augusta, Georgia, whose church forbade two African American college students from entering. She wrote, "Our church is not the same since we turned those people away. . . . We go to church. We explain it away. We say [the students] tried to get in just to show off or to get into the newspapers. We say all that, and we nod and agree that this is how it was. . . . I must confess, I was one who originally approved denying admission. I knew it would disturb the church if they were admitted. But what I did not know was that it would disturb us more deeply and fundamentally to keep them out. . . . We will never again feel so warm and good about our church . . . or about one another. Worst of all, I am sure our pastor, poor man, knows this—and like us, is troubled." McGill commented, "Troubled minds are a sign of change."[46]

◆ ◆ ◆

Church visitations by African Americans gave pastors who did not participate in sit-ins, marches, and other street demonstrations an opportunity to witness to the inclusive mission of the church. They were effective in many ways. Yeuell's actions accompanying black students at First Presbyterian Church in Tuscaloosa, Alabama, transformed his mother, who may have influenced other church members. First Presbyterian Church in Tuscaloosa now has an African American staff member and some African American members. Rev. Earl Stallings's witness, as revealed by Bass, outstripped the scant attention he received in King's letter. Stallings's followers were many and left First Baptist. Rev. Gilmore followed Stallings's lead and formed a new integrated Baptist church in the city of Birmingham. Segregationists were successful in expelling Miller and Holmes from their churches, but these churches did not survive. When Miller returned for a visit to Tuskegee in 2000, he found an empty First Presbyterian Church with plywood enclosing all windows, and Tattnall Square Baptist Church in Macon no longer has a congregation. Holmes wrote in the *Christian Index*, "Four other Baptist churches adopted open-door policies because of the adverse publicity given Tattnall Square," and Rufus Harris, president of Mercer University, finally broke his silence and apologized for what he called "an act of savagery and a denial of the relevancy of Jesus Christ as savior in Twentieth Century life."[47]

In the long run, the resignation of Rev. W. B. Selah from Galloway Memorial Methodist Church in Jackson produced results, but not until his replacement, W. J. Cunningham, resigned. As the historian Carter Dalton Lyon mentions, Selah's action was praised by bishops, ministers, people from across the nation, members and former members of Galloway Church. According to Lyon, one member, Verna R. Wood, wrote that Selah "had made her feel differently about the whole mess." In addition, Selah was invited back every year on the anniversary of his resignation to preach sermons, not unlike the one he gave that fateful day. Cunningham left feeling he had failed completely in his ministry. "It was a heavy burden to carry and I really didn't get over it for a few years," but his associate Clay Lee told him, "You shouldn't fault your-self. Jesus Christ himself would have failed." Cunningham continued to serve Methodist churches for another fifteen years and, as time progressed, began to believe that maybe he did accomplish something. Black members are now wel-comed at Galloway Church. As Cunningham modestly wrote in his memoir: "The church could not change the culture; the culture changed and carried the church along with it."[48]

◆ ◆ ◆

A northern Methodist minister, Rev. Pharis Harvey, who accompanied Tou-galoo students for the church visitations, reported to the group's sponsor, the World Council of Churches: "The visits contributed to the movement toward an open society . . . and helped the various congregations involved examine the Christian faith in regard to their congregational life. . . . Yet the most significant aspect of the church visits was the increasing JOY we found at the few oppor-tunities that were afforded us to enter the House of God in praise and prayer, and the real sense of celebration of thanksgiving for these high moments when we sat with other Christians in common worship."[49] This comment could be applied to all people who participated in church visitations.

As Stephen R. Haynes, professor of religious studies at Rhodes College, Memphis, Tennessee, has observed, African Americans are now welcome at most white churches, but, according to Rhett Jackson of Trenholm Road United Methodist Church in Columbia, South Carolina, "Except for a few iso-lated churches, the 11 o'clock hour on Sunday is still almost completely segre-gated." Larry Jackson, his twin brother, former associate minister of Central Methodist Church of Florence, South Carolina; retired president of Lander College in Greenwood, South Carolina; executor of its integration; and one of the compilers of the controversial *South Carolinians Speak* in 1957, has given the situation another perspective: "Black people are loyal to their own churches. Our black students will drive twenty to forty miles on Sundays just to go to their own church. Church attendance is a cultural thing and we're not going to change it." S. Jonathan Bass wrote in 2001, "Only a handful of interra-cial churches exist in the city [Birmingham, Alabama,] and blacks would be no more welcome in many of the area's white churches than they would have been in 1963. The peace that Martin Luther King sought . . . has remained an elusive dream."[50] In many individual cases, however, the witness of these ministers brought about change. They were true to their convictions that a Christian church should welcome all people.

═ 4 ═

THE MOVEMENT CONTINUES
Washington, DC; Chapel Hill; Selma; Louisville

> We didn't keep step. Someone had printed on a white cardboard, nailed to a slender piece of wood, "Presbyterians US." . . . As we walked down the street we were talking to one another. The streets were like Sunday morning, quiet and empty. I said to my companion, "You know, I have a feeling it's going to be like going to church."
> —CARL R. PRITCHETT, pastor of Bethesda (Maryland) Presbyterian Church, 1963

The March on Washington was a reprieve from the violence, warfare, nervous tension, and traumatic stress caused by boycotts, sit-ins, Freedom Rides, mass demonstrations, and protests occurring in the states of Alabama, Georgia, and Mississippi. The march was peaceful and well protected by Washington's Secret Service and police. The march enabled white people to say to African Americans, "We are with you!" Hundreds of white clergy participated, but those from the South did so in spite of southern hostility. This segment on the March on Washington contains the stories of three southern white ministers who dared to participate and let their stories be known: Rev. J. Randolph Taylor, Rev. Carl R. Pritchett, and Rev. Ed King. There may have been other southern white ministers who attended, but they did so without revealing their names.

In all four locations, DC, Chapel Hill, Selma, and Louisville, protestors marched, but in each location the marches were for different purposes. The March on Washington was for jobs and freedom; the Chapel Hill marches were for a public accommodations ordinance; the Selma marches were for voting rights; and the Louisville marches were for open public accommodations and open housing. The marches in Washington and Selma are commemorated each year and will never be forgotten in historical memory, but those in Chapel Hill and Louisville may be remembered by only participants, their friends, descendants, local librarians, and scholars.

Unlike Selma, desegregation in Chapel Hill and Louisville had steadily moved ahead, with schools partially integrated. African Americans could vote; a few were elected to municipal offices, served on the police force, and could generally patronize local business establishments. In both communities, however, majorities of African Americans still lived in poverty, lived in substandard housing, and were relegated to low-paying, menial types of work. There is no shortage of information about the marches in Washington and Selma, but information on the protests in Chapel Hill and Louisville is hard to come by. Demonstrations in Chapel Hill never made national headlines, but in 1965 John Ehle, a sociology professor at the University of North Carolina (UNC) and an educational adviser to Governor Terry Sanford, one of the few liberal governors in the South at the time, wrote *The Free Men*, an eyewitness account of the Chapel Hill demonstrations. The memoir is vital to the theme of this book, for lurking in the texts of its pages are the efforts of three white ministers: Rev. Robert Seymour, Rev. Charles M. Jones, and an eighty-year-old retired Episcopal priest, Fr. Clarence P. W. Parker.

In 1963 concerned citizens of Louisville, joined by Martin Luther King Jr. and several southern white ministers, marched to the state capitol to urge passage of an open accommodations bill for the entire state, but the bill did not become law until shortly after the passage of the federal Civil Rights Act of 1964. In 1967 small marches began to protest the lack of adequate housing for black people, Louisville's major problem, not easily solved. Southern white ministers again were involved in the marches for open housing—among them, Bishop Charles Marmion, Rev. Thomas Moffett, Rev. Gilbert Schroerlucke, and Rev. Grayson Tucker.

African Americans living in Selma, Alabama, in the Deep South would have been grateful for some of the advances existing in Chapel Hill and Louisville, the Upper South. Their situation was even more tenuous due to the presence of a brutal police chief, something that did not exist in Chapel Hill or Louisville. Demonstrations in Selma focused on voting rights, not an issue in Chapel Hill or Louisville. Another feature differentiating the three locations was the presence of white allies. Both Chapel Hill and Louisville were locations of major educational institutions, which guaranteed the presence of liberal-minded white sympathizers who were not afraid to speak out. This kind of presence did not exist in Selma. Chapel Hill was the site of UNC, considered one of the South's most liberal universities, and Louisville was home to the University of Louisville, desegregated since 1950, and two major theological seminaries: the Southern Baptist Theological Seminary (SBTS), liberal at the time, the largest Baptist seminary in the United States (and the world), and the Presbyterian Theological Seminary, a union seminary, connecting the southern and northern Presbyterian denominations.[1] Rev. Grayson Tucker and Rev. George Edwards, whose efforts are recounted in this chapter, were affiliated with the Presbyterian Theological Seminary. They were joined in their efforts by Presbyterian Rev. Thomas Moffett, Methodist Rev. Gilbert Schroerlucke, and Episcopal bishop Charles Gresham Marmion. Baptist Paul Turner, who helped integrate Clinton High School in Tennessee, studied at SBTS, as did Clarence Jordan, who established interracial Koinonia Farm in 1942, and Howard McClain, first executive director of the South Carolina Christian Action Council. Unlike the other locations, Louisville is a major city in the Upper South with a large population, and therefore it had a greater potential for white allies.

In Chapel Hill, the protest movements were led by young white people as well as African Americans, and in Louisville a strong white group supported protest efforts, but in Selma, white allies either did not exist or were hiding. The ministers who entered these crisis situations were brave and committed to helping African Americans. All four episodes contribute to an appreciation for the activities of southern white ministers and reveal how much easier it was for ministers in Chapel Hill and Louisville to express support for the civil rights movement than in Selma or even at the March on Washington.

Washington, DC, 1963

On June 22, 1963, Martin Luther King Jr. of the Southern Christian Leadership Conference (SCLC), Roy Wilkins of the National Association for the Advancement of Colored People (NAACP), and Asa Philip Randolph of the Brotherhood of Sleeping Car Porters and vice-president of the American Federation of Labor and Congress of Industrial Organization (AFL-CIO) informed President John F. Kennedy that "massive demonstrations would continue until the civil rights problem was settled." At a larger meeting that day, which included James Farmer of the Congress of Racial Equality (CORE) and Walter Reuther of the United Automobile Workers Union (UAW; AFL-CIO), it was announced that 100,000 blacks would march to the capitol in August to "pressure Congress into action on the civil rights bill," albeit with Kennedy's cautioning words to avoid "violence and undo pressure." To ensure nonviolence, Kennedy urged clergy throughout the nation to participate. "It is sad that the President of the United States has to call on churchmen to do what the Gospel requires," commented John C. Irwin of the Garrett Theological Seminary (Methodist) in Evanston, Illinois.[2]

The National Council of Churches, the National Catholic Council for
Interracial Justice, and the American Jewish Congress agreed to cosponsor
the march. The city of New York, the American Friends Service Committee,
the American Lutheran Church, the northern Presbyterian Church (PCUSA),
and the American Civil Liberties Union (ACLU) contributed funds. All thirty-
one members of the National Council of Churches gave their support. The
Methodist Conference on Human Relations endorsed the march, although the
House of Bishops of the Protestant Episcopal Church, representing both southern and northern bishops, was divided. The Presbyterian Church (PCUSA)
supported the march, while its southern counterpart (PCUS) refused. Bayard
Rustin, assistant to Randolph, sent personal invitations to clergy, political and
labor leaders, entertainers, and blacks and whites throughout the nation.[3]

The march took place on a warm summer day, Wednesday, August 28,
1963, with more than 200,000 Americans attending, mostly black. It became
the embodiment of nonviolent interracial and interregional cooperation,
together with the fanfare of a great celebration. It began at the Washington
Monument with the singing of impromptu freedom songs, "We shall not be
moved / Just like a tree that's planted by the water, we shall not be moved." It
proceeded to the Lincoln Memorial, where professional folk and gospel singers performed. Joan Baez sang, "Deep in my heart, I do believe, we shall overcome some day"; Peter, Paul, and Mary sang, "How many times must a man
look up before he can see the sky?"; Mahalia Jackson sang, "I been 'buked and
I been scorned"; and Marion Anderson sang, "He's got the whole world in his
hands." Then, from a podium at the Lincoln Memorial, the black leaders presented clear statements of purpose and need. Asa Philip Randolph declared,
"Yes, we all want public accommodations open to all citizens but those accommodations will mean little to those who cannot afford to use them. . . . We want
integrated public schools but that means we also want federal aid to education—all forms of education." As the son of a minister of the African Methodist Episcopal (AME) Church, Randolph emphasized the righteousness of the
cause: "We have taken our struggle into the streets, as the labor movement
took its struggle into the streets, as Jesus Christ led the multitudes through the
streets of Judea."[4]

As the march was being organized, Randolph and Rustin invited Rev. J.
Randolph Taylor (1929–2001), pastor of the Presbyterian Church of the Pilgrims in the heart of the city, to serve on the hospitality committee and provide space for delegates. Without hesitation, Taylor knew it was the right thing
to do. Born in China to missionary parents, he was three years old when the
family returned to the South, due to the death of his mother. He was raised
by family members in Charleston, South Carolina, and Nashville, Tennessee,
and educated at Davidson College in North Carolina; the Union Theological

Seminary in Richmond, Virginia; and Christ's College, the University of Aberdeen, in Scotland, where he completed a doctorate in theology. Upon his return from Scotland in 1956, Taylor was invited to be pastor of the Church of the Pilgrims, affiliated with the southern branch of the Presbyterian Church. In an interview, he related how, fresh from progressive learning at Aberdeen Seminary, he bravely told his white southern audience, including such distinguished segregationists as Senators Sam Ervin and B. Everett Jordan of North Carolina, "All people in the world are kin to each other." He called their political views terrible and reflected that he was able to teach the full Gospel only because there was intellectual freedom at the church: "They didn't mind my talking about the brotherhood of man or the fatherhood of God; nor did they mind my saying that we had to be concerned about the struggle of all people in this life." Although some members left because of his teaching, a nucleus of young civil servants with open minds remained to keep the church alive.[5]

Taylor related, "The hospitality committee had no idea how many people would be coming, but the plan was to make available large rooms that would hold several hundred people. We had two such rooms, our sanctuary and fellowship hall. We were asked to host two delegations, one from Vermont and one from Connecticut. I was relieved that they hadn't picked Mississippi or Louisiana, for I surely would have been lynched."[6]

In July, when the southern Presbyterian Church (PCUS) announced that it would not officially participate in the march, Taylor traveled to Richmond, Virginia, to the office of the *Presbyterian Outlook*, journal of the PCUS, to tell editors Rev. E. T. Thompson and Aubrey Brown that he would write an open letter expressing his disgust. "Brethren," he wrote, "all of us must be open to the fresh demands which the eternal Word of God places upon us to be relevant in our ministry to the age in which we live.... One of the crucial problems of our times is racial equality. The church is directly involved in its solution because of the imperatives of the gospel." He wrote from his heart as one who loved his church and his brethren. He implored southern Presbyterians to consider every ramification of their refusal: the adverse impression on world opinion and the disappointing and disillusioning effect on Presbyterians of African ancestry. "It is unlikely," he wrote, "that there will ever be another March on Washington in our lifetime." The letter was read to the General Assembly of PCUS two days before the march and had its influence. Two hundred or more southern Presbyterians (including ministers) responded and gathered at the Church of the Pilgrims for prayer and worship before moving into the streets.[7]

Taylor commented that he was elated. "I felt the spirit of the day. I was flying with angel's wings and I'm sure my congregation must have had some difficult feelings about me, but they backed me up. Some must have been proud of what I had done. While the march took place, we were officially not there. This meant that the other denominations and our northern brothers had their bishops, presbyters, and moderators, but we just had our own splintered southern group." As Taylor mentioned, for a southerner the process of renouncing segregation was like going to the "executioner's bench," but for those who marched it was an apology for the past and a confession that they were tired of being marked as segregationists just because they came from the South. Two weeks later, on the front page of the *Outlook*, there appeared a telling picture of southern Presbyterians, black and white, male and female, who risked careers and well-being to participate. They sat with smiling and proud faces under their simple, *unofficial* banner, "Presbyterians US." Editor Thompson attended, and Brown sent his photographer.[8]

Two months later a group met in Charlottesville, Virginia, and organized the Fellowship of Concern, dedicated to integration of the public schools, greater employment opportunities for African Americans, and increased opportunities for African Americans within the southern Presbyterian Church. Taylor related, "Members of the Fellowship of Concern actively joined the Civil Rights Movement. We were a source of information and we supplied white participants, perhaps a smaller number than we hoped for, but those who participated were the best of the ministry in the southern church. We went on the bus rides into Mississippi and Alabama and marched in demonstrations." The fellowship also helped pastors who lost churches because of participating in the March on Washington and other marches, but not all southern Presbyterians approved of the Fellowship of Concern or the March on Washington. The following year a group, Concerned Presbyterians, formed in opposition, thus drastically dividing the southern denomination. Concerned Presbyterians supported segregation while the Fellowship of Concern wanted an end to the laws of segregation forever.[9]

Although he could not reach all members of the southern denomination, Taylor influenced a great many. One pastor influenced by Taylor was Rev. Carl R. Pritchett (1909–1992), born in Salisbury, North Carolina, and pastor of Bethesda Presbyterian Church in nearby Maryland. Rev. Donald W. Shriver, then professor of church history at North Carolina State University in Raleigh (later president of Union Theological Seminary in New York City), wrote about Pritchett in his book *The Unsilent South*: "Pritchett was born with a good case of racial prejudice . . . but rose above his early upbringing to become a staunch supporter of black civil rights." In a sermon preached on the Sunday following the march, Pritchett told his congregation of his struggle in deciding whether he should participate. He declared that his approach in settling disputes had always been to engage in discussion, by parliamentary procedure, arbitration, negotiation, and courts of law. Like many ministers in his generation, he believed in appeal to reason, conscience, and the heart. It was not his way to march in the streets, but an invitation from three ministers in his presbytery to attend a worship service at the Church of the Pilgrims before the march tempted him to consider the possibility. He attended the service, and when he heard the sermon delivered by Rev. Taylor, he knew that he must participate: "Rev. Dr. Taylor is a southerner. I have known his family for years. He is as orthodox as anyone I know. He never has been a member of the communist party. He has never been in a riot. He explained to us why we were there in restrained theological and biblical language. . . . Another Presbyterian led us in a prayer of confession. It was thoughtful, probing, and painful. I sat there with my head bowed and said, 'Yes, Lord, that is exactly the way it is with us. We need to repent of past transgressions.'"[10]

The March on Washington was a moral and religious undertaking besides an effort to influence politicians. When the leaders were called to the podium, Rev. Eugene Carson Blake, chief executive officer of the United Presbyterian Church (PCUSA) and chair of the Commission of Religion and Race for the National Council of Churches of Christ, spoke apologetically, "If all the members and all the ministers of the constituency I represent here today were ready to stand and march with you for jobs and freedom . . . together with those of the Roman Catholic Church and the synagogues in America, then the battle for full civil rights and dignity would be already won." Matthew Ahmann, executive director of the National Catholic Conference for Interracial Justice, asked, "Who can call himself a man, say God created him, and at the same time take part in a system of segregation which destroys the livelihood, the citizenship, family life, and the very heart of the Negro citizens of the United States?" Rabbi Joachim Prinz, survivor of Nazi death camps and president of the American Jewish Congress, expressed a thought that had been articulated by Martin Luther King Jr. and many others: "The most important thing I learned in my life . . . is that bigotry and hatred are not the most urgent problem. The most urgent, the most disgraceful, the most shameful, and the most tragic problem is silence."[11]

King's speech, however, created a sensation. He listed grievances, called for action, but ended with vision, inspiration, and an expectation that better days would come: "I have a dream that my four little children will one day live in a nation where they will not be judged by the color of their skin, but by the content of their character."[12] But the better days would not come until after the bombing of the Sixteenth Street Baptist Church in Birmingham, Alabama; the killing of four young girls and two others in Alabama; the murders of African American James Chaney and white civil rights workers Andrew Goodman and Mickey Schwerner in Mississippi; the defeat of the Mississippi Freedom Democratic Party; the brutal slayings of African American Jimmy Lee Jackson, white Rev. James Reeb, white Viola Gregg Liuzzo, and white Seminarian Jonathan Daniels in Alabama; and ultimately the assassination of Martin Luther King Jr. in Tennessee.

The march had a tremendous effect on Revs. Taylor and Pritchett. In 1967 Taylor moved to Atlanta, and as pastor of Central Presbyterian Church became a leader for open housing, desegregation of schools, and open public facilities. Rev. Pritchett overcame his fear of violence and aversion to street demonstrations and continued guiding his congregation in the direction of greater involvement with the racial issue. Another white minister, Rev. James I. Lowry of all-white Meadowview Presbyterian Church in an all-white neighborhood in Louisville, Kentucky, experienced a transformation just from watching the event on home television. He told his congregation he cried when Marion Anderson sang "He's got the whole world in his hands." He said his tears were tears of joy and tears of shame. "I was proud to be a member of the human race, but I was ashamed to be part of a race that made demonstrations like this necessary." Lowry believed it was time for the Christian community to protest the ugliness in society. He urged members of his congregation to write to representatives in Congress asking them to vote for strong civil rights legislation, for improved employment opportunities, for an end to racial discrimination, and especially for improved housing conditions for African Americans.[13]

Pritchett believed there would have to be a moral revulsion to the humiliation of black people before any political action would take place. In his sermon that Sunday, he prevailed upon his congregation to pray that God would help them overcome their racial prejudice and help them to speak out for racial justice when it was courteous and appropriate to do so. Pritchett was transformed by the March on Washington. He no longer disapproved of street marching. He believed the corporate church was to blame for the racial problem being in the streets: "The Church forced it out in the streets. . . . If I should ever feel that my place is physically out in the street, it will be because my church has forced me out of the sanctuary . . . and into the street. If it embarrasses the church that one of its ministers is in jail, it is just too bad."[14]

Rev. R. Edwin King, forced into the streets, sent to jail, could well appreciate all that Pritchett spoke that Sunday. Ed King attended the March on Washington, heavily bandaged and recovering from his near-death auto wreck on a remote Mississippi highway. He came with his wife, Jeanette, and a group from Tougaloo College: Joan Trumpauer, a white student, veteran of the Woolworth's sit-ins; Bob, a black student, on his way to Harvard; and Anne Moody, a veteran of the Woolworth's sit-ins and church kneel-ins, all at great peril.[15]

◆ ◆ ◆

Eighteen days after the March on Washington, four teenage girls were killed in the bombing of the Sixteenth Street Baptist Church in Birmingham, Alabama. As stated by Ed King, "It was Alabama's answer to the March on Washington."[16]

Still heavily bandaged and recovering from reconstructive surgery, Ed King, along with a group from Mississippi, attended the funeral of the four girls. King openly cried when he saw the wreckage of the church with the body of Christ still visible in the stained-glass window, the head shattered to pieces, and he observed that two more children were killed that day. One black youngster of thirteen was shot by two teenage boys from a passing car while riding his bicycle, and a sixteen-year-old was shot by police, who claimed he threw a stone at them. Ed King wondered why the president and the Justice Department refused to heed the black leaders and a telegram from fifty moderate white citizens, including Rev. Alfred Hobart, pastor of the local Unitarian church, urging that federal troops be sent to Birmingham. Ed King wrote in a paper presented at Galloway Methodist Church in 2004, "If troops had been sent immediately after the bombing the additional murder of local black children would not have taken place." The SNCC workers were disgusted with Kennedy, and Ed King agreed, "It was time for John Kennedy to be at a funeral" (nor had Kennedy attended Medgar Evers's funeral at Arlington National Cemetery).[17] These were the anticlimactic events of the March on Washington.

Chapel Hill, North Carolina, 1963, 1964, and earlier

Chapel Hill, the site of the University of North Carolina (UNC), was considered by many to be the "liberal bastion" of North Carolina. Author John Egerton describes how UNC rose to its liberal status when Harold Odum established the Department of Sociology in 1920 and remained there until his death in 1954. Frank Porter Graham, president of the university from 1930 to 1949, also worked for progress, but was well behind Odum in speaking out against segregation. When Rev. Charles Jones (1906–1993), born in Nashville, Tennessee, arrived in Chapel Hill in 1941, there were no African American students at the university, and Chapel Hill was a typical southern segregated town. Jones, a graduate of the Union Theological Seminary, was called from a small church in Brevard, North Carolina, to First Presbyterian Church, near the campus of UNC. Graham, an active Presbyterian, was one of the church's elders.[18]

Jones welcomed his opportunity to minister in a university town. Mark Pryor, who spent many hours interviewing his grandfather for a biography, wrote, "His relaxed and approachable manner, his beautiful singing voice, and his persuasive speaking skills drew people to him—membership [at his church] broke the 200 mark in 1943." As the church grew, it became more closely associated with the university, and Jones included in his preaching discussions of community issues. From his first day, Pryor noted, "He maintained an open door policy welcoming people from all social and educational levels, including African Americans." He began a Sunday morning breakfast group, often inviting African American guests from Durham and Raleigh and once arranging for African American theologian Howard Thurman, dean of the School of Religion at Howard University, to preach for him. When some members of the church objected to the presence of occasional black visitors, Jones let it be known that "the Church would not be true to the teachings of Jesus if it should let color, creed, or race bar anyone to its fellowship." Jones received the support of Frank Porter Graham; Francis Bradshaw, philosophy professor at the university; and John Foushee, former mayor of Chapel Hill, but some in the church believed Jones was treating blacks "a little too much like equals."[19]

His real problems began in 1947 when a group of Freedom Riders sponsored by the Fellowship of Reconciliation, a New York–based peace and justice organization, left New York to test the 1946 Supreme Court ruling that segregation of passengers on motor carriers was unconstitutional. Two black men and two white men, Freedom Riders, sat in front of a Trailways bus, something that black people were not supposed to do in the South. When the bus got to Chapel Hill, the four men were forced off the bus and arrested. When James Peck, one of the white Freedom Riders, got off the bus to pay bail for the arrested men, he was slugged in the head by a white cab driver. An assistant from Jones's church saw the trouble and telephoned his pastor, who went immediately to get the Freedom Riders and brought them to the church's manse. A group of white cab drivers then piled into three cabs and followed closely, but Jones managed to elude them. Once the Freedom Riders were safely at Jones's house, the cab drivers rode away, but that was not the end of trouble. A few minutes later, he received a threatening phone call, "Get those men out of town by nightfall or we'll burn your house down." The Freedom Riders stayed at Jones's house, standing watch all night. The next morning three university students drove them to their next stop in Greensboro, North Carolina. After they left, Jones received more threatening phone calls. Students from UNC came to watch the house, and eventually the threatening phone calls stopped. News of the incident traveled throughout the state, and Jones, because of his involvement with the Freedom Riders, was blamed for causing division in his church and dissension in Chapel Hill. The *Atlanta Constitution*, very conservative at the time, considered the "freedom rides" to be Communist inspired.[20]

In 1952 a group from Jones's church petitioned the Council of the Presbytery of Orange County, North Carolina, to establish a second Presbyterian Church in Chapel Hill, one that would be more traditional. The petitioners claimed that Jones did not seem to be "a true Presbyterian," but Dorcas Jones, his wife, believed they did not approve of his interracial activities. The petition gave the council reason enough to investigate Jones. As recorded by Pryor, the questions were intimidating: "They wanted to know his views on the Bible, Jesus Christ, virgin birth, atonement, and the bodily resurrection of Christ." In their final report, the commissioners wrote, "The pastor of this church is deeply loved. There are those who frankly consider him an embodiment of Jesus. . . . Many indicate that . . . he is the 'finest Christian in the Community.' His sermons . . . the soul of the Church's spiritual life [are] seminars in religious experience," but the commissioners concluded, "We do not feel that the Pastor, the officers of this Church, or the members have always been true to the 'Record of God's Revelation' as it is interpreted in our denominational standards."[21]

Jones was dismissed in accordance with Paragraph 76 of the Presbyterian *Book of Church Order*, which stated that the presbytery may dismiss a minister "where the interests of religion imperatively demand it." Jones considered the decision arbitrary, but rather than challenge the presbytery and endure multitudes of hearings, he resigned and was joined by his deacons and elders.[22]

The national media announced on July 22, 1953, that "Jones had lost a final battle with the Orange Presbytery." Jones was quoted in *Time* magazine as saying, "I cannot place dogma above Christianity. . . . I believe [the Christian's] first loyalty is not to his denomination but to the church universal." Jones left Chapel Hill to work for Save the Children Foundation in the East Tennessee mountains, improving the education conditions in many one-room schoolhouses. Later that summer, a new community church organized on the campus of UNC with an ecumenical mission: "We are a fellowship of people from varied backgrounds, a church of open membership, free from denominational limitations, a spiritual home wherein there is unity in Christian essentials, liberty in non-essentials, and charity in all things; a fellowship dedicated to the worship of God and to outgoing Christian service." One of the founders of the new church was Phillips Russell, who brought Jones to First Presbyterian Church more than a decade earlier. Members of the new church called Jones to be their pastor and gave him the opportunity to return to the community he loved. His family moved into a manse in a quiet wooded area not far from Franklin Street, the site of his former church.[23]

Dorcas Jones commented, "Charles's religion was deep. Some people who knew him did not realize this. He had been raised very strictly as a Presbyterian in Nashville in a church that was part of the northern union at that time and therefore more liberal than the southern churches. It was instilled in him to fight injustice. He fought not just for blacks but for all people who were oppressed. . . . Part of his trouble was that students would come here, learn something new, and return to their small villages to tell people what they had learned, but their ministers and friends back home did not want to hear about racial injustice and liberalism."[24]

◆ ◆ ◆

Rev. Robert Seymour, an ordained Baptist minister born in 1925 in Greenwood, South Carolina, arrived in Chapel Hill in 1959, after the desegregation of UNC. Like Jones, he was active, outspoken, and committed to integration. Seymour attributed some of his ideas to Yale Divinity School, where he received a master's of divinity degree in 1948. At Yale, he discovered a vastly different world than the one he knew in South Carolina. White domestic servants cooked and cleaned while black students resided in his dormitory and shared his table in the cafeteria. Coming to a belief that segregation was morally wrong, he wrote a letter to his hometown newspaper in Greenwood denouncing a war memorial that listed names of white soldiers and sailors at the top and names of blacks at the bottom. His parents were mortified but soon adjusted to the fact that their son might be receiving a fine education. Seymour wrote in his memoir, "In later years, I would hear my father say with some sadness to his friends, 'I lost my son at Yale.'"[25]

At Yale, Seymour was transformed by what he called a "star-studded" faculty: H. Richard Niebuhr, professor of Christian ethics; Robert Calhoun, professor of historical theology; Halford Luccock, professor of preaching; and Liston Pope, professor of social ethics. From Niebuhr, he learned that the church should be against an evil culture, not its accomplice. From Pope, he learned that loving God with heart, mind, and soul is inseparably related to loving one's neighbor as oneself. Pope, a southerner from North Carolina and a graduate of Duke University, was an important person at the divinity school, later becoming dean. He often took students on field trips into Harlem for glimpses of poverty in America.[26]

Seymour went on to earn a PhD from the Presbyterian University of Edinburgh in Scotland, but he remained a Baptist. Being a Baptist meant to Seymour that he was free to follow his conscience in word and deed: "When a minister is called to a church, he needs to expect freedom of the pulpit. The church should not reflect the prejudices of the community." Shortly after the *Brown* decision, he introduced a resolution to the North Carolina State Baptist Convention calling for immediate integration of North Carolina's seven Baptist colleges. The leaders of the convention told him that school integration was not on their agenda, and he should forget it, but Seymour continued to introduce resolutions in support of integration at meetings of both the North Carolina Baptist Convention and the larger Southern Baptist Convention. As the years progressed, the conventions became more conservative, and Seymour was labeled "a person who was concerned with this issue and almost nothing else." In his words to interviewer Bruce Kalk, he was "ignored and isolated by North Carolina Baptist churches."[27]

Seymour welcomed his appointment to the Olin T. Binkley Memorial Baptist Church on the campus of UNC. The church took its name to honor Binkley, a progressive dean and later president of the Southern Baptist Theological Seminary in Louisville, Kentucky. Previously, Seymour had served as pastor at Mars Hill Baptist Church, Mars Hill, North Carolina, where he helped Oralene Graves become the first African American to enter Mars Hill College, a Baptist school. Graves was admitted in July 1961. (Seymour was no longer pastor of Mars Hill Church at that time.) Binkley Church had recently organized when the town's prevailing Baptist church refused to admit black students. Binkley's affirmation of faith made it clear that the church would welcome all people regardless of race.[28]

UNC had desegregated in 1955, without incident, by court order. By 1960 about thirty black students were enrolled, and at least one dozen worshiped at Binkley Church, but the public elementary and high schools remained segregated. Seymour worked diligently for school desegregation through a local organization, the Fellowship for School Integration, and through his church. He knew that if school integration was to succeed, it would have to come from the school board. Fred Ellis, a deacon at Binkley Church who had four daughters at each level of the school system, was convinced by Seymour and other deacons to run for the Board of Education. They promised Ellis that if he declared himself a school board candidate, he would be relieved of all his responsibilities as deacon. He agreed and was elected in 1961. Ellis's vote turned the tide on school integration. In 1961 Chapel Hill became the first school district in North Carolina to activate a plan for the total integration of public schools voluntarily.[29]

In 1962 an unexpected telephone call gave Seymour another opportunity to work for integration. The Union Theological Seminary in New York City invited Binkley Church to participate in its summer program for African American ministerial students by sponsoring the internship of James Forbes of Raleigh. Seymour liked the idea but needed to clear it with his deacons, who unanimously approved. The membership came to love Forbes as he directed the Vacation Bible School, made hospital visits, conducted retreats, and took charge when Seymour was on vacation. Later Seymour performed Forbes's wedding at a Pentecostal church in Wilmington, North Carolina, where Forbes had become pastor. Forbes attracted national attention as a gifted preacher and eventually became head pastor of New York's prestigious Riverside Church. In 1996 *Newsweek* magazine ranked Forbes as one of the top twelve preachers in the English-speaking world. Seymour can be said to have given Forbes a good start and to have opened the hearts of people in Chapel Hill.[30]

Seymour described Chapel Hill as an unlikely place for street demonstrations, once so peaceful and friendly it was called the "Southern Part of

Heaven." To him it was a town of "Camelot-like charm," where the university occupied the center and where quiet streets "wandered in all directions into heavily wooded neighborhoods," but appalling to Seymour was the segregated ambience outside the university. Local African Americans lived in poverty, serving as campus cooks and janitors at low wages: "Most restaurants were open to whites only, and the two local movie theaters did not even provide a balcony for blacks." Seymour, like Jones, would soon become involved in protest movements in Chapel Hill.[31]

Inspired by the Greensboro sit-ins in 1960, a group of high school students began Chapel Hill demonstrations soon afterward by picketing the Colonial Drug Store, near the black section of town, but where blacks were refused service at luncheon booths. The group was disorganized and quickly broken up by police, with some of the students becoming unruly. Seeking adult advice, they called on Rev. Jones at the Community Church. Jones was sympathetic and told them, "What you are trying to do is right, but it will take level-headed thinking, calm action, and cannot be done by explosion, but it is right." Jones made two proposals: "They must swear that under no circumstances would they return violence for violence, cursing for cursing, blow for blow"; and he also insisted they go through training sessions in which simulated episodes of possible picketing encounters would be acted out. Jones also arranged for Daniel Pollitt of the UNC law school to explain to them that picketing was a way of expressing free speech. They had the constitutional right, and if they picketed quietly and did not block doorways, they should receive police protection. After ten days of picketing, Jones delivered a passionate sermon at Community Church: "Since 1954 in this community, no advance has been made for the local Negro in race relations. . . . These young people need us and the businessmen [also] need us. They need to know that white people will not refuse to trade with them if they treat colored citizens with ordinary decency and equality."[32]

The picketing of Colonial Drug Store continued for several months, orderly, self-restrained, and with police protection, but the proprietor refused to give in. He simply removed the booths. Joining the picketers was Rev. Seymour and Fr. Clarence Parker.[33]

◆ ◆ ◆

A Kentucky native, the white Episcopal priest Clarence Parker (1883–1973) came to Chapel Hill in 1951 after many years as rector of St. Mark's Episcopal Church in Chicago's South Side. In Illinois, he was president of the Civil Rights Congress and active in peace, antifascist, and prolabor organizations. He was described by a friend as a man who "worked for practically every social cause this country has faced in the last fifty years." At the age of seventy, he developed pneumonia, and his bishop thought it best that he retire. He retired to Chapel Hill, not far from his wife's family and his son's farm; thus began his career as an activist in North Carolina.[34]

By 1963 the civil rights movement in Chapel Hill exploded, unrelated to the picketing of the Colonial Drug Store. A group of young activists refused to wait any longer for results. Pat Cusick, a white thirty-two-year-old veteran of the Korean War from Alabama and graduate of UNC, and nineteen-year-old African American Harold Foster, who commuted to the black state college in Durham, organized the Committee to Open Business (COB). The group's initial meeting, was held at St. Joseph's AME Church, was attended by Revs. Seymour and Jones, Fr. Parker, and several students and personnel from UNC. Foster and Parker became cochairs. The group was fighting for passage of a municipal accommodations ordinance that would end segregated businesses, finally and totally, but such an ordinance would have to be approved by the seven-member Board of Alderman of Chapel Hill.[35]

Demonstrations by COB began in July 1963, with simple marches, the first briefly described on a back page of the New York Times. About 450 persons, 120 white, marched quietly through the business district, pointing fingers at segregated business establishments. Police Chief W. D. Blake termed the protest the largest in the town's history, "without any disorders or arrests." On the steps of city hall, Rev. Jones delivered a sermon: "I am told that when they organized to climb Mt. Everest they established three requirements for participants in the enterprise: first, good health; second, some experience in mountain climbing; and third, faith that it could be done. So this march challenges every person: Do we have enough faith to make racial justice our personal Mount Everest?"[36]

Marches and picketing continued throughout the year. Attempts at negotiations were constant. Rev. Seymour pleaded with the aldermen to pass the public accommodations ordinance. They refused, in spite of the fact that one of their members, African American Charles Robinson, approved of the law. Telephone calls for support were made by the ministers and some UNC faculty, but opposition was virulent: "I'm for freedom—freedom of the businessman to run his own place of business"; "I believe a man has a constitutional right to discriminate." In response, Seymour preached in his church: "A man in business is required to operate his establishment within the framework of many laws. He is not free to pay his employees whatever he chooses . . . to hire children . . . to serve unhealthy food [from] a dirty kitchen. . . . His right of private property is contingent upon his acceptance of public responsibility. . . . [Some ask], 'Is it not lawful for me to do what I want with mine own?' . . . The answer must be 'No.'"[37]

Two new members were elected to the COB Executive Committee—John Dunne, a white scholarship student at UNC from Ohio, and Quinton Baker, state president of the NAACP Youth Chapters and a student at all-black North Carolina College in Durham, both on fire for racial justice. Cusick, Dunne, and Baker began training their associates in Gandhian civil disobedience: "no weapons of any kind, no resistance to police." If arrested, demonstrators were taught to go limp, a tactic meant not to help or hinder the police, and they were told to dress neatly, be cordial, be friendly, and display good manners: "After a reasonable amount of discussion . . . leave politely, thanking the person for his willingness to listen."[38]

John Ehle's eyewitness account reveals the extremist activities of COB, such as blocking the entrance lobby to the Merchant's Association Office Building in downtown Chapel Hill and singing freedom songs. As these extremist activities began, the police started making arrests. The *Chapel Hill Weekly*, in a front-page editorial, accused the activists of having "a lust for power . . . or a neurotic need for martyrdom." As the fall term approached, COB, under severe criticism and plagued with internal bickering, disintegrated. In its place, a local chapter of CORE organized, with Dunne, recently withdrawn from UNC to become a full-time activist, as its director. What followed were some of the most audacious actions performed by demonstrators and some of the most grotesque actions performed by businesspeople against them. A group, including Fr. Parker, blocked the entrance to the Pines, the most elegant restaurant in town. All were arrested and went limp, including Parker. In deference to his age, the police officers asked him to walk, but he refused. "I can't do different from the others," he told them as he was dragged along. A total of 150 people at several restaurants were arrested. Fr. Parker went to jail but was soon released. On December 22, 1963, he led a prayer march to the prison and delivered a consoling sermon.[39]

According to Ehle, the residents of Chapel Hill were furious. They asked, "Why have they picked on Chapel Hill? Didn't Chapel Hill have an excellent record in race matters?" The answer came back loudly and clearly that blacks in Chapel Hill lived in dire poverty with few business opportunities and were prevented from patronizing business establishments and other public facilities. These observations were substantiated by the North Carolina Advisory Committee to the Civil Rights Commission, a group consisting of both whites and blacks. According to the findings, blacks were held back from professional positions in North Carolina: only 2 percent of the lawyers, only 3 percent of the doctors, and only 6 percent of the dentists were black, whereas blacks made up 25 percent of the total population. The state medical society and even the North Carolina National Guard excluded blacks. The findings were significant because North Carolina had the long-held reputation as leader among the southern states in ameliorating racial discrimination.[40]

Asked to desist demonstrating by the mayor's Human Relations Committee, the young demonstrators became even more defiant. At a segregated grocery store, when Dunne and Baker refused to leave, the manager poured a bottle of ammonia down Baker's throat and ammonia over Dunne's entire body. Baker had to have his stomach pumped and was treated for first-degree burns. Dunne was treated for second-degree burns. The protestors were arrested, but no action was taken against the store's manager. More demonstrations followed, joined by a group of Duke professors, including three ministers from the religion department. At Watts Grill, Professor Al Amon of UNC's Psychology Department, one of the demonstrators, was severely kicked in the head, with spectators screaming, "Kill them, get the professors." They were thrown out bodily, and Amon bled from the head, becoming unconscious. The police soon took them all away. Amon died the following summer, leaving 1,600 photographs of the civil rights struggle in Chapel Hill. James Farmer of CORE came to town in January 1964, threatening to bring the full force of his organization to Chapel Hill if the public accommodations ordinance was not passed by February 1, 1964. According to Seymour, the ministerial association solicited 1,800 signatures on a petition to support the ordinance, while a petition against received less than 100 signatures. In spite of its overwhelming support, the ordinance failed to get the needed votes. It was the second time the aldermen rejected the legislation. Seymour attributed the defeat to Farmer's challenge, but Jones and Seymour continued appealing. Farmer's February 1 deadline came and went, with only silence from the aldermen. They would not be intimidated. The protestors became even more determined, and two days later, Ehle exclaimed, "Everything happened which could happen in a civil rights demonstration in a small town!"[41]

As hundreds of visitors entered the city for the UNC–Wake Forest basketball game, a group of about 110 protestors, including students and professors from Duke University, packed the main intersection approaching the university and sat down, immobile, blocking all traffic. With the addition of more groups, all four main highways serving Chapel Hill were blocked. Ninety-eight protestors were arrested, and traffic was held up for hours. According to Ehle, "Nobody seemed to know what could be done to stop further actions by masses of young people." After ten days Baker, Cusick, and Dunne decided they could not continue subjecting the young people to danger and stopped to consider another plan of action.[42]

The final attempt to convince the aldermen of the need for the ordinance consisted of a hunger strike staged on the front lawn of the post office, joined intermittently by Fr. Parker. The *New York Times* reported, "The group, with containers of water, sleeping bags and blankets is protesting the refusal of the Board of Aldermen to adopt a public accommodations law," but the *Times* never mentioned that the KKK met during that night at the Durham–Chapel Hill highway. As told by a *Durham Herald* reporter, "They stood under a full moon. . . . and from a twenty-five foot kerosene-soaked cross which burned against the sky, a record player played 'The Old Rugged Cross.'"[43]

In late March and early April 1964 the trials of 217 defendants were held at the Superior Court of Hillsboro, with Judge Raymond Mallard, known for his harsh treatment of demonstrators, presiding. Cusick, Baker, Dunne, and other leaders were each sentenced to one year of hard labor in North Carolina's prisons. The only minister in the group, Rev. Harmon Smith of Duke, a Millsaps College graduate, was sentenced to ninety days of hard labor on the state roads, but according to Ehle, appealed his sentence and posted $900 in bond.[44]

The story of the Chapel Hill demonstrations illustrates how a small group of intransigent segregationists were challenged by a determined group of radical young activists. A conflict also existed between liberal and radical integrationists. As Rev. Jones stated, "They [the local CORE group] went from one tactic to another, each more advanced than the other, each taking them further away from the main body of the liberal community, which could have been their chief source of strength." Floyd McKissick blamed the white liberals for not supporting the Freedom Committee of CORE: "I wish they would keep their mouths shut and send in their contributions. . . . They ought to stick with us, right or wrong." McKissick expressed intense disgust with white liberals, more of which would follow.[45]

The ministers in the narrative attempted to influence the aldermen to pass the public accommodations ordinance, but neither they nor the extremists were successful. As the demonstrations became more intense, the aldermen became more resistant and the police became more belligerent. Seymour was a peacemaker and negotiator, Jones an organizer and public advocate, and Parker a participant willing to go "all the way." After the sentencing, the eighty-year-old Parker told Bob Brown, one of the activists, "I'm getting ready. I told Mrs. Parker that my time had about come." Brown thought he was talking about dying, but Parker asserted that he was preparing to go to prison. "Yes," said Parker, "I'm going to prison along with the others. . . . I never did take part in the street blockings. . . . Some people say that the young people went too far, but I'll not say that about them. I know why they did what they did. The only reason I never did lie down in the streets myself was that I wasn't sure I could get up."[46]

Seymour, optimistic about Chapel Hill's ability to change, wrote that after passage of the Civil Rights Act of 1964, he paid a visit to the Pines Restaurant with the newly appointed basketball coach, Dean Smith, member of Binkley Church, and a black friend. They received a warm welcome "as if no past racial exclusion had ever existed," but Ehle was not quite so sure. Citing an instance of gunfire at an integrated private party and the refusal of a motel owner to admit the mother of one of the demonstrators, he wrote in 1965, "Small and large signs of resentment supply evidence that John Dunne and his colleagues, by stomping about in the Southern society, have broken a box of passions."[47]

Liberal citizens in Chapel Hill continued to work for progress in race relations. In 1969 Howard Lee, director of employee relations at Duke University, was elected as the city's first African American mayor. In a close election, he defeated his opponent, Roland Giduz, who had served as an intransigent alderman for twelve years.[48]

Selma, Alabama, 1963–1965

There was little white ministers in Selma, Alabama, could do or dared to do about the voting rights of African Americans. In 1963 there were over 15,000 black men and women of voting age in Dallas County, but only "about two hundred and fifty" were able to vote. Amelia Boynton, a graduate of Tuskegee Institute, related how her late husband, Sam, a Dallas County agent, brought her to the courthouse in Selma during the 1930s to register: "I had no trouble whatsoever, because I was a single person, just one." Long before the civil rights movement, Boynton and her husband organized the Dallas County Voters' League (DCVL) in an attempt to help other African Americans register, but unfathomable literacy tests, outright hostility on the part of the police, insults, and exorbitant poll taxes prevented any group larger than three from attempting to register. Nothing threatened the white power structure more than the black vote, and in central Alabama, where the black population exceeded the white by almost 10,000 people, the opposition was well organized and vicious.[49]

Rev. Ralph Smeltzer (1914–1976), an outsider, went to Selma from Washington, DC, in 1963 as an administrator for the Church of the Brethren to see what he could do to bring about racial harmony. Keeping away from demonstrations and maintaining a low profile, Smeltzer spoke to activists and segregationists alike, warning people that if they did not reduce racial tensions, greater troubles would ensue. During several trips, Smeltzer became acquainted with one of the few local white ministers, John L. Newton of the First Presbyterian Church, born in 1914 in Gainesville, Georgia, who was willing to talk to him about the explosive situation. As a progressive, Newton welcomed four black teenage girls into his church on September 29, 1963, after they were turned away from the all-white Baptist church. Several of his worshippers walked out and never came back. Harassing phone calls began, and white teenagers spread toilet paper and tin cans across his lawn. According to the historian Michael Friedland, Newton tried unsuccessfully to convince local clergymen to negotiate with black leaders and "adopt a resolution for freedom of speech regardless of racial position." Newton became frustrated and withdrew into silence, but he told Smeltzer, "Black demonstrations should continue because without pressure, the community would go on for another hundred years without making concessions."[50]

After struggling for two years trying to get support and resources from the black community, Amelia Boynton of the DCVL and local black leader Rev. Frederick D. Reese invited Martin Luther King Jr. and the Southern Christian Leadership Conference (SCLC) to make Selma "their next national focal point."[51] King and the SCLC staff arrived early in 1965 and began a series of demonstrations directed at the Dallas County courthouse, but by order of the Alabama Supreme Court, "Discussions of racial issues at any gathering of three or more persons" were strictly forbidden (a tactic reminiscent of the Black Codes of 1865). Speaking to a crowd of 700 gathered at Brown's Chapel AME, King challenged the order and rallied the black community, "We must be ready to march. We must be ready to go to jail by the thousands.... Our cry to the state of Alabama is a simple one. Give us the ballot." On February 1, 1965, he led a group out of Brown's Chapel down Sylvan Street. When asked to break the group into smaller groups, King refused, and 770 protestors, 500 of whom were children, were arrested. On February 5, in a paid advertisement, King's "Letter from a Selma Jail" appeared in the *New York Times*, reminiscent of his "Letter from a Birmingham Jail" and designed to expose the entire nation to the voting rights struggle in Selma: "This is Selma, Alabama," he wrote, "THERE ARE MORE NEGROES IN JAIL WITH ME THAN THERE ARE ON THE VOTING ROLLS" (included was a request for contributions).[52]

◆ ◆ ◆

No local white minister ever participated in the Selma demonstrations. Fear of reprisal and personal attacks, instructions from superiors, and outright disapproval of demonstrations prevented white ministers (and some black ministers) from going into the streets.

Rev. Newton, sympathetic to the cause, did not demonstrate, but Rev. Joseph Ellwanger, born in 1933 in St. Louis, raised in Selma, white pastor of Birmingham's black St. Paul's Lutheran Church, veteran of the Birmingham demonstrations, and president of the Birmingham Council on Human Relations, believed it was his duty to make an outspoken appearance in Selma. On Saturday, March 6, 1965, he led seventy white members of the Concerned White Citizens of Alabama—businessmen, housewives, and professional people who organized earlier that year to actively protest Alabama's racial violence and to fight for black voting rights—in a twelve-block march from Rev. C. C. Brown's all-black Reformed Presbyterian Church to the Dallas County courthouse. The group soon found themselves surrounded by 500 encouraging and cheering blacks and 100 menacing whites, screaming, "I think we ought to send them back to Birmingham" and "I think we ought to put them in the river right now," but they continued to the courthouse, where Ellwanger read the group's statement above the insults:

> We are horrified at the brutal way in which the police at times have attempted to break up peaceful assemblies and demonstrations by American citizens who are exercising their constitutional right to protest injustice. We are sickened by the totalitarian atmosphere of intimidation and fear officials have purposefully created and maintained to discourage lawful assembly and peaceful expression of grievances against the existing conditions. . . . We urge that the governor of our state and all elected officials—state and local—use their power and prestige to see to it that all open and subtle intimidation of persons seeking to register to vote be removed. . . . We finally plea for Federal help in terms of laws and registrars if these injustices are not removed forthrightly.[53]

After singing "America," the group returned to their starting point holding their placards, "Votelessness, Hopelessness" and "Decent Alabamians Detest Police Brutality," only to hear Selma's Lutheran clergyman, Rev. L. James Rongstad, greet them with a message, "We did not interfere in your problems and we do not need your interference in our problems."[54]

Ellwanger soon wrote for the publication of the Lutheran Human Relations Association an account of the incident and described his struggle. He wrestled with thoughts like, "You won't accomplish anything. . . . You're needlessly risking lives. . . . You're going to cause a division within the Church. . . . You will be called a communist," but when he thought of the black Lutheran pastors he knew and all the black people of Dallas County who "feared for their lives the moment they thought of registering to vote," he knew that he must lead the demonstration. He hoped the demonstration would "focus the eyes of the nation on injustices that should have been removed long ago."[55]

Ellwanger was no stranger to Selma, the town where he spent the major part of his youth. His father, also a Lutheran minister, was director of the Alabama Lutheran Academy and Junior College (for African Americans). Ellwanger's parents did not agree with their son's direct action approach, but Ellwanger made his move after much consideration and, finally, without hesitation. The group returned to Birmingham that evening, inspired by the response of their black spectators who sang "We Shall Overcome" at the courthouse steps. For some unknown reason, Sheriff Jim Clark's deputies did not arrest the white demonstrators, perhaps out of respect for Ellwanger's parents. (After the incident, a local beautician refused to allow Ellwanger's mother to enter her shop.)[56]

The next day, African Americans of Dallas County went ahead with plans for a fifty-mile walk from Selma to Montgomery in spite of Governor Wallace's warning that the march would not be permitted. On Sunday, March 7, the day following the petition of the white citizens, 525 African Americans left Brown's Chapel and attempted to cross the Edmund Pettus Bridge on their way to Montgomery, but as they reached the bridge, about 200 Alabama state troopers, joined by a posse of men on horses, advanced against them. The front line of the marchers was swept to the ground with tear gas and clubs, screaming. Seventeen protestors were hospitalized and forty more were given emergency treatment, among them John Lewis and Amelia Boynton, who both received concussions. Boynton lay half-conscious on the road as one trooper casually dropped a smoking gas grenade beside her. She lay there for ten minutes before troopers allowed ambulances over the bridge.[57]

White Episcopalian priest John Morris, returning to Atlanta from a meeting of the Episcopal Society for Cultural and Racial Unity (ESCRU), called his friend Andrew Young, assistant director of the SCLC, to inquire about the status of things in Selma. "I'm on my way there. Why don't you join me?" responded Young. They arrived just as the violence on the Edmund Pettus Bridge was beginning. Watching from their car, they could see what was happening. Returning to Brown's Chapel, they pitched in to help the wounded. "At some point," Morris related, "I told Andy that clergy from around the nation should be asked to come to Selma. He put me on the phone with Dr. King who was in Atlanta and I repeated the idea." For the next two days, Morris telephoned members of ESCRU, various denominational offices, and friends in Roman Catholic and Jewish organizations. King did the same, and on March 9 more than 450 white clergy and laity converged on Selma. All together about 1,500 people marched, five abreast, in spite of a federal court injunction and a plea against the march by President Johnson. The marchers were able to reach the bridge, but after the leaders knelt in prayer, they turned back. Violence was avoided except for one incident. That evening five white men attacked three Unitarian ministers after they had eaten dinner in a black restaurant. One of the three, Rev. James J. Reeb of Boston, thirty-eight years old, was struck on the back of the head and died after brain surgery. Rev. Reeb's death triggered national outrage and greater divisions among Selma's factions. As Julian Bond asserted, "No one in the black community questioned the value of Reeb's sacrifice, but they resented the silence that accompanied the ruthless murder of African American Jimmie Lee Jackson in nearby Marion by troopers" just nineteen days earlier.[58]

On the night of March 17, at a rally in Montgomery, King announced his plan for a five-day march from Selma to Montgomery. The next day Judge Frank M. Johnson Jr. ordered Governor Wallace and other Alabama officials to allow the peaceful mass march. The civil rights movement and its supporters had scored a victory. On Sunday, March 21, fourteen days after bloody Sunday, 3,200 people assembled, joyful and proud. An air of dignity and ceremony prevailed as participants, dressed in their Sunday best, had golden leis about their necks, sent from sympathizers in Hawaii. As they marched from Brown's Chapel, Martin Luther King Jr. led the way, flanked by African American dignitaries, and Cager Lee, grandfather of Jimmie Lee Jackson, who had been beaten the night Jackson was killed. No white people marched in the front line. As Rev. Randolph Taylor of the Presbyterian Church of the Pilgrims remarked, "That is how it should be; the black people are the leaders in this Movement and we white people are the followers."[59]

Of 3,200 marchers, 1,000 were white, and most of the white people were clergy. All major denominations were represented. Martin E. Marty, a Lutheran clergyman from the Lutheran Church–Missouri Synod and associate professor of modern church history at the University of Chicago Divinity School, went to Selma with ten of his colleagues and told a reporter for the *Vanguard* his reasons for going: "I rarely demonstrate. Most of my participation in the civil rights cause has been with my mouth or my pen. But there are times when one must put his body on the line." Rev. Joseph Ellwanger joined the marchers as they arrived in Montgomery with the contingent from Birmingham, disobeying the instructions from the presiding officer of the Southern District of the Lutheran Church–Missouri Synod that he should not demonstrate. In Montgomery, Rev. Raymond Davis of Our Redeemer Lutheran Church was told by the presiding officer of his American Lutheran Synod that he must keep out of harm's way during the Selma marches, but Davis opened his church, providing shelter for the participants. Davis recalled that during that time, if he went into any restaurant in Montgomery wearing his clerical collar, he would not be served.[60]

The Episcopalians were well represented with the presence of Presiding Bishop John Hines (native of South Carolina) and a huge contingent from the North, but some from the South as well. Rev. Morris mentioned that a Mrs. Heffernan, who had been forced out of McComb, Mississippi, for befriending Freedom Summer activists, walked beside him. Morris estimated that over 500 Episcopalian clergy and scores of laity participated in the Selma to Montgomery march, but when an attempt was made by an integrated group to worship at Selma's all-white St. Paul's Episcopal Church, they were denied entrance. When Suffragan Bishop of Michigan Rt. Rev. C. Kilmer Myers celebrated the Eucharist for an integrated group of over 150 clergy and laity at a sidewalk altar in front of Brown's AME chapel, it was considered a sacred moment, an "epiphany," by all those present.[61]

Morris reported that ESCRU had a staff in Selma during the entire march, helping in the orientation of new arrivals. One Episcopal priest spent a week driving trucks with supplies and then moved portable latrines during the march. A group of clergy of all faiths took care of food service and acted as "a buffer between walkers and guardsmen who weren't always the friendliest." An Episcopal priest from North Carolina helped out in communications, and many assisted in transporting marchers back to Selma, including Morris. After the Selma to Montgomery march, Morris sent an urgent plea to "All Bishops" for the continued involvement of churchpeople in Selma. He wrote, "The presence of visitors is necessary to hold down the harassment which has already started." He referred to an attempt to burn down Brown Chapel and several attempts to shoot local black people (no deaths or injuries were involved).[62]

Unfortunately, white seminarian Jonathan Daniels of Keene, New Hampshire, one of the Episcopalians who remained in the area under the auspices of ESCRU, was shot on his way to a grocery store in Hayneville, Alabama, by Tom Coleman, a part-time deputy sheriff of Lowndes County, and died instantly. Coleman was found not guilty by a grand jury. According to the historian Charles Eagles, federal authorities could have prosecuted Coleman "if his actions had involved a conspiracy." Morris and civil rights activists believed that Coleman was indeed involved in a conspiracy to have civil rights workers arrested and then released abruptly and killed, but the Justice Department and the Federal Bureau of Investigation (FBI) asserted they could find no evidence to substantiate the claim. As Eagles related in his book *Outside Agitator*, Coleman, when questioned, answered that he did what he had to do. "Someone had to stand up to the so-called priests who were trying to destroy this community." In 1990 Morris began efforts to include Daniels as a martyr in the church's calendar of Lesser Feasts and Fasts. In 1991, at the General Convention, his feast day was unanimously approved, and his martyrdom is remembered on August 14, 1965, the day of his arrest.[63]

Like Coleman, local white people considered outside clergy meddlesome intruders and publicity seekers who were disturbing their community, but Rev. Michael Allen, rector of St Mark's Episcopal Church in the Bowery, New York City, and one of Selma's marchers, told his congregation, "We went there to die: We did not go there to demonstrate. . . . There was death in the air of Brown's Memorial Chapel. It was the death that men might live, a beautiful death because men were bound together in holy fellowship."[64]

John Morris was one of the few southern Episcopalian priests who put himself in the forefront of the civil rights movement. On March 28, before the death of Daniels, Morris wrote an appraisal of Selma:

A number of good things can come out of Selma—Selma as an experience of national sin, national shame, and national repentance. But this regeneration must be truly national. President Johnson and Governor Wallace agree on this point . . . that racial injustice is an all-American problem, not simply a local or regional one. . . . The whole body of this nation suffers when one group or segment of it suffers. The white man cannot truly prosper at the expense of the colored man, or the rich at the expense of the poor.[65]

Some notables from the northern Presbyterian Church (PCUSA) attended the march, but the southern Presbyterians (PCUS) were the distinguished participants, many at the risk of their careers. Rachel Henderlite, the first woman ordained as a minister in the southern Presbyterian Church, explained why she went: "The decision was made for me when I projected myself ten years into the future, and standing there looking back on March 25, 1965, asked myself the question, 'Where were you when concerned people were marching for justice and freedom?' I found I could not say in answer to that question, 'I was in my office,' so I went." It was said of Rev. Henderlite that she acted on her belief "that the Gospel is relevant in areas where many have feared to tread."[66]

The *Presbyterian Survey*, the official periodical of the southern Presbyterian Church, listed the names of southern Presbyterian ministers, black and white, who attended the Selma march (in addition to Rev. Henderlite): Ernest Trice Thompson, former moderator of the General Assembly; James L. Mays of the Union Theological Seminary in Virginia; Malcolm Calhoun of Winston Salem, North Carolina, head of the Board of Christian Education; Rev. Irvin Elligan, Calhoun's associate; Rev. J. Randolph Taylor, pastor of the Church of the Pilgrims, Washington, DC; and Rev. Richard B. Hardie of the Westover Hills Presbyterian Church, Little Rock, Arkansas. The *Survey* did not include *all* the names of white pastors of southern churches who attended, as it would have meant their immediate dismissal, as the following published letter indicated: "I hope that our Presbyterian US ministers were there to preach the gospel and not to demonstrate."[67]

Two southern white Baptists from South Carolina also distinguished themselves by joining the march: Rev. T. C. Smith (1915–2011), born in Pineville, Louisiana, and a professor at Furman University, who helped transport marchers, and Martin England (1901–1989), born in Seneca, South Carolina; cofounder of Koinonia Farm in Americus, Georgia; and a Baptist missionary. Neither was a pastor of a church at the time, and they feared no retaliation.[68]

The presence of white people in the march may not have changed the hearts of segregationists or deterred hecklers along the way, but to black people it was a sign of encouragement and solidarity, as Rev. Henderlite wrote: "We knew why we marched when we saw the old people standing in front of their houses or waving from their porches.... We knew why we marched when I held the hand of a college student who was almost tongue-tied, because he had been brought up to hate all white people." Rev. Newton noted early in the dilemma that the white people of Selma could have avoided the violence, the notoriety, and the influx of outsiders had they only been willing to make concessions.[69]

Although segregationists condemned outsiders for intruding into Selma's problems, Dallas Blanchard, member of the Alabama–West Florida Methodist Conference, was glad they came: "They marched because we could not." Fred Reese of the South Carolina Methodist Conference was another southern white minister who would have liked to have marched but knew that if he went, it would have meant immediate dismissal from his church.[70]

The abortive bridge crossing, the notoriety, and the subsequent marches seemed to have changed Selma forever. According to Stephen L. Longenecker, "White moderates slowly became more visible, and the heavy-handed methods of the die-hards were increasingly discredited and seen as ineffective. Perhaps most important, blacks were registering to vote, which would provide them with unprecedented leverage to have an impact on Selma's power structure."[71]

Today in Selma there is a voting rights museum commemorating all the Selma marches; there is still a white majority, but blacks hold more positions in city government than in 1979. On the surface, peace prevails. Each year on a Sunday early in March, participants, black and white, gather to commemorate Bloody Sunday as they walk across the Edmund Pettus Bridge with the cooperation of state troopers and city and state officials. Joseph Ellwanger recently wrote, "I am profoundly encouraged by the accomplishments of the Civil Rights Movement. To now behold the changes that have occurred in the South is gratifying, I would even use the word 'awesome.' To go back to Selma, as I did in 2005, and to see all of the public places racially integrated, from consumer to paid staff, and to see black and white elected officials at every level is a vivid reminder that there is amazing power in people of faith coming together, focusing on specific justice goals, demonstrating nonviolently and sacrificially, making a clear call for change and speaking truth without fear to the power structure."[72]

◆   ◆   ◆

Opposite the magnificent falls of the Ohio River, on the south side, sits Louisville, so named for King Louis XVI of France, who aided Americans in the rebellion against Great Britain. With soil not conducive to farming, Louisville soon became an important industrial and transportation center and the most important city in Kentucky. Before the Civil War, it was a place where runaway

slaves gathered to make the treacherous journey across the rapids to freedom, and where, as free people, they came to find employment opportunities.
After the Civil War, the population swelled with Irish, German, and Jewish
immigrants, until by the time of the civil rights movement, it reached almost
350,000, with African Americans making up no more than 15 percent of the
total, but a very active and well-informed minority.[73]

The public schools were quickly desegregated in 1956 by the firm hand of
Superintendent Omer Carmichael, and blacks had been attending the University of Louisville since 1950. By 1963 two blacks served on the Board of
Aldermen, the municipal legislature. A black police officer commanded white
policemen at the Parke station, and the first black to play football for the University of Louisville was an assistant to the mayor and a law school student,
but according to Lyman Johnson, president of the Louisville Chapter of the
NAACP and longtime civil rights activist, by 1963 public schools had resegre-
gated. Affluent white families had moved to the suburbs, and discrimination
was widespread in downtown businesses and restaurants. Johnson declared,
"Everything the black people have won has been won . . . not by violence, but
by insistence. I was ready to bring out my people for a demonstration. . . . I
told the Mayor we would come marching on Saturday, and he said 'Could you
hold off till Tuesday; that's when the Board of Aldermen meets?' We held it off,
and that Tuesday, August 10, 1963, the aldermen passed an anti-bias ordinance
applying to all businesses serving the public, the first of its kind in any major
southern city." Governor Bert Combs of Kentucky extended the ordinance
by executive order to include the entire state. The problem of discrimination
in public accommodations seemed to have ended, but, according to William
Peeples of the *New Republic* magazine, "This proved to be the grand illusion
of 1963."[74]

The Louisville ordinance and the governor's executive order were never
enforced. During the 1963 gubernatorial campaign, Republican candidate
Louie B. Nunn conducted a blatantly segregationist campaign but lost the
election to Edward Breathitt, a Democrat who promised black voters to enact
the law. On a rainy day in March 1964, 10,000 Kentuckians, black and white,
assembled in front of the state capitol in Frankfort to urge passage of an open
public accommodations bill. They were led by Martin Luther King Jr., Jackie
Robinson, Ralph Abernathy, and many other African American activists.
Among the marchers was the white Episcopal bishop of Kentucky, Charles
Gresham Marmion (1905–2000), born in Houston, Texas. While serving a
parish in Texas in 1935, Marmion attempted to convince a mob not to lynch
two black teen-age boys accused of the rape and murder of a white girl, but
the lynching continued as planned. He went to Washington, DC, during the
1930s and 1940s to lobby for an antilynching law, but such a law never passed.

During the 1960s, although in a difficult position, he integrated Episcopal Church summer camps, marched in Louisville for desegregated businesses, and urged his communicants to support the civil rights movement. Shortly before his death in 2000, he told a newspaper reporter, "A lot of my people disagreed with me, but they knew where I stood."[75]

Despite all efforts, the public accommodations bill failed to make it out of committee. In protest, twenty-three of the marchers decided to have a sit-in and fast during the final week of the regular legislative session. Rev. Grayson Tucker (1924–2013), born in Laurel, Mississippi, and serving at the time as pastor to two black churches and as director of the two black community centers, became the only white minister in the group to participate. He recalled, "We were trained in techniques of passive resistance and brought books to help us pass the time. We slept on the floor or in the cushioned seats of the gallery, refusing all food, but drinking plenty of water. Generally nobody bothered us, although two of our members fainted and had to leave." Despite all efforts, the House rejected the bill for a second time before its adjournment. According to Tucker, the bill finally became law after passage of the federal Civil Rights Act of 1964, "not because of our efforts, but because the state did not want Washington interfering in Kentucky's right to enforce the new law." Finally, all hotels, restaurants, and public businesses were opened to African Americans.[76]

Tucker became sympathetic to the plight of African Americans while a student at the Presbyterian Theological Seminary. He worked at what was then called the John Little Presbyterian Mission, which included two black churches, Grace Presbyterian (PCUS) and Hope Presbyterian (PCUSA), and two community centers. The centers provided needed services to the black community, everything from well-baby clinics to activities for older adults. In 1954 he was called to the pastorate of all-white Bardstown Road Presbyterian Church (PCUS) but continued serving the John Little Mission. Finding the needs of the black community enormous, he decided in 1962 to resign his pastorate at the all-white church and accept a call to serve as pastor to the two black churches. The goal of the two churches was to unite into one church. With the support of church leaders and board members, the new church became a "union church" called Grace-Hope, with 300 black members and Tucker as pastor. The two community centers became the Presbyterian Community Center, with Tucker as director. It was at that time that he engaged in the sit-in, something other white ministers would not do. In 1966 Tucker joined the faculty of the Presbyterian Theological Seminary but remained determined to fight segregation after he and a black Scout leader were refused a table at a segregated restaurant in Louisville's east end.[77]

◆ ◆ ◆

The main problem for African Americans living in Louisville remained: there was no decent affordable housing. Black people were confined to living in the central section of town in an impoverished neighborhood, or in the West End, formerly all-white but rapidly changing.[78]

Demonstrations and street blockages in opposition to restrictive housing began on April 11, 1967, when 350 people led by comedian Dick Gregory and the SCLC's Rev. A. D. Williams King, brother of Martin Luther King Jr., marched from city hall to one of the city's busiest intersections at Broadway and Fourth Street and sat down, immobile, blocking traffic, like the Chapel Hill demonstrators. At one point Gregory told groups of black youth, "If the city has still refused to pass the open housing measure by Derby Day [May 6], it may be necessary for us to lie down on the track in front of the horses to keep those out-of-town folks from enjoying a city we can't even enjoy ourselves." On May 3 twenty protestors were arrested for demonstrating in front of Churchill Downs. One thousand police and National Guardsmen patrolled the tracks. On May 6 the Kentucky Derby was run without incident as open-housing leaders canceled demonstrations as an act of "good faith." After Derby Day, the president of the NAACP urged black families to refuse to be moved from urban renewal areas or from areas where highways were being built unless they were offered homes in white neighborhoods. Marches continued every night throughout white residential sections and continued in spite of restrictive injunctions.[79]

Between April 11 and May 9, 1967, over 300 people were arrested, among them white ministers George Edwards, Thomas Moffett, and three children of Rev. Gilbert Schroerlucke. On October 14 a federal three-judge panel voided six laws used against open-housing demonstrators, and on December 13 the city government passed the open-housing ordinance without the mayor's signature. According to Thomas Moffett, it was "an ordinance never enforced."[80]

Rev. Moffett was not born in the South but may be considered an adopted southerner. He was born in 1924 in Korea to missionary parents. After his education at Princeton Theological Seminary, ten years in three pastorates in West Virginia, and six years as an associate pastor in an integrated mission church in Kansas City, Missouri, he arrived in Louisville to serve as pastor to New Covenant Presbyterian Church (PCUSA) at the beginning of the open housing demonstrations. New Covenant was a church in the West End neighborhood that was in the later stages of "block breaking," whereby agents would sell one house to a black family, then make quick profits from frightened white people who bought homes elsewhere and from African Americans who paid inflated prices for houses being abandoned. By the time Moffett arrived, the West End was becoming black. Moffett welcomed the opportunity to be in an integrated church and struggled to minister equally to both races, but admitted that he may have been more solicitous to blacks than whites because many of the whites soon left the church.[81]

Open housing was the kind of issue that appealed to Moffett, and he marched along with other pastors (black and white), seminary professors, Roman Catholic nuns, and groups of liberal-minded citizens. He tried to convince his congregation to join him. One black member agreed, but others, white and black, would not participate, feeling it was undignified. Moffett was also asked to offer his church for rallies but decided not to approach the governing session, knowing it would not be approved. In time, he began to think he could work better for Christ as a member of a church rather than as a pastor. Moffett resigned his pastorate, preferring to no longer be called Reverend. He returned to school to study accounting and took a job at the Community Health Center in the West End, not far from the church he once served. He bought a small apartment in the same neighborhood and remains one of the few white people living in an African American neighborhood. He joined the black Grace-Hope Presbyterian Church in downtown Louisville, where white Rev. Grayson Tucker was the pastor. After retiring from the Health Center in 1994, Moffett spent nearly forty hours a week working for the Kentucky Alliance Against Racial and Political Repression, an organization established in 1976 by Carl and Anne Braden, liberal white activists in Louisville. Moffett maintained their books and advocated on issues of affirmative action, increased minimum wage, police reform, elimination of the death penalty, and aid for local victims of injustice.[82]

Moffett may not have been able to summon the New Covenant members to walk with him, but the demonstrations directed him to greater service to humanity. Somewhat disillusioned, he commented, "If churches were willing, they could bring about great changes, but it's hard to get them to move as a group on social issues. For the last thirty years I have tried to encourage as many people as possible in my church to be involved, either directly or through the Kentucky Alliance. I believe I am more effective now than I was as a pastor."[83]

◆ ◆ ◆

Rev. George Edwards (1920–2010), born in Memphis, Tennessee, described himself as hyper-religious: "Sunday school, morning worship, evening worship, preceded or followed by youth fellowship, and Wednesday night prayer meeting (devoted mainly to Bible study)." He admitted that he was not yet educated enough to choose sides in the liberal versus conservative debate. He read *The Meaning of Faith* and *The Meaning of Prayer* by Harry Emerson Fosdick, exponent of the social gospel, in his church's library and, with equal gusto, the writings of the conservative Presbyterian J. G. Machen, but the social gospel finally won out and led him to the Presbyterian Theological Seminary in Louisville.[84]

Edwards remembered quite well the difficulties he had in trying to be a church pastor. Married with a baby on the way, he welcomed an interview to serve a Presbyterian church in Trenton, in the western and very conservative part of Tennessee. The members of the selection committee indicated their desire to expand the church's membership. "Yes," he agreed. "I notice that you have a shoe factory here. Most of your members seem to come from the administration and management posts. I don't see why you don't have some rank and file folks here who do production work. You are not casting a wide enough net." The response was not noticeably negative, so Edwards decided to carry the topic a bit further. "Blacks," he submitted, "have their own churches and worship traditions, but some, in time, would probably find their religious home in Presbyterianism if we offered them a cordial welcome." The response was a long period of total silence, until one gentleman responded, "Well, Mr. Edwards, I guess we won't be taking you to look at the manse." The experience tarnished Edwards's expectations for serving as a pastor. He decided to accept the offer of a scholarship to study for a doctorate at the Graduate School of Religion at Duke University. While at Duke, he served several small Presbyterian churches in North Carolina (1951–1956). At a church in Pittsboro, he preached a sermon based on a verse from the Acts of the Apostles: "God hath made of one blood all nations of men for to dwell on all the earth." Edwards then explained to his congregation that it was erroneous to suggest that the blood of one race was different from that of another race and that blood transfusions should be available to all people regardless of race. The sermon was not well received. One elderly man approached him at the end of the service with a pointed finger, "It ain't in the blood, preacher, it's in the genes."[85]

From then on Edwards and his wife were careful to avoid adversarial relationships with members of their congregations. In 1958 he welcomed his opportunity to teach New Testament studies at his alma mater, the Louisville Presbyterian Seminary, and to follow more actively his passion for racial justice. He was one of twenty who were arrested for demonstrating with comedian Dick Gregory in front of Churchill Downs. Black student demonstrators went limp and had to be carried into the police wagon, but Edwards walked in. According to Edwards, the jail cells were just as horrible in Louisville as in Mississippi and Alabama: "We were all put into one cell with no mattresses on the steel cots. The jailors claimed that the mattresses would be torn apart." Jailed on other occasions, Edwards mentioned that members of the Klan were on the police force and supported the efforts of real estate brokers and banks to keep housing segregated, but black leaders were strong in the city, had good

lawyers, and were able to get prisoners released the next day. Many white ministers made efforts to help African American activists in Louisville, but, according to Edwards, "It hardly made a dent in changing the housing situation."[86]

The civil rights movement in Louisville transformed Edwards and his
wife, Jean. They became lifelong activists and with prayer, consistency, and
tenacity continued for over forty years to fight for issues of peace and social
justice. In 1970 Edwards and Jean organized the Louisville chapter of the Fellowship of Reconciliation (FOR), a New York–based peace and social justice
organization formed in 1915. From FOR came the Congress of Racial Equality
(CORE) in 1942. A FOR banner decorates the front entrance to the Edwards
home and asks for aid for their latest protégé, William Thomas Gregory, who
was imprisoned for rape in 1993 and served eight years in prison for a crime he
did not commit. Edwards and Jean raised $5,000 for DNA testing of a strand
of hair that cleared Gregory of all charges. He was the first person in Kentucky
ever released from prison solely on the basis of mitochondrial DNA testing, a
technology that was not available at the time he was sentenced to seventy years
in prison. George and Jean never met Gregory before his release, but their
efforts gave him new life. Gregory acclaimed, "They have helped me as if I were
their son. I'm a black dude, but they treat me like a human being instead of a
black person, purple, green, whatever. And they treat all people that way, not
only me. I love those two people with all my heart."[87]

◆　◆　◆

In 1967, 113 people were jailed during protest marches, among them the three
oldest children of white Methodist minister Gilbert Schroerlucke. Schroerlucke commented, "It remains a mystery to me as to why I was never arrested.
The police chief chose those to arrest and I was never chosen. The jailing of my
son and two daughters did not last long and their names were later stricken
from the books." Schroerlucke and his three oldest children participated in
most of the marches, even to the point of sitting down across the intersection
of Broadway and Fourth Street.[88]

Schroerlucke, born in 1923 in Jefferson County, Kentucky, grew up on a
farm in an ultraconservative family. He knew no African Americans, but he is
certain that if any black person ever came to his house at mealtime they would
have been served outside. He knows of no reason why he became liberal on
the racial question: "I guess I was always somewhat of a rebel. During my high
school years, I would go into Louisville and ride the buses. Although there was
no segregation, there was prejudice. Blacks would sit across the back and along
the side seats. If a black person was sitting next to a window and there was an
empty seat next to that person, whites would rather stand up than sit down,

but I would deliberately sit there because I felt compassion for those black people who were being shunned." He attributed much of his transformation to the education he received at Candler School of Theology at Emory University in Georgia, where such progressive professors as Malcolm Dewey took students regularly to concerts at the black colleges in Atlanta, and Boone M. Bowen urged his students to see the Book of Ruth as written by someone who asked, "How do you treat the person who is different?"[89]

He became a member of the Louisville Methodist Conference in 1953, showing signs of activism early in his career. It did not take much to antagonize his constituents. At the first church he served, he invited a black friend to sing at an evening service, and a few people left the church. In 1959 he was transferred to Cadiz in western Kentucky, where segregation was deeply entrenched, and again antagonized his congregation by inviting a black pastor to preach at a Sunday evening service. From Cadiz, he returned to Louisville to serve a large white church, when his district superintendent asked if he would be willing to move to the West Broadway Methodist Church in a neighborhood that was rapidly changing from white to black. After much prayer and discussion, the Schroerluckes decided that this would be the godly thing to do, and in 1966, with five children ranging in age from six months to seventeen years, they relocated to West Louisville from where white people were fleeing as quickly as possible. Could he become pastor of a black church? Schroerlucke knew that urban Methodist churches were closing throughout the nation because of white flight. He wondered if he could succeed where others had failed, but he made a personal declaration at the altar: "I promised God that I would give it the best that I had. I wanted the Methodist Church to survive, but only if it could survive as an authentic example of the body of Christ." Schroerlucke did his best and served the church for seventeen years, developing extensive activities for children and youth: piano lessons, tutoring, cooking, cake decorating, physical fitness, karate, movies, personal charm, street paint-ins, amateur musical programs, bicycle trips, and weekly teen dances. During the summer, as many as 1,000 people attended the programs, including his own five children, something his white associates could not understand. Again and again they asked, "Do you want your daughter to marry a black?" "You know I don't control who my daughters marry," he replied and added, "They have done marvelously well."[90]

Troubles developed for Schroerlucke in 1972 when black activist Rev. Ben Chavis and nine others were sentenced to thirty-four years in prison for allegedly fire-bombing property and conspiring to assault emergency personnel during racial disorders in Wilmington, North Carolina. A group from Louisville arranged for Angela Davis, a popular civil rights leader who happened to be a member of the Communist Party, to speak at a black Catholic church in the West End, but the local archbishop gave orders against it. Schroerlucke was approached and responded, "I saw it as just another ministry the church could render. My local church leaders gave their approval and we announced that the meeting would be held at our church." His decision had severe repercussions: "All hell broke loose. We received hundreds and hundreds of calls every day from Methodists, from Conference members, from everywhere." Schroelucke was about to "cave in under pressure" when he received inspiration from a downtown meeting of the planning committee: "When I saw people who had sacrificed and given much for human rights and had stood tall against the KKK and white racists, I soon became ashamed of my fear. I realized that if I had any faith at all, and if my commitment meant anything to me or to anyone else, there was no way I could renege on my word."[91]

The meeting with Angela Davis at West Broadway Methodist Church attracted over 800 people, with many standing outside at the windows. Schroelucke stated, "It was a great event with a lot of publicity and I'm not sorry I did it, but the Methodist Conference threatened to cut off my salary and considered me a traitor. The result was that I collapsed and had to be hospitalized, but the congregation wanted me back and I stayed at the church for seven more years with the financial support of the Conference." Schroerlucke's wife, Bettye, with a master's degree in education, started teaching in the Louisville school system, and the family of two adults and five children was able to survive. At the end of seven years, the bishop asked Schroerlucke to move to the western part of the state. Schroerlucke finally decided, at the age of sixty, to retire: "I wasn't going to ask my wife to give up her job. She had just begun teaching and was enjoying it." The Schroerluckes purchased a small house near the West End, finally a home of their own, and remained in Louisville, where he continued to be active in social reform issues. In his "Last Will and Testament . . . to the Louisville Conference," Schroerlucke wrote, "To my friends at West Broadway: Thanks for accepting and loving me and my family. You have enriched our lives with wealth more precious than fine jewels."[92]

Louisville, termed the "bridge city" between the North and South by Rev. Tucker, seemed to contain a bridge for black and white people to walk across during the years of the civil rights movement. Louisville never experienced the kind of violence that was raging in America's inner cities the very same year as the open housing demonstrations (1967). According to Rev. Edwards, capable black leaders, with the help of white liberal-minded citizens, were successful in finally establishing the legal right of blacks to purchase homes in any neighborhood in Louisville.[93]

Some thirty years later, during the 1990s, Rev. Louis Coleman complained, "Very few, if any, Kentucky cities have black mayors while such cities as Birmingham, Atlanta, and Jackson have black mayors, state senators, police chiefs, and tenured university professors. These positions are still unavailable to blacks in Kentucky." But as Thomas Moffett commented in 2012, "Of the positions named by Coleman as still closed to blacks in Louisville, only the office of mayor has still eluded them. We have had two black state senators, one black police chief, and quite a few black tenured university professors. In fact, the University of Louisville has outpaced a great many other well-known universities in its recruitment of black professors."[94]

◆ ◆ ◆

Southern white ministers risked everything to attend the March on Washington. The march transformed Revs. Taylor and Pritchett and many others. Southern white ministers demonstrated to remove all traces of segregation in business establishments in Chapel Hill, for voting rights in Selma (although they were a minority among outsiders), and against restrictive housing practices in Louisville. Revs. Jones and Seymour worked hard to organize nonviolent protest, but the faction led by Baker, Cusick, and Dunne, and spiritually supported by Fr. Parker, moved the protest to radical dimensions that were never attempted in other locations. In Selma, the efforts of southern white ministers such as Joseph Ellwanger and John Morris helped increase pressure on the federal government to pass the Voting Rights Act of 1965. In Louisville, many concerned white ministers made efforts to bring about a more open society, but they could do little to change the discriminatory practices of white real estate brokers and homeowners.

Protest movements varied according to locations, and the responses of the segregationists also differed. Alabama once again lived up to its reputation as a police state where demonstrators could not walk safely across a bridge, no less lie down across a major thoroughfare. The situation in Selma contrasted sharply with its faraway neighbors, North Carolina and Kentucky. Baker, Cusick, and Dunne might have been killed in Alabama. Their actions were much more daring and confrontational than those of Jimmy Lee Jackson, who was murdered for participation in a small civil rights march and for striking a policeman who attacked his mother, or of white participant Viola Liuzzo, a mother of five from Detroit, who was killed by the Klan as she transported marchers back and forth between Montgomery and Selma.[95]

In Chapel Hill and Louisville, white ministers were free to support demonstrations with minimal condemnation. If they were arrested, they were released the next day. In Selma, no local white minister or white person would dare to march. In Louisville, Gilbert Schroerlucke got into trouble with his Methodist Conference, not because of his marching, but because he allowed Communist sympathizer Angela Davis to speak at his church; yet many white people attended the event, including Rev. George Edwards. In some places, fear of Communism was greater than fear of integration. The right to vote had already been attained by black people in Chapel Hill and Louisville, but in Selma it took a catastrophe, the federal government, and throngs of outsiders to bring about change. The extreme measures in Chapel Hill never produced the desired results, nor did the constant marching by Louisville's activists. There again, change came about because of federal government action, but one could not say that the ministers' efforts were in vain. Clarence Parker and Joseph Ellwanger both accompanied Martin Luther King Jr. with groups of pastors, rabbis, ministers, and priests from across the nation to urge President Lyndon B. Johnson to approve civil rights legislation, nor could Johnson ignore the enormity of participation by white ministers in the Selma to Montgomery march.

As a result of the March on Washington and the efforts of Randolph Taylor, joining the civil rights movement became a worthy cause for many southern white Presbyterian ministers. The spirit was contagious. The ministers who marched in Chapel Hill and Louisville were not new to the cause of racial justice. They had worked for school desegregation and to open church doors to African Americans; they preached sermons to end racial injustice; and Charles Jones had lost his position as a Presbyterian minister because he came to the aid of the Freedom Riders.

A group of African American students walking to the newly integrated Clinton High School in Anderson County, Tennessee. Reporters and photographers are on the scene. Rev. Paul Turner, pastor of the First Baptist Church, is in the back row to the far right. He was severely beaten on his way home. *Knoxville Journal*, 1956.

Before he left Little Rock to become an assistant pastor of a Presbyterian church in Huntington, West Virginia, Rev. Dunbar Ogden visited Daisy Bates, state president of the NAACP and counselor to the nine students who desegregated Central High School in Little Rock. "I'm sorry I got you into this," she said to Rev. Ogden. "Don't feel sorry," he replied. "If I had to do it all over again, I would."

Bishop Duncan Montgomery Gray Jr. in his vestments, 2001. Gray served as seventh bishop of the Episcopal Diocese of Mississippi from 1974 to 1993. He served as rector of St. Peter's Church in Oxford and St. Paul's Church in Meridian during the critical years of the civil rights movement, and bravely spoke for an end to racial injustice and segregation. He is famous for attempting to quell the violence when James Meredith entered the University of Mississippi in 1962. Courtesy of Duncan Montgomery Gray Jr.

Rev. Marion A. Boggs, picking cotton in Arkansas, 1925. As pastor of Second Presbyterian Church, Little Rock, Arkansas, during the Little Rock school crisis of 1957, Rev. Boggs publicly advocated school integration and incurred ostracism from many Presbyterians. His church held integrated church services and fellowship meals with all-black Allison Memorial Presbyterian Church in spite of harassing phone calls and bomb threats. Marion A. Boggs Photo Collection, Columbia Theological Seminary, Decatur, Georgia.

A feeling of sadness is evident on the faces of participants in a summer-long voter-education project in segregated Warrenton, North Carolina, 1963, sponsored by the American Friends Service Committee. From left to right: Rev. Charles Webster, Glenda Gaspard, Liz Butter, and Gavin Wright. Payne Masuku, foreground. After being dismissed from the First Baptist Church of Clemson, South Carolina, Rev. Webster became a leader in the project. The other leader, Gavin Wright, became a professor of American economic history at Stanford University and author of *Sharing the Prize: The Economics of the Civil Rights Revolution in the American South*. Courtesy of Gavin Wright, David Spence, and Judith Bell Vaughan, *A Quiet Little Civil Rights Project*, Blog.com, 2013. Photo by Judy Howard.

The carpool vehicles used during the Montgomery Bus Boycott, parked in the lot of Trinity Lutheran Church, Robert S. Graetz, pastor. Because of his efforts, he was burned in effigy. Courtesy of Robert S. Graetz.

Secretly known as the "Core," progressive southern white ministers, members of the Alabama–West Florida Methodist Conference, worked for racial justice and integration during the 1950s and 1960s. Courtesy of the Archives of Huntingdon College, Montgomery, Alabama.

Andrew Turnipseed

Charles Prestwood

Dallas Blanchard

Donald Collins

Ennis Sellers

Floyd Enfinger

Powers McLeod

Thomas L. Butts

Rev. Dallas A. Blanchard and Rev. Joseph H. Griggs, copastors of Toulminville–Warren Street Methodist Church. In 1965 Revs. Blanchard and Griggs formed the first integrated Methodist church in Alabama, abandoned by most of the white members. Rev. Briggs remained at Toulminville–Warren Street Church until 1968, when he was appointed district superintendent of the Tuskegee District. After the separated Alabama Methodist Conferences merged, he became minister of St. Paul's United Methodist Church in Birmingham. After much harassment, Rev. Blanchard went on to become a professor of sociology at the University of West Florida in Pensacola. Courtesy of Edwena Seals, historian, Toulminville–Warren Street Methodist Church.

Rev. John Morris, compiler of *South Carolinians Speak*, an open forum on school desegregation; organizer of the activist Episcopal Society for Cultural and Racial Unity; leader of the Prayer Pilgrimage of 1961; one of the organizers of the Selma to Montgomery voting rights march of 1965 and the Southwide Conference of Black and White Elected Officials, 1968, held at the Dinkler Plaza Hotel, Atlanta, where in 1962, African American Ralph Bunche was denied a room. Courtesy of the Archives of the Episcopal Church, USA.

Trusties carry Rev. Ed King, Tougaloo College chaplain, to the paddy wagon after his arrest for protesting in front of the post office in Jackson, Mississippi, May 30, 1963. (AP Photo/Bill Hudson)

As pastor of the Church of the Pilgrims in Washington, DC, Rev. Dr. J. Randolph Taylor opened his sanctuary and fellowship hall to participants in the March on Washington, August 1963. In 1968 he became pastor of Central Presbyterian Church in Atlanta, as inner-city riots raged. Central provided many services to the city's poor. In 1985 Taylor became president of San Francisco Theological Seminary until his retirement in 1994. Courtesy of the Presbyterian Historical Society/the National Archives of the PCUSA.

Rev. Al Price, age twenty-three, preaching at Capitol Street Church of Christ, Jackson, Mississippi, that all people are welcome at the church regardless of race, 1964. Courtesy of Al Price.

Forced out of the First Presbyterian Church of Chapel Hill by the North Carolina Orange Presbytery, Rev. Charles M. Jones, civil rights activist, and his followers organized the nondenominational Community Church of Chapel Hill in 1961. Courtesy of Bettie Jones Bradford.

Fr. Clarence Parker, retired Episcopal priest, leading a prayer vigil in front of the city jail in Chapel Hill, North Carolina, for the release of prisoners who protested against segregated businesses in Chapel Hill, December 22, 1963. John Ehle Papers, Southern Historical Collection, Wilson Library, University of North Carolina at Chapel Hill.

A young Rev. W. W. Finlator photographed at the lectern of Pullen Memorial Baptist Church, Raleigh, North Carolina, 1956. He preached his conscience at Pullen for twenty-six years until his forced retirement. (Photo from the Pullen archives.)

At a special crisis session of the General Convention held at the University of Notre Dame in South Bend, Indiana, August 31, 1969, presiding bishop of the Episcopal Church, John Elbridge Hines, called for programs of support for those living in inner-city poverty. Some at the session demanded his resignation, but he asked those present to "dissolve their sharpness into one-ness. . . . No one with humility could receive the sacrament of the broken body and poured blood of Christ while anyone is denied access to decent housing and jobs and the right to self-determination." Courtesy of The Archives of the Episcopal Church, USA.

Joseph "Bo" Johnson and Clarence Jordan harvesting cotton, corn, and muscadines, along with the usual garden vegetables, during the 1950s. Johnson
was the first African American to join the common community at Koinonia. He
worked on the farm for several years after the death of his father, Candy Johnson, a sharecropper on the farm. Courtesy of Amanda Moore, Koinonia Farm
Archives.

Clarence Jordan and Peanuts at Koinonia
Farm, 1963. Peanuts (and later pecans) were
the major crops at Koinonia Farm. These
products were sent by mail order to customers because of violent attacks on the farm's
roadside stand in 1963. Courtesy of Amanda
Moore, Koinonia Farm Archives.

The annual meeting of the integrated and interdenominational South Carolina Christian Action Council (SCCAC) January 20,
2000. Left to right: Eva Elder, first woman board president of the SCCAC, 1973–74; Rev. Paul C. Jersild, Lutheran Theological
Southern Seminary, Columbia, South Carolina; Rev. Nate McMillan, Petra Ministries International, Orangeburg, South Carolina;
Rev. Gene Sparks, Cooperative Baptist Fellowship, Columbia, South Carolina; Rev. Amanda Jones, Disciples of Christ minister,
Columbia, South Carolina. Photo by author.

Rev. George William Floyd and his wife, Sarah Elizabeth. Floyd was pastor of Sylacauga Church of Christ, Sylacauga, Alabama, in 1963. He spoke passionately against injustice and was asked to resign his pastorate. Courtesy of Bill Floyd.

Rev. Al Price attending the February 2013 commemoration of the Selma to Montgomery march. Some members of his church did not approve. Courtesy of Al Price.

Will Campbell at his writing cabin, Mt. Juliet, Tennessee, 1995. His famous books are *Brother to a Dragonfly* (his memoir), *And Also with You* (about Bishop Duncan Montgomery Gray), and *Providence* (about Providence Cooperative Farm, Mississippi). Photo by Roy Lechtreck.

=== 5 ===

NEW DIRECTIONS

New Leaders, Riots, Voices of Southern White Ministers,
the Assassination of Martin Luther King Jr.,
and a Demand for Reparations

> Racial injustice is an all-American problem, not simply a local or regional
> one.... The whole body of this nation suffers when one group or segment
> of it suffers. The white man cannot truly prosper at the expense of the
> colored man, or the rich at the expense of the poor.
> —REV. JOHN BURNETT MORRIS, "Good Out of Selma," *The Living Church,*
> March 28, 1965

In the aftermath of the bombing of the Sixteenth Street Baptist Church in
Birmingham, Alabama, the rejection of the Mississippi Freedom Democratic
Party at the Democratic National Convention in 1964, the attack on peaceful
demonstrators in Selma in 1965, the shooting of James Meredith as he marched
through Mississippi in 1966, and the continuous arrests, torture, and murder
of civil rights activists, the spark that ignited the nonviolent civil rights movement was burning out. New leaders began moving black people in revolutionary directions. The result was rioting and violence.

New Leaders

Malcolm X (1925–1965), released from prison in 1963, began his diatribe
against the nonviolent civil rights movement: "The only revolution in which
the goal is loving your enemy is the Negro Revolution. It's the only revolution
in which the goal is a desegregated lunch counter, a desegregated theater, a
desegregated park, and a desegregated public toilet.... That's no revolution!"
Having heard many of his speeches on tape, Cleveland Sellers of the Student

Nonviolent Coordinating Committee (SNCC) became Malcolm X's advocate and invited Malcolm to Selma as a way to encourage students to demonstrate. Malcolm told students in Selma that they could bring a change to their conditions only by direct action, but he did not live long enough to witness the Selma march.[1] His assassination early in 1965 brought an end to his strident rhetoric. Others such as Stokely Carmichael, the Black Panthers, and James Forman continued his incendiary messages.

Riots

Beginning in 1964 in Harlem (New York City), young blacks took action against white police officers and others they considered their oppressors. They threw rocks, broke windows, looted stores and factories, and set fires with gasoline-filled bottles. One of the worst riots took place in the Watts section of Los Angeles in 1965. After five days of destruction, the final death toll was thirty-three. The number of injured treated at the hospitals was 874, and the number of arrests was 2,992. The amount of fire damage was estimated to be near $200 million.[2]

Most of the riots occurred in crowded northern ghettoes, but in 1966 the turbulence moved to Atlanta and followed a pattern similar to all riots, beginning with violent, often-unmerited police action. When police shot and seriously wounded a black youth fleeing from arrest as a suspected car thief, twenty-five-year-old Stokely Carmichael of SNCC rushed to the scene and allegedly told the mob, "We're going to tear this place apart." Carmichael was arrested and placed in solitary confinement at $10,000 bond. At one point fifty-five-year-old Mayor Ivan Allen Jr. walked into the middle of the angry crowd and told them, "This is no way to solve a problem." He asked them to join him at the Atlanta Stadium and talk about peace, but they did not respond. Instead, Allen was knocked down, his car rocked, and young blacks screamed, "White Devil," "Black Power." When the police began firing bullets over their heads and tear gas directly at them, the mob started to break up. Four days later rioting broke out again when two young blacks were shot from a car. One of the black youths died, at which point the crowd set fire to white-owned businesses and attacked newsmen's cars, demanding the release of Carmichael. After seven hours police subdued the violence, only to have it erupt again the following night with more cries of "Black Power."[3]

The African American *Atlanta World* blamed a small group of irresponsible black students and made significant recommendations: discourteous white and black policemen should be removed from the police force, the city sanitation department should clean up the area, a recreation area for teens and young adults should be established, and punitive action should be taken against police officers charged with brutality. No improvements were made, as evidenced by more rioting that occurred in March 1967, when five Black Muslims attacked police after their arrest. In June, after a "fiery speech" by Carmichael, blacks began throwing rocks at the police. Trying to disperse the crowd, the police fired shots, killing one black and wounding three others. Disorders plagued Atlanta again in October 1967, when 200 protesting blacks smashed store windows and set fire to white-owned businesses.[4]

In 1967 violence exploded everywhere, igniting all corners of the nation, seeming to come from extremists, both black and white. In Liberty, Mississippi, a bomb exploded in the office of a Head Start (preschool) program serving three counties in southwest Mississippi. In Fort Deposit, Lowndes County, Alabama, near the site of the murder of Viola Liuzzo, a black Baptist church was burned to the ground. In nearby Hayneville, site of the murder of Jonathan Daniels, a white Episcopal church, converted into headquarters for a federal antipoverty program, was bombed. Elsewhere in Lowndes County, snipers fired on police after Carmichael, released on bail and busy organizing the Black Panther movement, was jailed for confronting police during a riot in which forty blacks were trapped in a house by Klan members with guns. In Mobile, Alabama, a bomb destroyed the home of civil rights leader J. L. LeFlore, and another bomb destroyed a white-owned business in the black section of Birmingham. The riveting details occupied the front pages of newspapers across the country. In a letter to the *New York Times*, Martin Luther King Jr. suggested that to describe looting, assaults, and arson without exposing the provocations for such behavior was, in his words, "to do too little to relieve the agony of Negro life."[5]

Voices of White Ministers

Sympathetic white clergy searched for ways to respond to the uprisings of 1964–1968. Some spoke for toleration and understanding. Rev. Ralph Sockman (1889–1970), famous United Methodist preacher, seventy-four years old, returned to his former pulpit at Christ Church on Park Avenue in New York City to urge white Methodists throughout the nation to aid actively in the civil rights movement. He said he deplored the outbreaks of lawlessness but called for understanding: "We who enjoy full civil rights and social decencies should try to think how those people feel who have so long been denied them." A Lutheran leader, Rev. Philip A Johnson (1916–1991), head of public relations for the National Lutheran Council of the United Lutheran Church of America, proposed that the major faiths "forget about converting people for a while and concentrate on serving them."[6]

Most southern white ministers remained silent concerning the violence, but not John Elbridge Hines (1910–1997), presiding bishop of the Episcopal Church of the United States from 1965 until 1974. Hines, a southerner from Seneca, South Carolina, was able to speak out because he was standing in New York City at the helm of a national church. He was determined to make a difference, perhaps because he was the son of a pious and compassionate country doctor from South Carolina who treated African Americans with the same care he gave to his white patients and told his son to be concerned about the plight of "the least of these, our brethren." Hines responded to the riots by establishing the General Convention Special Program (GCSP) at the sixty-first General Convention in Seattle, Washington, on September 17, 1967. It was the "primary document of the era," with plans for distributing $3 million annually to community organizations largely controlled by African Americans and the poor in order to increase their "power for self determination [and restore] their dignity." He urged a "sacrificial response," a "token, a symbol . . . a sacrament." He called for an end to the "destructive bloody rioting," but asked Episcopalians to recognize that "people in the streets of Watts, Newark, Detroit, and Atlanta were fighting for the right of self-determination . . . for deliverance from discrimination . . . and nearly two centuries of oppression." Bishop Stephen Bayne of the General Convention Executive Council declared, "The Church is asked to pour out its life for others." It was Hines's and Bayne's answer to Malcolm X's attack on the white church. In consultation with the elected members of the Executive Council, Hines set up a special staff to administer the funds and named African American layman Leon Modeste to direct the program.[7]

An admirer of Hines, a southern minister of a younger generation, Rev. Kenneth Kesselus, born in 1947 in Bastrop, Texas, suggested that Hines's challenge changed forever the direction of the Episcopal Church. Although some Episcopalians rejected the plan, it met with majority approval. Among those white southerners who voted for it was Rev. Duncan Montgomery Gray Jr. (chapter 1), a member of the House of Deputies for the Episcopal Church from Mississippi at the time. Unfortunately, as the historian Gardiner Shattuck argues, the GCSP set in motion divisions within the Episcopal Church that would eventually lead to the demise of the GCSP. Many white churches withheld funds, and the president of the Union of Black Episcopalians, Frederick Williams, called it "the most sophisticated bit of paternalism to come from whites in many decades." The black Episcopalians complained that the GCSP had never been "their" program. By 1969 some Episcopal clergy and laity were calling for the end of the GCSP. At the 1973 General Convention it was decided to place all minority organizations of the Episcopal Church under one funding program, and the name of the GCSP was changed to the Commission on Community Action and Human Development. Modeste's position was terminated on December 31, 1973, but Hines had made his statement, and his voice was heeded by many white Episcopalians.[8]

◆ ◆ ◆

Most white ministers living in the South were silent concerning the riots, but not Rev. W. W. Finlator (1913–2006) , pastor of Pullen Memorial Baptist Church in Raleigh, North Carolina, and chair of the Public Affairs Committee at the North Carolina Baptist Convention, who called upon "Baptists and all men of good will to recognize and admit the human tragedy and deplorable conditions which spawned the violence." Finlator took the violence seriously, expressing fear that it soon might be "too late to avoid open rebellion and revolution within the borders of our nation." He stated, "None of us would passively accept for ourselves or for our children the intolerable conditions of the urban and rural ghettoes." His committee strongly urged "governments, federal, state, and local, to immediately undertake radical structural measures at whatever financial costs to achieve adequate and open housing, to provide health and education needs, job opportunities, and political enfranchisement for all African American citizens."[9]

The statement went unheeded at the North Carolina Baptist Convention and never made it to the larger Southern Baptist Convention. Surprisingly, however, the southern Presbyterian Church (PCUS) pledged $227,500 in emergency funds to fight the cause of riots, and a report issued by the Interdenominational Theological Center of Atlanta (predominantly African American) concerning responses of Atlanta's churches to the riots of 1966 and 1967 suggested that if all churches in Atlanta were as active as Central Presbyterian (PCUS), violence in Atlanta might have been prevented. The pastor J. Randolph Taylor, who may be remembered as having opened the sanctuary of the Church of the Pilgrims in Washington, DC, to participants in the March on Washington (chapter 4), accepted a transfer to Central Presbyterian during the height of the riots and continued the church's many services to the inner city: coaching basketball teams; opening Central's well-equipped gymnasium, kitchens, and sunny classrooms to its neighbors; helping with legal aid; and working in the church's oldest and best-known service project, the Baby Clinic, founded in 1922. More than 5,600 children received free medical care annually, and clinic nurses made follow-up visits to their homes.[10]

Central Presbyterian's service to its poor neighbors was exemplary, but the report of the Interdenominational Theological Center concluded that most of Atlanta's white churches did not help on the excuse that they either lacked the funds or conservative elements in their congregations were opposed to such action. The report made a disturbing conclusion: "Lessons of the past

three years have taught us . . . that riots are not born when a policeman shoots
or arrests a youth in a black ghetto or even when rats bite off the fingers of a
sleeping baby in a forgotten city hovel. They are born when the human spirit is
no longer moved to action by the plight of his brother."[11]

Rev. John Morris, executive director of the Episcopal Society for Cultural and Racial Unity (ESCRU), headquartered in Atlanta, and veteran of
the Selma march, had always been concerned about the plight of his fellow
human beings. The violence did not surprise him; rather, he saw the riots as
decomposing the equilibrium of white liberals in the North who had to finally
accept the fact that America's racial problems were not confined to the southern states. He told ESCRU audiences that it was possible that the South might
work through its racial problems sooner than the North: "We live more closely
together . . . so there is often some degree of 'knowingness' across racial lines
upon which we may eventually build."[12]

Rev. Frank McRae and the Assassination of Martin Luther King Jr.

One southern white minister, Rev. Frank McRae (1930–2014), born in Memphis, Tennessee, and district superintendent for the Methodist churches, saw
his role as mediator in a struggle between the deprived and long-suffering
sanitation workers and the intransigent mayor of Memphis, Henry Loeb. On
February 12, 1968, the sanitation workers in Memphis, 1,300 strong and almost
100 percent black, walked off their jobs, calling for higher wages, union recognition, safer and cleaner working conditions, and a dues payroll check-off. T. O.
Jones, former sanitation worker and president of the local American Federation of State, County, and Municipal Employees (AFSCME), emphasized the
need for safety in the aftermath of the accidental death of two sanitation workers swallowed up and mashed by a defective, antiquated barrel-type garbage
truck. As Joan Turner Beifuss, a local white activist, related, "There was no
workmen's compensation and neither man had life insurance."[13]

McRae had already earned a reputation as an outspoken, committed
integrationist. He attributed his support for the civil rights movement to his
beloved cook, Anna Jackson: "I could identify with black people through her.
Whatever touched her or those who were like her affected me. . . . On the busses, my brother and I always went to the back of the bus as sort of a protest
against an injustice that made no sense." Having graduated in 1954 from the
Candler School of Theology at Emory University, just as the race issue was
exploding, he defended school desegregation at his first assigned church in
North Memphis. He was told by a member of the church, "You're lower than
the dirtiest n____r, and if you ever come to my house, you can go to the back

door with all of the other n____rs. Dogs are better than you." McRae recalled
that in the 1950s and 1960s verbal abuse ran rampant. He attributed his survival to a supportive bishop, Ellis Finger, and the fact that he "didn't bruise
easily." In 1960, while he was at another church in Tennessee, the board members decided that they would not admit a black person to worship. McRae told
them, "Fine, but when this meeting is over, I will be going to my house and call
the bishop to tell him he needs to look for a new pastor. I will not serve in a
church where everybody is not welcome." He stayed another eighteen months.
The experience was repeated again and again as McRae was transferred from
church to church, but his responses were always the same. They threatened
his children. They sent mean and nasty letters. But he never left Tennessee.
He commented, "A lot of preachers ran off to the North or West because they
couldn't take it. I'm not saying I could take it any better, but there was nowhere
else I wanted to go. This was my home, and I was going to stay here and do
what I thought was right." Whenever he was criticized, he would say, "Well,
I don't know where you came from, but I was born right here in Memphis.
My father is from Mississippi and my mother is from Jackson, Tennessee. My
grandmother came from Mobile, Alabama, and my grandfather from Richmond, Virginia. I don't have any other roots except those that are southern."
McRae contended that in the heat of an argument it made sense to claim
southern roots and let people know that white insiders could be just as passionate about integration as white outsiders.[14]

The interracial, interdenominational Memphis Ministers Association knew
that McRae had a long friendship with Mayor Loeb and urged him to influence the mayor to end the strike. As a friend also and supervisor to Rev. James
Lawson, pastor of all-black Centenary United Methodist Church in Memphis
and supporter of the strike, McRae had complete sympathy for the people who
worked forty hours a week and lived in poverty, many of whom attended black
Methodist churches. As a child, Mc Rae could remember the sight of black men
with heavy metal containers, overflowing with garbage, on their heads and with
angry dogs at their heels. He thought how wonderful they were because they
drove horse-drawn wagons with huge wheels, but as he grew older, he realized
the hopelessness of their situation. As chairman of the Social Action Committee of the Minister's Association, McRae did everything he could to convince
the mayor to recognize the union, but Loeb took the position that the strike
was illegal and that the strikers had to return to work before grievances could
be discussed. Municipal council members agreed with him.[15]

On the sixth day of the strike, McRae arranged a talk between the mayor
and representatives of AFSCME. At the meeting, feisty Jerry Wurf, president of
AFSCME and soon to be a national executive for the AFL-CIO, arrived from
New York City and bluntly told Mayor Loeb, "We will not go back to work until

an agreement is reached. . . . We won't come on our knees begging for mercy."
McRae's own white Methodist church sent money to help feed the families of
striking workers, and Wurf gave $5,000.[16]

With no settlement in sight, an intransigent mayor, and a majority of white
Memphians supporting him, the black ministers of Memphis united with the
strikers and organized a demonstration for March 23, 1968, which came to be
known as Memphis's Pettus Bridge. J. Edwin Stanfield of the Southern Regional
Council cited conflicting versions of the march. In the marchers' version, "A
police cruiser [started] bumping and nudging the marchers, crowding them
closer to the curb." The *Tri-State Defender*, a black-owned weekly, reported
that the car stopped on a woman's foot and that the marchers tried to push
it off. The police reported that for unspecified reasons, an attempt was made
to overturn the squad car. For whatever reason, what followed was a vicious
attack on peaceful demonstrators. Almost the entire Memphis police force
began spraying the marchers with Mace, a new tear gas–like chemical causing temporary blindness and severe facial discomfort. Stanfield related that
they sprayed everyone in sight. When a cameraman for the *Tri-State Defender*
photographed the attacks, a policeman came at him, club in hand, screaming,
"Gimme that camera, n____r." The cameraman was able to get away and publish his photographs. The widespread spraying of Mace could not be denied.[17]

Boycotts and demonstrations against all downtown businesses, against
every barbeque and fried chicken restaurant and laundry bearing the name
"Loeb," and against the two daily newspapers that supported the mayor com-
menced. Small marches took place almost every day with demands not only for
an end to the strike but also for greater employment opportunities and better
housing for black people. A scattered number of white professors from Southwestern College and Memphis State University joined them. Marches were
quiet and orderly, with participants carrying placards: "Dignity and Decency
for Our Sanitation Workers," "Jim Crow Must Go," and "We Are Together Once
and For All," but additional talks between the mayor and the union produced
no results, and a decision was made to invite Martin Luther King Jr. to Memphis. The Southern Christian Leadership Conference (SCLC) was disturbed
that King would consider going to Memphis when his presence was sorely
needed in the planning stages for the "Poor People's Campaign." According
to Andrew Young, King promised, "I'll just make a speech and I'll be right
back." K. W. Cook of the *Memphis Commercial Appeal* described King's speech
as demanding confrontation and economic progress. King left soon afterward
to complete several tours to recruit people for his Poor People's Campaign but
promised to return to Memphis on March 28 to lead a second mass march.[18]

Taking place on the forty-fifth day of the strike, the March 28 demonstration proved to be a disaster. As the marchers, led by King, Abernathy, and

Lawson, made their way on Beale Street, with its rows of pawnshops and dry goods stores, they could hear the sound of breaking glass. Stanfield wrote, "So began the Memphis riots, which resulted in the death by police gunfire of a 16-year-old boy, injuries to sixty, mostly blacks, clubbed by police, and arrest of about 280 people." Another southern riot made its appearance. The black Memphis neighborhood appeared to be a battle zone, with police enforcing a strict curfew that lasted for five nights. The conservative *Memphis Commercial Appeal* focused on the violence and justification for police action and later accused King of instigating the riot. Although the rioters were but a fragment of the total marchers, they presented a serious challenge to King and the philosophy of nonviolent protest. According to the historian Michael Honey, King was greatly distressed by the riot, believing it was caused by a Black Power group that opposed him, but some black leaders suggested that the violence might have been avoided if the other marchers had somehow recognized the Black Power group. As in other riots, pent-up anger and bitterness had surfaced, but along with it was the dignity of the sanitation workers who proceeded down Main Street the next day, placards in hand saying, "I Am a Man."[19]

The white ministers of Memphis may have missed an opportunity. Had they joined the black ministers on March 23, the Mace attack might have been avoided, a settlement might have been reached, Martin Luther King Jr. might not have come to Memphis, the riots of March 28 might not have taken place, and King would not have returned to Memphis to be assassinated, but according to Honey, the black and white ministers could not communicate with each other. At one meeting, when an elderly white minister talked about loving our "Nigra brethren," a black minister angrily responded "The word N-E-G-R-O is not nigra. It's *knee-grow*. . . . You ministers talk about love, and black people can't even get in the doors of your churches." (Old-time white southerners often pronounced "Negro," "nigra," not intending it as an insult.) McRae went to see Loeb on his own in an effort to set up a meeting with the Memphis Ministers Association, but was bluntly told, "You're going to waste your time; all you're going to do is get yourselves in trouble with your congregations. . . . You're not going to change my mind one way or another."[20]

On the fifty-second day of the strike, McRae made one more attempt to avoid disaster. At a meeting of white clergy, he proposed a march to city hall. "We have no strategy of our own, so let's accept the strategy of our black brethren and take direct action to pressure the mayor." Some of the white ministers backed away and some left the meeting, but the next day a small group of ministers marched. The response was the same. The mayor would not change his mind.[21]

◆　◆　◆

The saddest day for the civil rights movement came on the evening of April 4, 1968, when King arrived in Memphis to lead a second march. As he leaned over the balcony of the Lorraine Motel, he was fatally shot by a white assassin. The historian Honey noted, "King's death shook what little faith black youth had in the possibility of working with whites." Memphis high school student Alice Wright stated, "I was so hurt when I heard about Dr. King's death, that I couldn't stand the sight of a white person." Another student wrote, "I wanted to go out and do as much damage to the white community as I possibly could." Violence accompanied the mourning in all inner cities. In Memphis, black people smashed windows and set fires. In Miami, in Jackson, Mississippi, and in Nashville, Tennessee, over 3,000 National Guardsmen were called to keep the peace. Outbreaks occurred in Harlem, Pittsburgh, Newark, Hartford, Los Angeles, San Francisco, Chicago, Detroit, Minneapolis, and Baltimore, but the worst was in the nation's capital, where eight people died.[22] According to Rev. McRae, it took the death of King to shake the white ministers of Memphis out of their complacency. The day after the assassination, a stunned group of white ministers held an interracial, interdenominational memorial service for King at St. Mary's Episcopal Cathedral, and at its conclusion, 112 white and thirty-two black Protestant, Catholic, and Jewish clergy walked solemnly by twos along the sidewalk— in many instances, a black minister beside his white colleague. Rabbi James Wax, president of the Memphis Ministers Association, marched with Rev. Henry Starks of the African Methodist Episcopal (AME) Church; Rev. McRae walked beside Rev. J. A. McDaniel, director of the Memphis Urban League. Two Baptist ministers, Brooks Ramsey and Bob Troutman, and Fr. William Greenspun of the Paulist inner-city project were also among the white walkers. The marchers were accompanied by three police cruisers and protected by 4,000 National Guardsmen in full gear. Once at the mayor's office, Rev. John William Aldridge, chair of the Christian Relations Committee of the Memphis Presbytery, read the resolution, basically an apology and something that might have been echoed by some white ministers across the nation: "We, as ministers of God . . . mourn with deep sorrow and a sense of unspeakable loss the murder of our brother, Dr. Martin Luther King, eminent preacher of peace, advocate of the power of nonviolent love, promoter and practitioner of true manhood. . . . We who are white confess our implication in this tragic event by our failure to speak and act, clearly and specifically, with conviction and courage, to the attitudes of prejudice and patterns of injustice that produced the society in which this act could occur. . . . We implore our mayor and city council to address themselves with swift dispatch to the forging of a mutually acceptable solution including agreement upon union recognition and dues check-off."[23]

Rabbi James Wax fervently asked the mayor not to hide any longer behind legal technicalities and slogans, but to obey "laws greater than the laws of Memphis and Tennessee . . . the laws of God." In spite of all entreaties, the mayor made only vague promises. At that, Rev. Dick Moon, Presbyterian chaplain to students at Memphis State University (not a southerner), called out, "We have heard this before and it gets us nowhere. I for one have had enough of it." With that, he began a hunger strike in city hall that lasted seven days.[24]

As Michael Honey wrote, "The liberal side of white Christianity began to be seen in Memphis for almost the first time. Methodists, Lutherans, Baptists, Presbyterians, and the Catholic diocese initiated discussions of urban issues," but complaints from white citizens flooded the Sunday newspapers. Some white people attacked Rabbi Wax for criticizing the mayor. One wrote, "King's death supplies the communist cause with exactly what it needs at this time: a martyr." Many white citizens considered white ministers sympathetic to the strikers to have lost their senses, but Honey, in his account, included the passionate words of William Dimmick, dean of St. Mary's Episcopal Church, who led the ministers' march: "Jesus was crucified on a garbage heap between two thieves. . . . If the cross and the reconciling love of Jesus Christ has no business on the street then I really don't know where its main business is."

The white backlash against the pro–civil rights ministers in Memphis was fierce. All received threatening phone calls and nasty letters, and suffered ostracism, including Frank Tudor Jones, pastor of Idlewild Presbyterian Church who supported civil rights organizations through many years of activities, and Fr. Nicholas Vieron of Annunciation Greek Orthodox Church, member of the Memphis Ministers Association, who knelt before African American minister Henry Starks of St. James AME Church asking forgiveness for white religious indifference to the plight of the sanitation workers. Rev. Brooks Ramsey (chapter 2), who supported demonstrators in Albany, Georgia, in 1962 and who returned to his home in Memphis to serve as pastor to Second Baptist Church, actively supported the strikers and participated in many marches. His parishioners criticized him for preaching tolerance and love instead of "hell fire and damnation." He was threatened and called a Communist. After a few years he left the ministry and became director of the Pastoral Counseling Center of Memphis. Rev. Malcolm Blackburn (originally from Canada), the white pastor at Clayborn Temple, the AME church where striking sanitation workers could find support and refuge, was called a "white n_____r" and eventually left Memphis. Rev. John Aldridge, who read the white ministers' apology, was also harassed and left Memphis, but Frank McRae and many others remained, working to bring reconciliation and racial peace to Memphis.[25]

Finally, at the request of a more yielding Mayor Loeb, the federal district court lifted the ban against marches so that a memorial parade to honor

King could be celebrated. Stanfield, in his final paper on the Memphis tragedy, described a solemn procession of more than 5,000 people coming from the entire nation, including labor leaders, church leaders, and activists, black and white. "Guardsmen with bayonets pointed upward were visible everywhere. . . . The principal address by Rev. Ralph Abernathy expressed determination. . . . 'We are on our way to Washington, but we are going to stay here in Memphis until this problem is solved.'" Walter Reuther announced a donation of $50,000 from the United Auto Workers (UAW) strike fund to the Memphis sanitation workers.[26]

McRae and the white ministers continued urging the mayor to recognize the union and its demands. In spite of everything, the mayor remained intransigent: "I'll never be known as the mayor who signed a contract with a black union. . . . I committed myself during my election that this city would never recognize this union." And for twelve days after the assassination, he kept his word, but business leaders of Memphis were beginning to feel a loss of revenue because of the violence. Honey estimated that the city may have sustained over $1 million in property losses and overtime for police since the strike began. Many white businesspeople urged Loeb to settle the strike. McRae related that eventually a wealthy Jewish man, Abe Plough, founder of Plough Incorporated, a nationally known pharmaceutical company, donated the money to pay the sanitation workers, and that's when Loeb finally gave in to their demands. "But the real heroes of the strike," McRae asserted, "were the sanitation workers who took risks and made sacrifices for sixty-five days for the good of all."[27]

McRae said that eventually people in Memphis changed, but he doubted that pastors had much to do with it: "I think the times changed. We had an attack of conscience in this city. People began to acknowledge what was wrong and escape from their indifference. We didn't want to know what was wrong. We didn't want to know how little sanitation workers were paid. We didn't want to know the injustice that was meted out to them. They could be sent home without pay. If they were injured on the job, they would not be compensated. . . . I saw attitudes change. There was a man who attended my church, a public official, very much opposed to me, who came to me years later and said, 'You know, you were right.' Some of the racism will always be here, and we know it exists elsewhere, but that doesn't excuse us."[28]

The historian S. Jonathan Bass mentioned the transformation of Roman Catholic bishop Joseph Durick (1914–1994), one of eight white Birmingham clergymen admonished by Martin Luther King Jr. in 1963 in his "Letter from a Birmingham Jail." The five clergymen had written a public letter urging King not to come to Birmingham and interfere in its racial problems (chapter 2). When he was transferred to Tennessee, Durick became a civil rights advocate and a supporter of King. During the strike, he donated $1,000 out of his discretionary fund to help the striking workers. Mayor Loeb was highly critical, and some Catholics in Memphis wrote letters condemning him for being more devoted to "rabble rousers" than to his own people, but Durick continued to support the strikers and participated in the memorial marches for King. Echoing the words of the "Letter from a Birmingham Jail," he told Catholics, "Society will be doomed if the Church remains silent on the vital issues of human rights and human needs. . . . We cannot hide the pulpit today behind the Gothic façades of ancient buildings and let the rest of the world go by." He was immediately branded a Communist and heretic. Often his speeches were boycotted, but he prevailed.[29]

Honey mentioned how City Councilman Jerred Blanchard, a staunch conservative, claimed he never liked labor unions, but he believed in civil liberties and human rights. Blanchard made efforts to resolve the strike, much to the chagrin of his followers. On the morning of King's memorial march, he lined up in the front row. "If some people had told me that I would have participated in a civil rights march I would have told them they were crazy," but Blanchard had been transformed.[30]

◆ ◆ ◆

Situated on a scenic cliff of the Mississippi River, once the capital of the cotton kingdom, Memphis today suffers from economic and racial problems. As Honey mentions, the departure of such corporations as Firestone, International Harvester, and RCA during the 1980s destroyed opportunities for the black working class. White flight left Memphis with the largest inner-city black population in the South. In spite of difficulties, the black people of Memphis honor the efforts and sacrifice of King, the sanitation workers, and all who helped in those difficult years. Five years after King's assassination, a sanitation worker told an African American news reporter that the strike would have been lost without King. He was grateful for the benefits of the victory: "Before he had worked six days a week; now he worked five. . . . He had breaks and overtime pay. . . . With a union, his wages and benefits had steadily improved." According to Honey, the whole moment in history gave black people in Memphis hope for a better future.[31]

More Voices of Southern White Ministers

Outside of Memphis, southern white ministers responded to King's death in a variety of ways. His enemies remained silent, but those who admired and loved him were genuinely grief-stricken. The evangelist Billy Graham said, "The slaying indicates that tens of thousands of Americans are mentally

deranged. It indicates the sickness of the American society and is going to further inflame passions of hate." Those who mourned in Raleigh, North Carolina, turned to W. W. Finlator, who preached to an overflowing congregation at
Pullen Memorial Baptist Church: "Truly a modern day prophet has been laid
to rest. . . . The prophets of the Old Testament told of the sins and transgressions of the people, but with abiding faith, they held out hope for forgiveness,
restoration, and pardon. This was the kind of prophet we had in Martin Luther
King, Jr." Finlator likened the King assassination to that of Abraham Lincoln
and John F. Kennedy, also killed by snipers' bullets.[32]

The Southern Regional Council, meeting in Atlanta, issued a statement to
the United Press International: "His leadership during his life and the pangs of
conscience white America feels in his death give all Americans the chance—
and all perhaps the last chance—to make the choice between the kind of society for which Dr. King lived and died and the kind of society which denies
equal opportunity and relies on force above justice and equality." Two hundred members of the council signed the statement, among them, southern
white ministers Rev. Duncan M. Gray Jr., Meridian, Mississippi; Rev. Powers
McLeod, Montgomery, Alabama; and Rev. Edward McDowell, Atlanta.[33]

In death, King brought some white churchpeople to their racial justice
senses, something that could not be done while he was alive. Grieving white
southern pastors began to feel that one of their own had died. Memorial services were held in white churches throughout his home city, Atlanta. One
prominent white pastor (name unknown) proclaimed at an interdenominational, interracial sunrise service in Atlanta stadium, "Dr. King's assassination
meant that the hour has struck that the peoples of Atlanta . . . and the world
must begin to take seriously what Jesus taught." He urged Christians to find
solutions to poverty and other social ills. "All that is lacking," he exclaimed,
"is the will to do so." Yet others responded contrarily. When a young white
businessman asked the pastor of his Atlanta church to provide lodgings for
mourners from the SCLC who would be in town to attend the funeral, he was
turned down: "It would create needless budget problems," he was told.[34]

Rev. Randolph Taylor, one of the few white members of the SCLC, opened
his church, Central Presbyterian, to mourners. He and Martin Luther King
Sr. exchanged pulpits frequently. In fact, Taylor and his wife were with King
Sr. at his home the day that Martin Luther King Jr. was killed and remained
with the family for several days thereafter. Theirs was a close relationship for
the eight years that Taylor remained in Atlanta. Taylor lamented, "The loss of
Martin Luther King, Jr., came at the critical point just when the Movement was
moving into the economic sphere." Episcopal bishop John Hines telegraphed
Coretta King, Martin Luther King Jr.'s wife, "His death shocks and saddens all
who care about justice and equality for all men." He called King a victim of

"irrational elements opposed to nonviolent protest and the exploitation of any man, particularly the black poor." Hines flew to Memphis to march in the memorial parade. In Meridian, Mississippi, Rev. Duncan Montgomery Gray Jr. devoted his entire Palm Sunday sermon to King in a region where King was despised and ridiculed; nevertheless, Gray likened King to Jesus: "A prophet is not without honor except in his own country. . . . And was not his life, itself, testimony to the truth of this?" King, Gray told his parishioners, gave his life for a dream of justice and brotherhood among all people. Gray asked his congregation to work for the fulfillment of King's dream and "erase every trace of racism; every trace of discrimination, injustice and bigotry . . . not only for the sake of this nation, but for the sake of our own souls." In Montgomery, where King and the bus boycott made national history, Rev. Raymond Davis was invited to speak at the Easter memorial service held at the football stadium to a crowd of thousands, black and white, the only white minister on the podium. He asked the people of Montgomery to honor King's dream that Montgomery, "the Cradle of the Confederacy," might be transformed into Montgomery, "the Cradle of Freedom and Justice."[35]

In Mobile, Alabama, where thirty-one white ministers signed the Mobile Bus Petition in 1958, Pastor Arnold Voigt of all-black Faith Lutheran Church, together with black leaders, organized a memorial march on Palm Sunday, April 7, beginning on Davis Avenue in the heart of the black business section and ending at Mobile's municipal auditorium with about 4,000 in attendance, including Pastor Voigt and other white participants. Pastor Voigt commented, "We were their allies. We mourned with them and helped where we could."[36]

Rev. Ed King in Mississippi believed the death of King to be the greatest tragedy that befell the civil rights movement. With Martin Luther King Jr.'s death, Ed King believed, the nonviolent aspect of the movement might be gone forever: "If King had lived, many of the problems would have been solved without separatism and without violence." Will Campbell was on the train that carried King's body from Memphis to Atlanta, helping to console mourners. Campbell lamented, "There will never be another Martin Luther King, Jr. There will never be another nonviolent black movement in America." Rev. Malcolm D. Calhoun, secretary of the Division of Christian Relations for the southern Presbyterian Church (PCUS), came from Richmond, Virginia, with his daughter Margaret. Unable to enter the sanctuary of Ebenezer Baptist Church, they stood in a roped-off section where thousands waited while 800 people entered. The choir sang King's favorite hymns, and his prophetic sermon, "A Drum Major for Justice," resounded from a loud speaker throughout the sanctuary and outside the church: "Tell them not to mention that I have a Nobel Peace Prize—that isn't important. . . . I'd like someone to mention . . . that Martin Luther King, Jr., tried to give his life serving others. . . . Say that I was a drum major for justice.... I was a drum major for peace." The coffin was pulled in a wagon by two mules as 50,000 people followed (Calhoun's estimate). As Calhoun and his daughter walked beside black people, they could hear the snarls of white onlookers. The procession ended at Morehouse College, where King's teacher and mentor Benjamin Mays delivered the eulogy: he spoke of a man "who had come preaching love and compassion and brotherhood rather than cynicism and violence, a man who, as a Negro, had every reason to hate America but who had loved her passionately instead and had sung of her glory and promise more eloquently than anyone of his generation, maybe of any generation."[37]

Walking in the funeral procession was white Baptist minister Francis E. Stewart of Cobb County, Georgia, working at the time for the Office of Economic Opportunity in downtown Atlanta. He was King's close friend and advocate since their college days at Crozer Theological Seminary in Chester, Pennsylvania. Stewart was moved to tears by the words of Benjamin Mays: "They killed the dreamer, but they cannot kill the dream." Stewart had been placed on a "watch list" in 1954 after he presented a motion at the Central Baptist Association that the association should accept the Supreme Court school desegregation decision. He lost his pulpit in Jasper County, Georgia, when he preached from the Book of Amos, "Let justice roll down like a river and righteousness like a never-failing stream," and he spoke of the double standard of justice in Jasper County, such as "No blacks on the juries." At the Monticello (Georgia) Baptist church, he did not lose his pulpit because the local dentist defended him: "We may not agree with our pastor, but he has a right to say what he believes God has called him to preach." Stewart was never called to serve another Baptist church in Georgia and became a chaplain in Milledgeville. Later, he worked for several agencies of Lyndon B. Johnson's War on Poverty program.[38]

In December 1968 in Atlanta, Rev. John Morris organized the Southwide Conference of Black and White Elected Officials. These officials came from all over the nation to discuss mutual problems. The conference was held at the Dinkler Plaza Hotel, where, in 1962, African American Ralph Bunche, Nobel Prize winner and undersecretary general of the United Nations, was denied a room. Rev. Morris gave the invocation: "As we meet, we also honor the memory of thy servant, Martin, whose vision of a beloved community still beckons, and whose death reminds us of the sacrifice of many who have gone before."[39]

◆ ◆ ◆

The rise of the Black Muslims, black nationalists, black separatists, and militant Black Power groups created a bittersweet success for the nonviolent movement. Angry young blacks idolized bold and fearless leaders like Malcolm X, Stokely Carmichael (Kwame Ture), Muhammad Ali, Sammy Younge, Huey Newton, Bobby Seale, Eldridge Cleaver, and James Forman. Older civil rights leaders such as Whitney Young, A. Philip Randolph, and Roy Wilkins opposed the "Black Power" concept. At a National Association for the Advancement of Colored People (NAACP) meeting, Wilkins declared, "No matter how endlessly they try to explain it, the term 'black power' means anti-white power. . . . It is a reverse Mississippi, a reverse Hitler, a reverse Ku Klux Klan." Not one of the new leaders was a Christian minister. The nonviolent ideas of Gandhi, Jesus Christ, and Martin Luther King Jr. seemed to have vanished. White liberals came to be seen as obstacles, paternalistic, hypocritical, and ineffectual by the extreme black nationalists, unable to understand the meaning of "Black Consciousness." Rev. Frank McRae, in Memphis, noted that the white liberal money, given so freely while King was alive, began to disappear with the rise of militant blacks. As Baptist minister McLeod Bryan suggested, "Liberals may talk of brotherhood and equality, but when it comes to making material sacrifices they retreat."[40]

New Directions, New Leaders

Twenty-five percent of SNCC members were white liberals, and in the opinion of many black members, they should no longer serve as organizers in black communities. In a dubious election, radical Stokely Carmichael replaced moderate John Lewis as SNCC chair, and white members were fired from leadership roles. To Will Campbell, this meant that he may have "pitched" his tent in the wrong camp for twenty years—the liberal camp where he worshiped "at the shrine of enlightenment and academia." In so doing he had denied the faith he professed, his own history, and his own people, like Thomas Coleman, murderer of his friend, seminarian Jonathan Daniels, or members of the Ku Klux Klan whom he came to know. His Christian faith now told him that these "sinners" and other "rednecks" were worthy of being forgiven by God:[41]

> We who left home, or were pushed from home when Mamma or Daddy couldn't understand, were just a little bit prideful of our alienation from them, and a little bit arrogant in our new-found liberation and assumed sophistication. We justified it in terms of the suffering, the injustices, the blatant hostilities, and economic deprivations black people had heaped upon them. There was drama and romance in the Civil Rights Movement and we who had *no* home at home sought that home in the black cause . . . like a lot of other white people in those days. We learned to cuss Mississippi and Alabama sheriffs,

learned to say "redneck" with the same venomous tones we had heard others, or ourselves, say n____r. . . . But then some of my black friends, like Stokely Carmichael started telling me, "Look . . . you wanna help out in this race-rela-tions thing? . . . You wanna help so bad, why don't you go where the problem really is—why don't you go to work on your own people?"[42]

Campbell began to see that the racist was perhaps the greatest challenge to be faced in his day, in both the North and the South: "the most unlovely and the most in need of love. . . . We must not abandon him in an attempt to pun-ish him to maturity." The "klanners" and "rednecks" were his people. They had been indentured servants set free after five or seven years into a new world, to fend in the wilderness for themselves at the mercy of wealthy landowners. At the request of a friend, he went to see a leader of the Klan who lived in North Carolina whose father left him when he was six years old, whose mother went to work in a sweat factory for thirty-seven years where her job was to sew the seam down the right leg of bib overalls. Her son, the Klan leader, was sent to reform school, ran away, and joined the army when he was fourteen: "For sev-enteen years, he was taught the fine arts of torture, interrogation, and guerrilla warfare." Campbell came to have compassion for Klan members. He decided to return to a ministry of what he called "grace" instead of "law." He would try to bring respectability to Klan members and in so doing might change them, but that was not his primary mission. His mission was to treat them as fellow human beings and minister to their needs, but his brother Joe argued against Campbell's new mission: "Will, these people are killers," but Campbell contin-ued to befriend Klan members.[43]

A Demand for Reparations

On May 4, 1969, African American James Forman (1928–2005), World War II air force veteran and executive secretary of SNCC, attracted the attention of the entire nation when he boldly interrupted the Sunday morning service at the Riverside Church in New York City with the Black Manifesto (a document repeating the revolutionary ideas of Malcolm X) and demanded $500 million in reparations from white Christian churches and Jewish synagogues. In the manifesto's words, "Total black control was the only solution to the economic problems of the black people who were victimized by the most vicious, rac-ist system in the world." The manifesto asked for compensation amounting to roughly $15 for every black person living in the United States. (Forman esti-mated that thirty million black people were living in the United States at that time.) Forman wrote the manifesto with the help of other black militants who had seized power at the final planning session of the National Black Economic Development Conference (NBEDC) held in Detroit in April 1969. As Forman's group reasoned, white Christian churches and synagogues possessed tremendous untaxed wealth and could afford to meet the $500 million demanded by the manifesto. (The NBEDC was sponsored by the Interreligious Foundation for Community Organization, established in New York City in the aftermath of the urban riots of 1965 and 1966 by the United Presbyterian Church [USA] and ten other religious organizations.)[44]

On May 6, in a gesture reminiscent of Martin Luther, Forman taped the manifesto with additional demands for $50 million and 60 percent of the church's yearly assets on the door of the national headquarters of the Lutheran Church of America (LCA) in New York City. On May 9 he met for two hours with officials of the Roman Catholic Archdiocese demanding $200 million and 60 percent of the church's yearly assets; he was served with papers barring him from further church disruptions, which he quickly burned. On May 13 he presented the manifesto to the presiding bishop of the Episcopal Church, John E. Hines.[45]

The Black Manifesto was not well received by the churches, especially southern churches, but the response of white southerner Hines was significant. He allocated 60 percent of the denomination's profits to the denomination's previously established General Convention Special Program (GCSP); $45,000 to the Malcolm X Liberation University in Durham, North Carolina (to be given in two successive grants); $25,000 to the Black Awareness Coordinating Committee (BACC) in Denmark, South Carolina; and other money to the NBEDC, but most white southern Episcopalians were repulsed. Thomas Fraser, bishop of North Carolina, immediately condemned Malcolm X University as "an unrealistic experiment in education and a direct threat to the essential interracial character of the Christian Church." Fraser charged that expenditures for Malcolm X University caused a deficit of nearly $165,000 in his diocesan budget, a reduction in donations from individual churches, and a limiting of diocesan contributions to the national church. Funding for Malcolm X University ceased. Additionally, the $25,000 grant to BACC was suspended when militants from BACC staged uprisings at Voorhees College, an industrial training school for African Americans in Denmark, South Carolina, sponsored by the Episcopal Church. James Stoney, a white priest from Alabama, called Hines's actions "cowardly, dishonest, hypocritical, immoral, and against the laws of God." Stoney suggested that Bishop Hines had "been living and working in New York for too long" and had forgotten his southern roots, but criticism did not deter Hines, who went on to proclaim to an interdenominational conference in Wisconsin that the church must continue to reform society.[46]

Due to the uproar caused by the manifesto in the Episcopal Church, Hines called for a special crisis session of the General Convention to be held at the

University of Notre Dame in South Bend, Indiana, from August 31 through September 3, 1969, the first such emergency session called by the Episcopal Church since 1821. Some Episcopalians, fearing trouble, urged Hines to cancel the meeting; some called for his resignation. Hines sent questionnaires to active bishops concerning their feelings about the emergency session. When it was discovered that 64 percent responded with unqualified support, he proceeded as planned. In his opening address, Hines called for unity and asserted that no one could "with humility receive the sacrament of the broken body . . . and blood of Christ while [anyone is] denied access to decent housing and jobs and the right to self-determination." He asked representatives to reach out to one another, whether "black, brown, white, young, old, not ordained, [or] ordained and move forward together—as people to whom God has committed the perilous ministry of servanthood and reconciliation." A dramatic moment came shortly afterward when a dozen black and white dissidents led by Rev. Paul Washington, a black Episcopalian priest, and Muhammed Kenyatta, on the NBEDC steering committee, hurried to the platform and seized the microphone. After a brief tussle, Hines took the microphone and asked for a show of hands to allow the group to speak. According to Kesselus, "Hands were raised and there were shouts for and against," but Hines, avoiding confrontation, declared, "The ayes have it." Rev. Washington introduced Kenyatta, twenty-five years old, who, like Forman, asked for large-scale reparations to black people. After several days, a compromise was reached. The convention voted to allocate $200,000 to the Interdenominational National Committee of Black Churchmen, but to please all concerned, the contributions would be channeled through the GCSP not through the NBEDC, much to Forman's disgust.[47]

The one and only southern group belonging to the Interreligious Foundation for Community Organization (IFCO), the southern Presbyterian Church (PCUS), also responded. Its Board of National Missions and Board of Christian Education told its members to listen "honestly to the manifesto message," but many in the group objected to the takeover of the NBEDC by Forman and his revolutionaries. One irate member queried, "Why did IFCO sponsor the Detroit thing in the first place?" Ultimately the Board of National Missions allocated $5,000 for economic development in the South, in cooperation with the Presbyterian Church (USA), the United Methodist Church, and the Center for Community Change, and $25,000 for a multicity metropolitan mission in Durham-Raleigh, North Carolina, but admitted the board could do no more due to a budgetary deficit. According to Rev. Joel Alvis, the Black Presbyterian Leadership Conference, organized in Atlanta, was not pleased. The black leaders charged, "We were perceived as 'objects of mission,' not as equals."[48]

In North Carolina, white firebrand Rev. W. W. Finlator did not ignore the manifesto and prepared a "Resolution on Reparations" for his state Baptist convention. He cited words from the *Standard Jewish Encyclopedia*: "Forgive-ness of sin depends upon true repentance while a wrong done to a fellow-man requires rectification and restitution before forgiveness is possible"; from the *New Catholic Encyclopedia*: "Restitution is an act of commutative justice whereby property has been restored to one who has been deprived of it by unjust damage or threat"; from Baptist theologian A. H. Strong: "True repen-tance is indeed manifested and evidenced by confession of sin before God and by reparation for wrongs done to men"; and from the Bible, the story of Zac-chaeus, the converted tax collector: "Behold, Lord," said Zacchaeus, "the half of my goods I give to the poor, and if I have defrauded anyone of anything, I restore it fourfold."[49]

The North Carolina Baptist Convention knew that reparations were a fundamental Christian principle, but drastically altered Finlator's resolution. It became a "Resolution on Restitution," and his words, "The Annuity Board will make available one third of its portfolio for high risk loans to business enterprises and economic development among minority groups," became "out of our own free will and volition we now move firmly and positively *to repair such damage to our relationship as possible.*" According to McLeod Bryan, the resolution was passed with the alternate wording, but when it came to provid-ing the funds, the convention apologized: "As tight as money is right now, we believe we can say there is no chance of special allocations being made to any project like this." As Bryan commented, "The voice of officialdom had won once again over the ethic of the Gospel."[50]

The larger Southern Baptist Convention rejected as "outrageous" the Black Manifesto—its demands, principles, and methods—but surprisingly, a group of young Baptist ministers at the convention called upon their elders "to move away from the classic Southern Baptist aloofness to social problems."

According to Duncan Montgomery Gray in Mississippi, there was much "screaming and hollering on the part of the press, citizens' councils, and die-hard segregationists," but Gray saw some good results. He indicated that although white Episcopalians in Mississippi may have disagreed with the idea of reparations, they recognized the injustices committed against African Americans and the need for restitution. Gray noted, "African American Head Start programs, housing projects, colleges and churches got a lot more contri-butions from church parishes and dioceses." The amount of money demanded by Forman was beyond the will or ability of the Episcopal Church to pro-vide, but Gray saw the Black Manifesto as quickening the consciences of all church groups to the economic needs of the black community. Gray attributed one of the reasons for a good response in Mississippi to the Committee of Concern, a group established by the Ministerial Association of Meridian (of which Gray was a member), well supported by Episcopalians in response to the bombing of a Jewish synagogue and the burning of black churches in Lauderdale County one year prior to the Black Manifesto. The violence, according to Gray, had an effect of sensitizing white people who had previously remained silent and equivocal about black civil rights. According to Gray, it was a turning point: "White people moved away from the leadership of the Citizens' Councils and began to do something creative and constructive about racial reconciliation. When the manifesto was issued with its demand for economic justice, the Committee of Concern, still operating, urged people to think of ways they could improve conditions for black people."[51]

◆ ◆ ◆

Southern white ministers responded in a variety of ways to the turbulent events of the mid and late 1960s. Most were far removed from the rioting in northern cities and remained out of harm's way, but some tried to understand the causes. Through outreach programs, some southern white church groups provided beneficial programs to needy people in depressed neighborhoods, and the larger national denominations such as the Episcopal Church created special funding and a specific organization (IFCO) to help the poor. The rioting awakened white people from all walks of life to the desperate need for such programs. But black people wanted more than charity; they wanted empowerment, and they no longer believed their empowerment would come from white people. The Black Power movement and the seeming demise of the civil rights movement challenged some southern white ministers also to move in new directions, as they became much more concerned about poverty, thus taking over Martin Luther King Jr.'s new goal. After serving as district superintendent in Memphis for five years, McRae became pastor of historic St. John's United Methodist Church in Memphis, an intentionally integrated church with many ancillary programs for the poor, such as soup kitchens, listings of job opportunities, literacy classes, and day care. Dr. Scott Morris, a member of McRae's church, a board-certified medical doctor, and a United Methodist minister, turned a former car dealership into a clinic and chapel, reaching over 30,000 people. McRae continued his social ministry by organizing the Association for Christian Service and Training in the church. In May 1989 Rhodes College in Memphis recognized his service to the community by conferring on him the Honorary Doctor of Divinity Degree. After his retirement and since 1997, he has been the community outreach director for Middle American Apartment Communities (MAAC), finding housing for families in medical crises (without charge) throughout the South. In 1993 McRae was featured along with other local people in the Emmy Award–winning production *At the River I Stand*, a documentary about the sanitation workers' strike and the death of Martin

Luther King Jr. In 1999 he appeared in the ABC presentation "The Century," in which he discussed issues relating to the sanitation strike. In 2003 the April Fourth Foundation awarded McRae the T. O. Jones Trailblazer Award for outstanding community service during the sanitation workers' strike of 1968. The T. O. Jones Trailblazer Award was only one of eighteen awards McRae has received for community service in Memphis during his lifetime.[52]

Will Campbell stated, "The black separatist movement never upset me the way it did a lot of white liberals . . . because I wasn't really trying to be an honorary black person." After the Black Power movement, Campbell went back to being what he had always been, a "preacher," the title his father, all his relatives, and a country preacher gave him when they ordained him in a little one-room church in Mississippi. He continued his ministry, not in a church building but at his thirty-acre farm in Tennessee, in a small cottage back in the fields where they might have Bible study, seminars, and prayer. If some of the gathering asked him to turn it into a regular church, Campbell, with his distaste for organizations and institutions, would refuse. "Pretty soon," he stated, "we would be arguing about whether we have communion with Welch's grape juice or Mogen David wine, and pretty soon I'm going to want to be the pastor because I have title to the house. . . . Church is not a big building with tall steeples and gymnasiums that are open only to members." Campbell also continued writing his books, sympathetic stories of race relations, stories about people he considered heroic, and the musings of a "bootleg preacher" (as he described himself). His books became best sellers among his followers, and to this day Campbell is considered something of a folk hero in the South.[53]

Rev. Ed King was probably more displaced than any other white minister because activism had been his whole life, and he knew he would have to look to other causes. He continued his career as a chaplain at Tougaloo College, volunteered for the Delta Ministry, and later taught at the University of Mississippi School of Medicine. He became a full-fledged member of the United Methodist Conference of Mississippi when the separated conferences united in 1974 and became a guest pastor at churches throughout Mississippi and the nation, lecturing about the civil rights movement and the continued need for interracial understanding. In 2003 Ed King stated, "After a number of years, the separatist movement with all its ancillary organizations petered out, knowing they could not achieve their goals without the cooperation of white leadership and white people," but at the time, it seemed to white progressive laypeople and clergy that they were forgotten and that their efforts were unappreciated.[54]

As director of ESCRU, first organized in 1959 as an unofficial arm of the Episcopal Church, John Morris led the organization into direct involvement in the civil rights movement. Black as well as white members engaged in Freedom Rides, sit-ins, and kneel-ins, and fought discrimination in education, housing, employment, and hospital facilities. Early in 1964 Morris and an integrated group, some from SNCC, the SCLC, and the NAACP, were arrested for attempting to enter a segregated cocktail lounge in Atlanta. Later that summer hundreds of Episcopalians went to Mississippi to help in the local voting rights campaign. Morris was present the night a black church and adjacent home were dynamited and bombed in McComb, Mississippi. ESCRU led the drive to raise funds for rebuilding the church and established Freedom House, a local community center. The involvement of ESCRU in the Freedom Summer campaign and the Selma campaign has been well documented, but as the old nonviolent ways seemed to be dying out, what Morris feared came to pass. ESCRU's services seemed no longer to be needed. ESCRU could not prevent the riots. The more militant members called for moving the office north and focusing on problems of inner cities and less on integration. The white staff, including Morris, did not want to leave the South; thus ESCRU began to realize that maintaining interracial unity was difficult and almost impossible, and that in many ways ESCRU had not accomplished all that it set out to do. Morris wrote in a 1966 newsletter that the Episcopal Church was far from integrated: parishes were still "privileged sanctuaries serving to further suburban white congregations. . . . The system of clergy placement still treated black clergy as though they were inferior human beings. . . . Christian education still reflected the image of false dignity and human separation," and the church's financial investments and building policies still perpetuated "economic and moral inequalities." The article called for repentance and renewal. According to Morris, ESCRU was becoming a fragment of its former self. Many white members anxious to become involved in protesting the Vietnam War withdrew their membership in spite of Morris's admonition that black civil rights, not war protest, was the main concern of ESCRU.[55]

Morris stepped down as executive director of ESCRU in 1967 and virtually faded from the scene, becoming a dealer in rare books in order to support his wife and four children. It was naturally a sad decision for the Episcopal minister, who first conceived of the idea of having an unofficial organization that would shake the American Episcopal Church out of its white middle-class complacency, open its heart and doors to its African American brothers and sisters, and truly live the emblem on the banner, "Behold, how good and joyful a thing it is, for brethren to dwell together in unity." Two years later he was given the Bishop Lichtenberger Human Rights Award for his dedication to ESCRU. In accepting the honor, he reflected, in a more optimistic tone, that the Episcopal Church was gradually taking over the goals of ESCRU and that the unofficial organization for cultural and racial unity was no longer needed, but between the lines one could feel Morris's pain.[56]

◆ ◆ ◆

Perhaps the lasting legacy to religionists from the Black Power movement is black theology. Proponents of black theology no longer worship a "white Americanized Christ," as presented by white segregated churches. Their Jesus is black and comes to liberate black people. In *God of the Oppressed* (1975) James Cone systematically traced the liberation cry throughout the Old and New Testaments and presented the theological construct of the black Jesus. Black people know Christ in a way that white people can never know him because, as Cone asserts, Christ, like black people, is rejected and misunderstood by his society. Cone argues that if Jesus is "not in the ghetto ... not where men are living at the brink of existence, but is rather, in the easy life of the suburbs, then the gospel is a lie." White southern evangelist Billy Graham knew and understood black theology. On his many mission trips to Africa, Graham told Afrikaners, "Jesus was not a white European. ... He was from the crossroads of the world where Africa, Asia, and Europe meet."[57] And because of the Black Manifesto, American church institutions have been forced to recognize their debt to African Americans and their need for restitution, repentance, reconciliation, and atonement.

As people of faith, the ministers and others could find strength in the arms of a savior. John Morris, who left ESCRU disillusioned, became a widower in 1980 and married Wright Cousins, the widow of Rev. Ralph Cousins, his friend and fellow compiler of *South Carolinians Speak*, the booklet that disturbed hundreds of South Carolina's segregationists (chapter 1). John and Wright found comfort and strength in often attending a black Baptist church in Augusta, Georgia, where they lived in their retirement years.[58]

═ 6 ═

THE WITNESS DOES NOT END

Jordan, McClain, Finlator, Moose, Sanderson, and Frank

It is not easy to be a minister in the South today. When a minister inter-prets the will of God in race relations, his attitude may be regarded as little short of treason. The ostracism he faces, whether economic or oth-erwise, is not a slight thing.

—REV. WILLIAM WALLACE FINLATOR, "Conscience in the South," statement prepared for the State Baptist Convention, October 3, 1960

Efforts of these southern white ministers to help African Americans began long before the civil rights movement and continued long after its decline. These ministers looked for and found ways to witness to the Christian mes-sage of inclusiveness and reconciliation in spite of opposition. The story of Clarence Jordan and his experimental cooperative interracial farm, founded in 1942 in Americus, Georgia, and modeled on the concept of *koinonia*, mean-ing, in Greek, "community," has become something of a sacred icon. People from many countries and parts of the United States come to serve as interns and residents and to keep alive Jordan's vision of a "demonstration plot for the Kingdom of God." Rev. Howard McClain became Jordan's protégé and admirer. As a master of divinity student at the Southern Baptist Theological Seminary in Louisville, Kentucky, in 1939, he became friendly with Jordan, who was studying for his doctorate and directing a small mission in the pre-dominantly black West End of Louisville. McClain joined him at the mission and followed in his footsteps. In 1950 McClain organized the Christian Action Council of Columbia, South Carolina, as an interracial, interdenominational ministerial association. The association is dedicated to all aspects of civil rights and social reform and still functions today with members from eighteen dif-ferent denominations.

Rev. W. W. Finlator has moved through several episodes of this book as an outspoken firebrand for change within his native state of North Carolina and the Southern Baptist Convention. From his pulpit at Pullen Memorial Baptist Church in Raleigh, North Carolina, Finlator spoke out in favor of the rights of labor, school desegregation, civil rights demonstrations, and equality for African Americans. He was truly a voice of conscience, and his witness continued during the Black Power movement as a person who helped some of the most hapless people behind prison bars. The Reverends David Moose and Joseph Sanderson were too young to be involved in the early episodes of the civil rights movement, but they found their opportunities in 1969 and 1970 during tense and explosive situations in eastern Arkansas. The story of Rev. Moose is especially poignant because he was eliminated from the scene before he was able to make a substantial contribution to racial reconciliation. Later he found opportunity in West Memphis, Arkansas, and never wavered in his efforts. Rev. Sanderson was able to make an amazing contribution on behalf of African Americans in a small community in eastern Arkansas, in spite of the disapproval of his parishioners. His is a story of struggle between love for his parishioners and love for justice.

Each of these ministers was born to a privileged white family, and each could have lived a comfortable life as a pastor in a peaceful country setting. Instead, each responded to the travails of his African American neighbors and each chose a thorny path, but one that opened doors to a better life for African Americans. Their stories are important because they show how some southern white ministers in their own individualistic ways found and made opportunities to make a Christian witness of love for fellow human beings. Their persistence and courage produced results in some cases.

Clarence Jordan

Clarence Jordan (1912–1969) is described by his biographer and friend, journalist Dallas Lee, as "southern through and through." His ancestors were "pure-bred Anglo Saxon who stalked Georgia, North Carolina, and Virginia as early as the seventeenth century. He looked southern, talked southern, walked southern, dressed southern. . . . Yet in 1942, while most of the region was physically or emotionally marching off to war, Jordan stepped counter to virtually all that the South was or ever had been." As one southern Georgian might have put it, "He just did not come out right."[1]

Jordan was born in Talbotton, Talbot County, southwest Georgia. W. E. B. Du Bois, traveling through southwest Georgia in the early 1900s, described it as a land of unfenced farms and forests, "where crouch on either hand scores of ugly one-room cabins, cheerless and dirty. Here lies the Negro problem in its naked dirt and penury." Jordan's father was the town banker, owner of the general store, and stern ruler of his family of seven children. Jordan should have matured into a conservative white segregationist, like his family, but instead he responded to scenes of the oppression and poverty of the black people who dwelled all around him: the beatings, the floggings, and lynchings; the black prisoners who spent most of their days in pillories or chained together in the yard of the jailhouse not far from the Jordan mansion; the ragged and hungry children; the ramshackle shacks with leaking roofs and broken windows.[2]

Jordan decided early in life to do something about this poverty and studied agriculture at the University of Georgia in Athens with the intention of teaching poor black sharecroppers the value of scientific farming (not unlike the aims of George Washington Carver at Tuskegee Institute). Later, in search of spiritual resources, he earned a master of theology degree and a doctorate in New Testament Greek at the Southern Baptist Theological Seminary in Louisville, Kentucky.[3]

In 1942 Jordan and his wife, Florence, with the help of Baptist missionary Martin England, transformed a run-down tenant farm into Koinonia Farm, one of the better-producing farms in the region. It had grown from an original 400 acres in 1942 to 1,100 acres by 1957. Ron Lemke, a member of the community, explained reasons for the farm's prosperity: "Jordan brought chickens to southwest Georgia at a time when most people believed chickens could not thrive in the Deep South. Jordan's egg and poultry business became a huge success. The farm also had pigs, cows, goats, geese, sheep, a slaughtering house, and produced cotton, corn, peanuts, pine trees, and muscadines as cash crops." Members of the community shared all farming tasks and held all goods in common, including the purse. According to Florence, outreach programs also prospered: an agricultural institute, a farm products market, a boys' club, neighborhood fellowship nights, craft classes, Vacation Bible School, and an integrated summer camp.[4]

Troubles began in 1956 when two African Americans asked for Jordan's help in enrolling in the segregated Georgia State College of Business in Atlanta. Their application needed the signature of two alumni of the Georgia university system. Jordan was one, and he convinced another alumnus, Rev. James Waldon, pastor of Oak Grove Methodist Church in Atlanta, to serve as the second sponsor. Their signatures were not accepted on the excuse that the application had to be signed by two alumni of the Georgia State College of Business, not merely of the university. The two students never applied, but local newspapers in Sumter County and Americus erroneously reported that an Americus man, a resident of Koinonia Farm, had signed applications for two African Americans to attend Georgia State College of Business, and the fireball of resistance

was ignited. Governor Marvin Griffin, an avowed segregationist, sent the sheriff to investigate "that Jordan fellow and what he was up to."[5]

The incident set in motion hostilities that had long been festering. Local
grocers stopped buying the farm's eggs, and all the carefully designed, hand-
made highway signs advertising their roadside market were pulled down, broken, or stolen. Fences were cut; garbage was dumped on their land; corn was
taken from their fields; sugar was put in their gasoline tanks; pistol shots were
fired at the roadside market and buildings, sometimes barely missing Koi-
nonians and their guests. Robert McNeill, a Presbyterian minister in nearby
Columbus, mentioned in his memoir, "A fruit orchard of over two hundred
trees was power-sawed down in one night." A local airplane company refused
to dust the boll weevil off their cotton crop; a local fertilizer company refused
to sell them fertilizer; a local auto dealer refused to repair their damaged vehicles; and the State Farm Insurance Company canceled all their insurance. The
Atlanta Journal reported local gasoline stations stopped supplying them with
gasoline to run their tractors. According to Will Campbell, who often visited
the farm, "The boycott was total and effective. They couldn't buy an aspirin.
They couldn't get the services of a doctor." The worst of the horror came on
the night of July 23, 1956, when dynamite destroyed the roadside market where
they sold ham, peanuts, and other products. The total damage was estimated at
$3,000, and their insurance company refused any form of compensation. The
farm was in ruins with only two families remaining. In an interview, Florence
Jordan reflected, "If it had not been for donations from our friends, we would
not have survived."[6]

Jordan began giving lectures to groups of American Baptists, National
Baptists, United Church of Christ, Brethren, Mennonites, and Lutherans. They
were transfixed by his earthy, plain-speaking, sometimes blunt translations of
the New Testament. Using his knowledge of Greek, Jordan emphasized that
God became human and dwelled among us: "The word in the Greek for 'dwelt
among us' is *eskēnōsen*," he told them, "which originally meant 'to pitch one's
tent.'" "In those days," he told his listeners, "people were wandering nomads
and . . . lived in tents. And so they said, 'God became one of us and lived among
us, pitched his tent in our midst.' Now today we might translate it . . . 'The
word became flesh and bought a home in our neighborhood—yeah, the black
bastard, and made the price of our property go down. . . . Jesus Christ is now
our brother. . . . So the advice we get from him is that the God-lover is also a
brother-lover.' Just a way of saying that from here on out, you can't have any
dealings with God unless you deal with your fellow man, for God has established residency on the earth."[7]

Concerning the racial conflict, he told his listeners that the solution was
not in government or law, but in God and grace. Jordan's heart was broken

because the integration struggle was not being resolved in the churches. He told Dallas Lee, his biographer, "The sit-ins never would have been necessary if Christians had been sitting down together in church and at Christ's table all these many years."[8]

Jordan's tremendous influence cannot be overlooked or understated. As Ben Willeford, a native of Charlotte, North Carolina, professor from Pennsylvania, and frequent visitor to the farm, asserted, "For years, *Koinonia* was on the cutting edge of the social applications of the Gospel, unacceptable to many, but an inspirational to others:"[9] Habitat for Humanity, Jubilee Partners,[10] and the Prison and Jail Project of Southwest Georgia[11] were all begun by people who had lived at Koinonia Farm and were inspired by Jordan. Over the years hundreds of volunteers, groups of ministers, and laypeople have continued to keep Jordan's witness alive. To this day Jordan's message resounds throughout southwest Georgia, in churches throughout the United States that participate in Habitat for Humanity, and as far away as Africa, where Habitat homes have been built.

Millard Fuller (1935–2009) was an Alabama millionaire who was transformed at Koinonia Farm. He graduated from Auburn University in 1957 and entered the University of Alabama School of Law. With fellow law student Morris Dees, he went into a direct-mail operation, publishing student directories, and a mail-order business sending cakes to students on their birthdays. Before the age of thirty, he had amassed a huge fortune. Fuller was also an active layman in the United Church of Christ and first went to the Koinonia Farm in 1965 to visit a friend who was staying there. As Jordan wrote, Fuller only intended to stay for a half-hour, but the half-hour stretched into a month, and his life was changed forever. He liquidated his assets, distributed them to charity, and became a fund-raiser for Tougaloo College, the black United Church of Christ school near Jackson, Mississippi, where white Rev. Ed King served as chaplain. In 1968 he wrote to Jordan during the most agonizing time in the farm's existence, when Jordan was experiencing the pains of "battle fatigue." Jordan and his wife were ready to call it "quits." Fuller wrote, "I have just resigned my job with Tougaloo. . . . I'm blank. . . . But wait. . . . Does God have something up his sleeve for both of us?"[12]

The two met at Oakhurst Baptist Church in Atlanta, a place where Jordan was to preach, and made plans for a new phase of the Koinonia experiment: Koinonia Partners, Inc., with over 1,000 acres ready to be organized. Partnerships were to be formed in farming, industries, and housing, to be financed by a "Fund for Humanity." Money for the fund would come from contributions, non-interest-bearing loans, and voluntary shared profits plowed back into the fund. In Jordan's words, the new plan would be a "practical application of the mission of *Koinonia* as a demonstration plot for the Kingdom of God." Farmland would be donated to farmers free of charge; industries such as pecan shelling, the fruitcake bakery, the candy kitchen, and the mail order business were already under way, as forty-two half-acre home sites were made available to displaced rural families. As Jordan stated, "An integrated Christian community was a practical vehicle with which to bear witness to a segregated society a decade ago, but now it is too slow, too weak, not aggressive enough." The Fund for Humanity, he believed, would provide "an inheritance for the disinherited . . . a means through which the possessed could share and invest in the dispossessed. . . . The houses we're building for the poor will be as good as or better than anything we ourselves are living in." Fuller immediately began surveying the land and negotiated for the state to put in roads at a twenty-one-acre site that would become Koinonia Village. Houses would be sold at cost, and non-interest-bearing mortgages would be held by Koinonia. Bo and Emma Johnson, displaced black sharecroppers, bought the first house in 1969 for $6,500, $700 down and $25 per month to be paid over a period of twenty years.[13]

The demand for the houses skyrocketed. Jordan and Fuller traveled throughout the United States raising funds as contributions poured in and the demand for new homes multiplied. Professional contractors built the first houses, but by 1970 Koinonia partners and volunteers made up the construction crews. Among the volunteers were Mennonites and Hutterites from the Forest River Colony of North Dakota. The original twenty-one-acre site soon filled up as demand for Koinonia's low-cost housing expanded. In 1976 the Fuller family moved into the town of Americus to establish the international headquarters for Habitat for Humanity. By 1982 Koinonia Partners, Inc., built 107 houses in Americus.[14]

Unfortunately, Jordan lived only briefly to see the success of the new venture. After completion of Koinonia's first house, he died of a heart attack while working on one of his many books in his study shack. He was fifty-seven years old, but his witness lives on.[15]

Howard Gordon McClain

Since early youth Howard Gordon McClain (1918–2003), born in Cooper, Texas, had the grandiose and idealistic dream of improving race relations and ecumenism throughout the South. As an undergraduate at Vanderbilt University's School of Theology during the years 1935–1939, he came under the spell of a professor of social ethics, Disciples of Christ minister Alva Taylor, until the chair was abolished in 1936 because members of the Board of Trustees objected to Taylor's progressive teachings on labor and race.[16] But for McClain, such teachings were profound.

Next, studying for a master's degree at the Southern Baptist Theological Seminary (SBTS) in Louisville, Kentucky, in 1939, he came under the spell of Clarence Jordan. McClain worked with Jordan at a small Baptist mission, the Fellowship Center, serving poor black people in the West End of Louisville. McClain, in pursuit of his life's dream of helping black people, took up residence at the Fellowship Center, teaching Bible classes and literacy classes, and helping to prepare meals. There he found longtime friend Barbara, who had recently earned a master's degree in social work from the University of California. She and McClain married and joined the Long Run Baptist Association (white Southern Baptist churches in and around Louisville). Together with the Jordans and like-minded theological students, they formed an informal on-campus discussion group.[17]

Barbara McClain recalled that at many of their meetings, Jordan shared his dream of bringing poverty-stricken black people back to a productive farming life. In 1942, armed with a degree in agriculture from the University of Georgia and a doctorate in Greek New Testament from SBTS, Jordan returned to his native Georgia to establish the interracial cooperative farm where all individuals had equal rights, had equal rank, and shared all possessions, as described in the Acts of the Apostles.[18]

That same year McClain returned to his home church in Texas to be ordained as a minister of race relations, something unusual in Baptist churches, but his pastor had an open mind and convinced the congregation that they should ordain Howard for this special ministry. With such a unique ministry, McClain knew that he might never be called to serve a Southern Baptist church, but he continued his studies as a Julius Rosenwald Fellow in the area of Christian ethics at the University of North Carolina and Duke Divinity School. His training and experience prepared him for the opportunity he found in 1950 in Columbia, South Carolina, when the South Carolina Federated Forces for Temperance and Law Enforcement was looking for a new leader. Formed during the 1930s by white ministers and laymen from Baptist, Methodist, and Presbyterian denominations, Federated Forces was the closest the state came to having a council of churches. Originally the group's goal was to lobby for continuation of the Eighteenth Amendment (Prohibition). When the goal was not achieved, members modified their purposes by promoting abstinence from the use of alcoholic beverages and the rehabilitation of those addicted to alcohol and drugs. Rev. Maxie C. Collins retired in 1950 and contacted his friend and fellow Baptist minister Howard McClain, who he knew could lead the agency into a new era."[19]

One of the first things McClain did as the new president was to insist that the group address all aspects of social reform, become interracial, and change its name to the South Carolina Christian Action Council (SCCAC). In 1952 the group merged with the South Carolina Association for Alcohol Education, which had as one of its members J. L. Mims, a public school leader and layman in the African Methodist Episcopal (AME) Church. The merger made SCCAC racially inclusive. Rev. Claude Evans, editor of the *South Carolina Methodist Advocate*, noted that the changes came within a period of four years because of McClain's "near genius in human relations" as he moved "church judicatories toward mutual trust and support."[20]

Under McClain's leadership the council became actively involved in integration activities. In 1952, when the school desegregation case *Briggs v. Elliot* was pending in the courts, the SCCAC (along with the League of Women Voters) immediately opposed a state constitutional amendment that would "relieve South Carolina of its obligation to provide free public school education for all children," but the amendment passed. It wasn't until the late 1960s that the right of all children in the state to attend public schools was officially restored.[21]

In 1958 the council invited evangelist Billy Graham to hold a rally on the grounds of the statehouse, knowing full well that Graham's rallies included black participants, but the request was denied by Governor George Bell Timmerman Jr. "It would be a violation of the principle of separation of church and state," Timmerman asserted. The SCCAC publicly disagreed through the media, stating that such a rally did not violate the First Amendment and did not support the authority of any one denomination over the state. Timmerman would not relent, replying that the SCCAC was pro-integration. The SCCAC then arranged for the rally to be held at nearby Fort Jackson military base. General Christian Clarke, commander of the base, welcomed Graham and encouraged some 60,000 military personnel to attend.[22]

Perhaps the most beautiful moment in the life of the council was its support for the entrance of African American Harvey Gantt to all-white Clemson University on January 27, 1963. Determined that this event should be peaceful and not like the violent entrance of James Meredith to the University of Mississippi the previous September, council president Rev. Neil Truesdell, Presbyterian, issued a statement: "The Christian Action Council calls upon every Christian, every citizen within the state, to proclaim to the world that we are a State of law, that we are motivated by the highest of all laws—the royal law of love." One hundred and twenty-one white ministers signed the statement, and, after Gantt's admission, another statement was issued: "Let not the Sovereign State of South Carolina be disgraced by violence." This was signed by the major officers of nine denominations, all members of the council: Horace Hammett (Baptist); Bishop Paul Hardin Jr. (Methodist); Karl Kinard (Lutheran); Bishop Alfred Cole (Episcopal); Bishop Francis Reh (Roman Catholic); Arthur Rogers

(Nazarene); Rev. Ira D. Crewdson (Christian); Bishop Gray Temple (Episcopal); and Arthur Martin (Presbyterian).[23]

As the civil rights movement gained momentum, McClain and the SCCAC became active behind-the-lines. McClain's approach was quiet and unassuming, urging people "to do the Christian thing." He provided ideas and strategies, helping churchpeople to see what they needed to do and what they could do, sometimes with a sense of humor. When white people in Greenville objected to swimming with people who had dark skin, a black Baptist minister asked for suggestions on how to get white authorities to open swimming pools for African Americans. McClain responded, "Why don't you tell them to bring a few seals into the pool to help white people get used to dark skins." A demonstration was organized, but pools were closed rather than opening them for African Americans.[24] This happened throughout the South. In the torrid heat of summer, children, black or white, could not swim in public swimming pools.

According to black activist Cleveland Sellers, "The Civil Rights Movement was not the same in South Carolina as it was in Georgia, Alabama, or Mississippi. There was never a mass movement. In South Carolina, being polite was more important than being right, and moderation was more important than confrontation," but the SCCAC continued to do what it could to change repressive laws. McClain attended legislative sessions of the General Assembly and kept SCCAC members informed as to happenings through a newsletter. The SCCAC also sponsored an annual legislative conference for ministers and laity to learn about issues and visit with legislators.[25] The SCCAC eventually became the only interracial, interdenominational ministerial association in South Carolina, and continues to this day.

In 1984 the South Carolina Baptist Convention honored McClain with its E. A. McDowell Award for outstanding service in the application of the gospel in public life. In 1985 the 164th annual session was dedicated to McClain for his thirty-five years of service as executive minister of the Christian Action Council. After thirty-five years of service, McClain, the gentle Baptist from Texas, was receiving recognition and tribute. Bishop Frederick Calhoun James of the AME Church, who served as vice-president of the council from 1987 to 1992, stated, "The Christian Churches of South Carolina may have witnessed more truly than they realize during the 1950s and 1960s. During this period the overwhelming majority of white churches *resisted* the suggestion to establish segregated public schools in church facilities. . . . Black and white ecumenical relations never ceased during these years. . . . I'm a South Carolinian and glad to be one!"[26]

The dreams of a young Baptist from Texas came true. Now in the twenty-first century, the SCCAC addresses social, racial, and ethical problems of South Carolina and includes black and white men and women, clergy and laity, from eighteen different denominations across the state, fully integrated and fully ecumenical. When asked whether it was difficult to achieve this goal, Barbara McClain answered on behalf of herself and her husband, "In South Carolina, we were opposed by many. If people didn't like our liberal ideas, they just called us eccentric and let it go at that."[27]

William Wallace Finlator

William Wallace Finlator (1913–2006) recalled that his father, a railroad man and later a lawyer, was the only person in his young life who had anything to say to him about the racial issue. Not his mother, grandparents, uncles, aunts, or cousins, but his father taught him from his earliest years never to use the "n" word. He told his son, "The black people are having a difficult time and it is not for us to stand in their way and make it more difficult."[28] Finlator spent his entire career as a Baptist minister attempting to ease the burdens of black people.

In 1977 Finlator donated to the Wisconsin Historical Society letters received, letters sent, his personal addresses, speeches, newspaper articles, and a variety of items on capital punishment, civil rights, civil liberties, conscientious objection, church-state relations, politics, and the Vietnam War. His collection has been preserved in what have become twenty-one reels of microfilm. The collection provides a vivid account of situations in North Carolina during the years 1951–1977 and of Finlator's long and continuous efforts for social and racial justice. In many ways Finlator was like Will D. Campbell, a freethinking Baptist fighting for the rights of black people and other oppressed minorities, but, unlike Campbell, he remained a pastor in one church for twenty-six years and would have remained longer if the deacons had not forced him to resign. The church was Pullen Memorial Baptist Church in Raleigh, North Carolina, designated by Finlator as the most liberal church in the South.[29]

Born in Louisburg, North Carolina, and raised in Raleigh, the capital city, in a pious Baptist family, Finlator left his home state only once, to attend Southern Baptist Theological Seminary in Louisville, Kentucky, where he recalled being asked by W. O. Carver, professor of missions and comparative religion, if any students ever heard the name "Walter Rauschenbusch." According to Finlator, "Not a single hand went up! I knew from the look on my professor's face that our ignorance was abysmal and shameful. I began to read Rauschenbusch (1861–1918), and the great Baptist prophet of social justice became my hero." At the Baptist seminary, liberal at the time, Finlator also became introduced to the ideas of Karl Barth (1886–1968), the Swiss theologian who denounced the National Socialist Party of Germany (NAZIs) and wrote about the discontinuity between the Christian message and the world. At a colloquium at Southeastern Baptist Theological Seminary in Wake Forest, North Carolina, in 1974, Finlator told seminary students, "Theologian Karl Barth said that the prophetic, up-to-date preacher should stand in his pulpit with the Bible in one hand and the morning edition of the newspaper in the other." Finlator, in his long career, applied the teachings of Rauschenbusch and Barth to his ministry.[30]

In 1956 he became pastor of the Pullen Memorial Baptist Church, whose members protested against the Klan (very active in North Carolina) and segregated schools, buses, and lunch counters. Because the church membership included writers, professors, and representatives of the Associated Press, the *Raleigh News and Observer*, and the *Charlotte Observer*, Finlator's social protest writings were often published, making him a well-known public figure in North Carolina. He seemed ideally suited to be pastor of Pullen Church, and the congregation did not seem to mind (at least at that time) that many of North Carolina's Baptists found his writings and sermons outrageous.[31]

Early in his ministry, he admonished pastors in Henderson for remaining silent during North Carolina's longest and ugliest labor strike in its history. He told the pastors emphatically that churches must cease being private clubs and become houses of prayer for all people. He called for an "unsegregated church in an unsegregated society," an idea not especially popular at the time. Rev. R. Donald Wagner of the Gatesville Baptist Church wrote to Finlator, "Stick by your guns and maybe a few of us other 'preachers' will rise up with you to assist in your demands for Christian ethics in all areas of living," but a Baptist layman attacked his integrity: "As for your advocacy of integration of our children with Negroes in our schools and churches—this would convince all rightly thinking people in any denomination . . . of your unfitness to hold a clerical office or position in any church."[32]

When, in 1960, he supported the gubernatorial primary campaign of Terry Sanford from the pulpit against staunch segregationist I. Beverly Lake, his former professor and Sunday school teacher at Wake Forest University, his readers were incensed. One woman wrote, "I just want to ask if you belong to the NAACP [National Association for the Advancement of Colored People]. I cannot see any other reason why you should strike at Beverly Lake, unless someone bribed you." An attorney in Greensboro wrote, "You prove yourself to be a man of extremely small stature by attacking the character of Doctor Lake." Even more vitriolic were the enclosures he received along with the letters, from the worst hate periodicals of the day (many published in the North), the kind of propaganda persuading masses of North Carolinians and others to oppose any form of integration: the *White Sentinel*, published by the White American News Service, Fort Lauderdale, Florida, with its classification of well-known Americans as Communist Party affiliates; the *Augusta Courier*, Augusta, Georgia, with its attack on the Supreme Court; *Are All White Men Israelites?*, a book about white supremacy by Theodore Fitch, Council Bluffs, Iowa; the *American Nationalist*, Los Angeles, emphasizing the evils of integration; *Tax Fax*, published by the *Independent American* of New Orleans, describing Communist infiltration in the churches; and someone from Raleigh who consistently argued with Finlator that the Bible supported segregation. Finlator may have influenced more people than he suspected. Terry Sanford won the primary election and the governorship and did his best to help North Carolinians accept a changing social order, but the flood of criticism against Finlator never ceased.[33]

Although Finlator rarely engaged in street demonstrations, he was designated "Baptist firebrand" by local Methodist minister Vernon Tyson because he called upon downtown merchants to integrate their businesses and paid for a petition to appear in the *Raleigh News and Observer* in September 1960, signed by Finlator and all who were willing.[34] Finlator's support for the civil rights movement came by way of sermons and newspaper articles, but as the movement progressed, he moved into the cutting edge of radical ranks, daring to defend revolutionaries and give aid to prisoners he believed were victims of oppression.

In 1967 he wrote an article in defense of Muhammad Ali, the world heavyweight boxing champion who refused to serve in the US Army during the Vietnam War on religious grounds. African Americans considered Finlator's article a masterpiece, while many in the white community considered it a monstrosity. He defended Ali's name change (from Cassius Clay): "In the American tradition it seems quite all right for Samuel Langhorne Clemens in literature to be known as Mark Twain or for Cornelius McGillicuddy in baseball to be known as Connie Mack." He defended Ali's claim to be a minister in the Black Muslim faith: "What makes his ordination inferior to mine, or for that matter, to that of the local Episcopal priest? . . . If the former Cassius Clay now insists that he is an ordained clergyman, who is to be the final judge? The point I wish to make, however, is that if ministers and rabbis and priests are granted automatic exemption from the draft why not Rev. Muhammad Ali?" One irate woman called Finlator a Communist and a traitor, among other things.[35]

Finlator's support for the revolutionary James Forman has already been cited, but his efforts on behalf of Rev. Ben Chavis, a black United Church of Christ minister and civil rights activist in Wilmington, North Carolina, where much racial unrest existed, are not widely known. Chavis had been charged with "accessory after the fact in an untried and unsolved crime with his bond set at $100,000." As chair of the North Carolina Advisory Committee of the Civil Rights Commission, Finlator wrote to the commission in Washington that the bond violated constitutional protections against excessive bail and was intended to keep Chavis in prison and removed from trial (a common court practice attempting to destroy civil rights activists). A different judge later reduced the bail to $15,000. Shortly thereafter, Chavis was arrested again along with nine others (the "Wilmington Ten") accused of fire-bombing a grocery store and conspiring to assault emergency personnel. Finlator notified Washington of Chavis's second arrest and excessive bond. He pointed out that men such as Chavis were respected members of society helping people in need. Finlator was convinced that Chavis, pastor of a black church in Wilmington and a member of the Commission on Racial Justice for the United Church of Christ, was being unfairly condemned. The historian Manning Marable affirmed Finlator's defense. In the case of Chavis, Marable wrote, "A jury of ten whites (some of whom admitted to membership in the Klan) and two elderly, intimidated blacks, gave sentences to the 'Wilmington Ten,' which totaled 282 years. . . . The FBI and the Alcohol, Tobacco, and Firearms division of the U.S. Treasury Department secretly paid three witnesses, two convicted criminals and a 15-year-old boy, to testify against Chavis." After a review of testimony by the Superior Court, Chavis and others were released on a $50,000 bond posted by the United Church of Christ in New York City, pending an appeal to the higher court. In 1977 Chavis wrote a stirring appeal to the 1977 Belgrade Conference based upon the Helsinki Accords guaranteeing protection for human rights and was eventually released.[36]

Finlator also asked leniency for James Grant, incarcerated in February in Charlotte, North Carolina (case of the Charlotte Three), on a conspiracy charge, with bail set at $100,000. According to Finlator, Grant held a PhD in chemistry from Pennsylvania State University. Finlator wrote to the attorney generals of North Carolina and the United States asking for a close watch on developments in Wilmington and Charlotte, where situations were exacerbated by a group called "The Rights of White People." Finlator firmly believed that activists were victims of white supremacist hate groups and should not be treated as common criminals.[37]

Finlator also aided "The High Point Four," who were arrested at a shoot-in at a house in High Point established by the Black Panthers to provide free breakfasts, free clothing, liberation schools, and adult political education programs for poverty-stricken black people. In January 1971 an eviction notice was issued to the occupants. Members of the Black Panthers exhausted every means available to stop the eviction, but the owner of the building would not relent, and on the morning of February 10, 1971, nearly 100 members of the High Point police, headed by Laurie Pritchett, known for his arrests of demonstrators in Albany, Georgia, in 1962 and recently relocated to High Point, attacked the house and arrested its four occupants: Randy Jennings, eighteen years old; Bradford Lilley, nineteen years old; George Dewitt, seventeen years old; and Larry Medley, sixteen years old. They were placed under $60,000 bond each, reduced to $4,000 after a bond reduction hearing. On September 20, 1972, Finlator went to Central Prison in Raleigh to see Jennings, DeWitt, and Lilly. He reported that Medley had recently been released on a bond paid for by Nell Hirschberg, a professor at the University of North Carolina. Medley still carried the bullet from the shoot-in in his body and desperately needed medical attention.[38]

The young men told Finlator that they belonged to a group called the National Committee to Combat Fascism and were in High Point to provide breakfast for young black children. According to their account of the shoot-in, the police, around 100 in number, arrived at 6:00 a.m. on the morning of February 10 and ordered them to come out of the house. When they saw how formidably they were surrounded, they were afraid to come out, remembering, as they put it, that some of the brothers in other places had been gunned down by the police. The police then fired tear gas at them, which was followed by heavy shooting with guns. After they emerged, they were charged with assault with intention to kill, assault on law enforcement officers, and interference with officers in performances of their duty. In the jail, where they had been for eight months, their chief complaint, they told Finlator, was the racist treatment they were receiving, not simply from the other prisoners but also from the guards. "Out in life," they said, "they could handle that kind of racism by simply walking away, but in the prison there was no exit." Finlator commented that the young men were fine looking and intelligent and "seemed to think that the hostility they encountered in High Point came from the white structure, a kind of jealousy over their success in doing for poor black children what the white community . . . had failed to do." Finlator asked for contributions. Their bonds were paid, and the three prisoners were released.[39]

Less famous prisoners were also Finlator's concern. In 1968, as chair of the North Carolina Civil Liberties Union, he contacted an attorney on behalf of Elmer Brown, an African American who had been placed in an institution for the criminally insane without a trial and with serious doubts that he had committed a crime. In 1970 Finlator marched with Coretta Scott King and others to protest the death penalty imposed on an eighteen-year-old black woman imprisoned in Raleigh. In 1972 he worked for the transfer of Roy Lee Fox, confined in Raleigh's Central Prison, to a prison in Asheville, where he could be closer to the home of his ailing mother and large family. In 1973 Finlator helped inmate Philip Walton secure work-release employment with the state highway commission and ultimately parole. He worked also for the parole of James Eugene Walker, imprisoned in what his mother called the "lock-up" and "the hole" for eight years. As chair of the North Carolina Civil Liberties Union, he fought for legislation to pay prisoners a minimum wage and helped establish a prisoners' union to deal with such matters as working conditions, workmen's compensation, educational and recreational opportunities, health, food, and visitation rights.[40] Finlator was peerless in his devotion to those he believed to be victims of oppression.

Mail condemning his efforts on behalf of prison reform poured into Finlator's office. His wife, Mary Lib, worried that her husband was allowing statements and enclosures to disturb him. When asked how he endured these vicious attacks, she responded, "After a while I stopped worrying because I suspected he was enjoying the battle."[41]

Finlator challenged people at Pullen Church for twenty-six years. He called for abolition of the death penalty, open housing, an end to literacy tests for voting, raising the minimum wage, pardon for civil rights activists, better treatment for prisoners, an end to all-white private academies at state expense, an end to censorship of textbooks, removal of discriminatory wording in North Carolina statutes (the words "Negro" and "colored" within North Carolina statutes were eventually removed), reparations for African Americans, and an end to the Vietnam War, until the fateful one that forced his retirement. The University of North Carolina was given $90 million by the Department of Health, Education, and Welfare (HEW) to desegregate all its facilities. The secretary of education was supposed to enforce it, but did not. Finlator kept writing to him, trying to persuade him to do so, but it didn't help. Finally, at the suggestion of the people on the Civil Rights Commission in Washington and as chair of the North Carolina Advisory Committee, he sent a telegram to President Carter to urge him to make his secretary of education enforce the law or withdraw the $90 million given to the university. People in the congregation who were employed at the university were furious. The deacons called for his immediate retirement and named the date. "I'll go to the congregation and they will sustain me," he thought, but immediately reconsidered. "Suppose I do that and win. I'm sixty-eight years old. What kind of Pyrrhic victory would that be?" Instead of retiring in six months as the deacons requested, Finlator agreed to retire in two years, in 1982.[42]

It was not easy for him to leave a church he loved, attended by his wife and three children, his mother, his sister and her family, his daughter-in-law, and his grandchildren, in the city in which he had resided for most of his life, all because he spoke his conscience. With his gift of longevity, he could have continued for at least another ten years. He sadly commented, "For twenty-six years, the congregation never asked me *not* to speak on controversial issues. I never got officially any word of disapproval. I never got an injunction to tell me to stop. It was an unprecedented action in a Southern Baptist church. The congregation, not the deacons, are supposed to make the decisions. It was mean and hurtful and something I can never fully understand." The forced retirement affirmed the long-held thesis of Baptist minister Rev. McLeod Bryan that no liberal minister could survive in the South. Bryan immediately contacted Finlator and began writing his book about Finlator, *Dissenter in the Baptist Southland*.[43]

Retirement did not stifle Finlator's enthusiasm for civil rights. He continued to serve on the North Carolina Advisory Committee to the United States Commission on Civil Rights, the governing board of the North Carolina Civil Liberties Union, and the advisory board of People of Faith Against the Death Penalty; continued expressing his opinions in dozens of newspapers and at meetings throughout the state; and continued to incur the wrath of those who opposed him. Finlator admitted that he never expected his resolutions and statements to be immediately approved. It was his intention to present to the public viewpoints other than those of the majority, to help people understand that there was always another side to every issue and that such divergent viewpoints might someday become acceptable. In the words of Warren Carr of Wake Forest University, "Bill Finlator takes the Christian ethic so seriously that he offends many, he scandalizes some, and is foolish in the view of others. In short, he is a prophet."[44]

In his last years Finlator's contributions to racial and social justice were recognized and appreciated. He received many awards, not only from the groups he served but also from Wake Forest University and the University of North Carolina at Chapel Hill. He received the coveted North Carolina Award for Public Service in 2001, and, at the age of ninety-two, he was inducted into the Raleigh Hall of Fame (September 8, 2005) by officials who, he noted, "in the past objected to many of my opinions." He told his audience, "I have no regrets. I accomplished what I set out to do, I spoke for justice." Finlator fought the good fight and dared to step in where others feared to tread. Someone from the white Christian community had to counter the opinions of Rev. James Cole, Grand Wizard of the Ku Klux Klan in Charlotte; Rev. James P. Dees, president of the North Carolina Defenders of States' Rights, Inc.; and Rev. Ebenezer Myers of Lenoir, North Carolina, author of *The Race Problem in a Nutshell*. Finlator once said, "A minister should be bold and brassy and something of a ham."[45] In the public eye, he fit that description, but privately and as a pastor, he was caring, kind, forgiving, and humble, much like the person of Jesus Christ.

David Moose

David Moose, a United Methodist minister, was born in 1941 when Clarence Jordan was just beginning to establish Koinonia Farm. Moose was born in

Little Rock but raised in Morrilton, Arkansas, a town cofounded by his grandfather. Moose attributes his openness toward black people to his mother. One of his early playmates was a black boy. Moose asked his mother, "Why can't Henry enter the house from the front door like my other friends?" His mother replied, "Henry is just as much your playmate as all the white children who come to play and should be treated just as kindly as you treat your white playmates."[46] Moose was too young to understand what segregation meant, but he would soon be aware of how angry white people could become. He was in senior high school in his hometown when the Little Rock crisis occurred: "I was casually dating a girl from Little Rock at the time, an out-and-out segregationist. She tried to argue with me that segregation was the way God meant it to be. In my limited understanding, I would argue back that she was taking scriptures out of context and ignoring a lot of scriptures that call us to an acceptance and openness toward all people. Well, we didn't date very long after that. The schools in Morrilton at that point were still segregated. We had a white high school and a black high school and it was obvious which one was better equipped."[47]

When Moose attended Hendrix College, an all-white Methodist school in Conway, Arkansas, he offered to room with a black student, but Hendrix officially refused his request. Desiring to prove the foolishness and injustice of exclusiveness, he made visits to the Philander Smith campus in Little Rock, a traditionally black college of the United Methodist Church, to interview local students and those from Africa and wrote articles about them for his campus newspaper. Soon after he graduated, Hendrix dropped its color bar.[48]

From college, Moose went to Saint Paul School of Theology, a United Methodist seminary in Kansas City, Missouri, where nonwhite students, both foreign and domestic, were equally accepted. Ordained by the Arkansas Methodist Conference, he was assigned a small Methodist church in Forrest City, the trading center and county seat for farming communities in the delta region (an expanse of rich alluvium soil created by constant flooding over thousands of years, extending along western Mississippi and eastern Arkansas). Moose, his wife, and two children arrived in Forrest City in 1969, at the beginning of what many remembered as Arkansas's long, hot summer. He commented, "My wife and I lived there many years that one summer."[49]

The family had entered a town in turmoil, and there was little he could do except to try to understand what was happening and why it was happening, and guide his congregation in the direction his conscience told him was just. All the components for full-scale agitation existed: black people pushed off farms due to mechanization, trying to find new opportunities in a town that had some industries, and white supremacist groups such as the Concerned Citizens' Committee, the John Birch Society, and the Ku Klux Klan determined to maintain the status quo of white supremacy. Trouble between the races erupted when Rev. J. F. Cooley, a civil rights activist, was fired from his teaching job at the local black high school, supposedly for insubordination. In retaliation, angry black students tore up desks and broke windows. Four black students were convicted of vandalism and sentenced to state juvenile training schools. Rev. Cooley and Rev. Cato Brooks, cochairs of the Committee for Peaceful Coexistence, planned a five-day, 140-mile march from West Memphis, Arkansas, to Little Rock to dramatize black poverty and alleged police brutality against black teenagers. Towns along the protest route announced they would be ready with police and shotguns, but there was a missing component. Orval Faubus was no longer in power, and liberal-minded Winthrop Rockefeller occupied the governor's office. Rockefeller went to Forrest City to investigate the trouble, meeting for seven hours with local black and white leaders, listening to twenty-five demands by black activists, including one to raise funds for black-owned businesses. As a result, Rockefeller promised to set up a special commission to work with the Committee for Peaceful Coexistence, and the scheduled march was postponed.[50]

Earlier that summer Brooks and Cooley had invited Lance Watson, popularly known as "Sweet Willie Wine," leader of the Invaders, a militant black activist group in Memphis, to help organize a boycott of downtown white merchants in an effort to get them to employ African American clerks. At times violence erupted. White vigilantes attacked Bonner McCollum, publisher of the local newspaper, because he printed articles about black protests. Three white newsmen, two black demonstrators, and Sweet Willie Wine were also attacked. After two white women claimed they had been raped by black teenagers, white residents began picketing and demonstrating in front of the police station and city hall, demanding law and order and the resignation of Mayor Robert Cope and Police Chief Marvin Gunn. The mayor finally called in the National Guard, and, as the summer ended, there seemed to be some degree of peace in Forrest City. Moose did his best to minister to his congregation, but he got into trouble anyway.[51]

Shortly after his arrival, Moose went downtown to make some purchases and noticed a small group of marchers making a protest. He asked a bystander what was going on. Someone recognized him, and immediately a false rumor circulated that the new Methodist preacher was marching with protestors. Moose received nasty telephone calls and a barrage of pamphlets on his front lawn from the Ku Klux Klan and the John Birch Society. Church attendance dropped, and after a brief stay of seven months, he was transferred to Fort Smith in western Arkansas as assistant pastor to the largest church in the conference. He stated, "I was just a new minister in town concerned about the community, trying to ease the desegregation process and calm the nerves of my congregation, but I got shot out of the water pretty quickly."[52]

At Fort Smith, a preschool program was being planned. As told by Moose, someone in the church asked, "Will we accept blacks?" John Bayless, the senior pastor, said calmly, "The Methodist Church does not discriminate based on race. Our program will be open to whoever needs it." Moose commented, "That seemed to settle the issue and I knew that times were slowly changing, but western Arkansas was not the same as the delta region."[53]

In 1995 Moose was transferred to a church in West Memphis, Arkansas, back in the delta region. While attending an event marking the thirtieth anniversary of the death of Martin Luther King Jr., Moose met fellow Methodist minister and black activist Rev. James Lawson, who had served at Centenary Methodist Church in Memphis. Moose asked Lawson how he could best minister to his white conservative members, especially those who genuinely feared blacks. Lawson advised him, "Talk about the hospitality of Jesus," knowing full well what would happen if Moose attempted anything more drastic. Moose took Lawson's advice and preached from his pulpit how Jesus offered openness and friendship to a Samaritan woman in spite of the fact that Jewish people in those days did not speak to Samaritans. Moose contended, "I never saw myself as an 'activist,' but I did see myself as one who desired to share God's grace and love with all people around me, black, white, or other. Sometimes, I had black ministers fill my pulpit, both in my absence and in my presence. . . . The Sundays of these visits were always announced in advance and, thankfully, we didn't have any 'issues' or noticeable absences, and after the services, members greeted the guests warmly. I'd like to think that my attitude and teachings contributed to the openness of my parishioners."[54]

In 2007 a white police officer shot and killed a black youth one block from Moose's church. The officer believed the black youth, DeAunta Farrow, was carrying a gun, and when "the suspect" did not drop the weapon, he opened fire. Only then did he realize that the "gun" was a toy gun and that he had shot and killed a twelve-year-old child. Family members and eyewitnesses believed DeAunta was shot without just cause and may not, in fact, have even been carrying a toy gun, but a bag of potato chips. The incident tore the community apart. Only a small number of white people attended DeAunta's funeral, among them Rev. Moose. He and his wife, Judy, led fifteen interracial dialogues at a local restaurant attempting to create "a bridge over troubled waters," but, Moose commented, "Tempers flared; there were people on both banks of the river trying to set fire to the bridge."[55]

Some good came out of the interracial dialogues, as Moose and his wife met and helped a young black couple begin a recycling business. They gave Dannie and Deresa Gatewood $200 toward a flatbed trailer and later loaned them money for a used pickup truck. Judy Moose helped with the bookkeeping, and the Moose home became a contact point for people wanting to drop off materials for recycling. Dannie once explained their friendship by telling

Rev. Moose, "You are the first white man who ever treated me with respect."[56] Although times are still difficult in West Memphis and Moose has retired from his pastorate, he continues to take an active part in racial reconciliation.

Joseph Sanderson

The experience of Fr. Joe Sanderson (1934–2015) in eastern Arkansas was as painful as that of Rev. Moose. Born in Town Creek, Alabama, the son of the town's mayor, Sanderson was a member of the elite white southern aristocracy. He remembered the sight of his grandfather, owner of a large plantation, beating his black farm laborers because they would not work quickly enough, but he could never reconcile such action with the love he felt for his black "mammy": "She was a beautiful lady and I was with her constantly for the first five years of my life. She stayed with me in my room and was more of a mother to me than my own mother at that time."[57]

At Seabury Western Episcopal Seminary in Chicago, Sanderson sat down to dinner with a black person on an equal basis for the first time and experienced another understanding of what it meant to be an African American. His fellow seminarian came from Birmingham, Alabama, and described for Sanderson the terrible, terrible feelings he had about having the money to go to the movies but not being allowed to go and not being allowed to go to the drugstore for a milkshake or a sundae. Greater visions of the black experience came after graduation from Seabury and ordination, when he came in contact with black activists. He was managing a coffeehouse for an Episcopal church in Nashville, Tennessee, frequented by Stokely Carmichael, Rev. James Bevel, Bernard Lafayette, Rafael Davis, Sweet Willie Wine, and Rev. James Lawson, all who came to enjoy good music (Nashville's specialty), good food (soul style), and conversation filled with anger and agony about their struggles. For the young white Alabamian, it was a revelation and an education, but in 1968, soon after the death of Martin Luther King Jr., he was assigned to St. Andrew's Parish in Marianna, Arkansas, a small town twenty-five miles south of Forrest City. For Sanderson, no place could be more unlike Nashville. The elite white minority, the town's planters, doctors, lawyers, and bankers, were the people of Sanderson's parish. He described them as "simply marvelous, gracious, loving, entertaining, fun to be with, but when the black issue was approached," he exclaimed, "their hearts trembled with terror! The boycotts and demonstrations of the 1960s threatened their way of life, creating resentment, fury, and hatred for blacks. Even the household help came to be feared."[58]

Sanderson's involvement in the movement came when he heard of the story of a black farm laborer who died one hot summer day while being driven to a hospital in Memphis because the local hospital would not take him. The laborer had been found lying in a field near a tractor with both his legs almost completely severed. A concerned person passing by put him in his Volkswagen bus and took him to the county hospital. When he was denied admission, the person started driving him to Memphis, some fifty miles north of Marianna, but the laborer died along the way. When Sanderson heard the story, he was appalled. "Somehow in my theology, I had to wrestle with what happened. I had to go to bed each night thinking about it and wake up each morning trying to figure out what this meant to me as a priest of the Episcopal Church in a small Arkansas town. What do I do with it? How do I react to something like that?"[59]

Shortly afterward, an old house in the black neighborhood was established as a clinic by the Volunteers in Service to America (VISTA) and staffed by a young doctor from New York, whom Sanderson described as "wide-eyed, bushy-tailed, and optimistic about what he was going to do." Although the clinic was called "Community Hospital," it was established primarily to serve black people, and Sanderson knew that this was his opportunity to help, but when he tried to solicit the interest of the influential whites—the planters, bankers, doctors, and lawyers—he was politely advised to "get out of the situation right quick and not do anything else about the hospital." Sanderson did just the opposite. He and his wife became hospital volunteers, and he functioned as a special liaison between the black and white communities. The Community Hospital became the seat of the NAACP and the place where strategies were planned.[60]

The next major campaign for civil rights in Marianna came during the summer of 1970 when school integration was about to happen, sixteen years after the landmark Supreme Court decision and one year after the desegregation of the Forrest City schools. The John Birch Society was already building a school for white children across the street from Sanderson's church. That summer the Arkansas Society for Racial Unity and the NAACP were planning a prayer vigil for the peaceful integration of the schools and were looking for white clergy who would help bring harmony between the races.[61]

Sanderson became the only white clergyman who offered to help. On a sultry Saturday in August, with the wind still and the air heavy, Sanderson delivered a sermon from Isaiah and prayed for the schools: "The wolf also shall dwell with the lamb, and the leopard shall lie down with the kid. . . . and a little child shall lead them." He was the only white man in the town square that day besides the head of the Society for Racial Unity: "My daughter and wife were the only white women among the large gathering of black people, and we all prayed for the peaceful integration of the schools." But once he gave his sermon, the attitude of his parishioners changed. His young son was shunned by playmates, and his daughter became the only white girl in her public school class.[62]

To members of the black community, however, Sanderson was a friend. Several months later the NAACP appealed to him for help with a group of young black activists who were threatening to burn the town down unless their grievances were addressed. Sanderson related, "I went to them and asked what could be done to prevent this from happening. They presented me with the list of grievances, and I, in turn, presented the list to the white community, predominantly those from my parish. They just laughed, saying I should not take the threat seriously. Well it was serious." On July 27, 1971, the town's news-paper reported, "A fire described as unquestionably arson gutted three build-ings on Main Street during the early morning hours." The next day "containers and fuel were found on the roof of the building and in other places leading to the conclusion that the fire's origin was definitely arson. The building exploded inward before the fire department arrived. . . . Reliable estimates placed the loss in excess of $200,000." In the aftermath of the fire, Sanderson, mentally and physically exhausted and suffering with a bleeding ulcer, collapsed and was admitted to a hospital in Memphis. A group from the church went to see him and asked what they could do. "You had a chance three weeks ago," he told them, "there's nothing you can do now." Sanderson did his best, but it took his collapse for his parishioners to accept the enormity of the situation. Sander-son recovered after several months and left Marianna to become a chaplain at a college in Jonesboro, Arkansas. In 1983 he returned to his native Alabama, where he became rector of the Episcopal Church of the Epiphany in Gun-tersville. There is not a large African American population in the north lake region of Alabama, but several black families attend his church, and several black friends lead him to the best spots for hunting and fishing.[63]

◆ ◆ ◆

These ministers did not demonstrate, did not agitate, and were undeterred by opposition. They looked for and found ways to witness for racial justice during the civil rights movement, the Black Power movement, and beyond. Jordan and McClain set in motion organizations that are continuing. The opposition and attacks to Koinonia Farm were unfathomable. Its survival to this day is extraordinary. In 2008 Koinonia Farm was the recipient of an International Peace Award from the worldwide Community of Christ, headquartered in Independence, Missouri. The award included a $30,000 honorarium, a bronze peace sculpture, and recognition that Koinonia Farm is "a sacred community . . . where we find the presence of repentance, forgiveness, speaking the truth in love, hospitality and reconciliation, the tender trust of knowing and being known, and the assurance that our friends in the community would lay down their lives for us." One must also think about all the intentional Christian communities that have been inspired by Clarence Jordan and Koinonia Farm, among them Don Mosley and Jubilee Partners, in Comer, northeast Georgia; Shane Claiborne and The Simple Way in Philadelphia, Pennsylvania; Jonathan

Wilson-Hartgrove and Rutba House in Durham, North Carolina; The Open Door Community in Atlanta; Communality, in Lexington, Kentucky; and as far away as the Grain of Wheat Community in Winnipeg, Manitoba.[64]

Rev. David Moose set an example for racial reconciliation in West Memphis, Arkansas, even when shunned by the all-black meeting of Concerned Pastors and Citizens in the aftermath of the DeAunta Farrow tragedy. Revs. Moose, Finlator, and Sanderson followed their consciences regardless of what white segregationists or black militants thought. Finlator's exposure and influence were great in North Carolina because of local news coverage and his participation as representative for national civil rights groups. As a result, he made friends and enemies. Sanderson felt compassion for blacks and braved a lonely path to help black activists in his own individual way, but he could not change most of the attitudes of people in his parish or in the Arkansas delta town of Marianna.

Travis Frank

Fr. Travis Frank, born in 1958 in Houston, Texas, served as rector of St. Andrew's Parish in Marianna, Arkansas, from 2002 to 2006 and followed in Sanderson's footsteps. In 2004 Frank was selected by the mayor of Marianna, an African American, to serve on the Community Action Committee when trouble was brewing in the desegregated public schools. Frank describes the Marianna public schools during that time as predominantly black, with "borderline chaos, and corruption that was legendary—money drained off to hand-picked contractors, teachers ill equipped to teach, and those who held on to the last day for retirement, all at the cost of children's education." In 2004 a boycott was conducted by black community members and students to make the school system better. At one of the committee meetings, Frank suggested to a black committee member that there were white people who would support the boycott. According to Frank, she responded, "We have always included our African American children in the fight for our rights," and she was dismissive of whites doing anything noteworthy. Frank told her, "I have seen photographs of the march in Selma in 1965, and the image was speckled with the white faces of Episcopal priests and others who were standing for black rights," but she did not respond. As Frank commented, "She seemed angry that I pointed out this fact of history. The black committee members were also angry that what their parents had fought so hard for—education—was being trashed because of the rap culture, teen pregnancy, drugs, alcohol abuse and the poor academic standards that had developed." According to Frank, "The delta has been left behind in culture, race relations, and the dread of poverty."[65]

In 2006 Frank was transferred to an all-white Episcopal church in Helena, Arkansas, where he tried to help poor black people in the region pay their bills with discretionary funds from the church. As told by Frank, "The need was overwhelming. The working poor lived just beyond the help of most government support, and there was little recourse for them except to ask help from churches and area agencies that had money from people in higher paying brackets. After I made public the use of the discretionary funds and the names of the blacks who had received the money, my congregants were furious. Many were heard to use racial slurs, much to my embarrassment and shame as their rector." Frank was soon forced to leave the church. He returned to his home state of Texas, where he continues to work on behalf of the poor and invisible.[66]

"I was frustrated with the way things were in the delta," he laments. "It is a world unto itself. The people who seem to thrive there have come from the powerful landed people with a name denoting such a place in their community. Most had their family names engraved in the stained-glass windows of the church. They believe it is not un-Christ-like to ignore the poverty and ignorance around them, using that good old Protestant work ethic as a philosophical groundwork: 'Those people choose this kind of life.' I was raised in a lower white middle-class family with a blue-collar dad and five siblings. It was my education that lifted me out of the cycle of near poverty and gave me an opportunity to become a priest, but the major difference between the people of the delta and myself is that while they believe in God, I believe God, and that changes how I respond to the needs around me."[67] In his willingness to address the pain and suffering he saw around him, Fr. Frank is very much like the ministers whose stories appear in this book.

Rev. David Moose comments, "I am glad that things were not as bad in West Memphis as they were in the delta." In answer to the question, "How effective were your efforts at racial reconciliation," Moose answered, "That's hard to say, but I believe Judy and I, particularly through the fifteen public dialogue sessions we led after the shooting of DeAunta Farrow, plus all the meetings I attended, helped West Memphis avoid the kind of civil unrest (even riots) seen in Ferguson, Missouri, in 2014, and Baltimore, Maryland, in 2015. And after I challenged the 'color bar' at Hendrix College in 1961, blacks were admitted starting four years later."[68]

On Martin Luther King Day, January 19, 2015, Rev. David Moose received a Lifetime Achievement Award from the Crittenden County (Arkansas) Christian Coalition, the first of what is to be an annual award. The coalition, headed by African American minister Rev. C. W. Campbell, is intended to be ecumenical and interracial, but is mostly black. Rev. Moose was the only non-black recipient to receive the award that year. He received it in recognition and appreciation for his lifelong efforts for racial reconciliation.[69] Wounds were beginning to heal in West Memphis.

═ 7 ═

DENOMINATIONS
Movers, Shakers, Dissidents, Reformers, Missioners

We have been part of a culture which has crippled the Negro and then blamed him for limping.
—FOY VALENTINE (1923–2006), executive secretary of the Christian Life Commission for the Southern Baptist Convention

Protestantism has been the dominant religious system of the South since colonial times, and among white Protestants in the South, there has been a Baptist-Methodist hegemony, with other groups in smaller numbers. According to a Gallup Poll of 1967, 57 percent of southern churchgoers were members of the Southern Baptist denomination; 30 percent were members of Methodist churches; 25 percent were members of Episcopal churches; 23 percent were members of Presbyterian churches; and 8 percent were members of Lutheran churches. Disciples of Christ and Churches of Christ were omitted from this sampling; in a poll conducted by American Geographers in 1965, the Churches of Christ membership was estimated at three million (mostly in Kentucky, Tennessee, and Texas, making it the third largest religious group in the South). It is obvious from these figures that Baptists were the most numerous religious group in the South. Will Campbell recalled that in rural Amite County, Mississippi, where he was born and grew up, everyone was Baptist. He knew of no Methodists, Presbyterians, Episcopalians, Catholics, or Jews.[1]

A review of the statements and resolutions of the governing boards of these major Protestant denominations reveals confessions to many sins and crimes committed against African Americans during the eras of slavery and segregation. Finally, these denominations began calling for a society opposed to discrimination and one in obedience to the highest law of all, the "royal law of love," but, according to scholars, most church members were more closely allied to the southern Jim Crow culture than to the "radical ethics of Christ."

The most eloquent statements came from the Southern Baptist Convention (SBC), but because Baptists follow a precept of "liberty of conscience" and govern through congregations, many Southern Baptist churches and ministers do not take the resolutions seriously. As independent Baptist minister Clarence Jordan (chapter 6) told his biographer, "If anybody has to bear the blame and the guilt for all the sit-ins and all the demonstrations and all the disorders in the South, it's the white-washed Christians who have had the Word of God locked up in their hearts and have refused to battle with it."[2] Eventually members of southern denominations changed, as this chapter shows.

The question asked is, "Did some denominational people change because the times changed or did they change because some ministers and elders within their ranks fought the battle for racial justice?" Or, as Pastor Robert Seymour of Binkley Baptist Church in Chapel Hill, North Carolina (chapter 4), suggested, "Perhaps it was the scattered church: people behind desks, in offices, behind counters, working in school cafeterias, parents, teachers, doctors, lawyers, carpenters, electricians, anonymous benefactors, women's organizations, a congregate church without a building, often unrecognized, but serving God and speaking out?" As written in the Bible, "Those who were scattered went from place to place, proclaiming the word." It seems that all factors worked together to bring about the transformation of southern denominations. According to Lutheran pastor Arnold Voigt, "My ministry in the South taught me that God works through many different people in many different ways and through many different denominations and associations."[3]

Baptists

In the Baptist tradition, the largest of the southern denominations, progressive ministers made concerted efforts to counter such outspoken segregationists as W. A. Criswell (1909–2002), born in Eldorado, Oklahoma, and pastor of the world's largest Baptist church (in Dallas, Texas), who expressed fears that integration would bring along with it liberal theology, socialism, Communism, and atheism. T. B. Maston (1897–1988), born in Jefferson County, Tennessee, taught, however, that all people are equal because of the redeeming work of Christ and that there was a more open way of looking at the situation. He taught Christian ethics for more than thirty years at Southwestern Baptist Theological Seminary in Fort Worth, Texas, and influenced many progressive Baptists. Rev. Brooks Ramsey, who supported Martin Luther King Jr. during the Albany, Georgia, movement of 1962 (chapter 2), was Maston's pupil during his student days at Southwestern Baptist Theological Seminary.[4]

Foy Valentine (1923–2006), born in Edgewood, Texas, spent a summer working at Koinonia Farm with Clarence Jordan, and entered Southwestern Baptist Theological Seminary, also becoming Maston's pupil and later a pastor and member of the SBC. As secretary of the Texas Christian Life Commission in 1957, Valentine wrote, "Jesus came preaching the gospel to the poor, giving sight to the blind, healing the sick, associating with social outcasts, and planting the seeds for the greatest social revolution in history." He urged Christians to be part of the social revolution. As executive secretary of the SBC's Christian Life Commission during the 1960s, he did his best to be the SBC's conscience. The historian David Stricklin indicates that Valentine became well known and counted as his friends journalist Bill Moyers and President Jimmy Carter. According to Alan Scot Willis, Valentine firmly believed (as did Clarence Jordan) that the civil rights protest movement came about because of the silence of Christians when they could have helped African Americans.[5]

During the 1970s the SBC showed little interest in racial issues; however, state Baptist conventions in North Carolina, Virginia, Arkansas, Mississippi, and Alabama began to hold joint meetings with black and white congregations, and the number of black churches in the SBC increased. Some were dually aligned with the National Baptist Convention. In 1979 Harper Shannon, president of the Alabama State Convention, stated, "This is the most significant thing that Alabama Baptists (both black and white) have ever attempted to do together in the history of our denomination," but the SBC that same year elected a conservative fundamentalist president, Adrian Rogers, who was allied with the religious Right on all political issues. Fundamentalists, although a minority, succeeded in gaining control of the SBC's agencies, boards, and seminaries. The historian Mark Newman wrote, "They were well organized, had a clear cut program, faced a divided and ill-prepared opposition." According to the historian Wayne Flynt, the moderates were ambivalent: "They desperately desired to maintain control and allow some theological diversity but were reluctant to become enmeshed in denominational politics." Baptist progressives who had championed civil rights and integration were no longer able to be influential, and some, like Robert Seymour (chapter 4) and W. W. Finlator (chapter 6), aligned their churches dually with the American Baptist Churches, U.S.A. Many progressives founded parallel organizations, such as the Southern Baptist Alliance in 1987 and the Cooperative Baptist Fellowship in 1991. Seymour moved his church into the Southern Baptist Alliance in 1992. Rogers attacked the Baptist Alliance and cooperative programs and was against moderates. In a history of the SBC, Rev. Jesse C. Fletcher argued that some moderates remained in the SBC because "they did not want to do anything to undermine their efforts to assert themselves as *real* Southern Baptists."[6]

The SBC, although conservative on most issues, has felt the influence of the civil rights movement and its progressive ministers. According to Fletcher, "Few aspects of Southern Baptist progress during this period have been more overlooked and eclipsed by its controversy than the Convention's remarkable progress regarding Blacks, Hispanics, and other ethnic groups. . . . Its current attitude can only be explained in terms of radical changes in the larger culture, paired with the slow but sure efforts of biblical principles as advocated by such Baptist pioneers . . . as Clarence Jordan, T. B. Maston, and Foy Valentine." Even W. A. Criswell, as president of the SBC in 1968, dramatically recanted his earlier segregationist position: "I don't think that segregation could have been or was at any time intelligently, seriously supported by the Bible." Infighting, schism, and division have always been a characteristic of the SBC, but it seems that on this one issue of racial reconciliation, the factions in the SBC have come together.[7]

In 1995 the SBC issued the largest mass expression of regret and repentance that had yet been made to African Americans on the event of the SBC's sesquicentennial anniversary. The SBC lamented "historic acts of evil" such as slavery and recognized that "the racism which yet plagues our culture today is inextricably tied to the past." Forgiveness was asked from African American brothers and sisters and a commitment was made "to eradicate racism in all its forms from Southern Baptist life and ministry." Rev. Charles T. Carter, pastor of Shades Mountain Baptist Church in Vestavia Hills, Alabama, and chairman of the Resolutions Committee that drafted the statement, added that the statement alone was not enough: "We must now move to putting words into action." Rev. Gary North of Youngstown, Ohio, the denomination's second vice-president and the first African American to reach that post, accepted the apology on behalf of "my black brothers and sisters."[8]

In 1995, the year of the apology, African American Nate McMillan (born in 1951 in Brooklyn, New York) was commissioned by the SBC as a "seed planter" to work for racial reconciliation and to bring more black Baptist churches into the SBC. Newman suggested it was tokenism, but for McMillan, it was an opportunity for interracial cooperation and reconciliation. In 1965 McMillan moved with his family to Orangeburg, South Carolina, and would not allow race to stop him from achieving success. He became a successful agent for the Liberty Insurance Company and an office manager in Greenville, South Carolina. In 1985 his company moved him to Orangeburg as the first black district office manager. In 1990 he began a ministry of reconciliation and preached his first sermon at the all-black Greater Faith Baptist Church in Orangeburg, interrupted by five years of service in Saudi Arabia during the first Gulf War. After his service, he returned to Greater Faith and became assistant pastor. He believed that God was preparing him for a special ministry to heal the bitterness that resulted from the killing of three students and the wounding of twenty-seven others by police officers on the campus of South Carolina State University in Orangeburg in 1968. The students were protesting against a bowling alley that had closed its doors to black people, the only bowling alley in Orangeburg. The incident was not easily forgotten by African Americans. McMillan believed that if racial reconciliation was to occur, it would have to be led by clergy. He was not yet an ordained minister when he approached white Rev. Bill Coates, pastor of the First Baptist Church. Coates liked McMillan, and together they planned a meeting of all Orangeburg pastors, black and white, to talk about their differences and the steps that could be taken for reconciliation. One white pastor at the meeting exclaimed, "I've been a racist all my life, but from this moment on, I'm going to ask God to deliver me." This meeting and subsequent meetings brought a new fellowship and a new era to Orangeburg. Change and forgiveness were "hot topics" on their agenda.[9]

In 1999 the SBC established an interracial Southern Baptist church in the Orangeburg area called the Petra Community Church. McMillan was invited to be the pastor and left his twenty-year career at the Liberty Insurance Company. His ordination was attended by over fifty pastors, black and white. Many could not believe that the Orangeburg-Calhoun Baptist Association would ordain a black minister. McMillan stated with a smile, "They wanted to see it for themselves." To this day, McMillan works to build bridges between blacks and whites and to witness to God's plan for his churches. McMillan is a member of the South Carolina Christian Action Council started by white Rev. Howard McClain (chapter 6). He supervises an insurance internship at South Carolina State University and is an active member of the local school board. He works directly with white minister Rev. Ron Heddle, director of missions for the Orangeburg-Calhoun Baptist Association, in an interracial ministry, conducting community-healing church services and mediating crisis situations in both black and white churches. Author Jack Schuler suggests that the experience of McMillan and Heddle has become a model for religious reconciliation throughout the South.[10]

Since the 1995 apology, the number of black members in the SBC has doubled to about one million throughout the United States. Almost 20 percent of its congregations is black, Latino, or Asian, and many of these people serve in leadership posts in state conventions, seminaries, and other organizations. Rev. McMillan serves as coach-consultant with the Church Multiplication Division of the South Carolina Baptist Convention. As Rev. R. Philip Roberts, member of the SBC, stated in 1999, "Today, we're talking about a Gospel that sees no color." On June 19, 2012, at a meeting in New Orleans, the SBC unanimously elected Rev. Fred Luter Jr., pastor of Franklin Avenue Baptist Church in New Orleans, as its first black president. An amazing act of reconciliation took place a few months later when Rev. Luter was invited to speak from the pulpit of First Baptist Church in Jackson, Mississippi, where Rev. William Douglas Hudgins defended segregation from 1946 until 1969.[11]

Baptists such as Will Campbell, W. W. Finlator, Herbert Gilmore, Thomas Holmes, Clarence Jordan, Howard McClain, Brooks Ramsey, Robert Seymour, Paul Turner, and Charles Webster, whose stories are in this book, may have been considered dissidents by conservative members of the SBC, but not dissident to the Baptist tradition of "liberty of conscience," and not dissident to their belief that "every human life is sacred, and is of equal and immeasurable worth, made in God's image, regardless of race or ethnicity."[12]

Methodists

What made some Methodist ministers brave and forthright in fighting segregation? Perhaps it was the comfort of knowing that they were appointed by the bishop, not the congregation, and they could remain in direct connection with their conference, even if they were dissident. Perhaps it was the Social Creed calling on Methodists to treat all human beings as brothers and sisters, to work for the improvement of society. Or perhaps it was the teachings of John Wesley to "love God with all your heart, mind, soul, and strength . . . and . . . do all the good you possibly can to the bodies and souls of as many people as you can."[13] For many reasons, a strong minority of southern Methodist ministers entered the struggle for black civil rights within the second-most numerous denomination in the South, but they had a double challenge: to support the civil rights movement and to unite their conferences, which had been divided by race since 1939.

The Methodist Episcopal Church South joined the northern Methodist Episcopal Church in 1939 on the condition that northerners would agree to segregate black Methodists into a separate Central Jurisdiction. Northerners agreed, and as the historian Peter C. Murray indicates, the new Methodist Church became "the most rigidly segregated church structure of any national Protestant denomination," but as the civil rights movement advanced, church leaders began to work for change. At the 1956 General Conference, race was the central issue. Amendment IX was added to the constitution, by which local churches and whole conferences of the Central Jurisdiction could voluntarily transfer into white annual conferences in their region. By 1968 all African American conferences had united, with the exception of twelve in the South. Plans to incorporate the Evangelical United Brethren (EUB), a denomination popular in Pennsylvania and the Midwest, into Methodism were delayed because EUB ministers would not approve union with a church that still observed racial segregation. At the 1968 Methodist General Conference, the segregated Central Jurisdiction was officially disbanded, and the target date of 1972 was set for uniting all separated southern conferences. This arrangement was approved by the EUB, and the United Methodist Church, as it is known today, was formed. In 1968 the Methodist General Conference also established a Commission on Religion and Race with the responsibility for monitoring inclusiveness throughout all boards, agencies, and committees of Methodist churches. Statements issued that year called on all Methodists to work for the removal of racial barriers in education, housing, employment, and public accommodations, and to support the right of black people to vote in all public elections; thus the United Methodist Church joined the civil rights movement, at least at the General Conference level.[14]

As Murray relates, merger was difficult. In Georgia, the North Georgia Conference approved a plan, but the white South Georgia Conference would not. Southwest Georgia, part of the South Georgia Conference, the location of Koinonia Farm, was controlled by segregationists during the 1950s and 1960s. Any minister or layperson who spoke for integration was subject to ostracism and even attack, but the minister of Lee Street Methodist Church in Americus, Rev. Edward Carruth (1920–1992), born in Summit, Mississippi, issued a resolution condemning the bombing of Koinonia Farm and devoted a sermon to the cause of restitution. He was forced to resign after serving the congregation for three years. Rev. C. G. Haugabook, born in 1928 in Montezuma, Georgia, was minister to five small Methodist churches in rural Sumter County when the bombing occurred. Someone in one of his Sunday school classes, a state employee at the local trade school, requested that the church support the renovation of the roadside market. Haugabook agreed, but when the church refused, he did not press the issue. The outspoken trade school employee lost his job, and Haugabook, transformed, told his parishioners in a sermon, "I don't want to ride in the back of a Jim Crow bus, go to the back of a Jim Crow station. I don't want anything to do with Jim Crow. . . . Jesus said something about doing 'unto others as you would have them do unto you.' . . . The time has come for all of us to be *Like a Bridge Over Troubled Water*." During the late 1960s, Carruth and Haugabook worked for the merger of the South Georgia Conference. Carruth never left the conference and became a district superintendent for Toombs County in 1971. He was able to directly influence the merger that took place that year.[15]

Haugabook reflected, "History is written in two forms: one is chronological history; the other is *kairos* history. *Kairos* is a Greek word meaning the right time. The nineteen fifties were the right time to bring love into a situation where change needed to occur. Clarence Jordan was trying with love to lift up the people who were at the bottom of the social and economic ladder and give them rights before the civil rights movement actually began, but we waited for the law. When the laws came, we didn't accept them. We rebelled. We bombed Koinonia's roadside stand. We turned dogs on people. We shot them down with fire hoses. *Kairos* is a time when God can act, when God can do something significant. It's a pregnant time when good things can be born, when good things can happen. If we miss that time, it becomes a tragedy. That is the tragedy of the Civil Rights Movement. We missed God's *kairos*." However, times have changed in Georgia. In 2007 black and white residents together had a unity community celebration in Americus, and in 2008 African American James R. King Jr., born in Ashland, Alabama, and former bishop of the Louisville, Kentucky, area, became bishop to the South Georgia Annual Conference.[16]

In South Carolina, it took six years for dedicated Methodist ministers and laypeople to complete the merger. According to Murray, merger in South Carolina was an important accomplishment because it was the largest single African American Annual Conference to be merged with a single white conference. In 1966 Methodist bishop Paul Hardin transferred from the white Alabama–West Florida Methodist Conference to the white South Carolina Methodist Conference. In Alabama, Hardin had been one of the ministers to whom Martin Luther King Jr. addressed his "Letter from a Birmingham Jail." Officially silent concerning beatings and bombings in Alabama and opposed to King's activities in Birmingham, Hardin seemed to have been reborn in South Carolina. Presiding over the white South Carolina Conference, he immediately appointed a committee to deal with merger issues: pensions, insurance, missions, social concerns, evangelism, and education. "The first task," he told the committee, was to elect a chairperson who would be willing to "devote long hours, days, weeks, and perhaps even years to accomplish the merger." One clergyman responded, "If a clergy person holds this position, it might not sit well with the congregation. I think a lay person should be our chair, and I nominate Rhett Jackson."[17] Jackson (1924–2016), born in Florence, South Carolina, was elected.

It became Jackson's responsibility to convince Methodists across the state that the merger was good and necessary. At some meetings in local churches, he barely escaped alive: "They kept asking me hostile questions like, 'Do you want your daughter to marry a black man?' I just said, 'Well if he were a nice man, it would be fine with me.' Changing our thinking was a slow process for all of us." Rev. Matthew McCollom, from the all-black Methodist Conference, was elected chair of the committee, and he and Jackson traveled together across the state. The Federal Bureau of Investigation (FBI) constantly followed McCollom, who was also field director for the National Association for the Advancement of Colored People (NAACP). Jackson related, "We would get into our car and an FBI agent would come and tell us that he was just going to drive around with us so we wouldn't get lost. He would ask us each day where we were going. 'Well,' we told him, 'today we're going to Greenwood and then to Spartanburg. If *you* get lost that's where you'll find us.'" Finally, in 1972, the Annual Conference approved the merger. Jackson commented that the merger was not perfect but worked well. Although individual Methodist churches are still pretty well segregated, at the conference level there is equality, and the Annual Conference has elected one black bishop.[18]

Warmth, sincerity, and unremitting effort enabled Jackson to reach many people, both black and white. His business establishment, The Happy Bookseller, in Columbia became a center for concerned racial liberals and moderates throughout the South. Jack Bass, professor of history at the College of Charleston and author of *The Orangeburg Massacre*, visited The Happy Bookseller in 1995, interested in getting a parole for African American activist Cleveland Sellers, convicted for one year for inciting violence in Orangeburg during 1968. As a member of the state's Probation, Pardon, and Parole Board, Jackson was able to obtain the pardon, which enabled Sellers to return to his home state and gain employment as a professor of African American studies at the University of South Carolina.[19]

In addition to Jackson, white Rev. A. McKay Brabham (1916–1997), born in Bamberg, South Carolina, also worked for change. In an interview with Susan Pierce Johnston, he articulated his belief that "a biracial society founded on special privilege for one race at the expense of the other is a sin against God and an affront to the dignity of all human life." After serving as a pastor for twenty years, Brabham became editor of the *South Carolina Methodist Advocate* in 1960. For ten years, Brabham gave opportunities to South Carolina's progressive Methodist ministers to express support for black civil rights and the merger of the two conferences. In editorial after editorial, Brabham pleaded for racial justice and school integration, but eventually he was forced to resign as editor by segregationist readers who would not tolerate his intercession on behalf of young people who had been arrested for a protest at the General Conference of 1970 in St. Louis, and his own brief arrest.[20]

In a sermon addressed to members of Bethel Methodist Church in Columbia in 1966, published in the *Advocate*, Rev. Fred M. Reese Jr. (1930–2016), born in Knoxville, Tennessee, and graduate of the Vanderbilt School of Theology, explained that in 1966 most African American Methodists did not favor the separate jurisdictional arrangement: "The Central Jurisdiction placed extreme hardship on District Superintendents who had to travel 900 miles across five states to serve their churches and their bishop had to supervise three Conferences across the Carolinas and Tennessee." Reese exhorted, "Such exclusivity has robbed the Church of its most able leadership among African Americans, especially in the South. . . . We in the South are given a tremendous role in history to witness to the inclusive nature of the Christian fellowship. We must not fail."[21]

As chair of the integrated South Carolina Council on Human Relations, Reese wrote a series of articles for the *Advocate* in 1967 giving reasons for South Carolina's lack of racial progress (reasons that could be applied to almost any southern denomination): South Carolina's Methodists were unwilling to look at the church in the light and life of the twentieth century; South Carolina's Methodists lacked seriousness to be a learning church; Methodists were proceeding at a snail's pace in entering human relationships with fellow Methodists in the Central Jurisdiction; and "the cultural captivity of the churches, which dulls the social conscience." The South Carolina Methodist Conference did not appreciate Reese's suggestions, and in 1969 he was forced to take a leave of absence to reassess the minister's role. With the help of Martin England, the itinerant Baptist minister in Greenville, he was provided with a fellowship to study at Harvard Divinity School in Cambridge, Massachusetts, where he worked as a pharmacist (his undergraduate degree) to help support his wife and six children. He returned to the conference one year later.[22]

In 1971 Rev. Eben Taylor (1925–2008), born in Florence, became a member of the Committee of Six, which helped prepare the final draft of the South Carolina Plan of Merger. When asked what compelled the committee to act on behalf of merger, Taylor responded, "For most of us, it was to let God, through us, love our neighbors, who were being terribly violated by the church and society. This commitment to justice and inclusion and affirmation of all persons still claims us!"[23]

Although the Methodist merger was difficult, the Commission on Religion and Race was able to report in 1972 that all southern conferences had merged, with the exception of Alabama, Mississippi, and parts of Arkansas.[24]

The struggle to end segregation in the Alabama and Mississippi Conferences took much time and patience. As Rev. Charles Prestwood (1932–1979) wrote in 1960, "There was no conspicuous progressive organization within the North Alabama Conference," and the liberal ministers within the Alabama–West Florida Conference kept leaving the state. In one year, 1968 to 1969, Dallas Blanchard recorded that the conference lost almost 20 percent of its pastoral ministers. (Revs. Donald E. Collins and Charles Prestwood were among the departing group.)[25] The stories of Dallas Blanchard, Thomas Butts, Floyd Enfinger, Ennis Sellers, and Andrew Turnipseed, members of the progressive coalition, have been told in this book. These ministers remained members of the conference, but were powerless.

Robert Gaines Corley, in his dissertation, related that segregationists from the North-Alabama Conference gathered at Birmingham's Highlands Methodist Church in March 1959 and formed the Methodist Layman's Union, declaring, "The Methodist Church is strictly Anglo-Saxon, and racial integration is a colossal blunder, a betrayal of unborn generations and a monstrous crime against civilization." According to Corley, Methodists in Alabama were told by the Layman's Union, "If your preacher doesn't preach segregation from his pulpit, you cut his salary to a dollar a year and sell his parsonage." The Layman's Union intimidated and publicly maligned Rev. Robert Hughes (among other Methodist ministers). Hughes was not minister of a church but was head of the Alabama Council on Human Relations, a branch of the Southern Regional Council and the only group in Alabama calling for racial justice at that time. In 1959 he wrote an article for the council's newsletter favoring merger. The Layman's Union quickly retaliated by sending letters to all Methodist ministers in the state condemning the council as a "small group of whites and Negroes who have been preaching full racial integration on all levels." Hughes and his family began receiving threatening phone calls and letters. Two months later a cross was burned on their front lawn. After years of harassment and finally arrest for giving information about Klan activities and racial injustice to a *New York Times* reporter, Hughes and his family left Alabama for missionary work in Africa.[26] Alabama was no easy place for pro-integration ministers.

A merger plan finally passed in 1972 because Rev. John Vickers, pastor to Governor George Wallace, stated, "We will adopt a plan of merger or an arbitration board will come give us a plan." The new plan, however, did not have good results for African Americans. Their career opportunities were limited, and many left the conference. White flight to the suburbs closed many inner-city churches, and much Methodist property was sold. Rev. Donald E. Collins indicates that beyond the local level, some progress has been made. African American Rev. E. D. Ridgeway was appointed to the Annual Conference Council in 1973, African American Terrence K. Hayes was appointed in 1986, and in 1992 Rev. William Wesley Morris became the first African American bishop in the Alabama–West Florida Conference. The North Alabama Conference has also appointed some African American ministers at the conference level, but not as bishops. The bishop in 2016 is a white woman, Rev. Debra Wallace-Padgett, but African American Rev. Clinton Hubbard Jr. is superintendent of the Cheaha District and executive director of Ethnic Ministries. According to Hubbard, "There are only about one or two mixed race churches; a lot of work remains to be done."[27]

The situation was also difficult in Mississippi, where four Methodist conferences existed—two African American and two white, with little contact between them. The historian Carolyn Renee Dupont captures the emotional drama that took place in 1971 when the Upper Mississippi (African American) Conference voted for merger, but the all-white Northern Mississippi Conference opposed merger. One African American pastor exclaimed, "My college roommate was lynched and if I were not a Christian, I could hate every white man." "God," he argued, "could use black Christians to make the church what it ought to be." The African American Conference voted overwhelmingly for merger, but a white Methodist layman argued, "The system of separate jurisdictions had been beneficial, preserving the distinctive social, political, economic, and cultural views of southerners.... The zeal of a very small minority [in the white conference] to integrate the races has ... benumbed their judgment and clouded their vision.... I am unalterably opposed to merger in any shape, form, or fashion." Dupont noted that lay delegates from the white conference opposed the plan at higher rates than their ministers. When Rev. D. McAlilly presented the plan, he emphasized the doctrines of church brotherhood and unity, but the plan was rejected by a vote of 173 to 24. One moderate Methodist, a lifelong Mississippian, lamented, "How few of us are willing to acknowledge and accept our black brothers.... May God have mercy on us all."[28]

In 1972 Rev. Mack B. Stokes (1911–2012) became bishop for all four Mississippi conferences and worked on a plan that provided for a transitional period but no immediate structural change other than to merge four conferences into two. In 1975 the Commission on Religion and Race declared the Mississippi plan unconstitutional because it seemed to preserve segregation. Stokes then appointed one African American district superintendent to each conference, and the Mississippi plan was finally approved.[29]

Dupont notes that merger in Mississippi came at a huge price, as Mississippi's Methodists joined conservative churches: "Between 1965 and 1972, white Mississippi Methodists lost nearly 14,500 members ... with a drop of nearly 4,000 between 1971 and 1972 alone." She quotes a Vicksburg layman, "Each time I attend a function ... at another denomination ... I see someone, who in the past was a Methodist."[30]

◆ ◆ ◆

Merger was delayed in Arkansas because the white Little Rock Conference rejected the request of the African American Southwestern Conference for an African American district superintendent, but in 1972 Bishop Eugene M. Frank (1907–2009), who had arranged the merger of the Missouri Methodist conferences, was appointed to the Arkansas conferences; African American district superintendents were appointed, and the merging of the separated conferences was achieved. In 1975 a gracious gesture of interracial friendship took place when two white delegates from the Little Rock Conference gave up their seats to two African Americans to enable them to attend the General Conference of 1976.[31]

◆ ◆ ◆

Ending the segregated structure of the Methodist Church in the South was most difficult, and as Rhett Jackson related, "Although there is integration at the Conference levels, most United Methodist congregations in the South are still pretty well segregated." Like the Baptists, the United Methodists had an official Apology for Racism at their General Conference, May 2–12, 2000. They acknowledged their sins of racism, particularly those that led to the formation of the African Methodist Episcopal, African Methodist Episcopal Zion, and Christian Methodist Episcopal denominations, and the Central Jurisdiction. With the creation of the Commission on Union and the Commission on Pan-Methodist Cooperation, the United Methodists have made efforts toward unity and repentance. The Council of Bishops called on all conferences to issue apologies during the year 2001.[32] South Carolina became the first southern conference to issue an apology.

In 2001 black and white leaders and members of the United Methodist Church in South Carolina joined hands with leaders and members of the African Methodist Episcopal Church in a ceremony of forgiveness and repentance. Apologies were offered and accepted, but African American congressman from South Carolina James E. Clyburn considered the ceremony only symbolic: "The real test of this reconciliation will be in the days to come. . . . Most people in word denounce racism, but their deeds clearly demonstrate the opposite." Clyburn was referring to a rash of black church burnings that took place in South Carolina during the 1990s.[33]

Episcopalians

Except for the interval during the Civil War, the Episcopal Church has always been a national unit with headquarters in New York City. Rev. Harold T. Lewis has written that order has always been the most important goal of the Episcopal Church. As long as tranquility prevailed between the races, the Episcopal Church "approved a *de facto* segregated church in a segregated society," but once discord became apparent, "the Episcopal Church became an advocate for racial equality as the social order demanded by Christian faith." In 1955, in response to the *Brown* decision, the General Convention declared, "All people and clergy of this Church . . . accept and support this ruling of the Supreme Court, and . . . they anticipate constructively the local implementation of this ruling as the law of the land." In 1958 two bishops; several priests, two of whom were African American; and several laypeople, northerners and southerners, met in Eaton, New Hampshire, and drew up a resolution that to deny anyone the right of equal education, housing, employment, and public accommodations on the basis of race or nationality is a "failure of Christian love."[34]

In 1963, one month after Martin Luther King Jr.'s "Letter from a Birmingham Jail" (and after much urging from African American sociologist and practicing Episcopalian Kenneth B. Clark), Rt. Rev. Arthur Lichtenberger, presiding bishop of the General Convention, issued a pastoral letter asking all Episcopalians to back the protest movement: "The freedom to vote, to eat a hamburger, to have a decent job, to live in a house fit for habitation are rights that should not be denied to anyone in the United States."[35]

As in the Methodist hierarchy, a minister was dependent for support from the bishop, but in the Episcopal Church, unlike the Methodist Church, bishops seemed determined to follow the central authority. According to Duncan Montgomery Gray Jr. (chapter 1) of the diocese of Mississippi, the majority of southern bishops and clergy supported integration. The controversy at the School of Theology of the Episcopal University of the South, Sewanee, Tennessee, illustrates how southern Episcopal bishops overcame their prejudices. In 1951 the Board of Trustees, composed of southern bishops, voted forty-nine to twelve *not* to comply with a resolution requiring them to admit African American divinity students. In protest, nine members of the seminary faculty resigned, and a hairsplitting division among the bishops resulted. One year later the trustees met, and this time a majority voted for acceptance of African American applicants. The father of Duncan Montgomery Gray Jr., Rt. Rev. Duncan Montgomery Gray Sr., bishop of Mississippi, was one of the trustees who voted for the African American applicants. Rev. Gardiner Shattuck mentioned that fourteen southern bishops pledged to remove their students from the School of Theology if it remained racially segregated.[36]

Frances Pauley, a feisty white activist from the Georgia Council on Human Relations, went often to southwest Georgia to arrange interracial meetings, which she called "plans for action," and spoke highly of Episcopalians: "Often in south Georgia, I used Episcopal ministers because the Episcopal bishop was so marvelous." The Episcopal bishop she was referring to was Albert Rhett Stuart (1906–1973), born in Washington, DC. Stuart was commemorated at the Ralph Mark Gilbert Civil Rights Museum in Savannah, Georgia, for organizing the Committee of 100, known as the Bishop's Committee, consisting of corporate heads and other white leaders interested in solving Savannah's racial problems. The plaque dedicated to Bishop Stuart reads: "During the 1960s, Rt. Rev. Stuart stated that no one should be refused admission to worship in any church in the diocese of Georgia. In spite of a strong revolt by segregationists in his wealthy Savannah parish, he stood firm and maintained a position that 'the church is open to all.'"[37]

Savannah was not an easy place for civil rights activists during the years of the civil rights movement. Another plaque in the museum tells the story of the African American pastor James Floyd, who displayed the banner carried by the Savannah NAACP contingent during the 1963 March on Washington at church and other meetings. In 1970 he was killed while on duty at the NAACP office. A mail bomb also killed Robert E. Robinson, an NAACP attorney.[38] Such events made the activism of Bishop Stuart all the more significant.

Pauley mentioned the wonderful relationship she had with Bishop Stuart: "He told me never to come to Savannah without coming to see him." Pauley told him about a minister in Terrell County, Georgia ("Terrible Terrell"), who shook hands with a black man on the street. "They just about ran him out," she commented. Pauley related how the bishop closed the church because of the way the congregation treated the minister.[39] In Stuart's view, it was better to lose a church than to allow harassment of a cleric.

Charles Marmion (1905–2000) (chapter 4), born in Houston, Texas, and bishop of Kentucky from 1954 to 1974, integrated Episcopal Church summer camps and participated in a 1964 march to Frankfort, Kentucky's capital, on behalf of open public accommodations. John Hines (1910–1997) (chapter 5) served as bishop of Texas from 1955 to 1965 before his election as presiding bishop. He integrated the Episcopal Theological Seminary of the Southwest, St. Stephen's Episcopal School in Austin, and upheld the right of black Episcopalians to attend white churches. Duncan Montgomery Gray Jr. considered Hines the most outstanding bishop in the history of the Episcopal Church: "He led us in the right direction during those difficult times."[40]

Another bishop considered outstanding by Gray was John Maury Allin (1921–1998), born in Helena, Arkansas, who, as bishop coadjutor of Mississippi during the Ole Miss crisis of 1962, helped Gray remain in Mississippi despite the wishes of many segregationists that he leave. Allin also raised funds to rebuild some fifty-four black churches that had been burned to the ground in Mississippi in 1964 and 1965. The work was done through the Committee of Concern, the first interracial and interdenominational group of its kind in Mississippi, founded by Allin and Gray. Shattuck mentioned that Allin was elected presiding bishop of the church in 1974 over the objections of the church's white liberal wing but surprised the liberals by furthering the advancement of African American Episcopal priests. Shortly after his election, he established the Office of Black Ministries (the "black desk") and appointed a black priest to his senior staff. Halfway through Allin's term, Charles Redford Lawrence was elected president of the House of Deputies, the first African American to hold the office.[41]

It can be seen that most Episcopal bishops, with the exception of Charles C. J. Carpenter of Alabama, supported priests who quietly and almost unnoticed contributed to a transformation of southern society. James Stirling (1894–1972), born in Lochwinnoch, Scotland, but raised in South Carolina, and rector of Trinity Episcopal Church, Columbia, South Carolina, gave his own money and the church's money to help a humble black woman with little education, Lugenia Hammond, transform one of the worst black slum areas of

Columbia into a decent neighborhood with electric power and paved streets. Trinity Church in central Columbia went on to become the diocesan head-quarters for South Carolina and continued a vast number of social services to the nearby inner city. Stirling became its dean. F. Bland Tucker (1895–1978), born in Norfolk, Virginia, welcomed NAACP Youth Council members into Christ Church, Episcopal, in Savannah without incident on August 21, 1960. Tucker told his church vestry that he would "take a reduction in salary" to offset any loss in pledges that might result from his actions. Edward Harri-son (1913–1996), born in Jacksonville, Florida, and rector of St. Andrew's Epis-copal Church in the heart of Jackson, Mississippi, helped Freedom Riders in 1961, organized interracial "plan of action" meetings, and welcomed African American worshippers into his church in 1963. Paul Ritch, born in 1928 in Columbia, South Carolina, welcomed visitors from Koinonia Farm into his Episcopal church in Americus, Georgia, almost an impossible accomplishment in Americus, and signed a statement calling for the prosecution of the perpe-trators of violence to the farm.[42]

In the words of Duncan Gray, "The years 1954–1974 were years of which the Episcopal Church can be justly proud . . . years that awakened the Church from slumber and complacency." African American churchman Harold Lewis noted many signs of racial progress, citing black bishops as leading three of the church's largest dioceses (although all in the North: Long Island, southern Ohio, and Connecticut). Struggling in this present day with such issues as the plight of Native Americans, the homeless, people with disabilities, and those living with AIDS, the Episcopal Church strives in the twenty-first century to become the church that John Hines envisioned during the years 1954 to 1974, a church reaching out to the dispossessed, friendless, and suffering people in the world, a church with "no outcasts."[43]

The Episcopal Church issued a mea culpa for slavery and segregation at the General Convention of 2004, with an admission of sin, an apology, and a promise to document its own complicity in "a fundamental betrayal of humanity." Deputies and bishops voted to find ways to repair the breach "both materially and relationally." Many responses came from African American Episcopalians. Billy Alford from the Diocese of Georgia called the discussion long overdue. Nelson Pinder from the Diocese of Central Florida exclaimed, "We were promised some mules and some acreage. We didn't even get a goat. It's time for America to come up to the plate." Great strides have been made by the Episcopal Church to bridge the gap between whites and African Amer-icans. Of significance was the announcement that on June 27, 2015, African American Michael Curry was elected in a landslide vote as presiding bishop of the 2.5-million-member church. Curry served as bishop of the Episcopal Diocese of North Carolina since 2000.[44]

Presbyterians

Southern Presbyterian Rev. E. T. Thompson (1894–1985), PCUS, once wrote that Christianity was a revolutionary movement, and when it ceased to be revolutionary, it became "salt without savor, fit for nothing but to be cast out and trodden under foot of men." Thompson, born in Texarkana, Texas, struggled for sixty-seven years of ministry to bring his denomination out of its nineteenth-century "Thornwellianism" (avoidance of involvement in social issues) into the twentieth century. As related by his biographer, Rev. Peter Hairston Hobbie, Thompson tried ministering to a small church for one year but soon decided that the academic life was his milieu; his writings became his sermons, and his students became his congregation. He taught Church history at Union Theological Seminary in Virginia for forty years, edited and wrote Sunday school lessons for Presbyterian journals until he was past ninety, and edited the *Presbyterian of the South* (later *Presbyterian Outlook*), the official journal of PCUS, for over twenty-five years. He reprinted articles concerning economics, race relations, issues of war and peace, church relations, and theology, rarely expressing his own opinions, but, as his biographer suggested, "by his choice of articles he subtly and effectively advanced his goals: racial justice; reunion with the northern church, and ecumenism, much like Methodist editor Brabham."[45]

Accused of heresy twice, Thompson was undeterred by attackers and continued to embrace liberal causes, encouraged by a host of young supporters who were always able to maintain majority control of the General Assembly. When the Supreme Court handed down the *Brown* decision, PCUS was the first denomination, southern or otherwise, to issue statements urging trustees of all institutions of higher education belonging to the different branches of the Church to open their doors to all races; sessions of local churches to "admit persons to membership and fellowship . . . on the scriptural basis of faith in the Lord Jesus Christ without reference to race"; and individuals and leaders in all churches to "practice the Christian graces of forbearance, patience, humility, and persistent goodwill." Not all southern Presbyterians welcomed the statements. Rev. Joel Alvis noted that many presbyteries across the South proposed repeal of the 1954 statements (Alabama and Mississippi), but the General Assembly, with the endorsement of many, "reaffirmed its decision by an even larger vote."[46] Thompson influenced Revs. Marion Boggs, Malcolm C. Calhoun, Charles Jones, John Lyles, Robert McNeill, Robert Miller, Dunbar Ogden, J. Sherrard Rice, Randolph Taylor, and H. Davis Yeuell, whose stories are told in this narrative.

As the years progressed, PCUS became more supportive of the civil rights movement. In 1967 the General Assembly ordered a special investigation of its Mississippi Synod in order to halt what it called "a strong anti-Assembly attitude." Chair of the investigating committee, Charles L. King (1892–1982), a retired minister from Houston, Texas, stated, "Ministers considered too liberal were subjected to a 'third degree' in order to insure that no one but a conservative got in." The committee also found that Mississippi presbyteries were rejecting the General Assembly on several counts: they refused to elect as commissioners "ministers whose views were different from those of the majority"; they refused to support church activities they considered too liberal; the majority of churches in Mississippi did not use Sunday school literature provided by the General Assembly; and they established their own seminary because they considered the church-affiliated schools too liberal. The Mississippi Synod was on the threshold of a schism that would occur in 1972 when ministers and elders met at the Briarwood Presbyterian Church in Birmingham, Alabama, and formed the Presbyterian Church in America (PCA), claiming to be Thornwell's theological heirs. PCUS was condemned and denounced as having been taken over by liberals. Rev. R. Milton Winter, pastor of First Presbyterian Church, in Holly Springs, Mississippi, noted that during the 1970s, half of Mississippi's PCUS congregations left to join the PCA, and a few years later others left to join the Evangelical Presbyterian Church. Winter suggests that many in Alabama and Mississippi considered secession an ancient and honorable means of resolving differences.[47]

In 1950 Rev. Malcolm C. Calhoun (1902–1989), born in Laurinburg, North Carolina, was infuriated by the smear campaign "highlighting issues of race and Communism" that caused the defeat of Frank Porter Graham, Presbyterian elder, candidate for Democratic senator from North Carolina. Calhoun took leave from his pastorate and returned to the Union Theological Seminary in Richmond to do a thorough study of the Scriptures concerning race relations in preparation for a PhD. After his extended education, he was appointed secretary of the Division of Christian Relations for PCUS and became the minister who prepared all the recommendations in support of integration that became official statements of the General Assembly of PCUS. In 1963 he went to Washington, DC, with a group of 250 religious leaders to discuss and advance proposed civil rights legislation, but Calhoun's most distinguished contribution to change came when he invited Martin Luther King Jr. to speak at the Christian Action Conference at the still segregated Montreat Conference Center in North Carolina in August 1965. Rev. L. Nelson Bell, who initiated a heresy trial of E. T. Thompson, suggested that the invitation be rescinded. Others deplored the use of church facilities for "topics other than spiritual matters." The controversy was finally settled by a vote, 311 to 120, in favor of the invitation.[48]

King's address mesmerized his audience. He repeated one of his major themes: "Too many Christians have remained silent behind the safe security

of stained glass windows. . . . The church needs to affirm the essential immorality of racial segregation." His address was long and elegiac. It was a call for
help from the white church: "A gospel true to its nature will be concerned, yes,
about heaven, but also about earth." After King spoke, one person asked a hostile question, suggesting that King was a Communist. The question referred to
a picture taken of him at the Highlander Folk School in Tennessee with a title
above it, "A Training School for Communists." King answered firmly, "I want to
say . . . that I consider the Highlander School one of the finest of its kind ever
to emerge in the South. The picture which purports to show me being 'trained'
by known communists at Highlander is almost humorous." King averred that
he had visited Highlander only once in his lifetime to make a forty-five-min-
ute speech. "Now that was a mighty short training course." One businessman
told Calhoun years later, "I want you to know something. I was converted by
Dr. Martin Luther King that day he spoke in Montreat."[49]

PCUS traveled a road full of thorns but reached a rainbow at the end. Its
1,492 black communicants were successfully absorbed into the white church
in 1968 with the abolishment of the all-black Snedecor synod. Another shaper
of the new PCUS, Rev. James H. Smylie, born in 1925 in West Virginia and
professor of church history at the Union Theological Seminary in Virginia
(1962–2003), traveled back and forth to Alabama and Mississippi to try to convince Presbyterians that General Assembly edicts were just and biblical. In his
history of the denomination, he wrote, "Presbyterians finally lived up to pro-
fessions of Christian faith and life. . . . In 1974, PCUS elected the Rev. Lawrence
Bottoms [African American] to be moderator of its highest governing body."[50]
The criticism foisted upon Presbyterians for ignoring their black brethren was
finally addressed.

The reunion of PCUS with its northern coreligionists occurred in 1983,
but not without the painful loss of many southern Presbyterian churches, the
most notable, historic First Presbyterian Church (FPC) of Columbia, South
Carolina, where James Henley Thornwell, supporter of slavery and segregation, preached from 1839 to 1841 and again from 1856 to 1861. J. Sherrard Rice
(1917–2005), born in Richmond, Virginia, and pastor of FPC from 1959 to 1966,
was caught in the conservative versus liberal dilemma. Rice believed firmly in
the doctrines of his Church but also in the goals of the civil rights movement
and the edicts of the General Assembly. The congregation never forgot the sermon he delivered one year after his arrival. He told of the sadness and embarrassment he felt when black students at the Union Theological Seminary in
Virginia had to eat in separate lunchrooms and ride in the back of busses. He
spoke of Peter, a Jew from Joppa, who overcame his prejudice against Gentiles.
"Change is coming," he told them. "Like Peter, we must not fear change." The
sermon was long, and he could sense the audience's uneasiness. Before it was

over, his voice quavered, and he had to stop. The clerk in the session called it "The Weeping Sermon." Rice continued to preach integration and became president of the integrated Columbia Ministerial Fellowship, but the session remained conservative. He resigned in 1966 and took a position as an administrator for PCUS.[51]

As the movement within PCUS to unite with the northern church became stronger, the session of the FPC consistently voted against it. Conservative members of PCUS prided themselves on their belief that "the southern church was the most spiritual and faithful body of Reformed Christians in the world" and that reunion would adulterate their denomination. A conservative pastor was chosen to succeed Rice in 1967, and eventually the congregation, by a close vote, rejected reunion with the northern church and became affiliated with another large conservative breakaway group in the South, the Associate Reformed Presbyterian Church (ARPC). Rice was disheartened but prayed that God would lead the FPC into a new unity and a fresh vision of its work and that "all our labors will not have been in vain." As Rice had prayed, all was not lost. In 1976 Peter Agbi Tabor of the Republic of Cameroon was welcomed as the first black member of the FPC since Reconstruction. Outreach activities to the nearby black community were established and continue to be outstanding.[52]

E. T. Thompson, after more than fifty years of struggle to defend the northern church, was one of three members of a special committee that recommended that the General Assembly of PCUS "adjourn *sine die*."[53] At the age of eighty-nine, Thompson was pushed in a wheelchair by his son along Peachtree Street in Atlanta in a joyful celebration parade. Rev. J. Randolph Taylor (chapter 4) became the first moderator for the newly reunited church. One of Taylor's first acts was to lead the new denomination in "grateful worship of God."[54] Thus Presbyterian leadership in the southern General Assembly did their best to change the attitudes of segregationists within their church structure, unfortunately, at the loss of many member churches.

Christian (Disciples of Christ) and Churches of Christ

In 1801 almost 25,000 people gathered on a bluff called "Cane Ridge" several miles southeast of Lexington, Kentucky, for a revival that became, according to the historian Grant Wacker, the most famous religious meeting in American history, with evangelists from all denominations working side by side. Barton W. Stone (1772–1844), ordained a Presbyterian minister and one of the leaders of the revival, broke away from the Presbyterians and began a movement called simply "Christians," and appealed for Christian unity and holy living. Stone also emphasized that slavery was incompatible with the teachings of Jesus.[55]

In 1807 another Presbyterian minister, Thomas Campbell (1763–1854), born in Northern Ireland, began preaching in western Pennsylvania. According to the historian Sydney Ahlstroim, he had no plans to begin a new denomination but only to promote Christian unity by preaching a simple gospel. His son Alexander (1788–1866) arrived two years later and soon took over the leadership of the movement. Alexander designated himself a reformer of the existing frontier denominations and zealously established many churches along the Ohio River valley. In 1824 Barton Stone and Alexander Campbell met, and the two movements came together with the famous handshake of 1832. Often referred to as the "Restoration Movement," the "Christians," "Reformers," or "Disciples," they spread rapidly, becoming the fifth-largest religious group in a region from Ohio to Texas and later to California. (Presidents James A. Garfield, Lyndon B. Johnson, and Ronald Reagan were members of the Disciples' denomination.)[56]

In 1863 the northern and southern groups began to pull apart when the American Christian Missionary Society, which had served many of their churches, passed a resolution of support for the Union. A final division came in 1906 over the use of instrumental music and the formation of missionary societies. This led to the loss of nearly 160,000 members, mostly in the South, who became officially the Churches of Christ, who to this day do not have instruments accompanying their worship services, do not belong to missionary societies, and remain silent concerning social issues.[57]

At their 1957 international meeting, members of the Christian Church (Disciples of Christ), considering themselves a denomination, gave instructions to local churches to make it unmistakably clear that Christian worship was to be inclusive. There have been southern Disciples ministers who have signed proclamations—for example, the Mobile Bus Petition of 1958 and a petition to support Harvey Gantt's entrance to Clemson University in South Carolina in 1963—and some have been members of the Southern Regional Council, but it can be assumed that most of the ministers in the southern Disciples' churches avoided the subject in their pulpits. As in the Baptist tradition, decisions concerning ministers were made at the congregational level and swiftly, as in the case of Roy Hulan (chapter 3). Colbert Cartwright, pastor of Pulaski Heights Christian Church, Little Rock, Arkansas, 1954–1963 (chapter 1), was completely outspoken, politically active, and determined to carry out his denomination's directives. He was able to maintain his position for nine years because of a large number of progressive members in his church, but no longer.[58] By contrast, Rev. Hulan may have believed in the inclusive message, but was never outspoken until the moment of crisis when his thoughts came streaming forth in a sermon, and his days at First Christian Church in Jackson, Mississippi, immediately ended.

The Churches of Christ, with a much larger constituency in the South than the Disciples, are estimated, according to C. Kirk Hadaway of the Hartford Institute for Religious Research, to have some 40,000 members in a region extending from Tennessee to Texas. Only loosely connected, Churches of Christ adherents do not consider themselves a denomination, although they are listed as a national denomination in the *Atlas of American Religion* because of their vast numbers and geographic spread. (They now have churches in every state, although some are very small.)[59]

Without a hierarchy of leadership, bishops, conventions, or central assemblies, professors at their colleges and journal editors have become their leadership voices, and these voices were generally protective of segregation during the civil rights movement. Rex Turner, president of Alabama Christian College, condemned Martin Luther King Jr. as a "rank modernist" and placed those white ministers who supported him "in the same category." Reuel Lemmons, editor of *Firm Foundation*, would not admit that the riots of the summer of 1967 had anything to do with "a downtrodden element of society struggling for its fair share of effluency." To Lemmons, the riots were simply "the signs of a decaying and dying society . . . [rejecting] eternal verities of moral conduct." These Churches of Christ spokespeople believed that the civil rights movement was "being surreptitiously directed by communist conspirators," that King was connected to international Communism and at best was a modernist who "denied faith in Jesus Christ as taught in the Bible." Richard T. Hughes of Pepperdine University opined, "The communist conspiracy theories and the inflamed rhetoric in which they were typically couched did much to increase the level of alienation between blacks and whites within the Churches of Christ."[60]

Yet within this loosely organized religious group were individual ministers who spoke out for racial justice. One was George William Floyd (1906–1975), who preached a sermon on the Golden Rule in the city of Sylacauga, Alabama. In 1963, after the bombing of the Sixteenth Street Baptist Church in Birmingham, in which four black girls died, he told his conservative congregation, "Jesus is asking us to look at conditions in the South from the point of view of the black man. Consider what you would do if you were in his shoes. We don't realize it yet, but because Martin Luther King, Jr., is preaching nonviolence, which is Jesus' way, someday, Martin Luther King, Jr., will be seen as the best friend the white man in the South has ever had." As he delivered the sermon, people in the sanctuary screamed, "You devil, you." Immediately, he was asked to leave the church.[61]

Floyd was born and grew up in the Calfkiller River valley of White County, Tennessee, and attended David Lipscomb College and Vanderbilt University. When he died, his wife's brother, Robert E. Keith, officiated at his graveside service and called George Floyd "the most courageous man he ever knew." His son commented, "That was not just the usual graveside platitude. My uncle knew Dad all of his life."[62]

Floyd started his career ministry in 1934, always *very* outspoken about racial problems and the failure of the Christian witness. He was often asked to leave his church. Many times he thought he would leave the ministry, but always another Church of Christ called him to be its pastor. It was as if God wanted Church of Christ people to hear Floyd's prophetic messages. He served several churches in Alabama, Florida, Georgia, Tennessee, and Texas.[63]

His son, William Kirk Floyd, born in 1935 in Sparta, Tennessee, known as Bill, followed in his father's footsteps, willing to speak out for racial justice. On September 4, 1957, as an undergraduate at Harding College (now Harding University) in Searcy, Arkansas, he happened to be in Little Rock for a doctor's appointment and decided to make his way to Central High School to observe the demonstrations. A man in a pickup truck gave him a ride and asked, "What do you think of the governor's action?" Floyd answered, "I think history will show Governor Faubus' action to be ill-advised." With that response, the driver flung open the passenger door and forced Floyd from the truck into the gutter. As Floyd lay stunned, the driver quickly put his truck in reverse gear. Floyd was nearly killed but escaped by jumping behind a telephone pole. The driver screamed, "No goddamn n____r lover is ever riding in my truck!" Floyd then went to see for himself the vicious mob, the soldiers, and the frightened children. The experience made him an activist and much respected by his fellow students. As president of the Harding student body, he organized a "Statement of Attitude," declaring that the majority of students at Harding College, according to their Christian consciences, were ready to accept black students into classrooms and living quarters.[64]

A total of 946 out of 1,276 students, faculty, and staff signed the document. Later, the president of Harding, George S. Benson, presented his own statement that few blacks desired to attend Harding and that those who had applied had received financial assistance from his own pocket to attend black colleges in Little Rock and Texas. Benson condemned the students' statement, but when the Civil Rights Act of 1964 passed in Congress and it was known that Harding would be required to desegregate to continue receiving federal funds, Benson reversed his position: "Effective immediately, three black male students will be admitted to Harding." According to Michael D. Brown of the *Arkansas Times*, "By the time the first black student association president, Lot Therrio, was elected in 1975, the early civil rights activism of Bill Floyd and the signers of the 'Statement of Attitude' had been long forgotten." William Kirk Floyd served as a Church of Christ minister, part-time, for fifteen congregations during the 1960s, but never became a career preacher. He pursued graduate studies and became a professor serving colleges and universities in both the United States and Canada teaching forensics, philosophy, and studies of the future, and continued to be outspoken.[65]

Another speaker for racial justice in the Churches of Christ was Carl Spain (1917–1990), born in Chattanooga, Tennessee; minister of the Hillcrest Church of Christ in Abilene, Texas; and Bible professor at Abilene Christian College (now Abilene Christian University). He announced at the college's annual Bible lectureship in 1960: "God forbid that Churches of Christ and schools operated by Christians shall be the last stronghold of refuge for socially sick people who have Nazi illusions about the Master Race. . . . I feel certain that Jesus would say, 'Ye hypocrites! You say you are the only true Christians . . . and have the only true Christian schools. Yet you drive one of your own preachers to [segregated] denominational schools . . . and refuse to let him take Bible for credit . . . because the color of his skin is dark!'" Spain's speech earned him notoriety, cancellations of speaking engagements, and nasty phone calls, but, as noted by Hughes, he changed the university. The college accepted blacks at its graduate schools in 1961 and as undergraduates in 1962.[66]

During the violent summer of 1968, John Allen Chalk, born in 1937 in Tennessee and minister of the Highland Church of Christ in Abilene, Texas, delivered a series of sermons on the *Herald of Truth* radio program heard on 400 stations in fifteen countries. As Harold K. Straughn noted, "The sermons . . . would be heard only once. . . . A single scriptural text dominated the whole series: 'Thou shalt love the Lord thy God with all thy heart and with all thy soul, and with all thy mind. This is the first and great commandment. And the second is like unto it. Thou shalt love they neighbor as thyself.'" Chalk preached that a true Christian is not a racist, that the God of time, space, and history who created all men "rules all men, sustains all men, and unifies all men. . . . Jehovah God . . . who confronts all men . . . is not a racist. . . . This is why no church, no congregation of regenerate men, can forbid the water of baptism and the fullness of fellowship to any other human being." During and after the series, letters condemned the sermons, but Straughn noted that such letters came from only 2 percent of the respondents: "The other ninety-eight percent regretted that the sermons were too little and too late to have any effect."[67]

In July 1968 white editor M. Norvel Young (1915–1998), born in Nashville, Tennessee, devoted the entire edition of the *20th Century Christian*, published in Nashville, to "Christ and Race Relations," featuring articles by black Church of Christ ministers and white progressives. As a result, circulation of the journal dropped from 40,000 to 20,000 subscribers. In one article, J. E. Choate, a white man born in 1916 in Wingo, Kentucky, and a professor at David Lipscomb College in Nashville, told the story of Marshall Keeble (1878–1968), an African American Church of Christ minister considered perhaps the greatest black evangelist of the twentieth century who preached for more than sixty years throughout the South and converted thousands of people, both black and white, but nevertheless suffered indignities because of his race. Keeble was president of the segregated Nashville Christian Institute (NCI) for the training of black Church of Christ ministers, alma mater of Fred Gray, civil rights attorney and Church of Christ minister from Tuskegee, Alabama, whose name is mentioned frequently in this book. Foy Wallace Jr. (1896–1979), editor of the *Gospel Advocate, Gospel Guardian,* and *Bible Banner* during the 1930s and 1940s, objected to the fact that white women became so enthralled with Keeble's preaching that they would shake his hand, "holding his hand in both of theirs." According to Wallace, "For any woman in the church to forget her dignity, and lower herself so, just because a Negro has learned enough about the gospel to preach it to his race, is pitiable indeed." Keeble bore the insult with dignity and was not involved in protests during the civil rights movement. Choate concluded, "Marshall Keeble . . . makes us ashamed for our having so long denied full justice to the American Negro. He has taught us again the great lesson of Christian charity in an age that so sorely needs it. . . . God used Marshall Keeble to show white people how wrong they have been!"[68]

Al Price (chapter 3) continued helping to change his Church. He returned to Mississippi in 1973 to begin a doctoral program in sociology at Mississippi State University and to preach for the Winona Church of Christ. What he did not know was that the minister's house, where he was to live, was occupied by a faction that had broken away from the church because an elderly black woman had been baptized in the church's baptistery. When Price and his family arrived at the house, they were threatened with guns. Price was knocked down by one of the men and warned not to enter, but locks were changed, items were removed, and the family moved in. The next day he preached with a swollen jaw. For Price, the experience was life-changing. He began to see ethnic and class discrimination issues on almost every page of the New Testament. He realized that during his formative years, the southern culture had adversely influenced his values. Price was determined to change.[69]

After many harassing experiences, the Price family moved again to Tennessee, where he began teaching sociology and preaching part-time. In Tennessee, he received a phone call from the man who assaulted him in Winona, but Price would not speak to him. Thirty-seven years later he answered the man's phone call. Immediately, the man told him how wrong he had been in that era. "I was angry and I hated black people, but I have changed. I have spent the rest of my life attempting to undo all the damage I did." Price was overwhelmed and commented, "We both had experienced redemption. Gradually, we began to see things differently." In 2011 Price met the man at a local restaurant in Winona, where they talked and prayed together. The man told him that the Winona Church of Christ was no longer divided or segregated and had several black members.[70]

Price, like the man from Winona, became outspoken for racial reconciliation. Since 2007 he has preached at joint services for black and white Churches of Christ in Tennessee. He focuses on the universal message of Jesus: "And it shall be that everyone (whosoever) calls on the name of the Lord shall be saved." Price speaks about the diversity in the early church: Parthians, Medes, Elamites, residents of Mesopotamia, Judea, Cappadocia, visitors from Rome, Jews, proselytes, Cretans, Arabs, and more. He marvels that such diversity can be united. By coming together, Price believes, "We see someone who is different from us as a human being worthy of dignity and rights." He calls his sermons "The Mighty Works of God." He tells his listeners how the Churches of Christ practiced segregation during the 1950s and 1960s, but they are changing. He speaks of the pain he felt when ushers at his church in Jackson kept black people from entering. He speaks of John Allen Chalk, who felt it was time for the Churches of Christ to address their racism and ungodly attitudes. Price's message is one of reconciliation, reform, and hope.[71]

On March 3, 2013, Price attended the forty-eighth anniversary of the Selma to Montgomery voting rights march. He commented, "For many years I wanted to attend, to tell my students in such classes as 'Race and Ethnic Relations,' that I had crossed the bridge to commemorate the moment that changed the course of United States history."[72]

The Churches of Christ have come a long way from extreme avoidance of the racial issue. In 1999 Royce Money, born in 1942 in Temple, Texas, made a public apology during the fiftieth anniversary Founders' Day celebration at Southwestern Christian College in Terrell, Texas, an African American institution established by the Churches of Christ because blacks were excluded from most Churches of Christ universities at the time. As president of Abilene Christian University (ACU), Abilene, Texas, he asked forgiveness for past sins of racism and discrimination: "I believe God is moving among us to bring us spiritual unity. ACU wants to do everything we can to heal old hurts. . . . We pledge to walk together with you as those in the body of Christ should always do. As Paul says in I Corinthians 12, we pray that 'there should be no division in the body, but its parts should have equal concern for each other.' . . . May God help us in word and in deed to be spiritually 'one in Christ.'"[73]

During his remarks, people shouted "Amen" and clapped. African American Andrew Hairston, a judge from Atlanta and a member of the Southwestern Christian College Board of Directors, hugged Money, and the crowd gave him a standing ovation. Attorney Fred Gray, chair of the Southwestern Christian College Board of Directors, was there to accept the apology. Six months later ACU appointed its first African American professor, Steven Moore, whose father had been denied admission to ACU some fifty-six years earlier. In 2004 Moore was voted ACU's "Teacher of the Year."[74] To this day, Churches of Christ colleges are racially integrated at the student and faculty levels.

Lutherans

In 1912 Rosa Young, a young African American woman, opened a small elementary school at her Methodist church in Rosebud, Wilcox County, Alabama. When the school experienced financial difficulties, she sought the help of Booker T. Washington at the Tuskegee Institute, who in turn told her to contact the missionary board of the Evangelical Lutheran Synodical Conference of North America. Missionary Rev. Nils Jules Bakke (1853–1921), from Wisconsin, went to investigate. At Bakke's recommendation, the Southern District of the Lutheran Church–Missouri Synod (LC-MS) agreed to finance the school. Young became confirmed as a Lutheran, and many African Americans joined her until, according to Jeff Johnson, "Wilcox County became the most rapidly growing mission field ever entered by a Lutheran Church denomination in U.S. History." Black churches and schools were established, and African Americans living in the rural regions of Alabama were given education and church affiliation.[75]

The pastors of the black churches, many of whom were white, taught in the schools during the week and performed pastoral duties on the weekend. In 1922 Young's original school moved to Selma, Alabama, and experienced phenomenal growth. In 1945 Walter Ellwanger (1897–1982), father of Joseph Ellwanger (chapters 2 and 5), went to Selma to preside over the school, then known as Alabama Lutheran Academy. Walter Ellwanger stated at the 1954 convention of the Southern District, "As we come to know the colored . . . we come to know them as precious souls . . . [and] segregation difficulties disappear." His son, Joseph, grew up in Selma, but as a white child he was not able to attend the all-black Alabama Lutheran Academy because of the state's segregation laws. As an adult, he became an avid integrationist and pastor of the all-black St. Paul's Lutheran Church in Birmingham, Alabama. Lutheran Academy is now known as Concordia College Alabama, the only historically black four-year college within the Concordia University system of the LC-MS. It is now racially mixed, with about 10 percent white students.[76]

According to African American Richard C. Dickinson, black Lutheranism in Wilcox County produced many African American pastors who longed to be accepted as full members of the denomination, but African Americans in the Southern District were treated as objects of mission, not as equals. As the civil rights movement progressed, the LC-MS began to consider removing racial barriers. At the 1957 pastors' conference, Paul Streufert (1903–1983), born in Chicago and president of the Southern District, declared, "God has blessed our work. . . . In the four states of our district [Alabama, Louisiana, Mississippi, and the western part of the Florida Panhandle], there are twenty-four pastors serving fifty African American churches, eight white pastors and sixteen African American pastors, with a combined communicant membership of 3,084." He urged his constituents, some of whom were staunch segregationists, to seek "a solution to the problem of synodical membership for our brethren." Finally, in 1963, after years of debate and discussion, the merger took place. Edgar Homrighausen, then district president, welcomed African American pastors and their congregations into the Missouri Synod. Homrighausen saw the merger as a victory for Christian unity and declared, "We are merely servants of the Lord who see a task and try to do it."[77] It was a dramatic step toward racial reconciliation.

Richard O. Ziehr, a white southern Lutheran pastor born in 1931 in Cisco, Texas, explains that because of their small southern presence, Lutherans in the South did not produce many pastors. White pastors for both black and white churches had to be imported from northern Lutheran seminaries. Homrighausen (1924–2017), born in New York City, was one of those pastors. He first served as vicar (intern) and later pastor at First English Lutheran Church in New Orleans, where black visitors were always welcomed and seated anywhere in his church. Stricken with polio at the age of three, at times Homrighausen had to overcome prejudice against a "limping pastor," but his preaching of the Word was so powerful that he was often featured on the radio program *Lutheran Hour*. When he was thirty-two years old, the Southern District of LC-MS elected him president-bishop and gave him the task of integrating the church because, as he said, "Nobody born in Pensacola, Tuscaloosa, Shreveport, or Jackson was going to do it." With an overwhelming segregationist membership, he could not officially endorse the participation of Lutheran ministers in civil rights demonstrations and still be welcomed at all-white Lutheran churches. "I had to keep the doors of segregated churches open to me. . . . I wanted the segregationists to trust me." Sometimes he was successful in his efforts, but not always. When he went to First Lutheran Church in Birmingham, Alabama, strictly segregated, he was told by some members, "We do not want n_____rs in our church." He responded, "The doors have to be open to everybody," but they replied, "The doors *are* open—for you to leave. . . . You came in with a limp and you will leave with a greater limp." Then someone threw a hymnal at his head, and he started bleeding.[78]

When new white pastors came to the South during the 1960s, he told them, "Do not say anything for one year. Just look and listen. Then after you are ingrained in the congregation, you can do good work." Homrighausen was keenly aware of the dangers and hostility white Lutheran pastors would face in the Deep South if they tried to move too quickly to change the customs of southern society. His strategy became negotiation. When Vicar James Fackler, born in 1930 in Toledo, Ohio, was beaten by the Klan in Tuscaloosa because he welcomed two African American teenagers into his church's youth group, Homrighausen paid three visits to Grand Wizard Robert Shelton, also living in Tuscaloosa: "My Lord wants me here to tell you that African American people want to be treated as equals. . . . Debate this issue but don't do cowardly acts like this." Each time he visited, he was asked to leave as quickly as possible. After the third visit, Klan members in pickup trucks chased him to his home in Cullman, Alabama, but he was able to lose them driving his small Fiat. Two days later a cross was burned in Cullman. He boldly confronted the cross burners, "Do you understand what you are doing, burning crosses?" They answered, "Yes, we know what we are doing. The cross means power and strength." Homrighausen replied, "Yes, but not the kind of power and strength that you are displaying." He never visited Shelton again, but went on television to confront the entire Klan: "You hide behind your pillow cases. I do not know who you are, but you know who I am and I am not going away. I am going to remain here and fight for African American people who need to be part of our lives."[79]

During the trouble in Selma in 1965, he received much notoriety from scholars because of his lack of support for Joseph Ellwanger's demonstration (chapter 5), but no mention was made of the seventy-two hours he spent in Selma appealing to Sheriff Clark and other officials for an end to racial discrimination. Homrighausen remained in the South from 1948 until his death in 2017. He wrote devotionals for radio station WSHO in New Orleans and served as pastor of the Village Church in LaCombe, Louisiana, an interracial church he founded in 1989, where the doors are open to everyone. The entire story of Homrighausen's journey for racial reconciliation has not been told by many scholars of the civil rights movement.[80]

Arnold Voigt, born in 1939 in Chicago but raised in Conover, North Carolina, was another Lutheran pastor in the LC-MS who contributed to the civil rights movement. Arriving in Mobile, Alabama, in 1965, he served as pastor of Faith Lutheran Church, a black congregation in the Toulminville area of Mobile, and also as administrator of Faith's elementary school, where 130 children were enrolled. Under his leadership, the congregation expanded, and the school became a leading parochial school in the state. Immediately, Voigt became involved in various community groups: the Christian Action Council of Toulminville, which worked to solve recreation, safety, and zoning issues; the Concerned Citizens for Equal Justice, which worked on voter registration; and the Interfaith Committee for Human Concern, which focused on summer programs for elementary and high school students. He was Toulminville's representative on the Mobile Area Community Action Committee, an arm of the federal antipoverty effort in Mobile. He also served on the Mobile Council on Human Relations and the board of Catholic Social Services of Mobile. Reports on his nonstop activities appeared in two local newspapers, the African American newspaper the *Mobile Beacon*, and the *Mobile Press Register*, which covered news articles for both the black and white communities. As the white community became aware of Voigt's interracial activities, he received harassing phone calls. His wife, who had been hired as a mathematics teacher at a predominantly white local high school, was told her contract was canceled because of "where your husband works." Mobile at that time (1966) was still resisting a federal court order to desegregate its schools. Voigt contacted the school board, the NAACP, and a community civil rights group (Neighbor Organized Workers), until his wife was rehired. In 1970 he was one of the speakers at an NAACP rally in support of Jackie Jacobs, the first black to run as a candidate for the Mobile Board of School Commissioners. Voigt's name soon became listed by the White Citizens' Council as one of the "ten most undesirable men in the county."[81]

After the assassination of Martin Luther King Jr., according to Voigt, "A sense of black empowerment arose in Mobile as more black leaders became involved in civil rights organizations." Voigt then turned his attention to working in his synod for the advancement of racial harmony. In 1970 he was elected to the Board of Directors of the Southern District of LC-MS and was appointed chair of the district's Social Ministry Committee. His committee developed "Operation Reconciliation," an effort to equip pastors and congregations to address racism and injustice and to help pastors deal with social change, but by 1975, after ten years in Mobile, Voigt became exhausted. He accepted a position in the Colorado District of LC-MS. Voigt never regrets his years in Mobile: "From the people in my parish, I learned much about the human condition and walking in other people's shoes. . . . In the name of our Lord, we kept dropping stones in the pond, trusting that somewhere and sometime the ripples would wash up change."[82]

The story of Raymond Davis (1929–2010) (chapter 1), born in Orangeburg, South Carolina, and a pastor in the United Lutheran Church of America (ULCA), Georgia-Alabama Synod, reveals how distressed a minister could become when rejected by his congregation. Upon his return to Our Redeemer Lutheran Church in Montgomery in 1964 after being transferred out in 1963, Davis became more active and forceful in the cause of racial justice. African Americans were welcomed as worshippers and members; luncheons for the integrated and interdenominational United Church Women's Fellowship were held in the church hall, with Our Redeemer's women cooking and serving the meals. It appeared to Davis that his congregation was advancing in race relations—until he proposed that an interracial preschool program be established within the confines of the building (as an extension to one in a nearby Catholic church). When Davis tried to explain the details of the program, to his astonishment, thirty people, the most active members of the congregation, rose in anger, left the room, and called for his immediate dismissal. Davis was devastated: "How could I have been so blind as not to see this coming?" Following biblical principles, he went to see the leader of the group, only to be told, "This is our church, and you won't tell us what to do." Shortly afterward, he was transferred to another church in the synod, but was no longer able to function. Always, he saw before him those thirty angry faces. Davis entered a rehabilitation program at Trinity Lutheran Hospital in Kansas City, Missouri, where ministers "suffering from congregational conflict" occupied an entire floor.[83]

Davis would not resign his ordination. It was not a crisis of faith from which he was suffering but an inability to accept the hostility of those in his Montgomery congregation. James R. Crumley 1925–2015), born in Bluff City, Tennessee, then pastor of historic Lutheran Church of the Ascension in Savannah, Georgia, helped Davis to recover, finding a place for him as celebrant, cantor, and teacher for lay readers. After many years, the synod realized that perhaps Davis should have been given more support in Montgomery, that many lies were told about him by members of the congregation, and that Davis was, after all, a loyal and faithful Christian. In many ways, the synod changed because of Davis's experience. In 2001 the Georgia-Alabama Synod honored Davis on the fiftieth anniversary of his membership. The entire assembly rose to their feet and applauded. Some of the pastors remembered Davis when he had been their adviser as chairperson for the synod's Parish Education Committee and ULCA's director of vacation and weekday church schools. Davis commented, "I was overwhelmed and greatly appreciative."[84]

The situation was not as difficult in the region of Columbia, South Carolina, as it was in Alabama. Rev. H. George Anderson of the ULCA, born in 1932 in Los Angeles, accepted a call to teach church history at the Lutheran Theological Seminary in Columbia, partly to understand how southern Lutherans were adjusting to the changing times. He taught that the Lutheran Church had to deal with change and reform since its earliest history and that Lutherans should welcome change and encourage the efforts of black people to achieve equality.[85]

With Anderson's help, the Lutheran Theological Seminary desegregated immediately and welcomed black pastors, not necessarily Lutheran, for evening classes. Anderson also arranged for the office of the integrated Christian Action Council of South Carolina to be housed at the Lutheran seminary and became an active supporter of the civil rights movement through an ecumenical group in and around Columbia known as "Displaced Pastors." This group of pastors without pulpits from Baptist, Methodist, Presbyterian, and

Lutheran denominations worked behind the scenes supporting demonstrations. According to Anderson, "We did the work quietly and made the peaceful
transition from segregation to desegregation possible." Anderson remained in
Columbia for twenty-four years, teaching from 1958 to 1970 and serving as
president of the seminary from 1970 to 1982. Later, he became presiding bishop
of the Evangelical Lutheran Church of America.[86] Columbia was a special location for activist Lutherans, no doubt because of Anderson's influence.

The Lutheran denominations, 90 percent white, have struggled through
divisions, schisms, and difficult race relations, but, like other denominations,
they have made great strides in changing attitudes toward race and in accepting African Americans as full members of their denominations. In 1966 African American Will Herzfeld (1937–2002), former pastor to all-black Christ
Lutheran Church, LC-MS, in Tuscaloosa, Alabama, and organizer of a local
chapter of the Southern Christian Leadership Conference (SCLC), harassed
and jailed by segregationists, became the first black executive of a Lutheran
Church Council in the USA, an ecumenical group of four Lutheran synods.
From 1984 to 1987 he served as presiding bishop of the Association of Evangelical Lutheran Churches, one of three Lutheran denominations that merged
to form the Evangelical Lutheran Church of America, of which H. George
Anderson served as presiding bishop from 1995 to 2001.[87]

White pastors such as Robert Graetz (chapter 2), Joseph Ellwanger (chapters 2 and 6), and Arnold Voigt (chapter 5) could be fully involved in the civil
rights movement because their congregations were black and supported their
efforts, but for many Lutheran ministers the obstacles were enormous. Conservative white Lutherans did not believe the role of clergy was to be politically
active. Some of the activist white Lutheran ministers were not southern-born
and were considered outsiders and intruders, but their help in educating African Americans has been considerable. Voigt notes that Rosa Young and Pastor
Nils Jules Bakke founded over thirty Lutheran schools and congregations in
central Alabama. African American pastor Christopher Drews estimated that
during the height of the segregation era, some 25,000 black Americans were
involved in some way with Lutheran churches and schools.[88]

Did white Lutheran ministers help change society? Pastor Richard O. Ziehr
believes that the black church and those associated with the SCLC, not the white
church, fostered change: "Would the Federal Government have acted as quickly
and as forthrightly to deal with civil rights matters if there had been no demonstrations and marches?" Ziehr contends that the black churches influenced
such activist Lutherans as Joseph Ellwanger and Will Herzfeld, both members
of the SCLC, who in turn influenced many moderate white Lutherans.[89]

Did the white ministers change the direction of the Lutheran denominations? At the LC-MS synodical convention in Detroit in 1965, progressive

Lutheran ministers were able to counteract the archconservatives of their denomination who saw the civil rights movement as "Communism," "rampant modernism," and "liberal ecumenism." As James C. Burkee has written, at the Detroit convention, "there were men who believed that a Lutheran could be at once theologically orthodox and socially active, conservative and evangelical, traditional yet ecumenical [and still] publicly affirm that Jesus Christ is the only way to heaven." Several years later, during the 1970s, as happened at the Southern Baptist Convention, the conservatives took over the LC-MS, and many who had been active in social change left the synod. Today, although he is still a pastor on the LC-MS register, Voigt, in retirement, attends a Lutheran church, ELCA.[90]

◆ ◆ ◆

During the civil rights movement, ministers from mainline denominations were the ones most likely to confront the South's racial patterns. This is also the conclusion of sociologist Nancy Tatom Ammerman in her 1962 study of seventy-two white clergy in Tuscaloosa, Alabama. She found that ministers belonging to mainline denominations, rather than small regional ones, supported the entrance of Vivian Malone and James Hood into the all-white University of Alabama—the reasons: mainline ministers were not "narrow in their perspectives" and were not "overly attached to their immediate local surroundings." Other influential factors included education, an urban childhood, strong denominational support, and being close to a university. Mainline denominations referred to by Ammerman were Episcopal, Lutheran, Presbyterian, Methodist, and Disciples of Christ. She also included Catholic and Unitarian churches and Reform Jews but excluded Baptists and small independent sects.[91] Mainline denominations cited in this book include Methodist, Episcopal, Presbyterian, Lutheran, and Disciples of Christ. The Southern Baptists and the Churches of Christ are also included, although in today's polls they are considered evangelical. The Southern Baptists produced many progressive ministers, perhaps not in Tuscaloosa, Alabama, or Little Rock, Arkansas, but elsewhere. The Churches of Christ produced only a few, but those few were strong in their convictions that churches and church schools should be inclusive. According to recent surveys, mainline denominations have lost many members, especially in the South. Part of the reason may be that they tried too hard to bring about a change that most of their constituents did not desire.

The years of the civil rights movement were also ecumenical years in the history of the mainline Protestant churches. Interdenominational and interracial conferences, ministerial alliances, committees, councils, and commissions flourished in the South and may still be flourishing in less organized ways as they mutually support inner-city soup kitchens, youth programs, poverty programs, and clinics. These ministries were often originated by ministers discussed in this narrative. In a brief questionnaire answered by twenty-eight of these ministers, all but three expressed a desire to see some form of cooperative movement, such as ecumenism promises. The idea of Christian unity, although biblical in origin, seems out of reach as the divide between conservative and liberal Christians becomes greater and the number of people who claim no religious affiliation (nones) keeps growing.

◆ ◆ ◆

The 1950s were a time of general prosperity among white elites. Mainline denominations were expanding, and the National Council of Churches (NCC), the largest ecumenical group of churches in the United States, consisting of thirty-seven mainline Protestant, Eastern Orthodox, African American, and historic peace churches, was a powerful organization housed in a huge, cathedral-size building, known as the "God-Box," in New York City. In 1952, in spite of opposition from southern church members, the NCC passed a resolution in support of an end to segregation: "The pattern of segregation is diametrically opposed to what Christians believe about the worth of men . . . . We must take our stand against it and work for 'a non-segregated church and a non-segregated community.'"[92]

Ten years later, almost too late, according to Will Campbell, the NCC established the Commission on Religion and Race, and on September 1, 1964, less than three months after the murders of civil rights activists James Chaney, Andrew Goodman, and Michael Schwerner, the Delta Ministry of the NCC officially began with offices in Greenville, Mississippi. The ministers emphasized that they came as a mission to the poor and a ministry of reconciliation and hoped that they would be welcomed, but from the outset, they faced strong opposition. Their leaders were northerners and considered ill-prepared to deal with Mississippi's problems. According to the historian Mark Newman, John M. Allin, bishop coadjutor of the Episcopal Church in Mississippi, complained that the project "had been ill-defined, ill-planned, ill-timed, and ill-announced." Edward J. Pendergrass, Methodist bishop of the Jackson area, and M. Maurice Grove, secretary-director of the Mississippi Christian Churches (Disciples of Christ), agreed.[93]

More than 200 Methodist churches in Mississippi voted to stop their financial support of the NCC; nevertheless, the ministry moved ahead with programs and projects in the Delta region and in the cities of Hattiesburg and McComb. During its first year, according to Newman, more than 300 clergy and laypeople from more than a dozen denominations, black but mostly white, volunteered for the ministry. Among the group was activist Rev. Ed King (chapters 2, 3, and 5), a white southern minister.[94]

In 1965 the Delta Ministry leased Mount Beulah, an African American college established in 1870 by the Disciples of Christ for newly freed African Americans but terminated in 1954 when students transferred to Tougaloo College. Because of its central location on twenty-three acres in Edwards, Mississippi, twenty-seven miles from Jackson, the Delta Ministry hoped to expand its ministry. The building became headquarters for many of the ministry's programs—it hosted conferences and workshops concerned with education, voter registration, and economic rehabilitation for more than 2,500 Mississippians. The Child Development Group of Mississippi (CDGM) used the building as an administrative and training center for its Head Start programs.[95]

After many complaints about the Delta Ministry, an investigation in 1965 led to the resignation of the first director, white Methodist minister Arthur Thomas, a native of Pennsylvania and a graduate of Duke Divinity School, and white suffragan bishop of the Episcopal Diocese of Washington, DC, Paul Moore, a native of New Jersey who was chairman of the Commission on the Delta Missionary. At the time of his appointment, Moore wrote, "God is working through this [civil rights] Movement, and it would be blasphemy for the Church to stand outside of it." The Delta Ministry, Moore claimed, was "intrinsically Christian," but the ministry was accused of mismanagement and failing to bring about reconciliation.[96]

In 1966 Owen Brooks, an Episcopal layman born in New York, became the director of the ministry, and Harry Bowie, an Episcopal priest from New Jersey who had directed the ministry in McComb, became his assistant. Both were African American. The new staff continued projects and programs until 1971, when the NCC cut off most of its funds and the Nixon administration showed little interest in antipoverty programs.[97]

Participants wondered why the Delta Ministry was so opposed. One answer seemed to be because the ministers worked with the existing black activist groups such as the Student Nonviolent Coordinating Committee (SNCC) and the Congress on Racial Equality (CORE), much hated by white segregationists. Another reason was that the ministry, outsiders, had entered the state without being asked by the existing white power structure, as Bishop Allin had suggested. Allin was not a segregationist, but believed in working out racial problems gradually through groups that already existed in the state.[98]

Although the ministry never achieved all its goals and many of its projects had to be discontinued because of lack of funding, it succeeded in distributing surplus government food and clothing to thousands of destitute people, both black and white. Under Brooks, it helped obtain federal funds for a community hospital in all-black Mound Bayou. The hospital provided health care for thousands of poor people in four counties in spite of the opposition of white Mississippi health officials. The ministry trained many black political candidates; assisted black elected officials; helped develop local leaders such as Thelma Barnes, L. C. Dorsey, and Kermit Stanton; and gave "research and administrative aid to Robert Clark, Mississippi's first African American legislator since Reconstruction." Even Hodding Carter III, newspaper editor in Greenville who initially opposed the ministry, had to concede in 1968, after the departure from Mississippi of SNCC and CORE, "There has been no other [more] effective civil rights and poverty organization in Mississippi. They have been a key factor in pulling in federal money to Mississippi."[99]

As the historian Paul Harvey has written, "Delta Ministry participants longed for a mutual relationship with white southern clergy." They expected attacks by militant segregationists, but were surprised by the opposition from Mississippi's white church leaders. The story of the Delta Ministry, so vividly told by Mark Newman in his book *Divine Agitators*, informs us of the vast divisions between conservative and progressive ministers within the denominations. The outside ministers had even more difficulty in working for change than did the native-born southerners. In spite of flaws and failures, the Delta Ministry may be considered one of the finest efforts of the ecumenical movement. As denominations decline, interest in the ecumenical movement has also declined. The NCC is now only a fragment of its former self. With a reduced staff and budget, it moved its headquarters from its large building in New York City to a suite of offices in Washington, DC.[100]

It may be remembered that Will Campbell (1924–2013) (chapters 1 and 5) became affiliated with the NCC in 1956 as an at-large minister and director of its southern project. The historian James Findlay writes that Campbell worked hard. "When local outbreaks of racial violence occurred," he always appeared. In Little Rock in 1957, he helped "organize ministers statewide to meet and then to protest Governor Faubus' attempt to prevent school desegregation. . . . By 1958, he was in frequent contact with the staff of the Southern Regional Council, a major civil rights organization. . . . In 1961, he participated in some of the earliest discussions about conditions in the South held by both the Justice Department and the Civil Rights Commission. . . . Eventually he became a part-time consultant to the commission." But by 1963, as Findlay argues, "individual negotiations and personal counseling at numerous flash points by a single individual were . . . not a very effective institutional policy, especially when most of the people Campbell talked to, including many white church people, refused voluntarily to make substantive changes in their daily acts of discrimination." Campbell resigned in 1963, and the southern project was phased out and replaced by the Delta Ministry. Campbell did not participate in the Delta

Ministry. In referring to his work with the NCC, Campbell called himself an "itinerant missioner," a "bridge between white and black," a "challenger of the recalcitrant," but he was not always sure that this was what he was called to be.[101]

Campbell later became field director for the Fellowship of Southern Churchmen, which he renamed Committee of Southern Churchmen. He changed it from a membership organization to a board organization of people like himself, committed to preaching the Gospel, traveling to trouble spots, and offering assistance to Christians seeking to find what he called "authentic Christianity," but after a few years he disbanded the group and became what he believed he was destined to be, simply a "preacher." He continued to write books and travel around to change one heart at a time, an "itinerant missioner."[102]

In an interview Campbell expressed disappointment with the NCC and disillusionment with all institutions: "Whether they are religious, educational, cultural, or whatever, [they] exist sooner or later for themselves and their own perpetuation. They are all self-protecting, self-loving. Anything that threatens their organization or institution cannot be accepted.... I think God and I get along fine. I call myself a Seventh Day Horizontalist."[103]

In his opinion, the NCC lacked religious grounds for what it was doing: "In their charter, they stated that they were an ecumenical group and did not get into theological matters.... For me, my involvement in the Civil Rights Movement *was* a theological matter. I was interested in the perpetuation of the Christian faith. I felt and still feel that the Christian faith has something to say about this issue [black civil rights] something at once redemptive and liberating." Campbell's story is important. As an insider, he knew that it would be difficult to eradicate racism in the South. He knew that white southerners had to be approached with humility and love, through their faith, not with outside pressure, cajoling, or force. As Findlay writes, "Campbell spoke to the segregationists of 'grace' and 'redemption,' and when applied to race these words meant that 'by this grace we are no longer Negro or white.... but we are part of a community that asks only one question and that has to do with redemption, not with color.'"[104] Yet Campbell was ecumenical in a sense and religious. In a 1976 interview he described his farmhouse in Mt. Juliet, Tennessee:

We have a guest house here, a sort of mini folk school back there in the fields, just a small cottage, you know, but a lot of things go on, seminars, or prayers. Every once in a while some of the neighbors [have been] in on this and sometimes we might have a service, like we had when the Catholic priest, who was gunned down with Jonathan Daniels in Lowndes County, came here for part of his later recuperation. He would say mass up there.[105]

As an "itinerant missioner," Campbell sometimes married people in a tavern, buried them in a field, went to a jail to try to get them released, or visited them in prison. Campbell's congregation consisted of anyone who came to see him, black or white, northern or southern, redneck or academic, a school dropout, a prison parolee, a successful businessperson, a farmer, a member of the Klan, a literary figure, a Nashville musician, or the unchurched.[106]

Perhaps Campbell's opinion of the NCC was not quite fair to those brave white ministers who ventured into Mississippi on behalf of the Delta Ministry. When asked why he went to serve in Mississippi, Bob Beech, a white Presbyterian minister from Minnesota who directed a Delta Ministry voting rights project in Hattiesburg from 1964 to 1966, responded with a passage from Luke (4:28): "The spirit of the Lord is upon me, because he hath anointed me to preach the gospel to the poor, he has sent me to heal the brokenhearted, to preach deliverance to the captives . . . to set at liberty them that are bruised."[107] Beech tried to form good relationships with white Mississippian ministers, but he suffered much harassment: a cross was burned in his yard; his home was fired upon with pistols; and he was personally attacked while shopping in a hardware store. His son was expelled from a private kindergarten, and he was asked to stop attending services at a local white Presbyterian church.[108]

◆ ◆ ◆

With the growth and rising power of conservative Christians in the South, mainline denominations have experienced a substantial loss of membership. A 2014 report on the religious composition of the South lists evangelical Protestants (Southern Baptist Convention, Assemblies of God, Churches of Christ, Lutheran Church–Missouri Synod, Presbyterian Church in America, and some nondenominational churches) as 34 percent of the population; mainline Protestants (the United Methodist Church; American Baptist Churches, USA; the Evangelical Lutheran Church in America; the Presbyterian Church, USA; and the Episcopal Church) as 14 percent; historically black Protestants (National Baptist Convention, Church of God in Christ, Church of Christ Holiness, African Methodist Episcopal Church, Progressive Baptist Convention, and others) at 11 percent; Catholics at 15 percent; nones at 19 percent; and all others (Mormon, Orthodox Christian, Jehovah's Witness, Jews) at 1 percent. This survey reveals the decline of the mainline denominations in the South and the increase of evangelical groups. Mainline members fled to more conservative religious groups (the Presbyterian Church in America, Association of Independent Methodists, Anglican Orthodox Church, Churches of Christ, and small independent evangelical groups) and to more liberal groups (Unitarian Universalists, Society of Friends, American Baptists, Independent Baptist Alliances, Lutheran ELCA, and even Buddhist societies).[109]

Eventually, a sense of racial reconciliation siphoned down to the evangelical groups. In 1973 an interracial group of concerned evangelicals drafted a statement that "bemoaned the conditions that allowed racism, materialism, hunger, blind patriotism, and women's inequality to flourish." They called for "total discipleship" and social action. From their efforts emerged Evangelicals for Social Action, whose members helped other evangelicals to recognize the social concern teachings in the Bible and the importance of racial reconciliation. Among this group of evangelicals was Jim Wallis, editor of *Sojourners Magazine*; Randall Balmer, Columbia University professor; Harold Ockenga and Richard Mouw, founders of Fuller Theological Seminary in Pasadena, California; and Mississippi-born African American evangelist John Perkins, a "missioner" of remarkable accomplishments who, with the help of northern whites and government programs, ministered among the poor in Mississippi (and elsewhere) for over forty years. In 1964 he established the Voices of Calvary Ministries (VOC) in Mendenhall, Mississippi. As Randy Sparks writes, "Perkins quickly realized that prayer was not enough: 'Our oppression was a political oppression. . . . You could pray all day and they wouldn't move. . . . Within a democratic society we would have to participate in that society to make changes.'" In Mendenhall and later Jackson and other Mississippi communities, the VOC established day-care centers, youth programs, health centers, adult education programs, thrift stores, and the Simpson County Housing Cooperative (which had built ten duplexes by 1980). With A. J. McKnight, a Roman Catholic priest from New York, black cooperatives were established throughout central Mississippi.[110]

It took many years for progressive evangelicals to overcome the rising religious Right, but during the 1990s the situation began to change. Representatives from the largely white National Association of Evangelicals and the National Black Evangelical Association called for the white church to repent of the sin of racism and for the black church to focus on a "constructive protest of racism." For the white Pentecostal Fellowship of North America, an end to racial separation came almost twenty-five years after the decline of the civil rights movement when representatives from the white group, meeting in Memphis in 1994, agreed to unite with leading black Pentecostals, the Churches of God in Christ and the Assemblies of God. At the thirtieth anniversary of the assassination of Martin Luther King Jr. held in Memphis, Tennessee, in 1998, Rev. Don Argue, president of the National Association of Evangelicals, stated, "In the 1960s, white Evangelicals should have been marching arm-in-arm with Dr. King, but they were silent. In some cases, they actually voiced opposition. That's a terrible stain on the history of white Evangelicals." According to Scott Thumma of the Hartford Institute for Religion Research, over 14 percent of evangelical congregations were considered interracial in the year 2010. This represented an increase of more than 50 percent since the institute's previous survey in 2000.[111]

What can we say about the efforts of southern white ministers who worked diligently within their mainline denominations for change: Methodists Ed King, Mackay Brabham, Rhett Jackson, Fred Reese, Eben Taylor, Ennis Sellers, Dallas Blanchard, Thomas Butts, and Andrew Turnipseed; Episcopalians Duncan Montgomery Gray, John Hines, John Morris, and Albert Rhett Stuart; Presbyterians E. T. Thompson, J. Randolph Taylor, Malcolm Calhoun, and J. Sherrard Rice; Lutherans H. George Anderson, Arnold Voigt, Edgar Homrighausen, Joseph Ellwanger, and Raymond Davis; and many others from all denominations not named? Were their efforts in vain? Not at all; although smaller in numbers, these denominations have apologized for slavery, have integrated black members, have elected black officials, and have established services to immigrants and those who are homeless, mentally challenged, or illiterate. Their churches have become less like clubs and more like inclusive houses of worship, places of learning for the young, of refuge for the tired, the lonely, the stranger, the elderly, and the oppressed. These denominations have weathered many storms. Their influence and numbers may be diminishing, but their resolutions and messages during the civil rights years were godly and important and may yet have a lasting influence.

The editors of *Christian Century* magazine expressed an interdenominational, evangelical Christian message in response to the decline of mainline churches: "Jesus chose a fallible church to tell the truth about Him . . . that He is the one who will bring all people and nations to their fulfillment. Telling and showing this truth is what we are called to do whether or not it brings institutional growth."[112]

═ 8 ═

CONCLUSION

We are thankful for those who in the mystery of life could find their path;
those who in darkness lighted a lamp for other men to see by; those who
could bring to utterance the sacred insights of the spirit; who have made
plain life's nobler way.
—CHARLES M. JONES, pastor, Community Church, Chapel Hill, North Carolina, 1963

A Protestant minister occupies a position of prominence and honor in southern culture. He or she is friend, counselor, interpreter of scripture, and shepherd to the flock, but in times of crises, the minister faces many challenges.
Does he or she remain silent in the face of injustice? What happens to important ministerial concepts such as "freedom of the pulpit"? Can he or she balance the prophetic with pastoral duties? Does a pastor ignore the inclusive
message of the Christian church for fear of losing a pulpit? In the course of
this book's narrative, these questions were addressed. These ministers did not
remain silent in the face of injustice. They believed in "freedom of the pulpit." They did not ignore the inclusive message of Christianity. Many lost their
pulpits, and some were never given pulpits. As Rev. James M. Wall, a southern
white minister who went north to serve as editor of the *Christian Century*
magazine for twenty-seven years, expressed, "These ministers carried a heavy
burden and many were truly prophets without honor in their own country."[1]

Rev. W. W. Finlator (chapter 6) preached social justice at the Pullen Memorial Baptist Church, the most progressive church in Raleigh, North Carolina,
for twenty-six years, but in 1979 his congregation decided he had gone too far
when he sent a telegram as chairman of the North Carolina Advisory Committee on Civil Rights to President Jimmy Carter demanding that the "federal government cut off its allocation to the University of North Carolina if
the university continued racial discrimination." Many people in his church
who were white employees in the university system and who might lose their
jobs were outraged. The following spring the deacons demanded his retirement. Rev. Brooks Ramsey (chapter 2) also chose the prophetic way. During

the Albany, Georgia, demonstrations in 1962, he stated publicly that Christ's church is open to all people. He also lost his pulpit.[2] The majority of white southern churchgoers did not want their ministers interfering in aspects of their personal lives and did not want to hear prophetic preaching during the civil rights movement.

Rev. Raymond Davis (chapters 1 and 7), a devout Lutheran and southern gentleman whose roots in the South went back 300 years to Quaker ancestors, suffered acute depression when his efforts to initiate a Head Start program in Montgomery, Alabama, were unappreciated by his all-white congregation: "The only way to defeat the program seemed to be by discrediting the pastor." When this author requested an interview with Rev. Andrew Turnipseed (chapter 2) in retirement in Comer, Alabama, he replied that he had an experience that he never wanted to remember. His son, with great admiration, related his father's story.[3]

Writing memoirs of their experiences was cathartic for several ministers. Rev. Robert McNeill, born in 1915 in Birmingham, Alabama, was forced to leave historic First Presbyterian Church in Columbus, Georgia, after seven years as pastor because he wrote an article for *Look* magazine stating that there should be "points of contact between the white and Negro people." In his memoir, he painfully asks, "How does a minister face a congregation to which he has just preached his last morning sermon while notice of his dismissal is read from the very same pulpit? Is the occasion like an impeachment, disbarment, or court martial?" For J. Herbert Gilmore (chapter 3), there was solemn resignation in the words written in his memoir as he left the First Baptist Church of Birmingham, Alabama: "Sooner or later the southern minister who would try to change this southern mystique must face the sad reality that most of his peers cannot be counted on for support. Indeed, most of them are prisoners in their own ecclesiastical houses." There was heartache in the memoir of Thomas J. Holmes (chapter 3) as he wrote of his dismissal from Tattnall Square Baptist Church in Macon, Georgia, for trying to welcome an African student: "The tragedy of this church is the nearly universal disgrace of all the churches—they might have led the way to community, but, alas, they would not!" Gilbert Schroerlucke (chapter 4) was forced to leave his all-black Methodist church in Louisville, Kentucky, where he had served for sixteen years, because he had provided a place for a black activist, considered a Communist, to speak to the community about racial injustice. He expressed sadness in the final words of his memoir. "As I look out on the landscape of closed churches . . . I . . . believe that . . . Kentucky United Methodism has failed its mission. It has turned in on itself making its preservation its primary mission. So it has turned a blind eye to the prophetic voice of God. Because of this, I weep."[4]

According to the historian David Chappell, "the prophetic stance has usually been a minority tradition," yet, as Chappell argues, prophetic preaching was exactly what changed the mores of the South. Most of Chappell's prophets are African American, all southern, some of whom have been mentioned in this narrative: Revs. James Lawson, Kelly Miller Smith, and Fred Shuttlesworth. Chappell also writes about secular prophets like John Lewis, who said the "movement was like a holy crusade," and Andrew Young, who told a reporter that there was a resurgence of religious feeling in the South because of the civil rights movement: "When folks start shooting at you, you do a lot more praying." Fannie Lou Hamer, a poor, black, rural southerner, was cited by Chappell as an authentic prophetic voice. Speaking of white churches and black churches alike, she declared, "They have failed to do what they should have done." When she spoke of Student Nonviolent Coordinating Committee (SNCC) volunteers in Mississippi, she said, "Some gave their lives for human justice. . . . There's more Christianity there than I've seen in the church." Chappell also writes about white ministers who were carried along into the "Great Crusade": Presbyterian Robert McNeill and white Southern Baptists Revs. Billy Graham, Dale Cowling, and Clyde Gordon, who preached against the curse of Ham; but those mentioned in this narrative—Robert Graetz, Will Campbell, Thomas J. Holmes, Ed King, Brooks Ramsey, Andrew Turnipseed—get only endnote recognition.[5]

The ministers I write about were all prophetic preachers. In a questionnaire, they were asked to identify one to three Bible verses that inspired their sense of racial justice. Almost all chose the verse from Amos 5:24: "Let justice roll down like a river and righteousness like a never-failing stream." In that verse, Amos is responding to the corruption, exploitation, immorality, and unfair economic and judicial practices that existed during the Golden Age of the northern kingdom of Israel: for Amos, justice is a "surging cleansing stream" that continues its force throughout the ages. The Hebrew prophets are biased toward the powerless, to those who otherwise are not heard. It seemed appropriate for some ministers to quote from this verse. In sermons, Dunbar Ogden Jr. called the verse "a plea for fair treatment" and "a command from the mouth of God."[6]

Many white ministers have also contributed to the "Holy Crusade." Whether I called them progressive, gradualist, desegregationist, integrationist, or prophetic, they all contributed something to pave the way for change in the South. The historian Carolyn Dupont calls them "moderates," ministers such as W. B. Selah (chapter 3), who acted on behalf of African Americans entering his church when the door was abruptly closed to them. She calls those who introduced supportive resolutions at general assemblies "religious

progressives." The religious historian Paul Harvey calls them "southern pro-
gressive religious elites," perhaps because many of them were born to southern privileged families. Bishop Duncan Montgomery Gray was the son of the
Episcopal bishop of Mississippi. Dunbar Ogden Jr. was the son of a minister of the largest and most distinguished Presbyterian church in the South.
Ogden's great-grandfather is said to have owned more slaves than anyone in
Mississippi. Rev. Dr. James Smylie, professor of church history at the Union
Theological Seminary in Richmond who traveled the Deep South trying to
convince Presbyterian churches to welcome African Americans, was the son
of a Presbyterian minister and also a descendant of one of the largest slave-
holders in Mississippi, another James Smylie who wrote numerous religious
tracts defending slavery. David Moose's great-grandfather was the founder of
the town of Morrilton, Arkansas. The father of Raymond Davis was a skilled
craftsman who owned a large business. Of course, not all the ministers had
elite backgrounds. Thomas Butts and Will Campbell were proud of their "redneck" forebears, but all the ministers were privileged during the segregation
era because they were white.[7]

As Roy Hulan wrote in 1963 for *The Christian*, the journal of the Disciples
of Christ, "I am a privileged person. I was born into the white community.
That has given me privileges not enjoyed by many fellow Americans." Hulan
was born in middle Tennessee, where the soil does not produce large crops
and slave plantations rarely existed, but some people had slaves and practiced
segregation. En route to the place of his birth, Shelbyville, one passes fields of
tall blue grass and grazing horses. Hulan's father, George Henry Hulan, was
the last of the line of skilled craftsmen who made harnesses for workhorses. In
addition to owning a harness factory, George Hulan was president of a local
bank and mayor of the town. Joseph Sanderson was also born to a privileged
family. His father was mayor of Town Creek, Alabama, in the heart of Black
Belt plantation land, but he tells how he sickened when he saw his planter
grandfather battering black workers because they weren't working fast enough.
Clarence Jordan's father was the town banker in Talbotton, southwest Georgia.
Jordan grew up in a mansion, but he responded to scenes of the oppression
and poverty all around him: the ragged and hungry children, the ramshackle
shacks with leaking roofs and broken windows.[8] These ministers were born to
privilege, but their status did not prevent them from feeling compassion and
entering the struggle for black civil rights.

Gilbert Schroerlucke, who grew up on a small farm in Kentucky, mentioned that "some of us were just rebels." Schroerlucke remembered going into
southern department stores in the larger towns and drinking from the "colored" water fountains. During his high school years, he would go into Louisville just to ride the buses. "Although there was no segregation as in other

southern cities, there was prejudice," he related. "Blacks would sit across the back and in the side seats. If a black person was sitting next to the window and there was an empty seat next to that person, whites would rather stand than sit down. I would deliberately sit there because I felt compassion for those black people who were being shunned." Growing up in Clio, South Carolina (population 600 at the time), Rev. R. Wright Spears's family had no servants, but he told how he came to love black people because of Roy Buchanan, who delivered ice in the summer, all for a "penny a pound." Buchanan owned his own horse and wagon, with a bell tied around the horse's neck to announce his coming. Spears remembered how Buchanan allowed the children to follow the ice wagon, giving them ice chips and thus "providing fun and a cooling treat on a hot day," and gaining their affection.[9]

Rev. Hulan wrote, "I was born into a town where my father was a leading businessman and that gave me other privileges. One of them was the privilege to go to good schools." Hulan graduated from Columbia Military Academy, Transylvania College, and the College of the Bible in Lexington, Kentucky. He did graduate work at Vanderbilt University and the University of Chicago. Many of these ministers, such as Will Campbell, left the South to attend Yale Divinity School. Others attended Columbia University, Union Theological Seminary, Hartford Seminary, General Theological Seminary, Garrett Theological Seminary, Seabury-Western Seminary, St. Paul School of Theology, Concordia University, and Boston University, and a few traveled as far away as the University of Edinburgh in Scotland, but most attended the South's most distinguished seminaries and universities: Candler School of Theology, Davidson College, Emory University, University of the South (Sewanee), Wake Forest University, Duke, Millsaps, Southern Baptist Theological Seminary, Southwestern Theological Seminary, Lutheran Theological Seminary, University of Georgia, Vanderbilt University, Troy State University, Wofford, Birmingham Southern, Washington and Lee, David Lipscomb College, and Maryville College. Education seems to have made a difference in their attitudes toward race. The sociologist Nancy Tatom Ammerman also concluded in her study of seventy-two white clergy in Tuscaloosa, Alabama, in 1962 that a progressive education was an important factor promoting white ministerial activism.[10]

One wonders what motivated these "progressive elites" to step outside the boundaries of their class, to sign proclamations, to organize interracial councils and interracial ministerial associations, to speak out against segregation, to accompany African American children as they tried to enter white schools, to invite African Americans into their churches, to join sit-in demonstrations, to march with activists, even to help felons behind prison walls. It may be remembered that Rev. George Edwards (chapter 4) and his wife, Jean, raised $5,000 for DNA testing of a strand of hair that cleared William Thomas Gregory, a black man, of all charges against him. Gregory was imprisoned for rape in 1993 and served eight years of a seventy-year prison sentence for a crime he did not commit. Gregory proclaimed, "I love those two people with all my heart." As Rev. Joseph Ellwanger commented, "To be silent in the face of injustice was to approve the *status quo*."[11]

Many of the ministers mentioned that they developed a basic love for African Americans because of the people who worked in their households. Marvin Whiting, growing up in Fort Valley, Georgia, where his father owned a factory, remembered Corley, who arrived at 6:30 a.m., fixed breakfast, and stayed until after supper, all for one dollar a day. "I could not have managed without her; she was always there for me, even when my mother was not," but to Whiting, the whole situation was so unjust. In later years, he wondered who took care of Corley's family.[12]

Sherrard Rice, son of Theron Rice, professor of ethics at Union Theological Seminary in Richmond, Virginia, told of his love for Mary, his cook, who encouraged him to "eat up" as she loaded his plate with potatoes and black-eyed peas. He told his congregation, "I love the Negro . . . in the way in which southern white people have always loved him, a way that outsiders never can quite understand." In the opening chapter of his memoir, Robert Seymour told how Rosa, elderly but stately and strong, came from Greenwood, South Carolina, his boyhood home, to Chapel Hill, North Carolina, to be present at his retirement liturgy at Binkley Memorial Baptist Church. She told the ushers, "I raised that good preacher." He introduced her to the congregation as his mother because she had been part of his life since early childhood, "as if she were family." Seymour truly loved her. According to Frank McRae, rich people had maids; the less rich had cooks. McRae learned to love black culture through his beloved cook, Anna Jackson. McRae admitted that he came to understand the civil rights movement through Anna Jackson: "Whatever touched her or those who were like her affected me. . . . I remember what it was like in public transportation. Time and again, Anna would have to go home in the afternoon making her way to the back of the bus through a lot of white people. My brother and I always went to the back of the bus as sort of a protest against an injustice that made no sense." As Rev. McRae commented, "We loved blacks as individuals but not always as a race," but McRae and others later changed their attitudes and came to love the whole race.[13]

Some white ministers were propelled into the civil rights movement by tragedies of enormous proportions. Such was the case with the Rev. Joseph Sanderson (chapter 6), rector of St. Andrew's Episcopal Church in Marianna, Arkansas. A black laborer was found lying in a field near his church with his legs severed by a tractor. A passerby drove the man to a nearby hospital that refused to admit him. The man then drove him to Memphis, some forty miles away, but before he could get him to a hospital, the laborer died. Sanderson knew that he could not stand idly by such egregious injustice. When Brooks Ramsey was twelve years old, he saw an old black man severely beaten in the head by his boss. He never knew what became of the man, but he never forgot the extreme compassion he felt for the old man's pain. At his first pastorate in the small country town of Jacksonville, Alabama, in 1949, Robert McNeill remembered a black family who lived in the back of his yard, whose cow frequently came to graze, and whose children came to play with his four-year-old daughter. One day McNeill learned that their thirteen-year-old boy had been stabbed to death. A professor at nearby Jacksonville State College telephoned McNeill asking for his help in rounding up witnesses. (McNeill emphasized that the professor was not a Yankee, but a South Carolinian with "an accent as thick as a cotton bale.") After a great deal of trouble, they were successful in obtaining a conviction, and both felt blacks would be much safer from then on. The incident launched McNeill into his "commitment to unqualified justice" for black people.[14]

Prejudice was so strong in Vicksburg, Mississippi, where Edwin King grew up, that his uncle, an avid baseball fan of the Brooklyn Dodgers (mainly because they opposed the New York YANKEES), swore he would never again listen to a Brooklyn game after they signed Jackie Robinson as their first black player. King pretty much accepted the status quo until 1953, when a tornado struck the town. There was massive property damage, and many people died, including one of King's friends. King, a high school senior, worked with the Red Cross, distributing food and clothing to storm victims, and, for the first time in his young life, he became aware of black poverty. The black neighborhood in Vicksburg was pretty well destroyed by the tornado. King noticed that the streets were not paved and that fire trucks and ambulances could not maneuver through the mud to save burning houses or injured people. King realized that the problem was due to segregation. "There was no such thing as separate but equal. . . . Before this I had been blind," King wrote. "I was ready for the school decision of the U.S. Supreme Court five months later."[15]

Duncan Montgomery Gray, who grew up in Canton, Mississippi, developed close relationships with African Americans who worked for his family and became repulsed by the harassment of black people by teenagers who threw rocks at their homes and called them names, but after graduating from Tulane University with a degree in engineering, Gray became particularly aware of the tragic effects of discrimination. Gray had taken a position with the Westinghouse Corporation in Pittsburgh, where he became friendly with an African American man who had an engineering degree from the Carnegie Institute. Although the man had good technical training and had served as a major in the US Army during World War II, the only employment he had at

Westinghouse was steam-cleaning motors. Such injustice, even in the North, had a strong effect on Gray, and he determined to work for racial justice upon returning to the South to study for the ministry.[16]

Some ministers were transformed by educational experiences. When Brooks Ramsey was attending Union University in Memphis, Tennessee, he worked on the weekends at a Baptist church, where the minister did not approve of seminaries. (Many Baptist ministers do not attend seminary.) Ramsey told the minister he intended to go to seminary; the minister responded, "If you go, you'll be contaminated—you don't need seminary," but Ramsey went anyway. At Southwestern Baptist Seminary in Fort Worth, Texas, the largest theological seminary in the world, he studied Christian ethics with one of the great liberal spirits of the Southern Baptist Convention, Thomas Bufford Maston. Ramsey remembered Maston's first lecture: "Young gentlemen, when you get out into the church field, you won't have the opportunity to examine all the issues confronting the church today, so I recommend that you read all the views and make up your mind what you believe so that you will have some resources."[17]

Ramsey had been told by conservatives that the famous Baptist minister Harry Emerson Fosdick was "of the devil," a liberal, a modernist, a Communist, and an arch-demon, so when Maston told him to "read all the views," Ramsey read six lectures by Fosdick called "The Meaning of Service," an interpretation of Christianity in terms of serving the world and helping the needy. Ramsey thought, "If Fosdick is 'of the devil,' then I will have to be a little on that side myself. This sounds more like the Jesus that I really believe in." Ramsey became convinced that racial justice was the major problem facing the churches.[18]

During the period December 2006 through January 2007, nineteen southern white ministers answered "A Brief Questionnaire, Part II," in which they were asked to rank factors such as faith, witnessing to black suffering, conscience, and so forth, as indicated in Table 1, according to first, second, and third choices, but the task was far from easy. For most ministers, all of the factors were important, and choosing the one that was most important was virtually impossible. The result was that they chose several factors for their first choice, several for their second and third choices. A tabulation of all of their answers revealed no definite first-place winner, but a tie score between "faith" and "witness to suffering and to gross injustice to African Americans," as Table 1 illustrates (factors are ranked in order of most chosen to least chosen).

These results highlight the impact of traumatic memories and the influence of faith. As people of faith, they believed that God could change people's hearts, and, in many cases, transformations occurred.[19]

It took forty-five years for Rev. William G. McAtee, born in 1934 in Shaw, Mississippi, great-grandson of slave owners, to publish the story of his

Table 1. Factors of Influence

FACTOR	NUMBER OF TIMES CHOSEN AS FIRST FACTOR	NUMBER OF TIMES CHOSEN AS SECOND FACTOR	NUMBER OF TIMES CHOSEN AS THIRD FACTOR
Faith	8	2	3
Witness to suffering and to gross injustice to African Americans	8	2	3
Personal acquaintance with African Americans	6	4	5
Conscience	3	5	1
Civil rights activists	3	4	1
Bible	2	3	3
Education	1	4	3
Theologians	1	2	3

transformation from a person silent on racial issues to someone willing to speak out about racial justice, harmony, and understanding. He calls himself a "recovering racist." McAtee became pastor of a Presbyterian church in Columbia, a small city in eastern Mississippi with a population of approximately 7,000, 60 percent white and 30 percent African American. He started his ministry in 1964, just a few days before activists James Chaney, Andrew Goodman, and Michael Schwerner were reported to have disappeared. Their dead bodies were later found in a sunken dam near Philadelphia, Mississippi.[20]

McAtee's transformation began that summer. While working on his master's thesis at the Presbyterian seminary in Louisville, Kentucky, he visited Oxford, Ohio, where SNCC, along with the National Council of Churches (NCC), was preparing students for work on the Mississippi voter registration drive. The only thing McAtee knew about SNCC and the NCC was what he heard from "archconservatives" in the Presbyterian Church in Mississippi, that they were "foreign anarchists," "Communists," and "subversives." He took the short drive from Louisville to Oxford to see for himself. In Oxford, he discovered a wide variety of what seemed like kind, generous people from all over the country, more whites than blacks, college students, professors, folk singers, guitar players, and working-class women from Mississippi, including activist Fannie Lou Hamer. There was disbelief among the group that a white minister would come all the way to such a meeting. They wanted him to make a speech, but he declined, knowing that it would cause severe repercussions in his church and presbytery. McAtee left with a feeling of despair, knowing that these people had no idea as to what was awaiting them in Mississippi.[21]

At the end of 1964 McAtee preached his first prophetic sermon. He told his congregation that "freedom" was not freedom to do anything you want. Christian freedom was summed up in the two great commandments: "'Loving God and loving your neighbor as yourself.' One may claim to love God with ease, but how one loves one's neighbor is more difficult." Whether the members of Columbia Presbyterian Church understood the challenge of McAtee's sermon is hard to say, but it is evident that one of his deacons, E. D. "Buddy" McLean, paid attention. In March 1965 McLean announced his candidacy for mayor. He said, "I am not unaware that the next four years as have been the past four, will be filled with problems and perhaps turmoil. . . . But I promise to use every ounce of my ability and the entirety of my time and efforts in our behalf." He won the election.[22]

Next, McAtee organized a biracial ministers' committee consisting of Rev. N. A. Dickson, pastor of First United Methodist Church in Columbia; Rev. Isaac C. Pittman, director of the Mississippi Rural Center in nearby Lampton; Rev. I. Z. Blankinship, pastor of Friendship (Missionary) Baptist Church in Columbia; and Rev. Amos Payton Sr., pastor of Owens Chapel (Missionary) Baptist Church in Columbia. McAtee and Dickson were white; Pittman, Blankinship, and Payton were black. Dedicated to peaceful solutions of racial problems, they first addressed the problem of segregated schools. On July 17, 1965, McAtee and Dickson wrote letters to local businesspeople warning that noncompliance with the law would surely bring outside agitators into Columbia, and normal life would be destroyed. They called for key individuals to "insist publicly on peaceful compliance with school desegregation." The Sunday following the letters, McAtee delivered another prophetic sermon:

> Too often we shut our eyes to the poor and the effects of poverty, then condemn the poor for being undeserving: we claim the business of the church is saving souls and not social reform; we do not recognize that charity without love destroys the giver and the receiver; we denounce every effort to meet the needs of the poor. . . . It would be staggering to describe the impact on this community if the church out of Christian conviction, together and individually, would take the lead in . . . doing things we have never done before. . . . But this just won't happen, it must be worked for.[23]

The letters and sermon bore fruit. On August 24, 1965, an acceptable plan for desegregation was approved by the school board by one vote. On January 3, 1966, twelve years after the *Brown* decision, an eight-year-old African

American girl, Dorothy Weary, entered all-white Columbia Primary School without incident.[24]

The mayor and the biracial ministers' committee were successful in maintaining peace and harmony in Columbia while violence blazed all around them. They made small gains and avoided friction until early 1966, when militant members of SNCC and the Mississippi Freedom Democratic Party (MFDP) came to Columbia to picket lack of employment opportunities for African Americans at several retail stores. Led by two African Americans, Curtis Styles and Willie McClenton, and one white activist from New York City, Ira Grupper, the leaders were arrested by local police for blocking a department store entrance and going beyond the picketing limits set up by the mayor and the biracial committee. Grupper was placed in a cell for whites, and Styles and McClenton in a cell for blacks; according to Grupper, little difference existed between the grimy cells After a few days the three convicts were released on bail, and the case was referred to the federal district court, where an indictment was never made.[25]

McAtee's memoir exposes two different approaches to solving segregation problems, one moderate and gradual, the other radical and extreme. Grupper, a leader in the MFDP, resented the fact that "his small ragtag group" was never included in an invitation to attend a meeting of the biracial committee, although a group of students from American University, who also came to protest, were included. Grupper criticized the biracial committee as being composed of the "most accommodating black ministers, too afraid to march," and he really did not want the students to attend the meeting because they might get the impression that things were not as bad as they really were. McAtee responded that his group wanted the students to be exposed to a set of Mississippi citizens who were working for desegregation in a peaceful, moderate way. McAtee feared that the presence of the extremists would have given the meeting a different dynamic. McAtee and Grupper (who later became friends) came to recognize that their tactics were different, but their goals were the same. Grupper believed that he was not breaking the law by blocking the entrance to the store. He felt he had First Amendment rights to protest egregious action by segregationists. The mayor, McAtee, and others also repudiated egregious injustice, but their approach involved working within the dominant power structure to bring about change. McAtee came to believe that many tactics were needed to change "separate and unequal into liberty and justice for all."[26]

McAtee left Columbia in October 1966 after three years of ministry in Amory, Mississippi, and two years in Columbia. Perhaps he was worn out. He does not say in his memoir. He moved his family to Richmond, Virginia, where he began service for the Board of Christian Education for the southern Presbyterian Church (PCUS). He wrote that his heart ached when he later learned that the Columbia Presbyterian Church broke away from PCUS and that several families left the denomination. His conclusion about the effectiveness of the civil rights movement is much the same as others: "for some, great changes have occurred," but not for everyone.[27]

McAtee was not the only minister transformed by the civil rights movement. Many whose stories are told in this narrative had similar experiences: Floyd Enfinger, Thomas Butts, Howard McClain, Sherrard Rice, C. G. Haugabook, and Bishop Paul Hardin. Like McAtee, these ministers were not activists but worked behind the scenes. Perhaps they could be called gradualists. They helped to gain white supporters who could pave the way for change. Some brought change to their denominations. The courageous effort of Bishop John Hines (chapter 5) transformed the Episcopal Church, probably forever. It is impossible to gauge the full extent of the influence of these ministers. Edgar Homrighausen (chapter 7) told white Lutheran ministers in Alabama to "love the hell out of the white segregationists," but we do not know how many of the Lutheran segregationists actually changed their attitudes. Even in their failures, these ministers were successful in bringing attention to the racial issue and making future successes possible.

In answer to the question, "Did their efforts bring about changes in the South?," I answer, "Yes." In Clinton, Tennessee, the courage of Rev. Paul Turner and his subsequent beating convinced the town's people that they must *not* vote for the segregationist town council. The booklet *South Carolinians Speak*, compiled by five southern white ministers, gave many pro-integration South Carolinians an opportunity to express their opinions and perhaps change some hearts (chapter 1). Some ministers brought about change on a personal level. Rev. Larry Jackson, who helped compile *South Carolinians Speak*, claimed the booklet had a tremendous effect on his brother Rhett, who helped bring about the merging of the two separated Methodist Conferences in South Carolina (chapter 7). The brother of Thomas Butts, once a member of the Klan, became active in an integrated Methodist church in Alabama because of his brother's influence (chapter 2). When Davis Yeuell was denied admittance to his family's church in Tuscaloosa, Alabama, his mother was transformed from a segregationist to an integrationist who condemned the governing body of First Presbyterian Church for having a closed-door policy (chapter 3). The long-lasting influence of Baptist Clarence Jordan in southwest Georgia is extraordinary (chapter 6). Martin Luther King Jr. is reported to have once remarked, "You know, when you can finally convert a white southerner, you have one of the most genuine, committed human beings that you'll ever find."[28]

Sometimes it took a long time and a new generation for change to occur. It took fifty-four years for the Washington Street Methodist Church of Columbia,

South Carolina, to apologize to Rev. Claude Evans (1917–2007) for dismissing him in 1942 because he preached a sermon on love and brotherhood.

What did Evans say in 1942 that was so offensive to the congregation and the governing board of the church? First, he told them that just to believe that "God is love" is not enough: "If you want to understand love, you have to get to concrete events. . . . The state constitution in South Carolina has kept blacks from voting. That is a simple violation of love. The poll tax has kept poor whites and blacks from voting and that is a simple violation of love." Then he repeated many times, "God has made of one blood all peoples of the earth." To him, that meant that blacks and whites shared a common heritage, had similar genes, similar DNA, and could share blood plasma: "There is no such thing as a permanently superior race or a permanently inferior race. The soul of the human being—the essence of life—is the same in all people. . . . 'All God's Children Got Soul.'" Then he went on to identify some very accomplished African Americans (perhaps with hyperbole, as he later admitted): "'Who is the best scientist in the world?' he asked. 'George Washington Carver,' he answered. 'Who is the best singer in the world?' he asked. 'Marion Anderson,' he answered. 'Who is the greatest pugilist in the world?' he asked. 'Joe Lewis,' he answered, "and if you don't believe this, you are [uninformed]." When he finished his sermon and left the pulpit, Evans thought the chairman of the Board of Stewards was coming forward to say something nice, but, to the contrary, he told Evans, "You have made the worse mistake of your life." At the stewards' next meeting, a vote was taken, eighty-seven to three, to ban Evans from ever speaking again at Washington Street Methodist Church. He told his story on July 21, 1996, at the church's Service of Reconciliation and said he had no resentment or grudge against anyone who played a part in the drama. He thanked the congregation with all his heart for inviting him back. When he left the pulpit, there was great applause and a standing ovation.[29]

In 1999 someone from a new generation spoke out. Joel Garrison, a white man born in 1973 in Memphis but raised in Earle, Arkansas, and a member of Rev. David Moose's Methodist church in West Memphis, Arkansas, was listening intently to stories that are contained in this book. At the end of the presentation, he made this comment: "I completely admire all those people who had the courage to speak out against racism at a time when it was unpopular and even dangerous to do so. I only wish I could have been there." Garrison, who saw action in Iraq, is now a lieutenant colonel in the army National Guard, stationed at the Pentagon in Washington, DC. He is also an active member of the Military Leadership Circle, which works to solve problems in inner cities peacefully. This was a sign that some people in a new generation might not have the same prejudices as their elders.[30]

Some ministers recalled their experience with pride and satisfaction. Rev. Randolph Taylor (chapters 4 and 5), who met with a measure of success in his endeavors in Washington, DC, during the March on Washington and later in Atlanta in 1967 and 1968, stated, "It was a wonderful time to be alive. When you have a clear, present duty, and a deserving cause to focus on instead of your own particular agenda, and an event forcing you to face an issue that you are embarrassed to face; it becomes an exciting and challenging time." Even Fr. Joseph Sanderson (chapter 6), who suffered much rejection in Marianna, Arkansas, when he aided African American activists, expressed good feelings: "It was a decade when people with hearts acted. It was a time when I felt useful. This was a cause to which we could devote ourselves. There was a marvelous kind of feeling that came as a result of becoming involved." Rev. Joseph Ellwanger (chapters 2 and 4), who led a protest march in Selma, Alabama, in 1965, was deeply encouraged by the accomplishments derived from the movement: "There is amazing power in people of faith coming together, focusing on specific justice goals, demonstrating nonviolently and sacrificially, making a clear call for change and speaking truth to power." The movement of white and black people coming together gave Ellwanger profound meaning to his life. He continued to work with a congregation-based justice group in Milwaukee, Wisconsin, helping to address the current needs: inner-city violence, gun usage, excessive incarceration, substance abuse, the continuing economic gap between blacks and whites, and de facto segregation of public schools and church congregations.[31]

Racial problems persist, as recent events demonstrate: police attacks on unarmed black youth; black church bombings; the massacre at Mother Emanuel African Methodist Episcopal (AME) Church in Charleston, South Carolina; the mass incarceration of black youth. Many good people still avoid confronting racial problems and discrimination as they have in the past, not only in the South but also in the North. According to the Southern Poverty Law Center in Montgomery, Alabama, hate groups have been on the rise throughout the United States since the election of Barack Obama as president in 2008.[32]

One hopeful sign is that African Americans have been returning to the South in large numbers since the 1970s. They are moving to the large cities—Atlanta, Nashville, Charlotte, and Houston. William H. Frey, a Brookings Institution demographer, has noted, "Segregation has declined mostly in the largest growing areas of the South and West," which partially explains a reason for the return. Atlanta is often considered a "Black Mecca" and a "Black Hollywood" because of the city's large number of black entertainers, business owners, and public figures. As Cicely Bland, a publishing company owner who left her home in Jersey City in 2006 for Stockbridge, an Atlanta suburb, expresses, "The business and political opportunities are here. You have a lot of African Americans with a lot of influence and they're in my immediate networks." Other African Americans, retirees, a smaller number, are returning to rural areas, regions they vowed they never wanted to see again, "many fleeing [northern] urban poverty for a place where vegetables grow readily." Bennie and Hilda Rayford left Toledo, Ohio, in 1990, when their teaching jobs in inner-city public schools became unbearable. In Hilda Rayford's school, a sixth grader was stabbed in the cafeteria, and another showed up in her classroom with a gun. The Rayfords returned to Tchula in the Mississippi Delta, where they had grown up. In Tchula, 80 percent black, the police force and county boards have become largely African American. Dusty roads have been paved. Hilda set up a reading program for children and adults who could not read, and Bennie became head of a local health center and vice-chair of the state prison industries. According to Greg Toppo and Paul Overberg of USA Today, "The quiet return of African American retirees and young professionals has the potential to reshape the South again over the next few decades much as the exodus to northern cities reshaped it in the twentieth century."[33]

The success of the civil rights movement in ending legal segregation and guaranteeing the voting rights of African Americans can be seen as contributing to this trend, but small cities and some rural regions are not as hospitable to African Americans as recent trends suggest. When Tonsa and Allen Stewart moved to Montgomery, Alabama, to teach at historically black Alabama State University, they found few friends and difficulty in getting a loan for a house in a town where blacks are still a minority, but they preferred to remain, in preference to California, where both had gone to college. The social realities in small towns have barely changed, according to Anthony Walton, who returned to Mississippi in the 1990s. Walton, born in Aurora, Illinois, to African American parents who left Columbia, Mississippi, in the 1960s, found that the society that his parents left was still a separate society, "although somewhat more equal than it had been before." The experience of Fr. Travis Frank in eastern Arkansas (chapter 6) also supports the consensus that in parts of the South, "everything has changed, but nothing has changed," but hope for change has not ended. As Rev. Clinton Hubbard Jr. of the North Alabama Methodist Conference states, "A lot of work remains to be done. We are working on awareness. We are working on a racial diversity initiative and racial reconciliation. We are trying to change things around."[34]

◆ ◆ ◆

As the narrative of this book has shown, the South produced some of the most radical and racially liberal white ministers in the nation at the time of the civil rights movement, but perhaps some were frightened away or silenced by the

opposition, the bombings, the cross burnings, the jailing, the beatings, the intimidation, the catcalls, the cursing, the threatening telephone calls, and sometimes
murder. These ministers, a courageous minority, did what they believed they had
to do for civil rights. They spoke from their hearts and consciences. As Thomas
Butts of Monroeville, Alabama, expressed, "I tried to make a positive witness for
justice. . . . If we did not make much difference in the Movement, the Movement
made a difference in us."[35] No doubt, there were not enough ministers willing to
stand up and be counted. How many ministers in today's society would be willing to sacrifice their careers for the "suffering other"?

Some questions explored in this narrative remain to be answered. Can a
minister safely be involved in social action? How much can he or she actually
achieve? Has the minister's prophetic role in society diminished, or even disappeared? And an even larger question: Is religious social action on behalf of
justice relevant in a troubled society? These are complex questions and cannot
easily be answered in one book or by one author, but as Chappell has suggested,
"Even opponents of religion . . . err in ignoring religion's persistence and unpre-
dictable power. . . . They need to learn from its wily durability in the past."[36]

NOTES

Acknowledgments

1. Marvin Yeomans Whiting, interview by author, Birmingham, AL, 15 August 1994.

2. Ibid.

3. Ibid.

4. Miller Williams, interview by author, Fayetteville, AR, 8 March 1999.

5. Ibid.

6. Lev. 19:18; Matt. 22:39; Mark 12:31; 1 John 4:12 RSV; Williams, interview.

7. Williams, interview; Miller Williams, letter to author, 13 February 2006; Walter N. Vernon, *Methodism in Arkansas, 1816–1976* (Little Rock, AR: Joint Committee for the History of Arkansas Methodism, 1976), 288–299. Miller Williams has published many books of poetry and was chosen to read his poetry at the inauguration of President William Clinton in 1997.

Introduction

1. Rev. R. Douglas Hudgins, pastor of First Baptist Church, Jackson, Mississippi, quoted in Charles Marsh, *God's Long Summer: Stories of Faith and Civil Rights* (Princeton, NJ: Princeton University Press, 1997), 89.

2. Rev. Laurence Neff, *Jesus: Master Segregationist*, 10, 7. The pamphlet has no publisher and no date, but according to archivist Danielle Theiss-White of the Emory University Archives, Neff was a Methodist minister, journalist, lawyer, and publisher of Emory University's Banner Press from 1919 until his retirement in 1960. Danielle Theiss-White to author, 19 December 2005; Matt.10:5 ESV.

3. Statement issued by the Arkansas Missionary Baptist Association in Little Rock, 1957, in Ernest Q. Campbell and Thomas F. Pettigrew, *Christians in Racial Crisis: A Survey of Little Rock's Ministry* (Washington, DC: Public Affairs Press, 1959), 38–39.

4. Rev. Ebenezer Myers, *The Race Question in a Nutshell*, 10 November 1959, W. W. Finlator Papers, reel 17:73, Wisconsin Historical Society, Madison.

5. James P. Dees, "Which Way the Nation—Which Way the South," an address to the Citizens' Council of Greater New Orleans (1961), Finlator Papers, reel 17:149–150. At the time, Dees was president of the North Carolina Defenders of States Rights, Inc. Later, in 1963, he founded the Anglican Orthodox Church in protest of liberal tendencies in the Protestant Episcopal Church, USA. David L. Chappell, *A Stone of Hope: Prophetic Religion and the Death of Jim Crow* (Chapel Hill: University of North Carolina Press, 2004), 111; verse is from Acts 17:26 RSV.

6. Marion A. Boggs, "The Crucial Test of Christian Citizenship," 7 July 1957, Boggs Papers, box 9:9, Presbyterian Historical Society, Montreat, NC.

7. Robert McNeill, *God Wills Us Free: The Ordeal of a Southern Minister* (New York: Hill and Wang, 1965), 8; Isa. 56:7; Amos 5:24 NIV. Also selected by Dunbar Ogden Jr. See Dunbar H. Ogden III, *My Father Said Yes: A White Pastor in Little Rock School Integration* (Nashville, TN: Vanderbilt University Press, 2008), 56.

8. Rev. Everett Tilson, "Racial Debate Props in Bible Called Scanty," *Nashville Tennessean*, 5 May 1958; "Segregation Called Immoral," *Nashville Tennessean*, 26 April 1960, both in Tilson Papers, Nashville Room, Nashville (TN) Public Library.

9. W. J. Cunningham, "If We Sound No Trumpet," sermon, quoted in W. J. Cunningham, *Agony at Galloway: One Church's Struggle with Social Change* (Jackson: University Press of Mississippi, 1980), 161.

10. Gal. 3:28–29, 5:14–15 NIV; George Edwards, Robert Graetz, and John Lyles, in answer to a questionnaire, "Which Bible verses have inspired your sense of racial justice?," March–April 2003, Elaine Allen Lechtreck, "Southern White Ministers and the Civil Rights Movement: 1954–1976" (PhD diss., Union Institute and University, 2007), 268, answers in author's possession.

11. 1 John 2:11 NIV; Dunbar H. Ogden Jr., "Beyond the Law," sermon, cited in Ogden, *My Father*, 42.

12. 1 John 4:12 NIV; Robert Hock, "Which Bible verses?"

13. Heb. 12:1–2; Matt. 22:37–40; Mark 12:31 RSV. H. George Anderson, Thomas Butts, Raymond Davis, W. W. Finlator, C. G. Haugabook, Larry A. Jackson, R. Edwin King, Frank McRae, David Moose, John B. Morris, Brooks Ramsey, Joseph Sanderson, Gilbert Schroerlucke, Robert Seymour, and more, "Which Bible verses?"

14. According to the *Book of Discipline* of the United Methodist Church (2000). See my unpublished paper, "Roots of Segregation within the Churches: An Inquiry into American Denominations from Their Origins until the Civil War," Union Institute and University, 24 September 2003. I include much detail about the ordination procedures of the denominations. "Rachel Henderlite and Myra Scovel: Lives of Dedication," *Presbyterian Heritage* 18, no. 1 (Winter 2004): 1. The Episcopalian Church also began ordaining women at the time but not in the South.

15. "Born of Conviction," 1 June 1999, *Mississippi Methodist Advocate* 2:1–4; Ellis Ray Branch, "Born of Conviction: Racial Conflict and Change in Mississippi Methodism, 1945–1983" (PhD diss., Mississippi State University, 1984), 98–101.

16. For a discussion of the Social Gospel movement, see James F. Findlay Jr., *Church People in the Struggle* (New York: Oxford, 1993), 6, 224; Chappell, *Stone of Hope*, 5; "Which term most closely describes your personal theology?" Questionnaire, March–April 2003, Lechtreck, "Southern White Ministers," H. George Anderson, Thomas Butts, Raymond Davis, W. W. Finlator, and more, answers in author's possession. See Anne Braden, *The Wall Between* (1958; reprint, with a new foreword by Julian Bond and a new epilogue by Anne Braden (Knoxville: University of Tennessee Press, 1999), 42.

17. Peter Hairston Hobbie, "Ernest Trice Thompson: Prophet for a Changing South" (PhD diss., Union Theological Seminary of Virginia, 1987), 85, 395. Hobbie cites ideas from Thompson's book *Changing Emphases in American Preaching* (Philadelphia: Westminster Press, 1943).

18. Kenneth Kesselus, *John E. Hines: Granite on Fire* (Austin, TX: Episcopal Theological Seminary of the Southwest, 1995), 3.

19. Joseph Ellwanger, letter to author, 20 December 2006.

20. Rhett Jackson, "Description of a Christian Progressive," *Zion Herald Christian Advocate* 178, no. 2 (2004): 38–39.

21. Charles Reagan Wilson, *Baptized in Blood: The Religion of the Lost Cause, 1865–1920* (1980; reprint, with a new preface by the author, Athens: University of Georgia Press, 2009), 16; Frank Lewis McRae, interview by author, tape recording, Memphis, TN, 14 May 1999 (and others).

22. Martin Luther King Jr., *Stride toward Freedom* (New York: Harper & Row, 1958), 209

23. Campbell and Pettigrew, *Christians in Racial Crisis*, 8.

Chapter 1. School Desegregation

1. Spoken by Carter at a panel, "*Brown v. Board of Education*: A Fifty-Year Retrospective: The History and Legacy of the Landmark Case and Its Meaning Today," program of the Organization of American Historians, Boston, Union United Methodist Church, 26 March 2004; Will D. Campbell, interview by author, tape recording, Mt. Juliet, TN, 18 August 1995.

2. Derrick Bell, *Silent Covenants: Brown v. Board of Education, the Unfulfilled Hopes for Racial Reform* (New York: Oxford, 2004), 95; Numan V. Bartley, *The Rise of Massive Resistance: Race and Politics in the South during the 1950s* (1969; reprint with a new preface by the author, Baton Rouge: Louisiana State University Press, 1999), 212–224, 77–78, 135, 81; Campbell, interview, 18 August 1995. The quotation from Marvin Griffin is in Bartley, *Rise of Massive Resistance*, 68.

3. "Statements of the Churches on Desegregation and Race Relations," in Campbell and Pettigrew, *Christians in Racial Crisis*, 137–172.

4. Campbell and Pettigrew, *Christians in Racial Crisis*, 7. Quotations from Hugh White and Baptist elders are in Carter Dalton Lyon, "Lifting the Color Bar from the House of God: The 1963–1964 Church Visit Campaign to Challenge Church Sanctuaries in Jackson, Mississippi" (PhD diss., University of Mississippi, 2010), 13–17; Randy J. Sparks, *Religion in Mississippi* (Jackson: University Press of Mississippi for the Mississippi Historical Society, 2001), 228; letter to Dr. Albert C. Barnett, July 31, 1958, Civil Rights and Methodists, box 1/R2, Mississippi Department of Archives and History.

5. G. McLeod Bryan, interview by author, tape recording, Winston Salem, NC, 8 August 2001; Cabell Phillips, "Integration: Battle of Hoxie, Arkansas," *New York Times*, 25 September 1955, Magazine Section, 12, 68; Bartley, *Rise of Massive Resistance*, 96–100, 202–210, 318, 330. See also Pete Daniel, *Lost Revolutions: The South in the 1950s* (Chapel Hill: University of North Carolina Press, 2000), 205–206; "Is Dixie Destroying Its Best Seed?" *Southern Patriot* 14, no. 8 (October 1956): 1, 4.

6. Phillips, "Integration," 68, 69; the second quotation is from Carolyn Renée Dupont, *Mississippi Praying: Southern White Evangelicals and the Civil Rights Movement, 1945–1975* (New York: New York University Press, 2013), 74.

7. Campbell and Pettigrew, *Christians in Racial Crisis*, 45–48, 53.

8. The last quotation is from Marion A. Boggs, "Lessons from the Little Rock Crisis," address at Columbia Theological Seminary, 2 November 1960, 22.

9. Bartley, *Rise of Massive Resistance*, 80; "The True Face of Clinton," *Time*, 17 December 1956, 21. The article mentioned other ties to the North: Clinton's voting record since the Civil War (Republican), and the fact of its name: it was originally named Burrville after Aaron Burr. When Burr was tried for treason, the town's name changed to Clinton in honor of Vice President George Clinton (from New York State).

10. Margaret Anderson, *The Children of the South* (New York: Dell, 1958), 8–10, 15; *New York Times*, 5 December 1956, 1:1; June N. Adamson, "Few Black Voices Heard: The Black Community and the Desegregation Crisis in Clinton, Tennessee, 1956," *Tennessee History Quarterly* 53, no. 1 (Spring 1994): 33; Arthur Gordon, "Intruder in the South," *Look* 21, no. 4 (19 February 1957), 28–30. Kasper became a hero to segregationists in Clinton. He also preached hatred for Jews and the law. See also Bartley, *Rise of Massive Resistance*, 148, 203–206.

11. Anderson, *Children*, 15–18. For more details, see ibid; Dorise Turner Haynes, interview by author, telephone, 3 March 2012.

12. *Time*, 17 December 1956, 21–22; Anderson, *Children*, 18. The church had a membership of 1,300 people in a town of 3,700. Mark Newman, *Getting Right with God: Southern Baptists and Desegregation: 1945–1995* (Tuscaloosa: University of Alabama Press, 2001), 117; G. McLeod

Bryan, *These Few Also Paid a Price* (Macon, GA: Mercer University Press, 2001), 111–113; John N. Popham, "Fifteen Seized by U.S. in Clinton Drive on School Bias," *New York Times*, 6 December 1956, 1:1. The two townspeople accompanying Turner were Sidney Davis, an attorney and chair of the Board of Deacons at Turner's church, and Leo Burnett, a textile mill employee.

13. Wilma Dykeman and James Stokely, "Courage in Action in Clinton, Tennessee," *Nation*, 22 December 1956, 531–533.

14. "Clinton Minister Lives His Faith," *Christian Century*, 19 December 1956, 1470; John N. Popham, "Violence Shuts Clinton School," *New York Times*, 5 December 1956, 1:1, 44:3–8; Anderson, *Children*, 18–19; *Time*, 17 December 1956, 22; *Commonweal* 65, no. 12 (December 1956): 301; Dykeman and Stokely, "Courage in Action," 532–533; Wayne Dahoney, ed., *Baptists See Black* (Waco, TX: Word, 1969), 12–16, cited in Bryan, *These Few*, 113; "Great Churches: First Baptist of Clinton, Tennessee," *Newsweek*, 28 January 1957, 92.

15. Dykeman and Stokely, "Courage in Action," 531; Haynes, interview; Will D. Campbell, interview by Orley Caudill, Mt. Juliet, TN, 8 June 1976, Will D. Campbell Papers, McCain Library and Archives, University of Southern Mississippi, Hattiesburg, 46.

16. Dr. Ralph Murray, letter to author, 17 February 2012; Jane Turner Murray, letter to author, 23 February 2012; Rev. C. R. Daley Jr., "Daily Observations," Middletown, KY: *Western Recorder*, ca. 1981, n.p.; James H. Wolfe, "'Burn Out' Hits Hardest at Achievers," unidentified newspaper article, n.d,, n.p. Wolfe's article is a review of the book *Burn Out* by Herbert Freudenberger (New York: Anchor Press, 1980). Wolfe noted that Freudenberger, a practicing psychologist, applied the term "burnout" to people who suffered from fatigue, frustration, and depression because of intense pressure and stress in their workplace or personal lives. Daley referred to Wolfe's article and called Turner's suicide a tragic case of "ministerial burnout." Daley and Wolfe's articles are from the personal papers of Dorise Turner Haynes in author's possession.

17. Haynes, interview.

18. According to a CBS television reporter, "The people in Clinton were on the verge of a lynching." "Clinton Near Lynching in Fall, TV Man Says," *Nashville Banner*, 1. The quoted phrase is from "Clinton Minister Lives His Faith," *Christian Century*, 19 December 1956, 1470:2.

19. Paul W. Turner, "The Minister's View of the Ministry," *Search* (Summer 1972): 33–39. See also Albert McClellan, "Attitudes That Hurt Pastors Are Fear, Self-Hatred, Anger, and Loneliness," 17 June 1974, 16–19, Haynes Papers.

20. Six African American children completed the year, but never without difficulties and harassment and the near destruction of the school. "Dynamite Wrecks Tennessee School Integrated in '56," *New York Times*, 6 October 1958, 34:1. In a smaller article, the *Times* quoted John Kasper as hailing the bombing as "a great victory for the white people of Tennessee." Kasper, the article stated, was in North Carolina to form a political party in line with his views. He was thus eliminated as a suspect in the bombing. "Kasper Hails Blast," *New York Times*, 6 October 1958, 34:2; Mike Bradley, "History Revisited," *Tennessee Alumnus Magazine* 83, no. 4 (Fall 2003). See also Clinton Beauchamp and Amanda Turner, "The Desegregation of Clinton High School: Trial and Triumph," www.jimcrow history.org.

21. Eric Snider, letter to author, 11 November 2015; www.greenmcadoo.org. The twelve students who integrated Clinton High School were JoAnn Allen, Bobby Cain, Theresa Caswell, Minnie Ann Dickey, Gail Ann Epps, Ronald Hayden, William Latham, Alvah McSwain, Maurice Soles, Robert Thacker, Regina Turner, and Alfred Williams. Many African American families left Clinton at the time because of harassment and violence against them.

22. Bartley, *Rise of Massive Resistance*, 261–262.

23. Will Counts's photographs were published in newspapers throughout the United States and internationally, among them the photograph of the black reporter kicked and beaten: "Violence in Little Rock: Alex Wilson, Negro Reporter Is Kicked at Central High by a White Man

Holding Brick," *New York Times*, 24 September 1957: 18: 2–5 (ill.); also the photograph of the
paratroopers: "With Bayonets Fixed, Troopers Escort Nine Negro Students as They Enter Little
Rock High School," *New York Times*, 26 September 1957: 1: 4–7 (ill.). See also Will Counts, *A Life
Is More Than a Moment: The Desegregation of Little Rock's Central High* (Bloomington: Indiana
University Press, 1999).

    24. Campbell and Pettigrew, *Christians in Racial Crisis*, 17; Marion A. Boggs, "Statement
Before the State Senate Committee on Segregation Bills," 18 February 1957, Boggs Papers,
Presbyterian Historical Society, Montreat, NC, box 4:6; Boggs, "Crucial Test of Christian
Citizenship," 1, 5.

    25. Marion A. Boggs, "Lessons from the Little Rock Crisis," address at Columbia Theologi-
cal Seminary, 2 November 1960, Decatur, GA, Boggs Papers, box 16:4, 24; "Faubus in Clash with
Ministers," *New York Times*, 17 September 1958, 25:2; Marion A. Boggs, "Statement to the Session
of Second Presbyterian Church, Little Rock, Arkansas, 24 April 1962," Boggs Papers, box 13:6.
For criticism of Boggs, see Paul Harvey, *Freedom's Coming: Religious Culture and the Shaping
of the South from the Civil War through the Civil Rights Era* (Chapel Hill: University of North
Carolina Press, 2005), 213.

    26. Virgil T. Blossom, *It Has Happened Here* (New York: Harper & Brothers, 1959), 15–18;
John A. Kirk, "Arkansas, the *Brown* decision, and the 1957 Little Rock School Crisis: A Local
Perspective," in *Understanding the Little Rock Crisis*, ed. Elizabeth Jacoway and C. Fred Williams
(Fayetteville: University of Arkansas Press, 1999), 71–74, 80. This action was one of the pupil
placement plans established by southern legislatures to give authority to local administrators to
place pupils in schools at their own discretion. Bartley, *Rise of Massive Resistance*, 77, 78.   .

    27. Blossom, *It Has Happened Here*, 33–34, 59, 39, 41, 43, 55–56.

    28. Ibid., 73–75; Daisy Bates, *The Long Shadow of Little Rock: A Memoir* (Fayetteville: Univer-
sity of Arkansas Press, 1986), 61, 64–65, 189; Benjamin Fine, "Little Rock Told to Integrate Now
Despite Militia," *New York Times*, 4 September 1957, 1:6.

    29. Ogden, *My Father*, 9, 38; Dunbar Ogden Jr., interview by Dunbar Ogden III, Berkeley,
CA, 1977, in Ogden, *My Father*, 22–23, 26, 32; Dunbar Ogden III, interview by author, tape
recording, Berkeley, CA, 25 September 1999; Bates, *Long Shadow*, 66.

    30. Relman Marin quoted in Walter Spearman and Sylvan Meyer, "Racial Crisis and the
Press," Series XVI, reel 218, 90:17, Southern Regional Council Papers, Auburn Avenue Research
Library, Atlanta. The Southern Regional Council, an Atlanta-based group of clergy and laity
working for integration, commended Marin for his eyewitness account. Benjamin Fine, "Little
Rock Told to Integrate Now Despite Militia," *New York Times*, 4 September 1957, 20:6–7, 5 Sep-
tember 1957, 20:4.

    31. Ogden, *My Father*, 28–29; Ogden, interview; Bates, *Long Shadow*, 66–67.

    32. Staff Correspondent [Anne Braden], "A Southern Profile: Little Rock Climaxes Spiritual
Journey," *Southern Patriot* 17, no. 7 (September 1959): 3–4, Beinecke Rare Book and Manuscript
Collection, Yale University, Folio S 30; Ogden, interview; Ogden, *My Father*, 50; Dunbar Ogden
Jr., sermons, Presbyterian Archives, Montreat, NC, unarranged files; "Those Who Favor Chris-
tian Principles and Law Should Speak Up, Little Rock Minister Declares," *Arkansas Gazette*, 30
September 1957.

    33. "Uncompromising Judge," *New York Times*, 5 September 1957, 20:2, 3. Bates reported
that in 1960, Little Rock's chief of police, Eugene G. Smith, "pumped three fatal bullets into his
wife . . . then turned the pistol on himself and fired a bullet into his head." Bates, *Long Shadow*,
182; Homer Bigart, "U.S. Troops Enforce Peace in Little Rock as Nine Negroes Return to Their
Classes; President to Meet Southern Governors," *New York Times* 26 September 1957, 1:8; Ogden,
My Father, 55; Campbell and Pettigrew quoted in Ogden, *My Father*, 62.

    34. Ogden, *My Father*, 84, 56, 85–87.

35. Ibid., 94–95, 103. Ogden conjectured that the guard may have thought that King was a member of the Green family.

36. Ibid., 147.

37. Colbert S. Cartwright, *Walking My Lonesome Valley: An Autobiography* (self-published), 40–44, 97–100, Colbert S. Cartwright Papers, Disciples of Christ Historical Society, Nashville, TN, box 3.

38. Ibid.; Colbert S. Cartwright, "What Can Southern Ministers Do?" *Christian Century* 73 (December 1956): 1505–1506; Cartwright's sermon was preached on 8 September 1957, quoted in Eleanor Humes Haney, "A Study of Conscience as It Is Expressed in Race Relations" (PhD diss., Yale University, 1965), 125, 129; Psalm 27:1 KJV; Sara Alderman Murphy, *Breaking the Silence: Little Rock's Women's Emergency Committee to Open Our Schools, 1958–1963*, ed. Patrick C. Murphy III (Fayetteville: University of Arkansas Press, 1997), 152.

39. Haney, "Study of Conscience," 127–130; Cartwright, *Walking My Lonesome Valley*, 7.

40. Campbell, interview, 18 August 1995; Will Campbell, "Speech to the Southern Regional Council," Atlanta, 2 November 1973, 4, Campbell Papers, M341, box 13:3; Thomas L. Connelly, *Will Campbell and the Soul of the South* (New York: Continuum, 1982), 81–82.

41. Will D. Campbell, *Brother to a Dragonfly* (New York: Continuum, 1994), 117–121; also Campbell, interview, 18 August 1995.

42. Campbell, *Brother to a Dragonfly*, 125–128. Campbell related that the University of Mississippi at that time would not even allow famed Oxford author William Faulkner to enter the campus because Faulkner spoke out against lynching and crimes against blacks. Campbell, interview, 18 August 1995; Campbell, interview by Caudill, 42, 52–53.

43. Campbell, interview by Caudill, 44–45, 48. The intention of the Southern Project was to respond to the crises precipitated by the *Brown* decision of 1954. Findlay, *Church People*, 22–23. Campbell served as director of the Southern Project for the National Council of Churches (NCC) from 1956 until 1963; Campbell, interview, 18 August 1995.

44. Ogden, *My Father*, 87, 131.

45. Ibid., 131.

46. Duncan Montgomery Gray, "The Church Considers the Supreme Court Decision," publication of the Diocese of Mississippi, Department of Christian Social Relations, 1954, in author's possession, 1–3; Will D. Campbell, *And Also with You: Duncan Gray and the American Dilemma* (Franklin, TN: Providence House, 1997), 138. Campbell greatly admired Gray and wrote a book about him.

47. Duncan Montgomery Gray, interview by author, telephone, 16 December 2004; James W. Silver, *Mississippi: The Closed Society* (New York: Harcourt, Brace and World, 1963), vii; Charles W. Eagles, *The Price of Defiance: James Meredith and the Integration of Ole Miss* (Chapel Hill: University of North Carolina Press, 2009), 146, 340–341, 347–348, 350–353. See also William Doyle, *An American Insurrection: The Battle of Oxford, Mississippi, 1962* (New York: Doubleday, 2001), 138–139, 144–149.

48. Duncan Montgomery Gray, interview by Donald Cunnigen, tape recording, Jackson, MS, December 1981, in Donald Cunnigen, "Working for Racial Integration: The Civil Rights Activism of Bishop Duncan Montgomery Gray of Mississippi," *Anglican and Episcopal History* 67, no. 4 (December 1998): 489; Duncan Montgomery Gray, interview by author, telephone, 9 August 2004; Campbell, *And Also with You*, 24–25, 27, 32; Eagles, *Price of Defiance*, 361–362; Doyle, *American Insurrection*, 128–129.

49. Cunnigen, "Working for Racial Integration," 491; Campbell, *And Also with You*, 26; Eagles, *Price of Defiance*, 361. An active member of the John Birch Society, Walker had been an important general in the US Army but was relieved of his command in Germany in 1961 after accusing former president Truman and Eleanor Roosevelt of being Communists and attempting

to influence his troops politically. Rather than take a demotion, Walker resigned and became an activist for segregation in his home state of Texas. "I Am a Walking Program," *Newsweek*, 4 December 1961, 21. Gray noted, "Walker went on television in Shreveport [Louisiana] and called for people to come from all over the South to Oxford to protest the forced integration. I think the hundreds and maybe even thousands of people who poured into Oxford that night and the next morning came because of Walker's going on television." Duncan Montgomery Gray, interview by author, Jackson, MS, 21 July 2007. Doyle also told about someone who came to Mississippi because he was told to by General Walker. Doyle, *American Insurrection*, 128.

50. Campbell, *And Also with You*, 3; Cunnigen, "Working for Racial Integration," 491–492; *New York Times*, 1 October 1962, 1:6; Eagles, *Price of Defiance*, 360–362, 369, 366; Gray, interview, 9 August 2004. See also Claude Sitton, "Negro at Mississippi U. as Barnett Yields; 3 Dead in Campus Riot 6 [incorrect, only 2] Marshals Shot; Guardsmen Move In; Kennedy Makes Plea," *New York Times*, 1 October 1962, 1:8. According to Campbell, 29 marshals were shot; 160 were hurt with bricks, pipes, bottles, and timbers. Campbell, *And Also with You*, 30.

51. Gray quoted in Campbell, *And Also with You*, 36; Gray quoted in Cunnigen, "Working for Racial Integration," 492–493. See also "Excerpts from Untitled Sermons by Duncan Gray," Campbell Papers, box 12:22.

52. A reporter from the *Los Angeles Times* wrote, "I feel free to picture him as a resolute, stubborn Scotsman with an inability to remain still when he feels that somebody is tampering with justice. And I wish I knew him." Dickson Preston of the *Rocky Mountain News* reported, "The Reverend Mr. Gray has a conscience. Because of it, he finds himself engaging massive forces in battle with weapons no more substantial than eloquence and the *Book of Common Prayer*." Gray, interview, 21 July 2007; Campbell, *And Also with You*, 36–37, 43–46; Duncan Montgomery Gray, letter to author, 9 August 2004. Gray also wrote, "The man who became Bishop Coadjutor in 1961 was the Right Reverend John M. Allin who became Presiding Bishop of the Episcopal Church in 1974." Gray added, "He, too, was supportive of my efforts."

53. Gray, letter to author; Ruth Gray quoted in Campbell, *And Also with You*, 61.

54. Gray, interview, 21 July 2007.

55. Tom Dent, *Southern Journey: A Return to the Civil Rights Movement* (Athens: University of Georgia Press, 2001), 339; Faulkner quoted in Carol Polsgrove, *Divided Minds: Intellectuals and the Civil Rights Movement* (New York: Norton, 2001), 5–6.

56. "Born of Conviction," 1 June 1999, *Mississippi Methodist Advocate* 2:1–4; Powell Hall, interview by author, tape recording, Hermitage, TN, 1 June 1999; Ellis Ray Branch, "Born of Conviction: Racial Conflict and Change in Mississippi Methodism, 1945–1983" (PhD diss., Mississippi State University, 1984), 98–101. Claude Sitton reported on the number of ministers under age forty-five in the Mississippi Methodist Conference. Claude Sitton, "3 Pastors Ousted by Mississippians," *New York Times*, 19 January 1963, 4:5. See also Joseph T. Reiff, "Born of Conviction: White Methodist Witness to Mississippi's Closed Society," in *Courage to Bear Witness: Essays in Honor of Gene L. Davenport*, ed. L. Edward Phillips and Billy Vaughan (Eugene, OR: Wipf and Stock, 2009), 124–142. See also Peter C. Murray, *Methodists and the Crucible of Race, 1930–1975* (Columbia: University of Missouri Press, 2004), 139–140.

57. *Methodist Church Discipline* (Nashville, TN: United Methodist Publishing House, 1960), 2026; Gal 3:26 RSV. See also W. B. Selah, *Puddles and Sunsets* (Huntsville, AL: Monte Sano United Methodist Church, 1990), Annex A, 2–3; Hall, interview; Branch, "Born of Conviction," 99–101.

58. For information on MAMML, see Lyon, "Lifting the Color Bar," 64–66. See also Branch, "Born of Conviction," 109–110. According to Branch, MAMML was reorganized on 31 March 1955 in Jackson from an earlier group called The Layman's Organization for the Preservation of the Southern Methodist Church, organized in 1938 in opposition to the reunification of the southern and northern Methodist Churches. MAMML officially opposed integration at

all levels of Mississippi Methodism. Branch, "Born of Conviction," 16, 47; Joseph Crespino, *In Search of Another Country: Mississippi and the Conservative Counterrevolution* (Princeton, NJ: Princeton University Press, 2007), 61; Campbell, *And Also with You*, 141.

59. Branch, "Born of Conviction," 102, 111, 123–125; Selah, *Puddles and Sunsets*, Annex A, 2–3; see also Sitton, "3 Pastors Ousted," 4:5–6; Reiff, "Born of Conviction," 125.

60. See also Selah, *Puddles and Sunsets*, Annex A, 2–3; Sitton, "3 Pastors Ousted," 4:5–6; Reiff, "Born of Conviction," 125.

61. Denson Napier, interview by author, Jackson, MS, 6 April 2000.

62. Hall, interview; John Herbers, "Church Burning Spreads in South," *New York Times*, 16 July 1964, 12.

63. Keith Tonkel, interview by author, tape recording, North Jackson, MS, 5 April 2000.

64. Cunnigen, "Working for Racial Integration," 500; see also Silver, *Mississippi*, 3; Reiff, "Born of Conviction," 140.

65. The placement law was passed in 1955 and declared constitutional by the Supreme Court, but school boards were warned "not to use it as a device to avoid desegregation," which, in fact, happened in many states. "Negro Students in Birmingham Denied a Desegregation Order," *New York Times*, 29 May 1963, 16:2; *Montgomery Advertiser*, 11 March 1962; *Birmingham Post-Herald*, 11 March 1962. See Dan T. Carter, *The Politics of Rage: George Wallace, the Origins of the New Conservatism and the Transformation of American Politics* (Baton Rouge: Louisiana State University Press, 1996), 96, 110. According to Carter, the phrase was "out n____red." Attorney Fred Gray quoted the statement made by Wallace as "out-segged." Fred Gray, *Bus Ride to Justice: Changing the System by the System* (Montgomery, AL: Black Belt, 1995), 143, 146, 193.

66. Rachel and Raymond Davis, interview by author, Charleston, SC, 8 March 2003; Raymond Earle Davis Jr., "Writing About My Life," 2001, unpublished paper in author's possession, photocopy, 1.

67. Rachel and Raymond Davis, interview.

68. Rev. Davis also recalled that he had a subscription to the *National Lutheran Magazine* sent to every home in his congregation. "Often blacks would be pictured on the cover which greatly disturbed many of the people. They didn't want their neighbors to know they were getting the magazine." Rachel and Raymond Davis, interview.

69. Gray, *Bus Ride*, 144.

70. Claude Sitton, "Alabama Tension on Schools Rising," *New York Times*, 1 September 1963, 40:4. Sitton calculated that African Americans outnumbered whites in Macon County by 22,000 to 5,000. See also Ennis G. Sellers, "Tuskegee, the Methodist Church, and School Integration," unpublished paper in author's possession, photocopy, 1964, 1.

71. Written from personal memories of the author's visit to Tuskegee Institute, 6 July 1994. Robert J. Norrell mentioned that author Ralph Ellison, a former Tuskegee student, stressed the ambiguity of the statue. Ellison was highly critical of the administration in his novel *The Invisible Man*. He characterized them as catering to the demands of wealthy white industrialists in preference to the needs of students. Robert J. Norrell, *Reaping the Whirlwind: The Civil Rights Movement in Tuskegee* (New York: Vintage Books, 1986), 182. See also Ralph Ellison, *The Invisible Man* (New York: Vintage Books, 1989).

72. For an excellent description of the different community groups in Tuskegee, see Norrell, *Reaping the Whirlwind*, 128–143.

73. 364 U.S. 339, 81 S.Ct. 125, 167 F. Supp. 405, 270 F. 2d 594 (1960). To convince the Supreme Court, Gray displayed an enlargement of a map showing the new city limits superimposed on the old. "You mean to tell me that Tuskegee Institute is now outside the city limits," asked Justice Frankfurter. "Yes, sir, Mr. Justice Frankfurter," replied Gray. Justice Frankfurter read the unanimous decision: "When a legislature thus singles out a readily isolated segment of a racial

minority for special discriminatory treatment, it violates the Fifteenth Amendment." The case became a landmark, preventing any other city from attempting racial gerrymandering. Gray, *Bus Ride*, 116, 121, 210; Ennis G. Sellers, interview by author, tape recording, Mobile, AL, 3 July 1997; Norrell, *Reaping the Whirlwind*, 136–138.

74. Sellers, interview.

75. Ibid.

76. Sellers, "Tuskegee," 5–6.

77. Ibid., 6–7; Claude Sitton, "Alabama Tension on Schools Rising," *New York Times*, 1 September 1963, 40: 3.

78. Norrell, *Reaping the Whirlwind*, 145; Sitton, "Alabama Tension," 40:3; Sellers, interview.

79. Claude Sitton, "Alabama Police Keep School Shut," *New York Times*, 3 September 1963, 26:6. In contrast to the problems incurred in Tuskegee, the *Times* reported that on 10 September 1963, "two African Americans entered Murphy High School in Mobile without opposition from 2,777 white students." In Huntsville, it was reported that four African Americans entered the high school without incident. John Herbers, "Mobile Is Orderly, Huntsville Stays Calm," *New York Times*, 11 September 1963, 31:1.

80. Sellers, "Tuskegee," 8–9; Sellers, interview.

81. "Proclamation and Order," *New York Times*, 11 September 1963, 31:1; Claude Sitton, "President Avoids a Show of Force," *New York Times*, 11 September 1963, 31:2; Sellers, "Tuskegee," 9–10.

82. Sellers, "Tuskegee," 11–16.

83. Sellers, interview.

84. Ibid.

85. Sellers, "Tuskegee," 17. The "Mission Ministers," as they were called, included Revs. Powers McLeod, Charles Prestwood, Dallas Blanchard, and Thomas Butts, in addition to Sellers, all members of the Alabama–West Florida Methodist Conference. Private papers of Dallas Blanchard in author's possession.

86. Walter Edgar, *South Carolina: A History* (Columbia: University of South Carolina Press, 1998), 522.

87. Ibid., 524.

88. The principal author of the "Southern Manifesto" was South Carolina senator Strom Thurmond. Edgar, *South Carolina*, 527–528.

89. John Morris to Ralph Cousins, 9 June 1957, John Morris Papers, box 1, South Caroliniana Library, Columbia, SC.

90. John Lyles, interview by author, tape recording, Cornelius, NC, 24 April 2002.

91. Daniel, *Lost Revolutions* 239; Morris Papers, box 1.

92. Larry Jackson, interview by author, tape recording, Greenwood, SC, 20 April 2002; Ralph E. Cousins, Joseph R. Horn III, Larry A. Jackson, John S. Lyles, and John B. Morris, comps., *South Carolinians Speak: A Moderate Approach to Race Relations* (self-published, 1957), v–vi, Morris Papers, box 1.

93. Cousins et al., *South Carolinians Speak*, 4, 18, 63, 72.

94. Daniel, *Lost Revolutions*, 241–242; John Morris, "A Final Report on *South Carolinians Speak*," 12 July 1958, 2, Morris Papers, box 1.

95. Lyles quoted in Donald W. Shriver, comp., *The Unsilent South: Prophetic Preaching in Racial Crisis* (Richmond, VA: John Knox, 1965), 27; Matt. 25:41–43 KJV.

96. Lyles, interview.

97. Ibid.

98. Larry Jackson, interview.

99. For more on Gantt and the Perry strategy, see Orville Vernon Burton, "Dining with Harvey Gantt," in *Matthew J. Perry: The Man, His Times, and His Legacy*, ed. W. Lewis Burke

and Belinda F. Gergel (Columbia: University of South Carolina Press, 2004), 187–188; Charles A. Webster, letter to author, 10 July 2003.

100. C. A. Webster Jr., "In Explanation of My Resignation," 31 March 1963, unpublished paper in author's possession, 1; South Carolina Council on Human Relations Papers, box 3 (South Caroliniana Library), courtesy of Will Gravely; C. A. Webster, interview by author, videotape, Buford, GA, 19 May 2003.

101. Webster claimed he was asked to leave Clemson because he escorted Gantt to the registrar's office to obtain an interview; he influenced students to criticize a film, *Operation Abolition*; and he arranged for Gantt to attend a student conference sponsored by the South Carolina Council on Human Relations. Webster, "In Explanation," 6–8; C. A. Webster, interview.

102. R. Wright Spears, *One in the Spirit: Ministry for Change in South Carolina* (Columbia, SC: R. L. Bryan, 1997), 150; Edgar, *South Carolina*, 538; C. A. Webster, interview; Al Webster, interview by author, videotape, Buford, GA, 19 May 2003.

103. Judith Bell Vaughan, *A Quiet Little Civil Rights Project* (Blog.com, 20 August 2013), 17, 41, 65; Gavin Wright, letter to author, 14 August 2013.

104. C. A. Webster, interview; Al Webster, interview. C. A. Webster thus prevented a cross burning. The burlap wrap was removed, and the cross remained in the Webster home until it was donated to a church.

105. "*Brown v. Board of Education*: Timeline of School Integration in the U.S.," in *Teaching Tolerance* (Montgomery, AL: Southern Poverty Law Center, Spring 2004), 25, online. In 1996 and 2006 a charter was denied to any sectarian or home-based private school by the General Assembly of the State of South Carolina, with the statement, "It is not the intent of the General Assembly to create a segregated school system, but to continue to promote educational improvement and excellence in South Carolina." 2006 Act no. 274, Section 1, eff. 3 May 2006.

106. "School Integration in South on the Rise," *New York Times*, 10 August 1963, 6:6; Gray, *Bus Ride*, 271.

107. Bell, *Silent Covenants*, 96–97; "Timeline of Supreme Court School-Desegregation Cases from *Brown* to *Fisher*," American Bar Association Annual Meeting, San Francisco, 8–12 August 2013, online.

108. Raymond Wolters, "From *Brown* to *Green* and Back: The Changing Meaning of Desegregation," *Journal of Southern History* 70, no. 2 (May 2004): 317–326, 321–322; "*Brown v. Board*: Timeline of School Integration in the U.S."

109. Bell, *Silent Covenants*, 112, 114, 164–179.

110. Gavin Wright, *Sharing the Prize: The Economics of the Civil Rights Revolution in the American South* (Cambridge, MA: Harvard University Press, 2013), 151, 177–180.

111. Elizabeth Jacoway, "Brown and the 'Road to Reunion,'" *Journal of Southern History* 70, no. 2 (May 2004): 308.

112. James Wiggins, letter to author, 6 June 2015.

113. Eric Snider, letters to author, 6 June 2015, 8 January 2016.

114. Sierra Cotham and Cierra Davis, interviews by author, telephone, 4 December 2015; Snider, letters to author, 6 June 2015, 8 January 2016.

115. DeMarea Whitt, J'Quan Thomas, and Kristopher Morrow, interviews by author, telephone, 4 December 2015

116. Snider, letter to author, 8 January 2016.

117. Debbie Elliot, "Nearly Six Decades Later, Integration Remains a Work in Progress," 13 January 2014, in *Code Switch, Frontiers of Race, Culture, and Ethnicity*, online.

118. Ibid.

119. Ibid. All quotations appear in the article.

120. Dykeman and Stokely, "Courage in Action," 532; Ogden, interview; also Ogden, *My Father Said Yes*, 27.

121. Boggs, "Lessons from the Little Rock Crisis," 28, 32.

122. For Campbell's discussion of Christian radicals, see Campbell, *And Also with You*, 136; Campbell, interview, 18 August 1995.

Chapter 2. The Heart of the Movement

1. King, *Stride toward Freedom*, 34–45.

2. Gray, *Bus Ride*, 61.

3. Donald E. Collins, *When the Church Bell Rang Racist: The Methodist Church and the Civil Rights Movement in Alabama* (Macon, GA: Mercer University Press, 1998), 19, 22, 27–31. Fraser is quoted on 28, and also in King, *Stride toward Freedom*, 116–117; parenthetic sentence from Crespino, *In Search of Another Country*, 60.

4. Active Core members, most of whom lost their pastorates, were: Andrew Turnipseed, Donald Collins, Fletcher McLeod, Charles Prestwood, Sam Shirrah, Ray E. Whatley, and James Zellner. Other members—Floyd Enfinger, Thomas Butts, Powers McLeod, James Love, and John Parker—managed to survive. Floyd Enfinger, interview by author, tape recording, Fairhope, AL, 12 August 2001; Collins, *When the Church Bell Rang*, 23–24.

5. Enfinger, interview.

6. Gardiner H. Shattuck Jr., *Episcopalians and Race* (Lexington: University of Kentucky Press, 2000), 77.

7. Robert S. Graetz, *A White Preacher's Memoir: The Montgomery Bus Boycott* (Montgomery, AL: Black Belt Press, 1998), 50, 121. Quotation is from Matt. 5:44 KJV.

8. During the early 1900s, German Lutheran missionaries went south to establish missions in black communities. Some communities disbanded as members left the farms for cities, while others continued with only a few members. These small churches were maintained as preaching stations, with Graetz serving two of them, one in Wetumka, twenty miles northeast of Montgomery, and the other in Clanton, about forty miles north of Montgomery. During the bus boycott, church members, fearing for Graetz's life, traveled with him as he went to his small outposts, especially Wetumka, considered Klan territory. Graetz, *White Preacher*, 45, 48, 139, 74–75, 80, 110. A photograph of the station wagons of the car pool lined up behind the parsonage of Graetz's church is pictured on page 117. Another photograph of Graetz, arms outstretched in prayer for the boycott, appears in King, *Stride toward Freedom*, 67; the account of violence toward Graetz appears in the *New York Times*, 11 January 1957, 1:5, 12:2.

9. Graetz, *White Preacher*, 85–87, 153–155; Bob Johnson, "Minister Finds His Actions Live On," *Birmingham Post-Herald*, 15 January 1998, A4:3.

10 Gray, *Bus Ride*, 68; Graetz, interview; Graetz, *White Preacher*, 77–78.

11 Gray, *Bus Ride*, 60.

12. "White Pastors Approve Plea on Bus Seating," *Mobile Press Register*, 5 March 1958, 1:3; Collins, *When the Church Bell Rang*, 39–44; *The Clerical Directory of the Episcopal Church* (New York: Church Hymnal Corporation for the Church Pension Fund, 1968); *Directory of the Episcopal Church, 1966*, Archives of the Episcopal Church, Austin, TX; *Revised Ministerial Directory of the Presbyterian Church in the United States* (Louisville, KY: Office of the General Assembly, 1983); "Bias Repeal Sought," *New York Times*, 5 March 1958, 18:3.

13. The *New York Times* reported that a large cross was burned the following night in front of the home of Rev. John T. Parker. *New York Times*, 11 March 1958, 22:3; Collins, *When the Church*

Bell Rang, 41–43; Spencer Andrew Turnipseed Jr., interview by author, tape recording, Montgomery, AL, 16 January 2001.

14. Marti had been a civil rights activist in Birmingham with Martin Luther King Jr. Her death left all who knew her stunned and bereaved. Turnipseed Jr., interview.

15. Thomas Lane Butts, interview by author, tape recording, Monroeville, AL, 10 November 1999.

16. Ibid.; Thomas Lane Butts, "Martin Luther King Celebration Address," Monroeville, AL, 19 January 2004.

17. Thomas Lane Butts, interview by author, tape recording, New York City, 3 July 2001. At the time, Rev. Butts was a guest preacher at Christ Church, New York City.

18. Ibid.

19. Ibid.

20. "Ban on N.A.A.C.P. Due for a Ruling," *New York Times*, 25 March 1964, 21:1. Butts, interview, 3 July 2001; Frank Price, "Town Saw Naked Truth, Suspended Minister Says," *Montgomery Advertiser*, 24 April 1983, 2A:4; Certificate of Exoneration issued by the Southeastern Jurisdiction United Methodist Court of Appeals, Atlanta, October 1, 1983.

21. "Another Thought," letter of Thomas Butts to Joanna Bosko, 4 April 2000, in author's possession; Butts, interview, 10 November 1999.

22. Thomas Lane Butts, "Alabama Bar Association Speech," Monroeville, AL, 18 July 2003, personal papers of Thomas Butts in author's possession.

23. Butts, interview, 3 July 2001.

24. "Resistance Groups of the South," 23 May 1957, 1–12, Series III, reel 111:0695–0707, Southern Regional Council Papers. The Southern Regional Council (SRC), an organization of white and black southerners, including many ministers, formed in 1944 to advance "equal opportunity for all the South's people," estimated a membership in pro-segregation groups to be more than half a million, with funding in excess of $2 million. The SRC reported on almost 100 resistance groups and also cited several that were led by ministers. In Georgia, the States Rights Council, with a total membership of at least 150,000, was headed by Baptist minister William F. Bodenheimer, from Ty Ty. Another Baptist minister headed the WCC in Memphis, Tennessee. The National Association for the Advancement of White People was incorporated in 1953 in Delaware with the goal of segregation of the races. In 1955 the attorney general of Delaware revoked the charter. The group organized again in Cincinnati, Ohio, in 1963. FBI, Freedom of Information Privacy Act: www.Fbi.gov.; *New York Times*, 17 July 1963, 30:4. STAND was a group united against the Mobile Bus Petition. R. Edwin King, interview by author, video recording, Brooklyn, NY, 15 November 2004; Robert Seymour, interview by author, tape recording, Chapel Hill, NC, 14 March 2001; Bible verse from Acts, 8:4 RSV.

25. John Hope Franklin, *From Slavery to Freedom: A History of Negro Americans*, 3rd ed. (New York: Knopf, 1967), 623; "Negroes in South in Store Sitdown," *New York Times*, 3 February 1960, 22:4; Joe McNeil statement is in Henry Hampton and Steve Fayer, *Voices of Freedom: An Oral History of the Civil Rights Movement from the 1950s through the 1980s* (New York: Bantam, 1991), 56–57.

26. "Negroes in South in Store Sitdown."

27. "Episcopal Group Backs Sitdowns," *New York Times*, 6 March 1960, 50:3.

28. "How to Practice Nonviolence" (Nyack, NY: The Fellowship of Reconciliation, n.d.), Nashville Special Collection, Nashville Public Library, Nashville, TN. Rev. Smiley also helped prepare "Suggestions for Integrating Buses" for the Montgomery Bus Boycott. He is pictured seated in the front of the bus with Martin Luther King Jr. on the first ride after the bus boycott. King, *Stride toward Freedom*, 163, 168.

29. Lawson quoted in Hampton and Fayer, *Voices of Freedom*, 54. Lawson had been to India and studied Gandhi's movement. He would later be expelled from Vanderbilt Divinity School because of demonstration activities. "Vanderbilt Crisis Deepens," *Christian Century*, no. 24 (15

June 1960): 716; Campbell, interview, 18 August 1995; Will D. Campbell, *Race and Renewal of the Church* (Philadelphia: Westminster, 1962), 26.

30. Will Campbell, "Baptist-Land: A Portrait," address to the Southern Baptist Alliance, draft, n.d., 2, Will D. Campbell Papers, McCain Library and Archives, University of Southern Mississippi, Hattiesburg, M341, box 13, f.3; David Halberstam, *The Children* (New York: Random House, 1998), 22, 122–123.

31. Hampton and Fayer, *Voices of Freedom*, 67; "Nashville Seizes 75 in Race Clash," *New York Times*, 28 February 1960, 51:1; Dallas Blanchard, interview by author, tape recording. Pensacola, FL, 16 August 1996.

32. Namely, Portsmouth, Virginia, and Chattanooga, Tennessee. "Negroes' Protest Turns into Melee," *New York Times*, 17 February 1960, 21:3–6; "Sitdown Erupts into Racial Riot," *New York Times*, 24 February 1960, 28:3; George Dugan, "Bishop Criticizes Sitdown Support," *New York Times*, 19 April 1960, 20:4.

33. "Episcopal Bishop Scored on Sitdown," *New York Times*, 11 April 1960, 25:6; John Morris, interview by author, tape recording, Augusta, GA, 13 April 2002.

34. George Dugan, "Called Ineffective," *New York Times*, 19 April 1960, 20:4–5. Shortly afterward, the northern Presbyterian Church (PCUSA) agreed overwhelmingly that "peaceable and orderly" civil disobedience was justified when laws favoring racial discrimination "violated the law of God." George Dugan, "Sit-Ins Endorsed by Presbyterians," *New York Times*, 26 May 1960, 20:1; "Southern Cleric Backs Negro Aim but Doubts Value of Pickets," *New York Times*, 7 November 1962, 62:2.

35. Blanchard, interview; first quotation, Dallas Blanchard to Donald E. Collins, 9 March 1994, in author's possession; second and third quotations, Dallas Blanchard, "Cracks in the Southern Universe," May 2000, unpublished paper in author's possession, photocopy, 13, 15. The final quotation is from the commemorative bulletin of Toulminville–Warren Street United Methodist Church, Mobile, AL, 3 September 2011, courtesy Edwena Seals.

36. Marsh, *God's Long Summer*, 122–123; see also Gray, *Bus Ride*, 178; also told by King, interview, 15 November 2004.

37. The white group was represented by white Montgomery attorney Clifford Durr. Gray, *Bus Ride*, 178–179; King, interview, 15 November 2004.

38. "Student and Negro Jailed in Alabama," *New York Times*, 8 June 1960, 33:4–5; King, interview, 15 November 2004; Gray, *Bus Ride*, 179; Marsh, *God's Long Summer*, 124.

39. As told by his older brother, Charles Evers. Charles Evers and Andrew Szanton, *Have No Fear: The Charles Evers Story* (New York: John Wiley & Sons, 1997), 78, 81; King, interview, 15 November 2004. After his expulsion from Vanderbilt Divinity School in 1960, practically every seminary in the country wanted Lawson, who decided to study at Boston University. Blanchard, interview; Halberstam, *Children*, 202–209; Marsh, *God's Long Summer*, 121.

40. Merrill Proudfoot, *Diary of a Sit-In*, 2nd ed. (1962, reprint, with an introduction by Michael S. Mayer, Urbana: University of Illinois Press, 1990), 2–6, 161–162, 207–208. Merrill Proudfoot, letter to Eleanor Humes Haney, September 1962.; Haney "Study of Conscience," 91; Michael S. Mayer, introduction to *Diary of a Sit-In*, xxvi–xxviii.

41. The SRC stated that no incident of violence had been reported in any of the places where desegregation occurred, and no store reported a loss in business from white patrons. Series XVI, reel 218:087–088, Southern Regional Council Papers.

42. James Peck, *Freedom Ride* (New York: Simon & Schuster, 1962), 96–97. See also "Freedom Rides-May '61," *Louisville Defender*, 8 June 1961, Series III, reel 111:0221, Southern Regional Council Papers. The photograph of Peck appeared in the *New York Times*, 18 May 1961, 27:2. The ACMHR was established in 1956 when the state of Alabama banned the NAACP. See Anthony Lewis, "Ban on N.A.A.C.P. Due for a Ruling," *New York Times*, 25 March 1964, 21:1; Peck, *Freedom Ride*, 101–103.

43. Lewis quoted in Hampton and Fayer, *Voices of Freedom*, 86. Seigenthaler, a southerner, was an important name in journalism, editor of the *National Tennessean* and later *Time* magazine; Campbell, interview, 18 August 1995; *New York Times*, 23 May 1961, 27:1–7; Farmer quoted in Hampton and Fayer, *Voices of Freedom*, 94–95.

44. King, interview, 23 November 2004.

45. "Bi-Racial Group Warns Southerners," Newport News, VA, *Times Herald*, 31 May 1961, n.p., Series III, reel 111:0221, Southern Regional Council Papers; Coffin's remarks are from *New York Times*, 25 May 1961, 26:3,4. Ed King participated in a later, peaceful Freedom Ride from Atlanta to Birmingham without incident; "Freedom Rides-May '61," *Louisville Defender*, 8 June 1961, Series III, reel 111:0223, Southern Regional Council Papers; King, interview, 23 November 2004.

46. Peck, *Freedom Ride*, 10. For the Sewanee crisis, see Shattuck, *Episcopalians*, 44–50, 115–116; see also *Southern Patriot* 11, no. 4 (September 1963): 2; John Morris, "ESCRU, The Episcopal Society for Cultural and Racial Unity: 1959–1967," paper presented at the Conference on Civil Rights and Christian Mission in the Episcopal Church, 9 June 1995, 13, 14, in author's possession.

47. John Morris, interview by author, tape recording, Augusta, GA, 15 August 2001.

48. Harold T. Lewis, *Yet with a Steady Beat: The African American Struggle for Recognition in the Episcopal Church* (Valley Forge, PA: Trinity Press International, 1996), 151; John Morris, reprinted in ESCRU newsletter, 31 May 1962, 1; see also ESCRU newsletters, November 1961, December 1962, December 1966, Archives of the Episcopal Church, Austin, TX.

49. W. E. B. Du Bois, *The Souls of Black Folk* (1903; reprint, with a new introduction by Randall Kenan, New York: Penguin Books, 1995), 143–144, 171, 184. Du Bois was a great supporter of the civil rights movement but died in Ghana in 1963 at the age of ninety-five, just hours before the March on Washington. Manning Marable, *Race, Reform and Rebellion* (Jackson: University Press of Mississippi, 1991), 76; Hampton and Fayer, *Voices of Freedom*, 98, Anderson quoted on 99–100. The goals were listed in the *New York Times* by Hedrick Smith, "Georgians Balk Albany Movement for Civil Rights," *New York Times*, 18 August 1962, 44:4.

50. Brooks Ramsey, interview by author, tape recording, Memphis, TN, 10 March 1999; Stephen Oates, "The Albany Movement: A Chapter in the Life of Martin Luther King, Jr.," *Journal of Southwest Georgia History* 2 (Fall 1984): 29; Anderson quoted in Hampton and Fayer, *Voices of Freedom*, 102.

51. "Georgia Impasse Hit by Kennedy," *New York Times*, 2 August 1962, 15:4; Hedrick Smith, "Outsider Issue Stirs Albany, GA.," *New York Times*, 13 August 1962, 13:2; Adam Fairclough, *To Redeem the Soul of America: The Southern Christian Leadership Conference and Martin Luther King, Jr.* (Athens: University of Georgia Press, 1987), 86; Ramsey, interview, 10 March 1999; Andrew Young quoted in Hampton and Fayer, *Voices of Freedom*, 104.

52. Oates, "Albany Movement," 29; *New York Times*, 19 December 1961, 1:1, 22 December 48:2, 23 December 28:1.

53. Ramsey, interview, 10 March 1999.

54. Ibid.; "Pastor Disappointed," *New York Times*, 21 August 1962: 28:5; *Atlanta Journal*, 21 August 1962.

55. Michael Chalfen, "Samuel B. Wells and Black Protest in Albany," *Journal of Southwest Georgia History* 9 (Fall 1994): 47; Ramsey, interview, 10 March 1999.

56. "Clergymen Arrive to Support Dr. King," *New York Times*, 8 August 1962, 63:3; Claude Sitton, "Albany, Georgia, Jails 75 in Prayer Vigil," *New York Times*, 29 August 1962, 14:1–2; John Wicklein, "Clergy and Laymen Form 'Army' to Aid Dr. King's Drive in South," *New York Times*, 16 September 1962, 1:4; "Albany Ministers Oppose Plan," *New York Times*, 16 September 1962, 70:5.

57. Brooks Ramsey, interview by author, telephone, 31 October 2006.

58. Ramsey, interview, 31 October 2006; Chalfen, "Samuel B. Wells," 47, 63–64; Robert Shelton, "Songs a Weapon in Rights Battle," *New York Times*, 20 August 1962, 1:6, 14:1.

59. "Mayor Bars Talk with Dr. King," *New York Times*, 2 August 1962, 15:4; Ramsey, interview, 31 October 2006.

60. Rowan quoted in Fairclough, *To Redeem*, 111; Theopolis Eugene "Bull" Connor, Commissioner of Public Safety, Birmingham, AL, in 1957, *Eyes on the Prize: America's Civil Rights Years, 1954–1965* (Boston: Blackside, PBS Video, 1987), episode 4, "No Easy Walk, 1962–1966." "Bull" Connor's opinions earned him election to three terms. Under his leadership, Birmingham was among few of the South's large municipalities not having blacks on the police force. Robert Gaines Corley, "The Quest for Racial Harmony, Race Relations in Birmingham, Alabama, 1947–1963" (PhD diss., University of Virginia, 1979), 75; Martin Luther King Jr., *Why We Can't Wait* (New York: Signet, 1964), 48–50.

61. John Rutland, *Mary and Me: Telling the Story of Prevenient Grace* (Pensacola, FL: Ardara House, 1996), 107–108.

62. Although airport, train, and bus terminals in Birmingham were desegregated, Commissioner Connor quickly arrested boycotters of segregated lunch counters, drinking fountains, and rest rooms. "Birmingham Sued by U.S. on Airport," *New York Times*, 20 June 1962, 17:1; "Negro Students Parade for Birmingham Boycott," *New York Times*, 16 June 1962, 17:2; King, *Why We Can't Wait*, 51–52; Joseph Ellwanger, interview by author, telephone, 5 February 2005.

63. Ellwanger, interview, 5 February 2005; see also Richard O. Ziehr, *The Struggle for Unity: A Personal Look at the Integration of Lutheran Churches in the South* (Milton, FL: CJH Enterprises, 1999), 70–71.

64. King wrote of the freedom songs as absolutely necessary for the movement: "We sing the freedom songs today for the same reason the slaves sang them, because we too are in bondage and the songs add hope…. I have stood in a meeting with hundreds of youngsters and joined in while they sang, 'Ain't Gonna Let Nobody Turn Me Round.' It's not just a song; it's a resolve. A few minutes later, I have seen those same youngsters . . . refuse to turn around before a pugnacious 'Bull' Connor in command of men armed with power hoses." King, *Why We Can't Wait*, 61. Foster Hailey, "Police Break Up Alabama March," *New York Times*, 8 April 1963, 31:4. Robert Fulton, a white Presbyterian clergyman teaching at all-black Miles College in Birmingham, was also arrested but released the following day. Foster Hailey, "Dr. King Arrested at Birmingham," *New York Times*, 13 April 1963, 1:5, 15:4–5.

65. Statement quoted in Sanford Wexler, *The Civil Rights Movement: An Eyewitness History* (New York: Facts on File, 1993), 170.

66. King, *Why We Can't Wait*, author's note, 76, 89–90; Wexler, *Civil Rights Movement*, 164. The historian S. Jonathan Bass defended the ministers who signed the statement as compassionate toward blacks but struggling to deal with the massive changes occurring in the South during the 1950s and 1960s. Bass agreed with King that they were gradualists, but that lack of "bold action left them vulnerable to criticism from all sides of the racial confrontation." S. Jonathan Bass, *Blessed Are the Peacemakers* (Baton Rouge: Louisiana State University Press, 2001), 212; Ellwanger, interview, 5 February 2005.

67. Wexler, *Civil Rights Movement*, 164–165; Hampton and Fayer, *Voices of Freedom*, 133; Foster Hailey, "Dogs and Hoses Repulse Negroes at Birmingham," *New York Times*, 4 May 1963, 8:5–8; Foseter Hailey "U.S. Seeking a Truce in Birmingham: Hoses Again Drive Off Demonstrators," *New York Times*, 5 May 1963, 1:1, 82:4–5; Claude Sitton, "Birmingham Talks Reach an Accord on Ending Crisis," *New York Times*, 10 May 1963, 1:8, 14:1–2; King, *Why We Can't Wait*, 55.

68. Ellwanger, interview, 5 February 2005.

69. Ibid.

70. King, interview, 15 November 2004; see also Marsh, *God's Long Summer*, 125–126.

71. COFO was a coalition of workers from SNCC, the SCLC, and the NAACP. In 1964 Freedom Summer in Mississippi was launched by COFO. Fairclough, *To Redeem*, 91; Julian Bond, ed., *Free at Last: A History of the Civil Rights Struggle and Those Who Died in the Struggle* (Montgomery, AL: A Project of the Southern Poverty Law Center, 1989), 29; King, interview, 15 November 2004.

72. Convictions of twenty-eight black and three white students for sit-in demonstrations at lunch counters in Alabama, Louisiana, North Carolina, and South Carolina were overturned; thus the Court applied the constitutional ban on racial discrimination to include private and well as public activity. Anthony Lewis, "Supreme Court Legalizes Sit-Ins in Cities Enforcing Segregation," *New York Times*, 21 May 1963, 1:8; King, interview, 15 November 2004.

73. King, interview, 15 November 2004; Ed King, "Bacchanal at Woolworth's," in *Freedom Is a Constant Struggle: An Anthology of the Mississippi Civil Rights Movement*, ed. Susie Erenrich, 29, 34 (Birmingham, AL: Black Belt Press, 1999).

74. King, interview, 15 November 2004; Jack Langguth, "3 in Sit-In Beaten at Jackson Store," *New York Times*, 29 May 1963, 1:7, 17:3–4; Jack Langguth, "Attacked Negro Hails 'Triumph,'" *New York Times*, 10 June 1963, 29:2.

75. King, interview, 15 November 2004; King, "Bacchanal," 31.

76. For more details of the arrest, see Anne Moody, *Coming of Age in Mississippi* (New York: Doubleday, 1968; reprint, New York; Delta Trade, 2004), 297.

77. King, interview, 15 November 2004; Taylor Branch, *Pillar of Fire: America in the King Years, 1963–65* (New York: Simon & Schuster, 1998), 121.

78. King, interview, 15 November 2004.

79. Jack Langguth "Jackson Police Jail 600 Negro Children," *New York Times*, 1 June 1963, 1:2; Jack Langguth, "Wilkins Is Seized in Jackson, Miss.," *New York Times*, 2 June 1963, 70:1, 17; "Jackson Negroes Ease Picketing," *New York Times*, 4 June 1963, 29:1; "State Court Bans Jackson Parades," *New York Times*, 7 June 1963, 14:3; "Atlanta Hotel Bars Dr. Bunche as Guest," *New York Times*, 29 June 1962, 21:6; "Bunche Says Racism Hurts U.S. Abroad," *New York Times*, 11 June 1963, 25:6.

80. King, interview, 15 November 2004; Claude Sitton, "N.A.A.C.P. Leader Slain in Jackson; Protests Mount," *New York Times*, 13 June 1963, 1:8; Jack Langguth, "Whites Adamant in Jackson Crisis," *New York Times*, 14 June 1963, 15:1; Claude Sitton, "Jackson Negroes Clubbed as Police Quell Marchers," *New York Times*, 11 June 1963; Rev. Ed King, "Christianity in Mississippi, Mourners in Prison," in *To Redeem a Nation: A History and Anthology of the Civil Rights Movement*, ed. Thomas R. West and James W. Moon (St. James, NY: Brandywine Press, 1993), 136, 138; see also Ed King, "Growing Up in Mississippi in a Time of Change," in *Mississippi Writers: Reflections of Childhood and Youth*, Vol. 2, *Nonfiction*, ed. Dorothy Abbott (Jackson: University Press of Mississippi, 1986), 382–383.

81. A photograph of police with dogs chasing demonstrators protesting segregated state fairs in Jackson appeared in the *New York Times*, 17 October 1961, 24:6–7. Moody told how dogs attacked students singing freedom songs at the black high school. Moody, *Coming of Age*, 299; Edwin King, "Birmingham Funerals," 16 (paper presented at the fortieth anniversary of the Birmingham church bombing of 15 September 1963 for the Christian Fellowship Sunday School Class, Galloway Methodist Church, 13 September 2004), Edwin King private papers in author's possession. Salter and Ed King had been traveling back and forth from a lawyer's office for several days picking up people at the airport, where it was noticed their car was being tampered with. On one occasion, the lug nuts had been loosened, almost causing a tire to fall off. It was accepted by all who knew of the incident that it was no accident, as an insurance agent reported. Ed King private papers; Florence Mars, *Witness in Philadelphia* (Baton Rouge: Louisiana State University Press, 1977), 105–106; Bond, *Free at Last*, 48–51, 64–65.

82. Will Campbell, interview by author, telephone, 7 August 2003. This was also Campbell's response to Orley Caudill when asked why he was not at the University of Mississippi when James Meredith attempted to enter. Campbell, interview by Caudill, 63.

83. Proudfoot, *Diary*, 10.

84. Ibid., 152.

85. Ellwanger, interview, 5 February 2005.

Chapter 3. Church Visitations

1. Andrew A. Snyder, jacket design for Thomas J. Holmes with Gainer E. Bryan Jr., *Ashes for Breakfast* (Valley Forge, PA: Judson Press, 1969).

2. Dallas Lee, *The Cotton Patch Evidence: The Story of Clarence Jordan and the Koinonia Farm Experiment, 1942–1970* (Americus, GA: A Koinonia Publication, 1971), 75.

3. Robert Seymour, *"Whites Only": A Pastor's Retrospective on Signs of the New South* (Valley Forge, PA: Judson Press, 1991), 78; "Baptists of South Exclude Negroes," *New York Times*, 4 November 1963, 31:3–6; Carter Dalton Lyon. "Lifting the Color Bar from the House of God: The 1963–1964 Church Visit Campaign to Challenge Church Sanctuaries in Jackson, Mississippi" (PhD diss., University of Mississippi, 2010), 143, 9.

4. H. Davis Yeuell, interview by author, Richmond, VA, 10 March 2003. In 1950 the Board of Directors of the Montreat Association allowed adult meetings to be desegregated. Not until 1954 was the entire facility desegregated. Joel L. Alvis Jr., *Religion and Race: Southern Presbyterians, 1946–1983* (Tuscaloosa: University of Alabama Press, 1994), 85–87.

5. Yeuell, interview, 10 March 2003.

6. Alvis, *Religion and Race*, 13–14; Yeuell, interview, 10 March 2003.

7. Yeuell, interview, 10 March 2003.

8. Ibid.

9. Ibid.

10. Stallings was one of the eight ministers who signed a statement on 16 April 1963 suggesting that the demonstrations in Birmingham were "unwise and untimely," thus provoking Martin Luther King Jr. to write his "Letter from a Birmingham jail." King commended Stallings for welcoming blacks into his church, but condemned the eight ministers for being only interested in law and order, not racial justice. King, *Why We Can't Wait*, 89–90; Bass, *Blessed Are the Peacemakers*, 76–77.

11. *New York Times*, 15 April 1963, 1:3–7; Bass, *Blessed Are the Peacemakers*, 76, 77, 79.

12. Bass, *Blessed Are the Peacemakers*, 77, 213, 219.

13. J. Herbert Gilmore Jr., *They Chose to Live: The Racial Agony of an American Church* (Grand Rapids, MI: Eerdmans, 1972), 11, 122.

14. Gilmore, *They Chose*, 136–137, 163; Betty Bock, interview by author, Birmingham, AL, 7 April 1995. Bock had been youth minister at First Baptist and was also to be voted on for dismissal because of her loyalty to Rev. Gilmore. She resigned with Rev. Gilmore and became an assistant at Church of the Covenant.

15. "Alabama Minister Quits in Racial Rift," *New York Times*, 14 June 1963, 17:5; "Looking Back: 6/10," Tuscaloosa News.com, 10 June 2013; Robert D. Miller, interview by author, tape recording, Elizabethtown, NC, 17 July 1996; Norrell, *Reaping the Whirlwind*, 134.

16. Jeanne Torrence Finley and Richard B. Faris, "'Making More Real the Church Universal': Francis Pickens Miller," *Journal of Presbyterian History* 82, no. 1 (Spring 2004): 23. The Bible verse is from James 2:17 KJV.

17. Norrell, *Reaping the Whirlwind*, 130.

18. Miller, interview; Robert D. Miller, "The End and the Beginning," sermon, 17 July 1964, First Presbyterian Church, Tuskegee, AL, in author's possession. The verse is from John 3:16 KJV.

19. Miller, "The End and the Beginning"; Norrell, *Reaping the Whirlwind*, 158. Black people in Tuskegee were denied the right to vote because of manipulation of the voting districts. The case, *Gomillion v. Lightfoot*, tried before the US Supreme Court in 1960, was decided for the plaintiff, Charles Gomillion, dean of students at the Tuskegee Institute and representative of the Tuskegee Civic Association. See Gray, *Bus Ride*, 118–119; Miller, interview; Norrell, *Reaping the Whirlwind*, 159

20. Robert D. Miller, letter to author, 8 March 2012; Bill McKee, "Lakeview Presbyterian Church: A Jubilee Center," unpublished paper in author's possession, 1992, photocopy, 5.

21. McKee, "Lakeview Presbyterian," 1, 5–7, 48–49.

22. First Presbyterian in Montgomery later united with PCA, a more conservative Presbyterian group in the South. McKee, "Lakeview Presbyterian," 5, 7; Miller, letter to author.

23. Lyon, "Lifting," 1; King, interview, 15 November 2004.

24. Marsh, *God's Long Summer*, 7; King, interview, 15 November 2004; Moody, *Coming of Age*, 310–311.

25. Moody, *Coming of Age*, 311–312; "Negroes Attend Jackson Church," *New York Times*, 17 June 1963, 12:4–5 (ill.). Ed King mentioned that they were seated at the back of the church.

26. W. B. Selah, "Puddles and Sunsets, Sermons of Dr. W. B. Selah, 1990" (Monte Sano United Methodist Church, Huntsville, AL, photocopy), 118; Cunningham, *Agony at Galloway*, 5–6. W. B. Selah Jr. mentioned that blacks occasionally would come to the church to listen to Selah, whose sermons were heard on the radio. They sat in the back inconspicuously, and no one objected until the 1960s. W. B. Selah Jr., interview by author, Huntsville, AL, 16 May 1999.

27. W. B. Selah, "Why I Left Galloway," in *Puddles and Sunsets*, Annex-A, 1–2; Lyon, "Lifting the Color Bar," 145.

28. William Jefferson Cunningham, interview by Orley B. Caudill, 6 August 1981, Mississippi Oral History Program of the University of Southern Mississippi, Hattiesburg, vol. 242, 44, 22; Cunningham, *Agony at Galloway*, 12.

29. W. J. Cunningham, "The Negro Question," sermon, Mississippi Oral History Program, Appendix A, 89–90; "A Sermon Preached in the Crisis," from Ezekiel 33:1–7 RSV, quoted in Cunningham, *Agony at Galloway*, 157–161.

30. Cunningham, *Agony at Galloway*, 69; Cunningham, interview, 34, 38, 29.

31. Cunningham, interview, 34, 44; Cunningham, *Agony at Galloway*, 96, 120–121.

32. First Christian Church, Jackson, Mississippi (Bulletin, 5 February 1956), frontispiece. Roy S. Hulan Papers, box 1, Disciples of Christ Historical Society, Nashville, TN.

33. Roy S. Hulan, "When Men Are at Odds," sermon, 16 June 1963, *The Christian*, 22 September 1963, 1209, Hulan Papers, box 1.

34. Edward and Normanda Huffman, interview by author, Shelbyville, TN, 20 May 2001; *Democrat*, Cynthiana, KY, 12 December 1963. Normanda Huffman is the sister of Roy Hulan.

35. Alvin H. Price, letter to author, 14 January 2013.

36. Eugene G. Patterson, foreword to Holmes, *Ashes for Breakfast*; Holmes, *Ashes for Breakfast*, 7, 2, 35, 14–16.

37. Holmes, *Ashes for Breakfast*, 35; personal interview by the author with a student on the Mercer University Campus, 12 June 1995.

38. Holmes, *Ashes for Breakfast*, 112.

39. Hugh Carter as told to Frances Spatz Leighton, *Cousin Beedie* [Hugh] *and Cousin Hot* [Jimmy]: *My Life with the Carter Family of Plains, Georgia* (Englewood Cliffs, NJ: Prentice-Hall, 1978), 319, 312–313.

40. Ibid., 311–312, 314–316.

41. Ibid., 317–319, Edwards quoted on 319–320.

42. Ibid., 320.

43. "Rev. Bruce Edwards Bids Farewell," *Spartanburg Herald*, 20 June 1977, 1:1.

44. Carter and Leighton, *Cousin Beedie*, 323–326.

45. Hal Glatzer, "Jimmy Carter's Ex-Pastor, Bruce Edwards, Now Has Hawaii, Not Georgia, on His Mind," *People* 8, no. 3 (26 September 1977): 99.

46. See John Egerton, *Speak Now Against the Day: The Generation before the Civil Rights Movement in the South* (Chapel Hill: University of North Carolina Press, 1995), 470–471, 548. Also *New Georgia Encyclopedia* online. The subjects covered by McGill are my personal assessment after perusing indexes of both newspapers carefully for the time period 1960–1970 at the Atlanta Public Library. Ralph McGill, *The South and the Southerner*, 2nd ed. (Boston: Little, Brown, 1963), 223.

47. Missy Pilkingon, secretary to Charles Durham, pastor of First Presbyterian Church, Tuscaloosa, AL, telephone conversation with author, 2 May 2013; "Holmes Returns to Mercer Staff," *Christian Index*, 27 October 1966, 3, quoted in Alan Scot Willis, "A Baptist Dilemma: Christianity, Discrimination, and the Desegregation of Mercer University," *Georgia Historical Quarterly* 80, no. 3 (Fall 1996): 614; *Atlanta Constitution*, 28 September 1966, quoted in Holmes, *Ashes for Breakfast*, 100.

48. Cunningham, interview, 43, 51; Lyon, "Lifting," 145; Cunningham, *Agony at Galloway*, 96, 121, 151; R. Edwin King, interview by author, video recording, Medgar Evers College, Brooklyn, NY, 15 November 2004.

49. Harvey quoted in Lyon, "Lifting," 155.

50. Stephen R. Haynes, *The Last Segregated Hour* (New York: Oxford University Press, 2012); Rhett Jackson, interview by author, tape recording, Columbia, SC, 17 April 2002; Larry Jackson, interview; Bass, *Blessed Are the Peacemakers*, 232.

Chapter 4. The Movement Continues

1. *Encyclopedia Americana*, 1948 ed., s.v. "Louisville."

2. Tom Wicker, "Kennedy Asks Broad Rights Bill as Reasonable Course in Crisis; Calls for Restraint by Negroes," *New York Times*, 20 June 1963, 1:8, 17:1–5. The editor of "The News of the Week," *New York Times*, on 16 June 1963, concluded that "the Negro protest movement was still gathering momentum," "violence was increasing," "the time when 'tokenism' could satisfy Negroes was long past," and "large areas of discrimination were extremely difficult to eradicate through Federal law." "A Critical Week in the Deepening Crisis over Desegregation," *New York Times*, 16 June 1963, 1:1–5; Marjorie Hunter, "Negroes Inform Kennedy of Plan for New Protests," *New York Times*, 23 June 1963, 1:1, 63:3–4; Wicker, "Kennedy Asks Broad Rights Bill," 1:8, 17:1–5; "Churchmen Exhorted to Aid Race Progress," *New York Times*, 22 June 1963, 10:7–8.

3. *New York Times*, 8 August 1963, 13:2–5, 9 August 1963, 10:4, 10 August 1963, 6:3, 8, 11 August 1963, 1:3, 13 August 1963, 1:4, 7:3, 22:3, 14 August 1963, 21:1, 31 August 1963, 6:5; "A Further Word About the March on Washington," Presbyterian Archives, Montreat, NC; Branch, *Pillar of Fire*, 133. Bayard Rustin quoted in Hampton and Fayer, *Voices of Freedom*, 169.

4. E. W. Kenworthy, "200,000 March for Civil Rights in Orderly Washington Rally; President Sees Gain for Negro," *New York Times*, 29 August 1963, 16:5, 21:1–8.

5. J. Randolph Taylor, interview by author, tape recording, Montreat, NC, 7 October 2001.

6. The church, located at Dupont Circle in Washington, DC, was well protected by police, who were instructed to prevent molesters from assembling anywhere in the city, especially during the time of the march. J. Randolph Taylor, interview.

7. J. Randolph Taylor, interview; J. Randolph Taylor, "Letter from Washington," *Presbyterian Outlook* 145, no. 31 (September 1963), 5–6, Presbyterian Archives.

8. J. Randolph Taylor, interview; "Washington March," *Presbyterian Outlook* 145, no. 33 (September 1963), 1.

9. See also *Presbyterian Survey* 53 (November 1963): 8, cited in Alvis, *Religion and Race*, 72.

10. Pritchett quoted in Shriver, *Unsilent South*, 99–100, 102.

11. "March on Washington" folder, Presbyterian Archives; *New York Times*, 29 August 1963, 21:1–8.

12. *New York Times*, 29 August 1963, 21:5.

13. Lowry quoted in Shriver, *Unsilent South*, 110.

14. Pritchett quoted in Shriver, *Unsilent South*, 107, 105.

15. R. Edwin King, interview by author, telephone, 25 April 2005.

16. King, "Birmingham Funerals," 15–18.

17. Ibid.

18. Egerton, *Speak Now Against the Day*, 62, 63, 620, 422.

19. Mark Pryor, *Faith, Grace, and Heresy: The Biography of Rev. Charles M. Jones* (New York: Writer's Showcase, 2002), 91–92, 98; Dorcas Jones, interview by author, tape recording, Chapel Hill, NC, 29 July 1999.

20. In *Irene Morgan v. Commonwealth of Virginia*, 328 U.S. 373 (1946), the Supreme Court ruled that segregation of passengers on motor carriers was unconstitutional. Jones, interview; James Peck, *Freedom Ride* (New York: Simon & Schuster, 1962), 16–17; "An Example of 'Commies' at Work," *Atlanta Constitution*, 20 April 1947, 1, in Pryor, *Faith, Grace*, 124–127.

21. Jones, interview; Pryor, *Faith, Grace*, 135, 168, 170.

22. Jones was dismissed on a rule from the 1952 edition of the *Book of Church Order*. A Presbyterian minister could not be dismissed today for the reasons for which Jones was dismissed in 1953. Jones, interview; Pryor, *Faith, Grace*, 288.

23. Jones quoted from *Time*, 27 July 1953, in Pryor, *Faith, Grace*, 278; Statement of Purpose of Community Church of Chapel Hill, quoted in Pryor, *Faith, Grace*, 291–293.

24. Jones, interview.

25. Seymour, *"Whites Only,"* 40.

26. Seymour, interview.

27. Seymour quoted in Virtie Stroup, "Progress in Race Relations Noted," Winston Salem paper, n.d., n.p., Robert E. Seymour Papers, Southern Historical Collection, Manuscripts Department, Wilson Library, University of North Carolina, Chapel Hill, #4554; "Slow Integration Progress in Tarheel Churches Scored," *Durham Morning Herald*, n.d., n.p.; Robert Seymour, interview by Bruce Kalk, 21 May 1985, Southern Oral History Collection, Manuscripts Department, vol. 4007, C-20, 7.

28. Seymour, *"Whites Only,"* 67, 76; John Robinson, "Maverick Baptist Pastor in a University Town," *Chapel Hill Weekly*, c. 1982, North Carolina Collection, Clipping File, University of North Carolina, Chapel Hill. Shortly after the arrival of Seymour, an item appeared in the *Durham Morning Herald*, "Negro Joins White Church." One reader responded, "I was shocked and grieved when I saw that one who professed to be a Christian . . . had committed such a sinful thing as to take a Negro in his church. I'm a Baptist and believe the teachings of God, and He taught segregation from cover to cover." Another reader wrote, "I think it is a demonstration of genuine Christianity." Seymour, *"Whites Only,"* 77, 78.

29. Seymour, *"Whites Only,"* 94.

30. Ibid., 93; "Senior Minister Emeritus," http: www.theriversidechurchny.org; *Christian Century*, 12 July 2005, 25.

31. Seymour, *"Whites Only,"* 89, 74–75.

32. Pryor, *Faith, Grace*, 331–333; Charles Jones, "The Chapel Hill Crisis," sermon delivered in the Community Church, 13 March 1960, in author's possession, 4–5.

33. In 1960 the Southern Regional Council reported Chapel Hill as one of twenty-seven places that had opened lunch counters to African Americans, but failed to mention that about

25 of 200 places of business still practiced segregation. Series XVI, reel 218:87, 95, Southern Regional Council Papers; Jones, interview.

34. Leon Rooke, "On the Path of Father Parker," *North Carolina Anvil*, 25 August 1967, 4:2–3, North Carolina Clipping File through 1975.

35. John Ehle, *The Free Men* (New York: Harper & Row, 1965), 36. The book is part of the Southern Historical Collection, Manuscripts Department, Wilson Library, University of North Carolina, Chapel Hill; Seymour, *"Whites Only,"* 96.

36. "450 March in Chapel Hill in Anti-Segregation Protest," *New York Times*, 5 July 1963, 44:8; Ehle, *Free Men*, 46–47; Charles Jones, "On Love and the Quest for Peace," in *From the Sermons of Charles M. Jones: A Memorial on the Occasion of the Dedication of the Charles M. Jones Community Building*, Chapel Hill, NC, 24 September 1995, Dorcas Jones personal papers in author's possession, 10.

37. "Chapel Hill Freedom Committee Report," Christmas, 1963, North Carolina Collection, Cp326, c74c1; Seymour, *"Whites Only,"* 98; Ehle, *Free Men*, 69, 73.

38. "Some Background Information on the Chapel Hill Committee for Open Business, Suggested Guidelines, 1963," North Carolina Collection, Cb971.68, c46c4.

39. Ehle, *Free Men*, 84–85, 105, 131; *Chapel Hill Weekly* quoted in Ehle, *Free Men*, 88.

40. Ehle, *Free Men*, 39–40. See also "Chapel Hill Freedom Committee Report"; "North Carolina Keeps Color Bar," *New York Times*, 7 April 1963, 53:1.

41. Ehle, *Free Men*, 123–132, 141–147, 154–155, 312, 191; "Sanford Warns CORE," *New York Times*, 16 January 1964, 18:4; Seymour, *"Whites Only,"* 101. Because of Amon's photographs included in Ehle's book, the truth of Ehle's details is verified.

42. Ehle, *Free Men*, 192–197, 119–120.

43. Ibid., 248–249, 256–257; Ben. A. Franklin, "5 Enter Fourth Day of Fast in Civil Rights Protest at Chapel Hill," *New York Times*, 25 March 1964, 21:2–6.

44. Ehle, *Free Men*, 276–277, 271, 267.

45. C. Jones and McKissick quoted in Ehle, *Free Men*, 326.

46. Parker quoted in Ehle, *Free Men*, 288–289. Parker never was called for a trial.

47. Seymour, *"Whites Only,"* 103; Ehle, *Free Men*, 309–310, 319–320. Ehle resigned his position at UNC to write the account and work for the parole of the prisoners.

48. "Negro Voted Mayor of Chapel Hill, North Carolina," *New York Times*, 7 May 1969, 1:2, 31:1.

49. John Herbers, "Alabama Police Rough Up 4 as Selma Negroes Seek to Vote," *New York Times*, 8 October 1963, 37:5; "Whites in Selma," 77:1. Referring to the 1960 census report, Herbers identified 32,687 blacks and 23,952 whites in the entire Dallas County.

50. Stephen L. Longenecker, *Ralph Smeltzer and Civil Rights Mediation* (Philadelphia: Temple University Press, 1987), 27–34; Michael B. Friedland, *Lift Your Voice Like a Trumpet: White Clergy and the Civil Rights and Antiwar Movements, 1954–1973* (Chapel Hill: University of North Carolina Press, 1998), 116. Newton left Selma in 1974 for a church in Atlanta. *Revised Ministerial Directory of the Presbyterian Church in the United States* (Atlanta: Darby Printing, 1986), 535.

51. David J. Garrow, "Bridge to Freedom," (1965), introduction to chapter 6, *Eyes on the Prize Civil Rights Reader*, ed. Clayborne Carson et al. (New York: Penguin Books, 1991), 205. At this time, Martin Luther King Jr. was marked by the FBI as the "most dangerous Negro of the future of this nation." Branch, *Pillar of Fire*, 150.

52. King quoted in Branch, *Pillar of Fire*, 554–555; "A Letter from Martin Luther King from a Selma, Alabama Jail," *New York Times*, 5 February 1965, 15:4–8.

53. Ellwanger may be remembered as a participant in the initial planning session for Project Confrontation in Birmingham and for picketing merchants in 1963. He also read the scriptural lesson for the funeral of Denise McNair, one of the four girls killed in the bombing of the Sixteenth Street Baptist Church in Birmingham. McNair's father, Chris, a member of Ellwanger's church, asked Ellwanger to participate in the joint funeral for three of the four

girls. Joseph Ellwanger, interview, telephone, 29 December 2004; "Birmingham Pastor Leads 'Concerned White Citizens' in March in Selma," *The Vanguard, Lutheran Human Relations Association of America* 12, no. 2 (March–April 1965): 1:1; Ziehr, *Struggle for Unity*, 175; Roy Reed, "White Alabamians Stage Selma March to Support Negroes," *New York Times*, 7 March 1965, 1:2, 46:3–8. For more about the Concerned White Citizens of Alabama, see Maurice Baer, "The Concerned White Citizens of Alabama and Their Appearance in Selma, Alabama on March 6, 1965," Mervyn H. Sterne Library, University of Alabama at Birmingham.

54. "Birmingham Pastor Leads," 1:1; Ellwanger, interview, 29 December 2004; Rongstad quoted in Reed, "White Alabamians," 46:7.

55. Ellwanger quoted in "Birmingham Pastor Leads," 1:1; Ellwanger, interview, 29 December 2004; Tom Heinen, "Bombing Revealed the Danger of Silence," *Milwaukee Journal Sentinel*, 17 January 2004, jsonline.com/news/metro/jan04/200643.asp.

56. "Birmingham Pastor Leads," 1:4; Ellwanger, interview, 29 December 2004.

57. Another woman was hit so hard that she needed five stitches in her scalp and all her front teeth became loose. Roy Reed, "Alabama Police Use Gas and Clubs to Rout Negroes," *New York Times*, 8 March 1965, 1:1, 20:1; "An American Tragedy," *Newsweek*, 22 March 1965, 19:2–3.

58. Morris, "ESCRU," 20; Roy Reed, "Dr. King Leads March at Selma," *New York Times*, 10 March 1965, 1:8, 22:3; "Three Held in Assault on Boston Cleric," *New York Times*, 11 March 1965, 20:6–8. Longenecker noted that President Johnson sent yellow roses to Reeb's widow and assigned Air Force One to fly her to Selma, but nothing like that was done for Jimmy Lee Jackson. Jackson had participated in a peaceful night march of about 200 people in Marion, Alabama, when they were ordered to stop by the police chief and a line of state troopers. As they stopped, the streetlights went out and the troopers began swinging their clubs, striking marchers at random. Jackson and his mother headed into a nearby café for safety. The troopers followed, continuing to club and beat people. Jackson's grandfather was hit in the head with a club. When Jackson attempted to leave the café to take his grandfather to the hospital, troopers laid him on the floor and started beating him. His mother tried to stop the troopers by hitting them with a bottle. When Jackson saw a trooper strike his mother, as Julian Bond related, "Jackson lunged for the man without thinking." Jackson was clubbed by one trooper and shot in the stomach by another. Taken to the Good Samaritan Hospital in Selma, he died eight days later. Charges were never brought against the troopers. Longenecker, *Ralph Smeltzer*, 179–180; Bond, *Free at Last*, 72–75.

59. Ben A. Franklin, "U.S. Court Allows Alabama March; Enjoins Wallace," *New York Times*, 18 March 1965, 1:8; "The Big Parade: On the Road to Montgomery," *New York Times*, 22 March 1965, 1:4–7 (ill.); J. Randolph Taylor, interview. The celebrities were also there: Leonard Bernstein, Harry Belafonte, Mahalia Jackson, Pete Seeger, Sammy Davis Jr., James Baldwin, Ella Fitzgerald, and Floyd Patterson, among others. Ben A. Franklin, "Top Entertainers in Alabama Tonight," *New York Times*, 24 March 1965, 33:2. By the time the marchers arrived in Montgomery, David J. Garrow cited the best estimate at 25,000 marchers, most of them black. David J. Garrow, *Bearing the Cross: Martin Luther King, Jr., and the Southern Christian Leadership Conference* (New York: Morrow, 1986), 412.

60. Many Lutheran ministers from the North joined him. "Lutheran Minister Tells Why He Went to Alabama to Join Demonstrators," *Vanguard* 1:5; Rachel and Raymond Davis, interview. Reeb's murder gave the superior of Rev. Davis much cause for concern.

61. "500 Episcopal Clergymen Took Part in Alabama Drive," *New York Times*, 29 March 1965, 36:7; *ESCRU Newsletter*, 4 April 1965, ESCRU Papers, Archives of the Episcopal Church, Austin, TX; Morris, "ESCRU"; Morris, interview; "St. Paul's: More Shame in Selma," *ESCRU Newsletter*, 14 March 1965, 8, ESCRU Papers; "Eucharist Celebrated on Church Sidewalk in Selma," *Church in Metropolis* 5 (Spring): 24, ESCRU Papers.

62. "Churchmen in Selma," *ESCRU Newsletter*, 4 April 1965; John Morris, "To All Bishops," 27 March 1965, 3:24, ESCRU Papers.

63. See William J. Schneider, *American Martyr: The Jon Daniels Story* (Harrisburg, PA: Morehouse, 1992), 41–47; Charles W. Eagles, *Outside Agitator: Jon Daniels and the Civil Rights Movement in Alabama* (Chapel Hill: University of North Carolina Press, 1993), 251–253, 262–264; Morris, "ESCRU," 21.

64. Allen quoted in "Alabama, Terrible Events," *The Living Church*, 28 March 1965, 9, ESCRU Papers.

65. John Morris, "Good Out of Selma," *The Living Church*, 28 March 1965, 9, ESCRU Papers.

66. Rachel Henderlite, "Life of Dedication," *Presbyterian Heritage* 18, no. 1 (Winter 2004): 1.

67. "Presbyterians US Take Part in Selma Negro Voter Rights Demonstrations," *Presbyterian Survey* 55, no. 5 (May 1965): 40, Presbyterian Historical Society, Montreat, NC; Hardie's name is mentioned in Murphy, *Breaking the Silence*, 145. W. Williams to the editor, Tucker, GA, *Presbyterian Survey* 65, no. 7 (July 1965): 7, Presbyterian Historical Society.

68. Stephen M. Fox, letter to author, 6 March 2012.

69. Rachel Henderlite, "The March to Montgomery," *Presbyterian Outlook*, 19 April 1965, 5:1–3, Presbyterian Historical Society; Newton quoted in Friedland, *Lift Your Voice*, 116.

70. Blanchard, interview; Fred Reese, interview by author, tape recording, Linville Falls, NC, 15 November 1999.

71. Longenecker, *Ralph Smeltzer*, 214.

72. Ellwanger, interview, 29 December 2004; Robyn Harris, "In Memory of Those in the Past," *Selma Times-Journal*, 8 March 1998, 1:1–2; Ellwanger to author, 20 December 2006.

73. *Encyclopedia Americana*, 1948 ed., s.v. "Louisville."

74. Johnson quoted in Chester Morrison, "Louisville, Kentucky: The City That Integrated without Strife," *Look* 27 (13 August 1963), 41, 44; William Peeples, "Hunger Sit-In," *New Republic* 150 (25 April 1964), 9.

75. "Remembering the 1964 March on Frankfort," *The Owl*, newsletter of the University of Louisville Libraries 20, no. 1 (February 2005): 1; "Kentucky's House Is Scene of Sit-In," *New York Times*, 17 March 1964, 25:8; Doris Dissen Marmion (widow of Charles Marmion), interview by author, Louisville, KY, 8 August 2001; Peter Smith, "Retired Episcopal Bishop Charles G. Marmion Dies," *Louisville Courier-Journal Metro*, 8 December 2000, 1.

76. Peeples, "Hunger Sit-In," 10; Grayson Tucker, interview by author, telephone, 1 March 2005; John Herbers, "Kentucky Capitol, Ignoring Fasters," *New York Times*, 18 March 1964, 20:4; "Two in Rights Fast Faint in Kentucky," *New York Times*, 19 March 1964, 14:6.

77. Tucker, interview.

78. Johnson quoted in Morrison, "Louisville," 41, 44. For an informative exposé of housing problems in Louisville, see Anne Braden's 1958 book, *The Wall Between*.

79. Ben A. Franklin, "Louisville Scene of Rights Protest," *New York Times*, 12 April 1967, 29:5–8, Gregory quoted on 29:8; "Negroes and Whites March through White Area," *New York Times*, 9 May 1967, 28:8, 46:3; *New York Times*, 2 June 1967, 25:5.

80. "Revs. A. D. W. King, L. Lesser Jr., and H. James among 50 Seized during Night March," *New York Times*, 19 April 1967, 21:1; "125, Including Rev. C. B. Tachau, Held in Jail," *New York Times*, 23 April 1967, 64:4; "A. D. W. King and 6 Others Jailed," *New York Times*, 2 May 29:1, 4; Douglas Robinson, "Louisville Jails 7 Protest Chiefs," *New York Times*, 2 May 1967, 29:1; "150 Demonstrate in Nearly Deserted Downtown Streets," *New York Times*, 7 May 1967, 40:1; "Negroes and Whites March through White Area," *New York Times*, 9 May 1967, 28:8, 46:3; *New York Times*, 2 June 1967, 25:5; "Louisville Passes Open Housing Rule," *New York Times*, 14 December 1967, 68:6; "Without Mayor's Signature," *New York Times*, 17 December 1967, 17:1; Thomas Moffett, interview by author, tape recording, Louisville, KY, 9 August 2001.

81. Braden related that "block breaking" was something promoted by banks and white real estate agents. Braden, *Wall Between*, 40. After a period of five years, Moffett mentioned that only about fifteen white people remained in the church, but the total number of 150 had not changed because of a merger with a small black congregation in the area. Moffett, interview.

82. Moffett, interview; "Kentucky's House Is Scene of Sit-In," *New York Times*, 17 March 1964, 25:8.

83. Moffett, interview.

84. George R. Edwards, interview by author, tape recording, Louisville, KY, 8 August 2001. Louisville had a law known as the Day Law, which allowed black students to attend classes but not occupy dorm space. George R. Edwards, letter to author, 3 April 2002.

85. Duke has United Methodist affiliation but is, according to Edwards, "ecumenical in outlook and practice." Edwards, interview, 8 August 2001. The Bible verse is from Acts 17:26 KJV. The words "one blood" do not appear in newer Bible versions.

86. Edwards, interview, 8 August 2001; George R. Edwards, interview by author, telephone, 23 March 2005. Two more white ministers who marched for open housing were mentioned in the *New York Times*: Rev. R. Brooke Gibson, an assistant pastor at Central Presbyterian Church who, with a group of white ministers, was splattered with mud by passing automobiles bearing Confederate flags. Gibson was punched in the mouth to the point of bleeding by a white heckler but did not fight back. Rev. Ralph Leach, a Methodist minister, marched in a seventy-five-member delegation in the city's white South End. Stones pelted the windows of his station wagon as he drove a group of marchers home at the end of a housing demonstration. "Stones Are Thrown at Car in Louisville Housing March," *New York Times*, 25 May 1967, 14:8. Edwards also mentioned that several faculty members were purged from the faculty of Southern Baptist Theological Seminary (SBTS) because of their support for the Louisville demonstrations: Rev. Glenn Staffen went to teach at the Fuller Theological Seminary in California; Rev. Paul Simmons went to teach a course in ethics at the University of Louisville; and Glenn Hanson abandoned SBTS to establish a "moderate" Baptist theological school in Richmond, Virginia.

87. Evan Silverstein, "Absolved by DNA," *Presbyterians Today*, March 2001, 20–22.

88. Gilbert Schroerlucke, interview by author, tape recording, Louisville, KY, 9 August 2001; Franklin, "Louisville Scene of Rights Protest," 29:5–8.

89. Schroerlucke, interview.

90. Ibid.; Gilbert Schroerlucke, Last Will and Testament of Gilbert Schroerlucke to the Louisville Conference, personal papers of Gilbert Schroerlucke in author's possession, April 1989, 4.

91. Chavis and others were released on a $50,000 bond posted by the United Church of Christ in New York City, pending an appeal to the higher court. "Chavis Released from Central Prison," *New York Times*, 11 December 1972, 28:5; Schroerlucke, interview; Schroerlucke, Last Will, 7–8.

92. Schroerlucke, interview; Schroerlucke, Last Will, 7–8.

93. Tucker, interview; Edwards, interview, 23 March 2005.

94. Louis Coleman Jr., *The Struggle for Freedom Continues in Kentucky* (Louisville, KY: self-published, 1987), 2–7; Thomas Moffett, letter to author, 4 March 2012.

95. Bond, *Free at Last*, 72–73, 76–77. After the murder, the Klan circulated ugly lies about Liuzzo's character, which were completely refuted by people who knew her. Her husband, an official for the Teamsters' Union, commented, "She was one who fought for everyone's rights." "Mrs. Liuzzo Felt She Had to Help," *New York Times*, 27 March 1965, 10:6.

Chapter 5. New Directions

1. Malcolm X, "Message to the Grass Roots," in Carson et al., *Eyes on the Prize Civil Rights Reader*, 252–253; Cleveland Sellers quoted in Hampton and Fayer, *Voices of Freedom*, 220–221; John Herbers, "Speed Negro Vote in Alabama," *New York Times*, 5 February 1965, 17:1.

2. Gladwin Hill, "Calm Returning to Los Angeles; Death Toll Is 33," *New York Times*, 17 August 1965, 1:8.

3. The accounts as told by reporters from the *Atlantic Constitution*, *New York Times*, and *Atlanta Daily World* were similar, each exposing police brutality: "In Middle of Mob—-the Mayor," *Atlanta Constitution*, 7 September 1966, 1:7–8, 12:1–4; Gene Roberts, "Atlanta Negroes Riot After Police Wound a Suspect," *New York Times*, 7 September 1966, 1:4, 38:2; Dick Hebert et al., "Negro Youth Here; 15 Injured as Hundreds of Negroes Riot, Toss Rocks at Police, Smash Cars, Defy Allen, Repulsed by Tear Gas," *Atlanta Constitution*, 7 September 1966, 1:7–8, 6:1, 12:1; Roy Reed, "S.N.C.C. Assailed on Atlanta Riot," *New York Times*, 8 September 1966, 1:4, 37:1; Roy Reed, "Negro Is Slain in Atlanta, Setting Off New Violence," *New York Times*, 11 September 1966; see also "Fire Bombs Exploded in Boulevard Violence," *Atlanta Constitution*, 12 September 1966, 1:8; Harmon G. Perry, "Police Quell Disturbance in Summerhill Community," *Atlanta Daily World*, 7 September 1966, 1:6–7, 6:1; "Fire Bombs Exploded in Boulevard Violence, Allen Posts Reward in Slaying," *Atlanta Constitution*, 12 September 1966, 1:8, 7:1; Bill Shipp, "New Boulevard Melee Flares as Snick Grabs Control of Peace Talk," *Atlanta Constitution*, 13 September 1966, 1:6; "City Posts $10,000 Reward for Information on Person Who Fatally Injured Boy," *Atlanta Daily World*, 13 September 1966, 1:5; "A Tragic Saturday Night," editorial, *Atlanta Daily World*, 13 September 1966, 1:1.

4. "No One Group to Blame for Riot, Council Holds," *Atlanta Daily World*, 8 September 1966, 1:7; "SNCC Not Wanted in Summerhill Says Residents," *Atlanta Daily World*, 9 September 1966, 12:4; "Black Muslims Charged With Assault to Commit Murder," *New York Times*, 6 March 1967, 23:1; "Negro Killed, Three Others Wounded After Negroes Began Throwing Rocks at Police," *New York Times*, 21 June 1967, 1:2; "About 200 Negroes Charging Police Brutality Smash Store Windows, Set Minor Fires," *New York Times*, 23 October 1967, 39:1.

5. Martin Luther King Jr. to the editor, *New York Times*, 2 August 1967, 36:5.

6. "Sockman Returns to His Old Church for Plea on Rights," *New York Times*, 3 August 1964, 22:5; "Churches Urged to Serve People," *New York Times*, 3 August 1964, 22:6.

7. Kesselus, *John E. Hines*, 3; Matt. 25:31–40 KJV. Hines is quoted in Kesselus, *John E. Hines*, 92, 260–262; see also *Episcopal Dictionary of the Church*, online.

8. John E. Hines, "Opening Address, 62nd General Convention," Archives of the Episcopal Church, Austin, TX, RG 238; Duncan Montgomery Gray, telephone conversation with author, 26 July 2006; Shattuck, *Episcopalians*, 180, 208–210; *Episcopal Dictionary of the Church*, online.

9. W. W. Finlator, "Statement on Rioting," Finlator Papers, reel 18, frames 0982, 0983, 0992.

10. *New York Times*, 1 March 1968, 22:4, 15 March 1968, 36:2; bulletin of Central Presbyterian Church; "Atlanta Churches in Crisis," 16 March 1969, Series XVI, reel 248:0462, Southern Regional Council Papers.

11. "Atlanta Churches in Crisis," 30, reel 248:476.

12. Morris, "ESCRU," 22.

13. Joan Turner Beifuss, *At the River I Stand: Memphis, the 1968 Strike and Martin Luther King* (Memphis, TN: St. Luke's Press, 1990), 37–38.

14. McRae, interview, 14 May 1999.

15. Ibid.; J. Edwin Stanfield, "In Memphis: More Than a Garbage Strike," 1–2, Series XVI, reel 221, 243, Southern Regional Council Papers. Lawson may be remembered as an organizer of sit-ins in Nashville in 1960.

16. Beifuss, *At the River*, 85–87; McRae, interview, 14 May 1999.

17. Beifuss, *At the River*, 149; Stanfield, "In Memphis," 9.

18. Loeb's family made money through a chain of "Barb-B-Ques" and laundries in black neighborhoods. McRae, interview, 14 May 1999; *New York Times*, 27 February 1968, 85:6, 28 February 1968, 15:1, 1 March 1968, 24:6, 3 March 1968, 66:2; Stanfield, "In Memphis," 12, 14–15, 20; see also Beifuss, *At the River*, 178–180. Andrew Young quoted in Hampton and Fayer, *Voices of Freedom*, 459; K. W. Cook, *Memphis Commercial Appeal*, 19 March 1968, commercialappeal.com.

19. J. Edwin Stanfield, "In Memphis: Tragedy Unaverted," Supplement to Special Report of 22 March 1968, Series XVI, reel 221, 245, Southern Regional Council Papers. As Stanfield wrote, "Damage from the fire was very light." "Juveniles Spark Violence, Looting as King Leads March," *Memphis Commercial Appeal*, 29 March 1968, commercialappeal.com; see also J. Garrow, *Bearing the Cross*, 610–614; Michael Honey, *Going Down Jericho Road: The Memphis Strike, Martin Luther King's Last Campaign* (New York: Norton, 2007), 362–363, 385. Photographs of the sanitation workers with their placards appeared in Alice Faye Duncan, *The National Civil Rights Museum Celebrates Everyday People* (Memphis, TN: Bridgewater Book, 1995), 46; and Stephen Kasher, *The Civil Rights Movement: A Photographic History* (New York: Abbeyville Press, 1995), 228–229.

20. Honey, *Going Down Jericho Road*, 414.

21. McRae quoted in Beifuss, *At the River*, 361; McRae, interview, 14 May 1999.

22. Honey, *Going Down Jericho Road*, 472, 481; Richard Lentz, "Guardsmen Return; Curfew Is Ordered," *Memphis Commercial Appeal*, 5 April 1968, 1:1; Roy Reed, "Johnson Orders Troops into the Capital as Looting and Arson by Negroes Spread," *New York Times*, 6 April 1968, 1:8; Ben A. Franklin, "Washington Turmoil Subsides; Hundreds Homeless, Eight Dead," *New York Times*, 8 April 1968, 1:6.

23. Earl Caldwell, "Martin Luther King Is Slain in Memphis; A White Is Suspected; Johnson Urges Calm," *New York Times*, 5 April 1968, 1:8, 24:1; Beifuss, *At the River*, 418, 474; J. Anthony Lukas, "Memphis Approves a Memorial Parade; Clergy and Teachers Assail Mayor," *New York Times*, 6 April 1968, 24:2–7. The quotation from the resolution is in Stanfield, "In Memphis: Mirror to America?" 5–6, Series XVI, reel 221, 246, Southern Regional Council Papers; also McCrae, interview, 14 May 1999.

24. Wax quoted in Lukas, "Memphis Approves," 24:6. At home, Rev. Moon continued his fast until the strike was finally settled. Moon quoted in Beifuss, *At the River*, 422–424.

25. Honey, *Going Down Jericho Road*, 470–471; Ramsey, interview, 10 March 1999; McRae, interview, 14 May 1999.

26. Stanfield, "In Memphis," 17–19, 22.

27. Ibid., 23–24; Honey, *Going Down Jericho Road*, 468, 487, 489; McRae, interview, 14 May 1999.

28. McRae, interview, 14 May 1999.

29. Bass, *Blessed Are the Peacemakers*, 192–194; Honey, *Going Down Jericho Road*, 455.

30. Honey, *Going Down Jericho Road*, 475.

31. Ibid., 503–506; Memphis Census Report, 2010, online.

32. "Dismay, Anger and Foreboding Are Voiced by Leaders Across U.S. After Slaying," *New York Times*, 5 April 1968, 26:1–2. Even former governor of Alabama George Wallace, then segregationist candidate for president, called the assassination regrettable and senseless. Violence accompanied the mourning in all inner cities. Roy Reed, "Johnson Orders Troops into the Capital as Looting and Arson by Negroes Spread," *New York Times*, 6 April 1968, 1:8, 22:1; Finlator Papers, reel 20:431; Finlator, interview by author, telephone, 19 October 2005.

33. Southern Regional Council Papers, Series XVI, reel 219:175.

34. "Atlanta Churches in Crisis," Series XVI, reel 219:252.

35. J. Randolph Taylor, interview; Hines quoted in Kesselus, *Hines*, 291; Gray quoted in Campbell, *And Also with You*, 178; Gray, interview, 16 December 2004; Rachel and Raymond Davis, interview.

36. Arnold Voigt, interview by author, telephone, 1 February 2014; *Mobile Beacon-Alabama Citizen*, 13 April 1968, 3.

37. King, interview, 23 November 2004; Connelly, *Will Campbell*, 107; Will D. Campbell, interview by author, tape recording, Mt. Juliet, TN, 20 March 2001. Stephen B. Oates mentioned that President Lyndon B. Johnson did not attend but sent Vice President Hubert Humphrey in his place. Stephen B. Oates, *Let the Trumpet Sound: The Life of Martin Luther King, Jr.* (New

York: Harper & Row, 1982), 495–496. The sermon "A Drum Major for Justice," in anticipation of his death, was delivered by King at Ebenezer Baptist Church, Atlanta, 4 February 1968. Clayborne Carson and Peter Holloran, eds., *A Knock at Midnight: Inspiration from the Great Sermons of Reverend Martin Luther King, Jr.* (New York: Warner Books, 1998), 85; Malcolm P. Calhoun, *With Staff in Hand* (Asheville, NC: Atwood Printing, 1996), 155–156; Mays quoted in Oates, *Let the Trumpet Sound*, 497.

38. Francis E. Stewart Sr., *From Iowa Cornfields to Fernwood: My Life and Stories* (self-published, 2011), 112, 121, 122, 135, 141–145. Born on a farm in Iowa in 1923, Stewart moved as a child with his parents to Jasper County, Georgia, his father's ancestral home. Francis Stewart died in 2011.

39. "Atlanta Hotel Bars Dr. Bunche as Guest"; "Bunche Bids Race Press for Rights," *New York Times*, 7 July 1962, 18:2; John Morris, "A More Just Society," Series XVI, reel 219:174, Southern Regional Council Papers.

40. Muhammad Ali, a boxing champion who embraced the Nation of Islam, became a conscientious objector on religious grounds during the Vietnam War. He was sentenced to prison and stripped of his heavyweight title. Gerald Gill, introduction to chapter 11, in Carson et al., *Eyes on the Prize Civil Rights Reader*, 339–441. Younge grew up in a middle-class family in Tuskegee, Alabama, where he was able to get 100 blacks registered to vote in one day, but he was killed in Tuskegee when he tried to use a segregated rest room at a gasoline station. His murder led to a violent uprising by blacks in Tuskegee. For details, see Bond, *Free at Last*, 84–85. Newton, Seale, Cleaver, and Forman were organizers of the militant Black Panther movement in Oakland, California, and Lowndes County, Alabama. Carson et al., *Eyes on the Prize Civil Rights Reader*, 345–361. Wilkins quoted in Fairclough, *To Redeem*, 320; McRae, interview, 14 May 1999; Bryan, interview.

41. See Cleveland Sellers and Robert Terrell, *River of No Return: The Autobiography of a Black Militant and the Life and Death of SNCC* (New York: William Morrow, 1973; reprint, with an afterword by Sellers, Jackson: University Press of Mississippi, 1990), 156–157; Campbell, interview by Caudill, 59; Campbell, *Brother to a Dragonfly*, 222.

42. Campbell, *Brother to a Dragonfly*, 226; Marshall Frady, *Southerners: A Journalist's Odyssey* (New York: New American Library, 1980), 367.

43. Campbell, *Brother to a Dragonfly*, 226, 244–245, 227, 242.

44. "The Black Manifesto, to the White Christian Churches and the Jewish Synagogues in the USA and All Other Racist Institutions," presented by James Forman, delivered and adopted by the National Black Economic Development Conference in Detroit, 26 April 1969, 1–2, 11, Interreligious Foundation for Community Organization (IFCO) Papers, New York Public Library, Schomburg Center for Research in Black Culture, Manuscripts, Archives, and Rare Books Division, box 16:1, box 15:9.

45. "Chronology," 9 May 1969, IFCO Papers, box 15:10. See also "Forman Burns a Court Order Barring Disruption in Church," *New York Times*, 10 May 1969, 32:5. According to the *New York Times*, the burning of the orders "did not appear to be in itself an act of contempt of court." Forman, *Black Revolutionaries*, 546; Emanuel Perlmutter, "Black Militant Halts Service at Riverside Church," *New York Times*, 5 May 1969, 37:1. See Elaine Allen Lechtreck, "'We Are Demanding $500 Million for Reparations': The Black Manifesto, Mainline Religious Denominations and Black Economic Development," *Journal of African American History* 97, nos. 1–2 (Winter–Spring 2012): 47–48; "New Jersey Council of Churches/Council News: Church's Response to the Black Manifesto," 3 May 1969, IFCO Papers, box 15:10; see also Shattuck, *Episcopalians*.

46. Shattuck, *Episcopalians*, 198–201, Stoney is quoted on 195; see also Kessel, *Hines*, 325.

47. "Response to the Executive Council," 22 May 1969, IFCO Papers, box 15:3; Kesselus, *Hines*, 309–314, 317; "Black and White Militants Disrupt Episcopal Parley," *New York Times*, 1 September 1969; "A Chronological Digest of the Response of the Churches to the Black

Manifesto," 4 September 1969, IFCO Papers, box 15:10. The Episcopal Church in various southern locations contributed generously to African American social causes. In Nashville, Tennessee, a "liberation school" established at St. Anselm's Chapel Episcopal Student Center lost funding from the federal government when it was accused of teaching white hatred. The accusation was denied by Rev. James Woodruff, chaplain of St. Anselm's, who stated the school would continue without federal money. *Nashville Banner*, 5 August 1967, Nashville Collection, Nashville (TN) Public Library.

48. "PCUS and Its Relations with IFCO"; "Funds Voted for Presbyterian Black Clergy, Laity Conference," IFCO Papers, box 16:1; Alvis, *Religion and Race*, 128–129.

49. The quotation is from Augustus Hopkins Strong, *Systematic Theology* (Rochester, NY: E. R. Andrews, 1886), n.p., in "Resolution on Reparations," Finlator Papers, reel 18:1013. The Bible verse is from Luke 19:8 NSV

50. "Resolution on Restitution," Finlator Papers, reel 18:1037; W. W. Finlator, interview by author, tape recording, Raleigh, NC, 12 May 1999; quotation from B. J. Collins to the North Carolina *Biblical Recorder* (4 April 1970), quoted in G. McLeod Bryan, *Dissenter in the Baptist Southland: Fifty Years in the Career of William Wallace Finlator* (Macon, GA: Mercer University Press, 1985), 111.

51. George Dugan, "Young Baptists Challenge Southern Convention," *New York Times*, 12 June 1969, 36:6; Duncan Montgomery Gray, interview by author, telephone, 17 December 2006. Harold E. O'Chester, a white Baptist pastor and a member of the Committee of Conscience, spoke out to his church congregation against the burning of seven black churches in four months in Meridian, Mississippi, and through the Committee of Conscience, O'Chester raised more than $10,000 in cash for replacing the burned churches. As a result of his action, the Meridian police placed him on a list for violent action, he received threatening phone calls, and his children were threatened, but some people in the congregation supported him. Harold E. O'Chester, "A Stand Against Violence," *Baptist Press Features*, 14 August 1968, SBC Historical Commission, Dargan-Carver Library, Nashville, TN, online.

52. Public Broadcasting System's *Religion and Ethics Newsweekly* cited Rev. Morris's "Hope and Health Center" on 6 February 2000 for its great service to the nation and Memphis, where one-fourth of the people are poor and have no medical insurance. "The Reverend Frank Lewis McRae, D.D.," unpublished paper in author's possession, photocopy, 2; David Appleby, Allison Graham, and Stephen Ross, "At the River I Stand," a production of Memphis State University, Department of Theater and Communication Arts, 1993; Frank Lewis McRae, interview by author, telephone, 1 May 2006.

53. Campbell, interview by Caudill, 59, 48, 70; Campbell, interview, 18 August 1995; Campbell quoted in *God's Will*, a documentary produced at the University of Alabama, 2000. Reference to the musings of a "bootleg preacher" is from Will D. Campbell, *Soul among Lions: Musings of a Bootleg Preacher* (Louisville, KY: Westminster John Knox, 1999).

54. King, interview, 23 November 2004.

55. Morris, "ESCRU," 8–24; John B. Morris, "McComb," *The Episcopal Society for Cultural and Racial Unity*, Newsletter, 14 March 1965, 1, 26 December 1966, 1, ESCRU Papers.

56. Morris is referred to as a minister. Morris explained that high church Episcopalian clergy are called "Father" and are designated as priests, whereas he and other low church clergy are called "Reverend" and are designated as ministers. Morris, interview, 15 August 2001; Psalm 113; Morris, "ESCRU," 25.

57. James H. Cone, *God of the Oppressed* (New York: Seabury Press, 1975), 133; James H. Cone, *Black Theology & Black Power* (New York: Seabury Press, 1969), 37; "Billy's Bountiful African Harvest," *Life*, 21 March 1960, 29.

58. John and Wright Morris, interview by author, Augusta, GA, 15 August 2001.

Chapter 6. The Witness Does Not End

1. Lee, *Cotton Patch Evidence*, 5.

2. W. E. B. Du Bois, *The Souls of Black Folk* (1903; reprint, with a new introduction by Randall Kenan, New York: Penguin Books, 1995), 149; Lee, *Cotton Patch Evidence*, 4–7, 10, quotation is on 7; also in Florence Jordan, interview by Ray Rockwell, tape recording, Americus, GA, c. 1987, personal collection of Ray Rockwell, Plains, GA, in author's possession.

3. Lee, *Cotton Patch Evidence*, 8–10.

4. John Pennington, "Americus' Bi-Racial Farm: A Cancer on Community?" *Atlanta Journal*, n.d., Koinonia Archives, Americus, GA. Jordan and Martin England also planted pecan trees when they first arrived, but such trees take a long time to produce. Ron Lemke, interview by author, tape recording, Koinonia Farm, Americus, GA, 15 June 2000. By 2000 Koinonia no longer existed as an intentional community. The farm is now run as a cooperative, with many members owning their own homes on or near the property, and much of the work is done by volunteers from all over the world. Lemke served as volunteer property manager for the year 2000; Florence Jordan, interview by Rockwell.

5. Jordan never actually signed the application because he was not permitted to do so. "A Farm in Georgia," *Nation*, 22 September 1956: 237.

6. Robert Lee, "The Crisis at Koinonia," *Christian Century*, 7 November 1956, 1290; Joyce Hollyday, "The Dream That Has Endured: Clarence Jordan and Koinonia," *Sojourners* 8, no. 12 (December 1979), 14; *Atlanta Journal*, 17 April 1957; Lee, *Cotton Patch Evidence*, 107; McNeill, *God Wills Us Free*, 153; Campbell, interview by Caudill, 60; Clarence Jordan, "To the Friends of Koinonia Farm," 26 July 1956, personal letter. Koinonia Archives, Americus, GA; John Pennington, "Koinonia Farm," *Atlanta Journal*, n.p., Koinonia Archives; Florence Jordan, interview by Rockwell; also quoted in Hollyday, "Dream That Has Endured," 14. A news item in the *Macon Telegraph* mentioned that damages to the farm were estimated at $20,000, in addition to bank and business establishments cutting off credit, trade, and services. The article mentioned that the Macon Council on Human Relations condemned the acts of violence and began a fund to aid residents. *Macon Telegraph*, 18 February 1957, n.p., Koinonia Archives. During the boycott, Jordan began harvesting his pecans, and a thriving mail-order business also saved Koinonia from extinction.

7. "According to Clarence," *Newsweek*, 26 February 1968, Koinonia Archives; Lee, *Cotton Patch Evidence*, 181; Clarence Jordan, *The Substance of Faith and Other Cotton Patch Sermons*, ed. Dallas Lee, A Koinonia Publication (New York: Association Press, 1972), 25.

8. "According to Clarence," 61; Lee, *Cotton Patch Evidence*, 181, 190; Jordan, *Substance of Faith*, 25.

9. Ben Willeford, interview by author, Americus, GA, 7 December 2000. For stories of people inspired by Jordan, see Kay N. Weiner, ed., *Koinonia Remembered: The First Fifty Years* (Americus, GA: Koinonia Publication, 1992).

10. Jubilee Partners, Inc., patterned after Koinonia Farm, was established in Comer (northeast Georgia) in 1979 by Don Mosley and his family as a place of refuge for refugees from around the world. Mosley had been a director of Koinonia for nine years and helped found Habitat for Humanity. He was also national chairman of the Fellowship of Reconciliation from 1984 to 1986 and helped lead delegations to many war-torn parts of the world. Don Mosley with Joyce Hollyday, *With Our Own Eyes: The Dramatic Story of a Christian Response to the Wounds of War, Racism, and Oppression* (Scottdale, PA: Herald Press, 1996), 299.

11. John Cole Vodicka, founder of the Prison and Jail Project, went to Koinonia Farm with his family in 1990 after living in several other intentional communities. A conscientious objector during the Vietnam War, Vodicka served a prison sentence and determined to help victims of prison abuse. During the mid-1990s, Koinonia, deeply in debt, almost closed down again and

could no longer support the Prison and Jail Project. Vodicka and his family moved to Americus, where he was able to obtain funds from several charitable foundations. Since 1990 the Prison and Jail Project has been fighting for justice for African American prisoners in Georgia and has been successful in establishing community centers in Georgia's southwestern counties. John Cole Vodicka, interview by author, Americus, GA, 17 January 2001.

12. Clarence Jordan, "A Personal Letter from Clarence Jordan to Friends of Koinonia," 21 October 1968, 1, Koinonia Archives.

13. Oakhurst Baptist Church was a church that welcomed diversity. The church was expelled from the Southern Baptist Convention in 1969 and established the Decatur (Georgia) Cooperative Ministries. www.oakhurstbaptist.org.; Jordan, "Personal Letter," 1, 3–5; Clarence Jordan, interview by Walden Howard, *Faith at Work* 83, no. 2 (April 1970): 17. Koinonia's mission statement appears on packaging of all its mail order items, its newsletters, and its brochures: "Koinonia Partners, Inc. is a Christian organization seeking to be a 'demonstration plot for the Kingdom of God.' We are committed to non-violence and peaceful solutions to society's problems, reconciliation among all people, Christian discipleship and the empowerment of the poor, the neglected, and the oppressed. We come together, united in our belief in God, to participate in community life, outreach ministries, and business enterprises."

14. Avis Crowe, "The Story of Low Cost Housing at Koinonia Partners," c. 1982 (Koinonia Partners, mimeographed), 6, 11, 19.

15. Ibid., 6.

16. Alva W. Taylor, "My Chair Was Abolished," New Year's letter of 1952, Taylor Papers, Disciples of Christ Historical Society, Nashville, TN, box 1.

17. In 1939 Jordan became the first full-time superintendent of missions for the Long Ridge Association as well as director of the Fellowship Center. Lee, *Cotton Patch Evidence*, 21; Barbara and Howard McClain, interview by author, tape recording, Chapin, SC, 14 November 1999. Howard McClain was present at the interview but, due to a stroke, was unable to speak. Barbara McClain spoke for the two McClains.

18. Barbara and Howard McClain, interview, 14 November 1999; Lee, *Cotton Patch Evidence*, 197–220.

19. R. Wright Spears, *Journey toward Unity: The Christian Action Council in South Carolina, 1933–1983* (Columbia, SC: Crowson-Stone, 1983), 5.

20. Ibid., 5–6; Spears, *One in the Spirit*, 141, 142. Evans is quoted in Spears, *One in the Spirit*, 156.

21. Spears, *Journey*, 10.

22. Ibid., 11–13.

23. Ibid., 14; Spears, *One in the Spirit*, 148.

24. Barbara and Howard McClain, interview, 14 November 1999.

25. Cleveland Sellers, "Voices from the Civil Rights Movement in South Carolina: Personal Testimony," The Citadel Conference on Civil Rights in South Carolina, Charleston, 8 March 2003; Barbara and Howard McClain, interview, 14 November 1999.

26. South Carolina Annual Baptist Convention Bulletin, 1985, in author's possession; Frederick C. James quoted in Spears, *Journey*, 17.

27. Barbara and Howard interview.

28. Finlator, interview, 12 May 1999.

29. Ibid.

30. "The Minister as Prophet," Address at Southeastern Baptist Theological Seminary, Wake Forest, NC, 25 March 1976, Finlator Papers, reel 18:216; G. C. Berkouwer, *The Triumph of Grace in the Theology of Karl Barth* (Grand Rapids, MI: Eerdmans, 1956); W. W. Finlator, "The Pastor and Social Issues," 1974, Finlator Papers, reel 18:161.

31. Pullen's constitution demanded sermons related to problems facing Christians all over the world. "A Statement of Principles and Goals," Pullen Memorial Baptist Church, May 1956, Finlator Papers, reel 18:813–814.

32. Employees at the Harriet Cotton Mills in Henderson tried to form a branch of the Textile Workers Union and had been out of work for over one year. According to Finlator, the church never "said a mumbling word." Finlator admonished them: "Surely, my brethren, this is what Martin Luther would call 'wicked silence.'" W. W. Finlator, "Four Areas of Concern," *Biblical Recorder*, 7 November 1959, 13, Finlator Papers, reel 17, frame 79; W. W. Finlator, "Until Our Churches Repent of This Denial," *Raleigh News and Observer*, 25 October 1959, Finlator Papers, reel 17:1–2; Wagner to Finlator, 22 October 1959; Baptist layman to Finlator, October 1959, Finlator Papers, reel 17:6–7.

33. Letters to Finlator, June 1960, Finlator Papers, reel 17: 105, 139–143, 156, 163–199, 67–81, 406–407. These publications were also identified in the Southern Regional Council Papers, "Resistance Groups," Series III, reel 111:0695–0707. The annual report of the National Council of Christians and Jews (of which Finlator was the Raleigh chair) pictured Sanford signing the Brotherhood Week Proclamation in 1961. Finlator Papers, reel 19:0182. In 1963, as governor, Sanford appealed to the aldermen of Chapel Hill to pass the public accommodations ordinance. In 1964, although he did not approve of the extreme tactics of the Chapel Hill demonstrators, he nevertheless commuted the sentences and fines for fifteen of the group. See John Drescher, *Triumph of Good Will: How Terry Sanford Beat a Champion of Segregation and Reshaped the South* (Jackson: University Press of Mississippi, 2000).

34. Told by Timothy Tyson in *Blood Done Sign My Name* (2006), Tyson's biography of his father. Divinity Online, www.divinity.duke.edu/publications/2005.01/.

35. W. W. Finlator, "Muhammad Ali Case Calls for Debate," *Charlotte Observer*, 4 July 1967; Letter to Finlator, 6 July 1967, Finlator Papers, reel 19:538, 540. The woman was especially angry because she had a son fighting in the Vietnam War.

36. Finlator to the US Commission on Civil Rights, Washington, DC, n.d.; Finlator to Jacob Schlitt, US Commission on Civil Rights, 23 March 1972; Finlator wrote also on behalf of T. J. Reddy, a poet and painter whose works were soon to be published by Random House and who was arrested with the "Wilmington Ten." Finlator Papers, reel 19:718, 735, 754; *New York Times*, 11 December 1972, 28:5; Manning Marable, *Race, Reform, and Rebellion: The Second Reconstruction in Black America, 1945–1990*, 2nd ed. (Jackson: University Press of Mississippi, 1990), 127–128.

37. Tom Wicker wrote that Grant and two others (the "Charlotte Three") were later convicted and sentenced to prison terms of twenty-five, twenty, and ten years, respectively, for allegedly setting fire to the Lazy B. stables in Charlotte when they were refused the right to ride. (Numerous horses died in the blaze.) It later came out, according to Wicker, that the federal government had secretly paid $4,000 to each of the prosecution's two main witnesses and given them immunity from prosecution on other charges. Tom Wicker, "The Most Repressive State?" *Fayetteville Times*, 27 December 1975; Finlator to I. T. Creswell Jr., Asst. Staff Director, US Commission on Civil Rights, Washington, DC, 26 May 1972. Finlator wrote, "Wilmington has been for a long time the scene of violent contention between the races. . . . Years ago, Wilmington was the scene of one of the worst race riots in the nation's history." Finlator to the Office of the Attorney General, Department of Justice, Washington, DC, 27 March 1972. Charlotte was also the headquarters for the North Carolina chapter of the Ku Klux Klan. Finlator Papers, reel 18:208, reel 19:740–741, 754, reel 20:319–322.

38. Paul and Keenan, Attorneys at Law, Greenville, NX, to Finlator, "On the Case of the High Point Four," 9 August 1971, Finlator Papers, reel 18:13.

39. Finlator Papers, reel 18:15.

40. Finlator to Charles Lambeth, attorney, 16 January 1968, Finlator Papers, reel 5:11; Finlator, interview, 12 May 1999; Bryan, *Dissenter in the Baptist Southland*, 111; Finlator to Stanley Blackledge, Warden, Central Prison; Finlator to the Board of Parole, 17 March 1972; Finlator to Dept. of Personnel, City of Raleigh, 12 September 1973; W. W. Finlator, "Press Release, An Act to Pay Prisoners a Minimum Wage for Their Work," 1973; Wilbur Hobby and W. W. Finlator, "Suggestions for a Joint Press Release Regarding the Prisoners' Union," Finlator Papers, reel 19:479, 484–491, reel 20:983.

41. Finlator, interview, 12 May 1999.

42. As chair of the North Carolina Branch of the ACLU's legislative committee, Rev. Finlator stated that one of the ACLU's chief goals, abolishment of capital punishment, was consistently "killed in the [NC] House. "Civil Liberties' Bills Unveiled," *Raleigh News and Observer*, 23 April 1969, Finlator Papers, reel 19:288. According to Tom Fisher, the four items—abolition of the death penalty, open housing, elimination of literacy tests, and recommendation that sale, use, or possession of marijuana be made a misdemeanor rather than a felony—were all goals of the North Carolina Civil Liberties Union and did not pass the state legislature. "Civil Liberties Package Meets Lukewarm Legislation, *North Carolina Anvil*, 17 May 1969; W. W. Finlator, "The Need for a State Minimum Wage Law," c. 1957; W. W. Finlator, "They Are 'Christian Academies'?" *Smithfield Herald*, 26 August 1969, Finlator Papers, reel 19:304, 136, reel 17:956. The Twin County Fundamentalist Ministerial Association (Edgecombe and Martin Counties) had banned two literature textbooks on the accusation that they contained stories that used the word "damn," attacked "parental authority," were written by known Communists or writers who, if not Communists, were "pretty far out." In Finlator's estimation, the textbooks were banned because of prejudicial attitudes against the authors: Langston Hughes, Richard Wright, Woody Guthrie, Malcolm X, Martin Luther King Jr., and Dick Gregory (all African Americans except for Woody Guthrie, folk singer and composer of protest songs). W. W. Finlator, "School Board, Spare That Text," address to the Kiwanis Club of Rocky Mount, 14 January 1971, Finlator Papers, reel 17:1052; Finlator, interview, 12 May 1999.

43. Finlator, interview, 12 May 1999.

44. One letter of attack read, "The unchristian left's views aren't in the Gospels or the Constitution of the United States. What religious people like W. W. Finlator refuse to admit is that our Forefathers had in mind to build this great country on Christian principles. What these gentlemen and the Apostle Paul would find appalling is how far to the unchristian left we have let our country fall in the last 40 years." Larry Edwards, letter to the editor, *Raleigh News and Observer*, 24 July 1998, Finlator Papers; Warren Carr, letter to the editor, *Biblical Recorder* 135 (24 May 1969):10, quoted in Bryan, *Dissenter*, 179. See also the comment of Shelton Smith of the Duke Divinity School, "How have you managed to be so prophetical and successful in a denomination and region that is, on the whole, so amazingly conservative?" Bryan, *Dissenter*, 51.

45. Finlator, interview, 19 October 2005. Rev. James Cole was noted by the B'nai B'rith to have told an audience near Salisbury, "A n___r who wants to go to a white swimming pool is not looking for a bath. He's looking for a funeral." That same year, dynamite blasts were reported at a Jewish synagogue, at the home of a white woman, and at the home of a black tenant farmer, all in the vicinity of Charlotte. White ministers who preached brotherhood and desegregation were warned that they would receive the same treatment as all enemies of the pure white race. "Klan Revival," Finlator Papers, reel 20:320. Myers, a retired Methodist minister, included this thought in his pamphlet: "Some people in the North are using all available means to force the Southern people to accept their ideas of race-mixing. Zionists and communists have started the racket and these enemies of ours join them; even bishops and other church leaders whom we think should have more sense are in the racket." Meyers, *Race Question in a Nutshell*, reel 17:73; Finlator quoted in Yonat Shimron, "Church to Honor Finlator," *News and Observer*, 19 August 2001, 4B:6.

46. David Moose, interview by author, tape recording, West Memphis, AR, 9 March 1999.

47. Ibid.

48. Ibid.

49. Ibid.

50. Ibid.; "Arkansas Moves to Block Protest," *New York Times*, 17 August 1969, 60:6; Martin Waldron, "Whites in Arkansas Town Cry for 'Law and Order,'" *New York Times*, 29 August 1969, 14:1.

51. Moose, interview; "Arkansas Whites Continue Protest," *New York Times*, 30 August 1969, 13:3–4.

52. Moose, interview.

53. Ibid.

54. Ibid.

55. David Moose, letter to author, 26 January 2012.

56. Ibid.

57. Joseph Sanderson, interview by author, tape recording, Guntersville, AL, 16 November 1995.

58. Ibid.

59. Ibid.

60. VISTA was established in 1965 as part of President Johnson's War on Poverty to provide services on the home front, much like the Peace Corps abroad. Philip L. Groisser, *Basic American History*, vol. 2 (New York: Keystone Education; 1969), 165; Sanderson interview.

61. Sanderson, interview.

62. Isa. 1:6 KJV; Sanderson, interview.

63. *Marianna Courier-Index*, 27 July 1971, 1:7, 29 July 1971, 1:7; Sanderson, interview.

64. Yearbook of the 2012 Koinonia Reunion and various Internet sites.

65. Travis Frank, letter to author, 22 August 2015.

66. Ibid.

67. Travis Frank, letter to author, 27 August 2015.

68. David Moose, letter to author, 10 August 2015.

69. David Moose, letter to author, 22 August 2015.

Chapter 7. Denominations

1. Rankings have been compiled by Edwin Scott Gaustad, "Religious Demography of the South," in Samuel S. Hill Jr., *Religion and the Solid South* (Nashville, TN: Abingdon Press, 1972), 146; Gallup Poll of 1967, cited by Gaustad in Hill, *Religion and the Solid South*, 147; Orley D. Caudill, "An Oral History with Will D. Campbell," Mt. Juliet, TN, 8 June 1976, McCain Library and Archives, University of Southern Mississippi, Hattiesburg, 8.

2. The phrase "the radical ethics of Christ" appears in John B. Boles, "The Discovery of Southern Religious History," in *Interpreting Southern History: Historiographical Essays in Honor of Sanford W. Higginbotham*, ed. John B. Boles and Evelyn Thomas Nolen (Baton Rouge: Louisiana State University Press, 1987), 543; "According to Clarence"; Lee, *Cotton Patch Evidence*, 181, 190; Clarence Jordan, *The Substance of Faith and Other Cotton Patch Sermons*, ed. Dallas Lee, A Koinonia Publication (New York: Association Press, 1972), 25.

3. Seymour, interview; Bible verse from Acts 8:4 RSV; Arnold Voigt, letter to author, 6 February 2014.

4. Criswell denounced all forms of integration in 1956 before the South Carolina Baptist Convention and the South Carolina legislature: "We don't want to be forced by laws or statutes to cross into those intimate things where we don't want to go." Quoted in Andrew Scott Manis, "'Dying from the Neck Up': Southern Baptist Resistance to the Civil Rights Movement," *Baptist*

History and Heritage 34, no. 1 (Winter 1999): 36; T. B. Maston, *Bible and Race: A Careful Examination of Biblical Teachings on Human Relations* (Nashville, TN: Broadman, 1959), 45; Ramsey, interview, 10 March 1999.

5. Mark Newman, *Getting Right with God: Southern Baptists and Desegregation: 1945–1995* (Tuscaloosa: University of Alabama Press, 2001), 71; David Stricklin, *A Genealogy of Dissent: Southern Baptist Protest in the Twentieth Century* (Louisville: University Press of Kentucky, 1999), 75; Valentine quoted in Willis, *All According*, 29, 176. For Clarence Jordan's writings about white-washed Christians, see Lee, *Cotton Patch Evidence*, 190, quoted in chapter 6.

6. Newman, *Getting Right*, 196–200, 63; Flynt, *Alabama Baptists*, 543; Stricklin, *Genealogy of Dissent*, 70; "A Short History of Pullen," Pullen Memorial Baptist Church website online; Courtland Smith and John L. Humber, *Olin T. Binkley Memorial Baptist Church, a Twenty Year View: 1958–1978* (University of North Carolina Archives digitalized, CP 286.09, Archives.org/details/olintbrinleymemo 00smit, 1978), 2–4; Jesse C. Fletcher, *The Southern Baptist Convention: The Sesquicentennial History* (Nashville, TN: Broadman & Holman, 1994), 292, 323, 331–333, 345, 359, 375, 380.

7. Fletcher, *Southern Baptist Convention*, 273–274, 4. Newman (*Getting Right*, 85) agrees with Fletcher; Criswell quoted in Newman, *Getting Right*, 63. Manis notes, "Though Criswell spoke [in a 1970 sermon] of a truly Christian church being one that is open to all persons regardless of race, his recanting of his earlier views did not specifically mean he now approved of the civil rights movement." Manis, "Dying," 46, endnote 3.

8. Extracts from "Resolution on Racial Reconciliation on the 150th Anniversary of the Southern Baptist Convention," Atlanta, 20–22 June 1995; Bible verse: Genesis 1:27; Greg Garrison, "Southern Baptists Repent Over Racism," *Birmingham News*, 21 June 1995, 1:1–3, 10:1–2; John Dart, "Southern Baptists Vote to Issue Apology for Past Racism," *Los Angeles Times*, 21 June 1995, 28:1–3; Greg Garrison, "Black Baptist Churches Join Southern Baptist Churches," *Birmingham News*, 2 May 1999, 1:1–2.

9. Nate McMillan, interview by author, Orangeburg, SC, 10 July 2003. For more details on Nate McMillan, see Jack Shuler, *Blood and Bone: Truth and Reconciliation in a Southern Town* (Columbia: University of South Carolina Press, 2012), 149–156; McMillan is quoted on 154. For more details on the Orangeburg violence, see Jack Bass and Jack Nelson, *The Orangeburg Massacre* (Macon, GA: Mercer University Press, 1984).

10. Nate McMillan, letter to author, 3 April 2012; Schuler, *Blood and Bone*, 156.

11. Ed Stetzer, "Changing Names Is Good, Changing Actions Is Better," *Baptist Press*, 23 February 2012; McMillan, interview, 10 July 2003; Jacqueline L. Salmon, "Southern Baptists Diversifying to Survive; Minority Outreach Seen as Key to Crisis," *Washington Post*, 16 February 2008, A1; Fletcher, *Southern Baptist Convention*, 274–275; Karen Willoughby, "Fred Luter, Elected SBC President," *Baptist Press*, 19 June 2012, 30; Roberts quoted in "Southern Baptists Seek More Blacks, *New York Times*, 20 June 1999, 1–3; Adelle M. Banks, "SBC Elects First Black President," *Christian Century*, 11 July 2012, 14. The historian Carolyn Renée Dupont writes about the invitation to Luter in *Mississippi Praying*, 237. For more about Hudgins, see Marsh, *God's Long Summer*, 82–115.

12. The quotation (Genesis 1:27) is taken from "Resolution on Racial Reconciliation on the 150th Anniversary of the Southern Baptist Convention," Atlanta, 20–22 June 1995.

13. The "Social Creed" was adopted by northern Methodists in 1908 and by southern Methodists in 1913, and restated by each successive General Conference. General Board of Church and Society, *Social Principles of the United Methodist Church* (Nashville, TN: United Methodist Publishing House, 2004), 1–2; "Our Social Creed," *The Book of Discipline of the United Methodist Church* (Nashville, TN: United Methodist Publishing House, 2000), 166; Wesley, *Christian*

Perfection, 1739. Wesley is also reputed to have influenced prime minister of England William Wilberforce to end the British slave trade in 1807.

14. Peter C. Murray, *Methodists and the Crucible of Race* (Columbia: University of Missouri Press, 2004), 3–5, 84–85, 186–187, 208–209; A. V. Huff Jr., "The Methodist Church," in *Encyclopedia of Religion in the South*, ed. Samuel S. Hill and Charles H. Lippy, with Charles Reagan Wilson (Macon, GA: Mercer University Press, 2005), 498; *The United Methodist Church and Race* (Division of Human Relations, Board of Christian Social Concerns of the United Methodist Church, 1968), 2–4; Rhett Jackson Papers, South Caroliniana Library, box 2.

15. C. G. Haugabook, interview by author, tape recording, Plains, GA, 17 January 2001; C. G. Haugabook, letter to author, 4 March 2001; C. G. Haugabook, "The Static Heart of Man," to the Americus circuit, 1956, unpublished sermon in author's possession, photocopy, 5.

16. Haugabook's reflection is in letter to author; "Bishop James R. King, Jr.," *South Georgia Annual Conference* (Summer 2008), online.

17. Murray, *Methodists*, 222; Rhett Jackson, interview; Rhett Jackson, "The United Methodist Church Had Two Annual Conferences in South Carolina—-One for White Methodists, One for Black Methodists; the Conferences Merged. How Did it Happen?" unpublished paper in author's possession, 2; Huff, "Methodist Church," 498; A. McKay Brabham Jr., "The Committees of the Conferences Meet," *South Carolina Methodist Advocate*, 18 May 1967, 2.

18. Rhett Jackson, interview; "A Progress Report by the General Commission on Religion and Race of the United Methodist Church" (1976 General Conference Records), private papers of Rhett Jackson in author's possession; see also Murray, *Methodists*, 211–222, 227, 229.

19. Bass and Nelson, *Orangeburg Massacre*, 240.

20. A. McKay Brabham, "I Have a Great Sorrow," *South Carolina Methodist Advocate*, 30 April 1970, 5; Susan Pierce Johnston, *One Editor's Stand* (Columbia, SC: Trustees of the *South Carolina Methodist Advocate* and Friends of Rev. McKay Brabham, 1992), 4, 23–26.

21. Fred Reese Jr., "Dilemma and Hope Seen in Church's Race Structure," *South Carolina Methodist Advocate*, 17 March 1966, 4–5.

22. Reese, interview.

23. Eben Taylor, interview by author, telephone, Lawrence, SC, 29 January 2003.

24. Murray, *Methodists*, 221.

25. Charles M. Prestwood, "Social Ideas of Methodist Ministers in Alabama since Unification" (PhD diss., Boston University, 1960), 112–113, 367–369. See also Murray, *Methodists*, 105; Dallas Anthony Blanchard, "Some Social and Orientative Correlates of Career Change and Continuity as Revealed among United Methodist Pastors of the Alabama–West Florida Conference, 1960–1970" (PhD diss., Boston University, 1972), 1; Bachman G. Hodge, bishop from 1956 to 1961, described by Collins as weak and ineffectual, did nothing to curtail the activities of the Methodist Layman's Union. Collins also criticized Bishop Paul Hardin (1961–1969) for failing to speak out against the beatings and bombings that occurred in Birmingham during the tumultuous years of the 1960s. Collins, *When the Church Bell Rang*, 58–60, 77. Thomas Butts maintained that Collins's indictment of Alabama Methodists was mild. Butts, interview, 10 November 1999.

26. Corley, "Quest for Racial Harmony," 181–189; "Robert Hughes, thirty-two, left his post as director of the Alabama Council on Human Relations early in 1961 to serve as a missionary in Southern Rhodesia," quoted from "Robert Hughes Leaves Post," *Methodist Christian Advocate* (Nashville, TN: United Methodist Publishing House, 1960), 3–4:151.

27. Collins, *When the Church Bell Rang*, 150–152, 159, 161–162, 165; Vickers is quoted on 150; Clinton Hubbard Jr., interview by author, telephone, 1 March 2016.

28. Dupont, *Mississippi Praying*, 225–226. See also Murray, *Methodists*, 228.

29. Murray, *Methodists*, 228–229.

30. Dupont, *Mississippi Praying*, 227.

31. Murray, *Methodists*, 221–222; Vernon, *Methodists in Arkansas*, 388–389.

32. Text of 30541-CS-R1-U, General Conference, Cleveland, OH, 12 May 2000.

33. James E. Clyburn, "South Carolina Takes Lead with Racism Apology," *Capitol Column*, Columbia, SC, 4 June 2001.

34. First quotation is from John Kater, "Experiment in Freedom: The Episcopal Church and the Black Power Movement," *Historical Magazine of the Episcopal Church* (March 1970): 68–69, cited in Lewis, *Yet with a Steady Beat*, 147–148; Resolution of the General Convention of the Episcopal Church, September 1955; John H. Fenton, "Churchmen Urge a Stand on South," *New York Times*, 18 September 1958, 21:3.

35. *Atlanta Journal*, 26 May 1963, 10:4; Shattuck, *Episcopalians*, 125. The last quotation is in Shattuck, *Episcopalians*, 129. See also Lewis, *Yet with a Steady Beat*, 149.

36. Gray, interview, 21 July 2007; Donald S. Armentrout, "The Integration Crisis at Sewanee," *Historiographer of the National Episcopal Historians and Archivists* 27, no. 2 (Summer 1995): 11–12; Gray, interview, 21 July 2007; see also Shattuck, *Episcopalians*, 49. Gray's statement that the majority of bishops and clergy supported integration and edicts handed down from the General Convention was corroborated by the sociologist Charles Y. Glock, who conducted a survey to determine how parishioners and clergy felt concerning a whole range of resolutions passed by the Triennial Conventions. In total, 100 bishops, 259 priests, and 1,530 parishioners completed questionnaires. Glock and associates found that bishops and priests were more supportive of the principle "that the Church has a responsibility for the secular society of which it is a part" than were church members. Charles Y. Glock, Benjamin B. Ringer, and Earl R. Babbie, *To Comfort and to Challenge* (Berkeley: University of California Press, 1967), vii, 8, 135.

37. Frances Pauley, interview by Cliff Kuhn, 3 May 1988, Special Collections, Georgia State University, Atlanta, 35, 34; plaque on view at the Ralph Mark Gilbert Civil Rights Museum, Savannah, GA, 24 April 2002.

38. Ralph Mark Gilbert Civil Rights Museum, courtesy of Sharon Dillard Johnson.

39. Pauley, interview, 34.

40. Marmion, interview. Marmion also tried to stop a lynching in his home state in 1935. "Retired Episcopal Bishop Charles G. Marmion Dies," *Louisville Courier-Journal Metro*, 8 December 2000, 1. A much younger white southern Episcopal minister, Rev. Kenneth Kesselus (born in Austin, Texas, in 1947), came to know Hines through his sermons, articles, press releases, interviews, and written statements, and was inspired, like Gray, by Hines's Christ-like devotion to the underprivileged and dispossessed in society. In a biography about Hines, Kesselus demonstrated that Hines's devotion to racial justice began early in his career in the South. Kesselus, *John E. Hines*, 9, 166–170, 181; Gray, interview, 21 July 2007.

41. Joel Alvis Jr., "Racial Turmoil and Religious Reaction: The Right Reverend John M. Allin," *Historical Magazine of the Protestant Episcopal Church* 50 (March 1984): 1, 85–86, Mississippi Department of Archives and History, Jackson; Shattuck, *Episcopalians*, 212. Gray mentioned that Allin was opposed because of his objections to the Delta Ministry in Mississippi in 1964. Gray, interview, 21 July 2007; Shattuck, *Episcopalians*, 212; Lewis, *Yet with a Steady Beat*, 166–167.

42. Gray, interview, 21 July 2007; for Hammond's story, see Spears, *One in the Spirit*, 180–184; Roger K. Warlick, *History of Christ Church*, Ralph Mark Gilbert Civil Rights Museum, courtesy of Sharon Dillard Johnson; "Negroes Attend Jackson Church," *New York Times*, 17 June 1963, 12:4–5 (ill.); dates for ministers courtesy Archives of the Episcopal Church, Austin, TX; Helen T. Bradley, "Terrifying Memories, 1954–1957," in Weiner, *Koinonia Remembered*, 40–41.

43. Gray, interview, 21 July 2007; Harold T. Lewis, "Racial Concerns in the Episcopal Church since 1973," *Anglican and Episcopal History* 67, no. 4 (December 1998): 476–477; Barbara

Ramnaraine, "Episcopal Church: The Church of No Outcasts," *Anglican World*, Easter, 1998, 31. Ramnaraine believes the church has a long way to go to become "The Church of No Outcasts."

44. *Episcopal News Service*, 1 July 2006; *Christian Century* 132, no. 15 (22 July 2015): 17.

45. Rev. E. T. Thompson, *Presbyterian Standard*, 2 September 1925, quoted in Hobbie, "Ernest Trice Thompson," 153, 343.Thompson also produced eight comprehensive volumes of the history of the southern Presbyterian Church. Hobbie, "Ernest Trice Thompson," v–vi.

46. Report of the Council on Christian Relations, quoted in Campbell and Pettigrew, *Christians in Racial Crisis*, 160–161; the session of South Highland Presbyterian Church in Birmingham, Alabama; the Tuscaloosa Presbytery; and the Synod of Alabama all voiced disagreement. Alvis, *Religion and Race* 58; "Churches Begin Belated Drive for Brotherhood," *Southern Patriot* 12, no. 7 (September 1954): 3.

47. Walter Rugaber, "Church Liberals Quell 2 Revolts," *New York Times*, 11 June 1967, 46:1; Alvis, *Religion and Race*, 132–133; R. Milton Winter, "Division and Reunion in the Presbyterian Church, U.S.: A Mississippi Retrospective," *Journal of Presbyterian History* 78, no. 1 (Spring 2000): 67.

48. Malcolm P. Calhoun, *With Staff in Hand* (Asheville, NC: St. Andrews College Press, 1996), 1–4, 36–38, 49–50, 130–133.

49. Ibid., 142; King's entire speech is quoted on 256–273.

50. Alvis, *Religion and Race*, 14–15; Ernest Trice Thompson, *Presbyterians in the South*, vol. 3 (Richmond, VA: John Knox, 1963), 547; James H. Smylie, *A Brief History of the Presbyterians* (Louisville, KY: Geneva, 1996), 130. Smylie was transformed by the civil rights movement in spite of his ancestor, another James Smylie, also a Presbyterian minister, who convinced many southerners "that slavery was built upon the foundations of God's law and natural law and Christians had no moral obligation to seek its abolition." The pre–Civil War Smylie's defense of slavery, published in 1836, was considered to have triggered the abolitionist movement in the North. Thomas H. Long, "Preaching in the South," in *Encyclopedia of Religion in the South*, ed. Samuel S. Hill, 3–8 (1984; reprint, Macon, GA: Mercer University Press, 1997), 594b.

51. Sherrard Rice, interview by author, tape recording, Columbia, SC, 21 January 2001; David B. Calhoun, *The Glory of the Lord Risen Upon It: First Presbyterian Church, Columbia, South Carolina, 1795–1995* (Columbia, SC: R. L. Bryan, 1994), 262; "The Weeping Sermon" is quoted on 260–261.

52. Calhoun, *Glory*, 276, 309, 293, 297. Presbyterian missionaries had converted Tabor. This author has witnessed FPC's expansive outreach programs during personal visits to FPC.

53. From the Latin, meaning coming to an end without setting a specific time or date.

54. Hobbie, "Ernest Trice Thompson," 604–605; J. Randolph Taylor, interview; Smylie, *Brief History*, 142.

55. Jon Butler, Grant Wacker, and Randall Balmer, *Religion in American Life: A Short History* (New York: Oxford University Press, 2000), 184–185; *Our Story: A Brief History of the Global Family of Christian Churches, Churches of Christ, and Disciples of Christ* (Nashville, TN: The World Convention of the Churches of Christ, 1995), 2–4; Richard T. Hughes, *Reviving the Ancient Faith: The Story of Churches of Christ in America* (Grand Rapids, MI: Eerdmans, 1996), 271; see also Ahlstrom, *Religious History*, 432–435.

56. Ahlstrom, *Religious History*, 447–449; D. Newell Williams, *A Case Study of Mainstream Protestantism: The Disciples' Relation to American Culture, 1880–1989* (Grand Rapids, MI: Eerdmans, 1991), x; The World Convention, *Our Story*, 4.

57. Hughes, *Reviving the Ancient Faith*, 274–275, 281; Richard T. Hughes and R. L. Roberts, *The Churches of Christ*, student edition (Westport CT: Greenwood, 2001), 8–9; Roger W. Stump, "Spatial Patterns of Growth and Decline among the Disciples of Christ, 1890–1980," in *A Case*

Study of Mainstream Protestantism: The Disciples' Relation to American Culture, 1880–1989, ed. D. Newell Williams (Grand Rapids, MI: Eerdmans, 1991), 451–452.

58. The Disciples' document suggested that the idea of inclusiveness was open to interpretation: "For some this may mean the employment of a multi-racial staff; for others it may mean an active evangelism program among persons of 'other' races; for still others it may mean public announcements [such as] . . . 'We welcome all people.'" Disciples of Christ, International Convention, Indianapolis, IN, 11–18 October 1957, cited in Campbell and Pettigrew, *Christians in Racial Crisis*, 146; Southern Regional Council Papers, Series 1, reel 622:800–868. After leaving Little Rock, Cartwright served Central Christian Church in Youngstown, Ohio. He returned to the South in 1971 to serve South Hills Christian Church in Fort Worth, Texas. Colbert Cartwright biography, University of Arkansas, Special Collections, MC 1026.

59. William M. Newman and Peter L. Halvorson, *Atlas of American Religion* (Walnut Creek, CA: Alta-Mira Press/Rowman & Littlefield, 1999), 60–61

60. Hughes, *Reviving the Ancient Faith*, 297–298.

61. William K. Floyd, letter to author, 9 June 2012.

62. Ibid.

63. Ibid.

64. W. K. Floyd, "Why I Could Not Be a Career Preacher," in *Voices of Concern, Critical Studies in Church of Christism*, ed. Robert Meyers (St. Louis: Mission Messenger, 1966), 163; Michael D. Brown, "Despite School Sentiment, Harding's Leader Said 'No' to Integration," *Arkansas Times*, 6 June 2012, 1, 3, 4–6.

65. Floyd, letter to author; Brown, "Despite School Sentiment," 3–6; Robert Meyers, introduction to W. K. Floyd, "Why I Could Not Be a Career Preacher," in Meyers, *Voices of Concern*, 155.

66. Hughes, *Reviving*, 289–290.

67. Chalk's sermons have been published in *Three American Revolutions* (New York: Carlton Press, 1970). Chalk, *Three American Revolutions*, 83–86; Harold K. Straughn, foreword to Chalk, *Three American Revolutions*, v–vi.

68. Hughes, *Reviving*, 302; J. E. Choate, "Marshall Keeble: An Uncommon Man," *20th Century Christian* 30, no. 10 (July 1968): 49–50. Choate also wrote a book about Keeble, *Roll, Jordan, Roll: A Biography of Marshall Keeble* (Nashville, TN: Gospel Advocate, 2001). Hughes, *Reviving*, 282.

69. Al Price, letter to author, 14 January 2013.

70. Ibid.

71. Bible verse from Acts 2:21. Alvin H. Price, "The Mighty Works of God," sermon delivered at College Hills Church of Christ, Lebanon, TN, 20 June 2007, in author's possession.

72. Al Price, letter to author, 26 March 2013.

73. *Abilene Christian University News*, 22 November 1999, 1

74. *Abilene Christian University News*, 1 February 2013; Paul A. Anthony, "Multicultural Effort Builds Campus Community," *ACU Today* (Fall 2012).

75. Jeff G. Johnson, *Black Christians: The Untold Lutheran Story* (St. Louis: Concordia, 1991), 167–168; Richard C. Dickinson, *Roses and Thorns: The Centennial Edition of Black Lutheran Mission and Ministry in the Lutheran Church–Missouri Synod* (St. Louis: Concordia, 1977), 65–67; Clair S. Hollerup, "Nils Jules Bakke and the Colored Missions of the South," paper (Mequoa, WI: Wisconsin Lutheran Seminary, 18 April 1984), 9–13.

76. Johnson, *Black Christians*, 170; Kathryn M. Galchutt, *Andrew Schulze: Lutherans and Race in the Civil Rights Era* (Macon, GA: Mercer University Press, 2005), 52, 168–169; Walter Ellwanger quoted in Ziehr, *Struggle for Unity*, 28.

77. Richard O. Ziehr, interview by author, telephone, 29 December 2013; Dickinson, *Roses and Thorns*, 12, 70–72, 192, 194; Streufert quoted in Ziehr, *Struggle for Unity*, 39–41; Homrighausen quoted in Ziehr, *Struggle for Unity*, 125.

78. Ziehr, interview; Edgar Homrighausen, interview by author, telephone, 31 January 2014.

79. Homrighausen quoted in Ziehr, *Struggle for Unity*, 101; Ziehr, *Struggle for Unity*, 71–72; Homrighausen, interview.

80. Ziehr, *Struggle for Unity*, 184–185; Homrighausen, interview. For limited coverage of Homrighausen, see Kathryn M. Galchutt, *Andrew Schulze: Lutherans and Race in the Civil Rights Era* (Macon, GA: Mercer University Press, 2005), 201–202, 212–213.

81. "Faith Lutheran Church School Long Established," *Mobile Press-Register*, n.p., n.d.; Arnold Voigt, "Social Action Must Stem from Church's Doctrine," *Mobile Press-Register*, 6 July 1966; "Toulminville Anti-Poverty Council," *Mobile Beacon*, 15 April 1967, n.p.; "Pastor Leaving," *Mobile Press Register*, n.d., n.p., "Area Civil Plan Starts Monday," *Mobile Press-Register*, 15 June 1969, 13:1–5; "Miss. NAACP Head, B'gham, Editor Speak at Jackie's Rally," *Mobile Beacon*, 7 May 1970, n.p.; personal papers of Arnold Voigt in author's possession.

82. Voigt, letter to author; "Pastor Leaving"; Arnold Voigt, interview by author, telephone, 11 January 2014.

83. Rachel and Raymond Davis, interview; Davis, "Writing About My Life," 3.

84. Rachel and Raymond Davis, interview. Crumley later served as bishop of the Georgia-Alabama Synod from 1980 to 1987.

85. H. George Anderson, "Milestones in ELCA Work Related to Poverty and Social Justice," paper presented at the ELCA Forum on Poverty and Wealth, 8 November 2003, 5, in author's possession.

86. H. George Anderson, interview by author, New Haven, CT, 25 April 2004. The group consisted of Lauren Brubaker (1914–2010), Presbyterian minister, chair of the Religious Studies Department at the University of South Carolina in Columbia; Rev. R. Wright Spears, president of the Methodist women's college in Columbia; Arthur Martin, executive of the Presbyterian Synod of South Carolina; Rev. J. Claude Evans (1917–2007), editor in chief of the *South Carolina Methodist Advocate* from 1952 to 1957; Rev. A. McKay Brabham (1916–2000), editor in chief of the *South Carolina Methodist Advocate* from 1961 to 1971; Rev. A. Harold Cole, executive secretary-treasurer of the South Carolina Baptist Convention from 1970 to 1982; and Baptist Howard G. McClain (1919–2003), executive minister of the Christian Action Council of South Carolina from 1950 to 1985, all southern-born. Lauren Brubaker, interview by author, Mitchell-ville, MD, 14 August 2004. From 1995 to 2001 Anderson served as presiding bishop of the Evangelical Lutheran Church in America, formed in 1988 from the merger of the Lutheran Church in America, the American Lutheran Church, and the Association of Evangelical Lutheran Churches, with a combined membership of over five million people. ELCA online.

87. Dickinson, *Roses and Thorns*, 205; James Thomas, "Remembering Bishop Will Herzfeld," *Cresset* 74, no. 3 (2001): 24–27.

88. Faith Lutheran Church School, n.p., n.d.; Christopher Drews, *Half a Century of Lutheranism among Our Colored People* (St. Louis: Concord Publishing House, 1927), 109.

89. Ziehr, *Struggle for Unity*, 199–200.

90. James C. Burkee, *Power, Politics, and the Missouri Synod: A Conflict That Changed American Christianity* (Minneapolis: Fortress Press, 2011), 57–67, 172–176; Lutheran Forum 18 (Spring 2011): 19; Voigt, letter to author.

91. Nancy T. Ammerman, "The Civil Rights Movement and the Clergy in a Southern Community," *Sociological Analysis* 41, no. 4 (1981): 339–350.

92. The NCC began as the Federal Council of Churches in 1908, and expanded through merger with several other ecumenical organizations to become the National Council of Churches in 1950. The NCC has lost much power and influence. See Jacob Lupfer, "The Rise and Fall and Rise of the National Council of Churches," *Commentary*, www.religious news.com/2014/09/26.

93. Mark Newman, *Divine Agitators: The Delta Ministry and Civil Rights in Mississippi* (Athens: University of Georgia Press, 2004), 24.

94. Ibid., 29, 43.

95. Ibid., 31, 109. Mt. Beulah was leased over the objections of the local Disciples' churches. See also "The Delta Ministry: A Project of the National Council of Churches in Mississippi," *Newsletter*, Greenville, MI, 2, no. 2 (October 1965): 1–8, online. See also Findlay, *Church People*, 151.

96. Newman, *Divine Agitators*, 14–16, 32, 111, 120.

97. Ibid., 113, 120–121, 219–220; Findlay, *Church People*, 153–155.

98. "Delta Ministry," 6. As bishop coadjutor of Mississippi, Allin supported Duncan Montgomery Gray as he was being harassed by segregationists. As organizer of the Committee of Concern in Mississippi, Allin raised funds to rebuild fifty-four bombed-out churches in Mississippi in 1964 and 1965. See chapters 1 and 7; Alvis, "Racial Turmoil," 85–86.

99. Newman, *Divine Agitators*, 175–176, xii, 220–221.

100. Harvey, *Freedom's Coming*, 210; Crespino, *In Search of Another Country*, 155. For more violence against the Delta Ministry, see Findlay, *Church People*, 141; Lupfer, "Rise and Fall."

101. Findlay, *Church People*, 23–27; Will D. Campbell, *Forty Acres and a Goat: A Memoir* (Atlanta: Peachtree Publishers, 1986), 5, 47–48.

102. Findlay, *Church People*, 26; Merrill M. Hawkins Jr., *Will Campbell, Radical Prophet of the South* (Macon, GA: Mercer University Press, 1997), 48–51; Edmund Willingham, "Council of Churches Director Quitting," *Nashville Tennessean*, 16 April 1963, n.p., Special Collections, Nashville Room, Nashville (TN) Public Library; Campbell, interview, 18 August 1995. For essays by the Committee of Southern Churchmen, see Will D. Campbell and James Y. Holloway, eds., *The Failure and the Hope: Essays of Southern Churchmen* (Grand Rapid, MI: Eerdmans, 1972); Will D. Campbell and James Y. Holloway, eds., *Callings!* Deus Books Series (New York: Paulist Press, 1974).

103. Will Campbell, interview by author, tape recording, Mt. Juliet, TN, 20 March 2001.

104. Ibid.; Findlay, *Church People*, 26.

105. Campbell, interview by Caudill, 70.

106. Campbell, interview by Caudill, 70; Campbell, interview, 18 August 1995; Campbell quoted in *God's Will*, documentary produced at the University of Alabama, 2000.

107. Newman, *Divine Agitators*, 21.

108. Harvey, *Freedom's Coming*, 210; Crespino, *In Search of Another Country*, 155. For more violence against the Delta Ministry, see Findlay, *Church People*, 141.

109. U.S. Religious Landscape Survey, Pew Research Center Religion and Public Life, Washington, DC, 2014, http://religions.pewforum.org. At the thirtieth commemorative celebration of the Selma to Montgomery march, there were a sizable number of Americans marching with their banner from the Atlanta Buddhist Association.

110. Brian Steensland and Philip Goff, *The New Evangelical Social Engagement* (New York: Oxford University Press, 2014) 8, 273; Sparks, *Religion in Mississippi*, 267–268; Stephen E. Berk, *A Time to Heal: John Perkins, Community Development and Racial Reconciliation* (Grand Rapids, MI: Baker Books), 141–143. Sparks and Berk narrate many details in Perkins's life.

111. Steensland and Goff, *New Evangelical*, 269; Lyn Cryderman, "Do the Hard Thing," *Christianity Today* 34, no. 6 (April 1990): 12; Larry Stammer, "Era of Racial Separation Ending for Pentecostal Religion," *Los Angeles Times*, 17 October 1994, 1 (the article includes the Cox quotation); Don Argue, "Where Are We Today? Where Are We Going?," public apology before an interracial group commemorating the thirtieth anniversary of the assassination of Martin Luther King Jr., *Commemorative Journal*, Pilgrimage to Memphis Committee, Memphis, TN, 3–5 April 1998, 84, in author's possession; Scott Thumma, "Racial Diversity Increasing in U.S. Congregations," *HuffPost, Religion*, 24 May 2013, http://www.huffingtonpost.com/scott-thumma-phd/racial-diversity-increasing-in-us-congregations.

112. "What the Pew Data Tells Us," *Christian Century* 132, no. 12 (10 June 2015): 7.

Chapter 8. Conclusion

1. A native of Georgia, Wall had earned a degree from Emory University in journalism in 1949 and went north to attend graduate school at the University of Chicago Divinity School. Focusing on pastoral care, he intended to return south to teach in that area, but about halfway through his academic program, he took a job at the United Methodist magazine as an associate editor and later became managing editor and then editor of a second Methodist magazine, the *Christian Advocate*. He combined journalism with theology and ended up getting two master's degrees in religion. In 1972 he became editor and publisher of the *Christian Century* in Chicago, where he remained until his retirement in 1999. From 1999 to 2008 he served as senior contributing editor. After 2008 he became one of the contributing editors. James M. Wall, letter to author, online, 20 July 2012.

2. Finlator, interview, 12 May 1999. For more about Finlator's forced retirement, see Bryan, *Dissenter in the Baptist Southland*, 49, 119; Ramsey, interview, 10 March 1999.

3. Rachel and Raymond Davis, interview; Davis, "Writing About My Life," 1; S. Andrew Turnipseed Sr. interview by author, telephone, 5 July 1995.

4. McNeill, *God Wills Us Free*, 1; J. Herbert Gilmore, *They Chose to Live: The Racial Agony of an American Church* (Grand Rapids, MI: Eerdmans, 1971), 16; Holmes, *Ashes for Breakfast*, 10; Gilbert Schroerlucke, *I Did What I Could: A Memoir* (Louisville, KY: Book Locker, 2009), 289. Angela Davis was protesting the unfair treatment of jailed African American minister Rev. Ben Chavis of North Carolina, but she was an avowed Communist. See chapters 5 and 7.

5. Chappell, *Stone of Hope*, 88, 76, 99, 72, 133, 116.

6. "A Brief Questionnaire," March–April 2003, 268–269. See Lechtreck, "Southern White Ministers," Appendix B, 268–269. Exegesis on Amos 5:24 is taken from Rev. Dale Paul's sermon, "Back to Amos, God's Warning to His Chosen People, Then to Us Who Feel Chosen Now," Stamford (CT) Church of Christ, 20 February 2016, in author's possession; Ogden, *My Father Said Yes*, 56. The verse from Amos 5:24 was also beloved by Martin Luther King Jr.

7. Harvey, *Freedom's Coming*, 212; Gray, interview, 21 July 2007; Ogden, interview; James H. Smylie, interview by author, tape recording, Richmond, VA, 31 March 1998; Moose, interview; Rachel and Raymond Davis, interview; King, interview, 15 November 2004; Butts, interview, 10 November 1999; Campbell, interview, 18 August 1995.

8. Roy S. Hulan, "When Men Are at Odds," *The Christian* 22 September 1963, 1209; Edward Huffman (brother-in-law of Roy Hulan), interview by author, tape recording, Shelbyville, TN, 20 May 2001; Sanderson, interview; Lee, *Cotton Patch Evidence*, 6–8; also in Florence Jordan, interview by Rockwell.

9. Schroerlucke, interview; Spears, *One in the Spirit*, 12–13. In addition to owning a draying business, Buchanan was sexton at the Methodist church. He was proud of his son Essie, who won a scholarship to college.

10. Information about the colleges attended by the ministers has been gathered during interviews and from memoirs. See Lechtreck, "Southern White Ministers," Tables 2.1–2.7, 264–266; Nancy Tatom Ammerman, "The Civil Rights Movement and the Clergy in a Southern Community," *Sociological Analysis* 41, no. 4 (1981): 344, 348–349.

11. "Absolved by DNA," *Presbyterians Today*, March 2001, 20–22; Ellwanger, interview, 29 December 2004.

12. Whiting, interview.

13. Rice quoted in David B. Calhoun, *The Glory of the Lord Risen Upon It: First Presbyterian Church, Columbia, South Carolina, 1795–1995* (Columbia, SC: R. L. Bryan, 1994), 260–261; Seymour, *"Whites Only,"* 1–2; McRae, interview, 14 May 1999.

14. Sanderson, interview; Ramsey, interview, 10 March 1999; McNeill, *God Wills Us Free*, 85.

15. King, "Growing Up in Mississippi," 378, 380.

16. Gray, interview, 16 December 2004; see also Donald Cunnigen, "Working for Racial Integration: The Civil Rights Activism of Duncan Montgomery Gray," *Anglican and Episcopal History* 67, no. 41 (December 1998): 484–486.

17. Information about Southwestern Baptist Seminary in Edward Miller, "Texas," in *Encyclopedia of Religion in the South*, ed. Samuel S. Hill (Macon, GA: Mercer University Press, 1984), 766; Ramsey, interview, 10 March 1999.

18. Ramsey, interview, 10 March 1999. When John D. Rockefeller, also a Baptist, built Riverside Church in New York City in 1930, he requested that Fosdick be the pastor.

19. "A Brief Questionnaire, Part II," in Lechtreck, "Southern White Ministers," 270, answers in author's possession.

20. William G. McAtee, *Transformed: A White Mississippi Pastor's Journey into Civil Rights and Beyond* (Jackson: University Press of Mississippi, 2011), x, 63, 9, 18.

21. Ibid., 64–67.

22. Ibid., 64–67, 82, 89, 99.

23. Ibid. 96–98, 110–111. Dickson was one of the twenty-eight young Methodist ministers who signed the "Born of Conviction Statement" in support of public school integration in 1963. He was not dismissed from his pulpit as were most of the young ministers. Neither were Dickson and McAtee dismissed from their pulpits for writing their letters.

24. Ibid., 118, 152.

25. Ibid., 152, 164, 207–208. Grupper said they were never tried again.

26. Ibid., 209–211, 214–215.

27. Ibid., 129, 196, 268, 260.

28. King quoted in Harvey, *Freedom's Coming*, 216.

29. The verse "God has made of one blood all peoples of the earth" is from Acts 17:26 KJV. J. Claude Evans, "As the Twig Is Bent, So Will the Tree Grow," sermon delivered at Washington Street Methodist Church, 21 July 1996, audiotape in author's possession. It may be that vestiges of bitterness remained among people in the congregation because Washington Street Methodist Church (WSMC) was burned to the ground by Sherman's troops during the Civil War. According to Evans, "The troops were looking for First Baptist Church, the site of the original secession, and were directed to WSMC by [First Baptist's] janitor. The pastor of WSMC traveled throughout the South telling the story and soliciting funds to build a new church." Evans, "As the Twig Is Bent."

30. The presentation attended by Garrison was part of a program of the West Memphis Lions Club, of which Rev. Moose was president. At the time of his statement, Garrison was managing an Arkansas State University satellite center in West Memphis. He also served as a reserve officer in the Arkansas Army National Guard and as vice president of the Lions Club. Moose, interview; Joel Garrison, interview by author, West Memphis, AR, 9 March 1999; military leadershipcircle.com; Joel Garrison, letters to author, 25 April 2012, 19 October 2017.

31. J. Randolph Taylor, interview; Sanderson, interview; Ellwanger, interview, 20 December 2004.

32. "892 Active Hate Groups in U.S.," Publication of SPLC Southern Poverty Law Center, Montgomery, AL, 15 March 2016.

33. Sabrina Tavernise and Robert Gebeloff, "Many U.S. Blacks Moving to the South, Reversing Trend," *New York Times*, 25 March 2011, A1; Vern E. Smith and Daniel Pedersen, "South toward Home: Facing Long Odds and Painful History, Blacks Are at Last Moving Back to the Old Confederacy," *Newsweek*, 14 July 1997, 36–37; also http://www.usatoday.com/story//news/nation/2015/02/02/ migration:reversal; B. Clark, "Why Are Blacks Returning to the South?" *Melanoid Nation*, 13 November 2014, http://melanoidnation.org/why-are-blacks-returning-to-the-south.

34. Smith and Pedersen, "South toward Home," 37; McAtee, *Transformed*, 260–261; Frank, letter to author, 22 August 2015. The quotation "Everything has changed, but nothing has changed" was expressed by activist Luis Overbea, "Rosa Parks Took Her Stand for Civil Rights—By Sitting Down," *Christian Science Monitor*, 29 November 1985 1, 56, in Leon F. Litwack, "'Fight the Power!' The Legacy of the Civil Rights Movement," *Journal of Southern History* 75, no. 3 (February 2009): 28; Clinton Hubbard Jr., interview by author, telephone, 1 March 2016.

35. Butts, interview, 10 November 1999.

36. Chappell, *Stone of Hope*, 180.

BIBLIOGRAPHY

Manuscript Collections

Marion A. Boggs Papers. Presbyterian Historical Society, Montreat, NC.
Will Campbell Papers. McCain Library and Archives, University of Southern Mississippi, Hattiesburg.
Civil Rights and Methodists Papers. Mississippi Department of Archives and History, Jackson.
Colbert S. Cartwright Papers. Disciples of Christ Historical Society, Nashville, TN.
Colbert S. Cartwright Scrapbooks, University of Arkansas, Fayetteville.
John Ehle Papers. Manuscripts Department, Wilson Library, University of North Carolina, Chapel Hill.
Episcopal Society for Cultural and Racial Unity (ESCRU) Papers. Archives of the Episcopal Church, Austin, TX.
W. W. Finlator Papers. Wisconsin Historical Society, Madison.
Roy S. Hulan Papers. Disciples of Christ Historical Society, Nashville, TN.
Interreligious Foundation for Community Organization Records 1966–1984. Schomburg Center for Research in Black Culture, Manuscripts, Archives, and Rare Books, New York City Public Library.
Rhett Jackson Papers. South Caroliniana Library, Columbia.
John Morris Papers. South Caroliniana Library, Columbia.
North Carolina Collection. Clipping File. University of North Carolina Library, Chapel Hill.
Robert E. Seymour Papers. Southern Historical Collection, Manuscripts Department, Wilson Library, University of North Carolina Library, Chapel Hill.
South Carolina Council on Human Relations Papers. South Caroliniana Library, Columbia.
Southern Patriot Collection. Beinecke Rare Book and Manuscript Collection, Yale University, New Haven, CT.
Southern Regional Council Papers. Auburn Research Library, Atlanta.

Primary Sources

Bates, Daisy. *The Long Shadow of Little Rock: A Memoir.* Fayetteville: University of Arkansas Press, 1986.
Blossom, Virgil. *It Has Happened Here.* New York: Harper & Brothers, 1959.
Book of Church Order. Louisville, KY: Westminster John Knox, 1999.
Book of Discipline of the United Methodist Church 2000. Nashville, TN: United Methodist Publishing House, 2000.
Bulletin of Central Presbyterian Church, Atlanta. "Churches in Crisis." March 1969. Southern Regional Council Papers, Auburn Research Library, Atlanta.

Calhoun, Malcolm P. *With Staff in Hand.* Asheville, NC: St. Andrews College Press, 1996.

Campbell, Will D. *Brother to a Dragonfly.* New York: Continuum, 1994.

Campbell, Will D. *Soul among Lions: Musings of a Bootleg Preacher.* Louisville, KY: Westminster John Knox, 1999.

Cousins, Ralph E., Joseph R. Horn III, Larry A. Jackson, John S. Lyles, and John B. Morris, comps. *South Carolinians Speak: A Moderate Approach to Race Relations.* Self-published, 1957.

Cunningham, W. J. *Agony at Galloway: One Church's Struggle with Social Change.* Jackson: University Press of Mississippi, 1980.

Drews, Christopher. *Half a Century of Lutheranism among Our Colored People.* St. Louis: Concordia Publishing House, 1927.

Evans, Claude. "As the Twig Is Bent, So Will the Tree Grow." Sermon delivered at Washington Street Methodist Church, 21 July 1996, audiotape in author's possession.

Finlator, W. W. "Four Areas of Concern." *Baptist Biblical Recorder,* 7 November 1959, 13.

First Christian Church, Jackson, Mississippi. Bulletin, 5 February 1956. Roy S. Hulan Papers, box 1, Disciples of Christ Historical Society, Nashville, TN.

Forman, James. *The Making of Black Revolutionaries.* New York: Macmillan, 1972. Reprint, with a new preface by Forman and a new foreword by Julian Bond. Seattle: University of Washington Press, 1997.

Gilmore, J. Herbert, Jr. *They Chose to Live: The Racial Agony of an American Church.* Grand Rapids, MI: Eerdmans, 1972.

Gilmore, J. Herbert, Jr. *When Love Prevails.* Grand Rapids, MI: Eerdmans, 1970.

Graetz, Robert S. *A White Preacher's Memoir: The Montgomery Bus Boycott.* Montgomery, AL: Black Belt, 1991.

Gray, Duncan Montgomery. "In Defense of the Steeple." *Katallagete* 2, no. 1 (1968): 141–145. Beinecke Rare Book and Manuscript Collection, Yale University.

Holmes, Thomas J., with Gainer E. Bryan Jr. *Ashes for Breakfast.* Valley Forge, PA: Judson, 1969.

Hulan, Roy S. "When Men Are at Odds." *The Christian,* 22 September 1963, 1209. Roy S. Hulan Papers, box 1, Disciples of Christ Historical Society, Nashville, TN.

King, Martin Luther, Jr. *Stride toward Freedom.* New York: Harper & Row, 1958.

King, Martin Luther, Jr. *Why We Can't Wait.* New York: Signet Books, 1964.

Malcolm X, and Alex Haley. *The Autobiography of Malcolm X.* 1964. Reprint, New York: Ballantine, 1999.

Mars, Florence. *Witness in Philadelphia.* Baton Rouge: Louisiana State University Press, 1977.

McAtee, William G. *Transformed: A White Mississippi Pastor's Journey into Civil Rights and Beyond.* Jackson: University Press of Mississippi, 2011.

McNeill, Robert. *God Wills Us Free: The Ordeal of a Southern Minister.* New York: Hill and Wang, 1965.

Moody, Anne. *Coming of Age in Mississippi.* New York: Doubleday, 1968. Reprint. New York: Delta Trade, 2004.

Peck, James. *Freedom Ride.* New York: Simon & Schuster, 1962.

Rutland, John. *Mary and Me: Telling the Story of Prevenient Grace.* Pensacola, FL: Ardara House, 1996.

Schroerlucke, Gilbert. *I Did What I Could: A Memoir.* Louisville, KY: Book Locker, 2009.

Selah, W. B. *Puddles and Sunsets: Sermons of Dr. W. B. Selah.* Huntsville, AL: Monte Sano United Methodist Church, 1990.

Sellers, Cleveland, with Robert Terrell. *The River of No Return: The Autobiography of a Black Militant and the Life and Death of SNCC.* New York: William Morrow, 1973. Reprint. Jackson: University Press of Mississippi, 1990.

Seymour, Robert. *"Whites Only": A Pastor's Retrospective on Signs of the New South.* Valley Forge, PA: Judson, 1991.

Shriver, Donald W., comp. *The Unsilent South: Prophetic Preaching in Racial Crisis*. Richmond, VA: John Knox, 1965.

Silverstein, Evan. "Absolved by DNA." *Presbyterians Today*, March 2001, 20–22.

South Carolina Annual Baptist Convention. Bulletin. 1989.

Spears, R. Wright. *Journey toward Unity: The Christian Action Council in South Carolina, 1933–1983*. Columbia, SC: Crowson-Stone, 1983.

Taylor, J. Randolph. "Letter from Washington." *Presbyterian Outlook* 145, no. 31 (September 1963): 5–6. Presbyterian Historical Society, Montreat, NC.

Ture, Kwame (Stokely Carmichael), and Charles V. Hamilton. *Black Power: The Politics of Liberation*. 1967. Reprint, with an afterword by the authors, New York: Vintage, 1992.

Upchurch, Thomas Adams. *A White Minority in Post-Civil-Rights Mississippi*. Lanham, MD: Hamilton Books, University Press of America, 2005.

Secondary Sources

Ahlstrom, Sydney E. *A Religious History of the American People*. New Haven, CT: Yale University Press, 1972.

Alvis, Joel L., Jr. *Religion and Race: Southern Presbyterians, 1946–1983*. Tuscaloosa: University of Alabama Press, 1994.

Anderson, Margaret. *The Children of the South*. New York: Dell, 1958.

Bartley, Numan V. *The Rise of Massive Resistance: Race and Politics in the South during the 1950s*. 1969. Reprint, with a new preface by the author. Baton Rouge: Louisiana State University Press, 1999.

Bass, S. Jonathan. *Blessed Are the Peacemakers*. Baton Rouge: Louisiana State University Press, 2001.

Bell, Derrick. *Silent Covenants: Brown v. Board of Education, the Unfulfilled Hopes for Racial Reform*. New York: Oxford University Press, 2004.

Beifuss, Joan Turner. *At the River I Stand: Memphis, the 1968 Strike and Martin Luther King*. Memphis, TN: St. Luke's, 1990.

Bond, Julian, ed. *Free at Last: A History of the Civil Rights Struggle and Those Who Died in the Struggle*. Montgomery, AL.: A Project of the Southern Poverty Law Center, 1989.

Braden, Anne. *The Wall Between*. 1958. Reprint, with a foreword by Julian Bond and an epilogue by the author, Knoxville: University of Tennessee Press, 1999.

Branch, Taylor. *Pillar of Fire: America in the King Years, 1963–65*. New York: Simon & Schuster, 1998.

Branch, Taylor. *At Canaan's Edge: America in the King Years, 1965–68*. New York: Simon & Schuster, 2006.

Bryan, G. McLeod. *Dissenter in the Baptist Southland: Fifty Years in the Career of William Wallace Finlator*. Macon, GA: Mercer University Press, 1985.

Bryan, G. McLeod. *These Few Also Paid a Price*. Macon, GA: Mercer University Press, 2001.

Burkee, James C. *Power, Politics, and the Missouri Synod: A Conflict That Changed American Christianity*. Minneapolis: Fortress Press, 2011.

Butler, Jon, Grant Wacker, and Randall Balmer. *Religion in American Life: A Short History*. New York: Oxford University Press, 2000.

Calhoun, David B. *The Glory of the Lord Risen Upon It: First Presbyterian Church: Columbia, South Carolina, 1795–1995*. Columbia, SC: R. L. Bryan, 1994.

Campbell, Ernest Q., and Thomas F. Pettigrew. *Christians in Racial Crisis: A Survey of Little Rock's Ministry*. Washington, DC: Public Affairs, 1959.

Campbell, Will D. *And Also with You: Duncan Gray and the American Dilemma*. Franklin, TN: Providence House, 1997.

Carey, John J. *Carlyle Marney: A Pilgrim's Progress*. Macon, GA: Mercer University Press, 1980.

Carson, Clayborne, and Peter Holloran, eds. *A Knock at Midnight: Inspiration from the Great Sermons of Reverend Martin Luther King, Jr*. New York: Warner Books, 1998.

Carson, Clayborne, David J. Garrow, Gerald Gill, Vincent Harding, and Darlene Clark Hine, eds. *The Eyes on the Prize Civil Rights Reader*. 1987. Reprint, New York: Penguin, 1991.

Carter, Dan T. *The Politics of Rage: George Wallace, the Origins of the New Conservatism, and the Transformation of American Politics*. Baton Rouge: Louisiana State University Press, 1996.

Carter, Hugh, as told to Frances Spatz Leighton. *Cousin Beedie and Cousin Hot: My Life with the Carter Family of Plains, Georgia*. Englewood Cliffs, NJ: Prentice-Hall, 1978.

Chalk, John Allen. *Three American Revolutions*. New York: Carlton Press, 1970.

Chappell, David L. *A Stone of Hope: Prophetic Religion and the Death of Jim Crow*. Chapel Hill: University of North Carolina Press, 2004.

Collins, Donald E. *When the Church Bell Rang Racist*. Macon, GA: Mercer University Press, 1998.

Connelly, Thomas L. *Will Campbell and the Soul of the South*. New York: Continuum, 1982.

Counts, Will. *A Life Is More Than a Moment: The Desegregation of Little Rock's Central High*. Bloomington: Indiana University Press, 1999.

Crespino, Joseph. *In Search of Another Country*. Princeton, NJ: Princeton University Press, 2007.

Daniel, Pete. *Lost Revolutions: The South in the 1950s*. Chapel Hill: University of North Carolina Press, 2000.

Dent, Tom. *Southern Journey: A Return to the Civil Rights Movement*. Athens: University of Georgia Press, 2001.

Dickinson, Richard C. *Roses and Thorns: The Centennial Edition of Black Lutheran Mission and Ministry in the Lutheran Church–Missouri Synod*. St. Louis: Concordia, 1977.

Doyle, William. *An American Insurrection: The Battle of Oxford, Mississippi, 1962*. New York: Doubleday, 2001.

Du Bois, W. E. B. *The Souls of Black Folk*. 1903. Reprint, with an introduction by Randall Kenan. New York: Penguin, 1995.

Dupont, Carolyn Renée. *Mississippi Praying: Southern White Evangelicals and the Civil Rights Movement, 1945–1975*. New York: New York University Press, 2013.

Eagles, Charles W. *Outside Agitator: Jon Daniels and the Civil Rights Movement in Alabama*. Chapel Hill: University of North Carolina Press, 1993.

Eagles, Charles W. *The Price of Defiance: James Meredith and the Integration of Ole Miss*. Chapel Hill: University of North Carolina Press, 2009.

Edgar, Walter. *South Carolina: A History*. Columbia: University of South Carolina Press, 1998.

Egerton, John. *Speak Now Against the Day: The Generation Before the Civil Rights Movement in the South*. Chapel Hill: University of North Carolina Press, 1995.

Ehle, John. *The Free Men*. New York: Harper & Row, 1965.

Fager, Charles E. *Selma 1965: The March That Changed the South*. New York: Scribner's, 1974.

Fairclough, Adam. *To Redeem the Soul of America: The Southern Christian Leadership Conference and Martin Luther King, Jr*. Athens: University of Georgia Press, 1987.

Findlay, James F., Jr. *Church People in the Struggle*. New York: Oxford, 1993.

Fletcher, Jesse C. *The Southern Baptist Convention: The Sesquicentennial History*. Nashville, TN: Broadman & Holman, 1994.

Flynt, Wayne. *Alabama Baptists in the Heart of Dixie*. Tuscaloosa: University of Alabama Press, 1998.

Franklin, John Hope. *From Slavery to Freedom: A History of Negro Americans*. 3rd ed. New York: Alfred A. Knopf, 1967.

Friedland, Michael B. *Lift Your Voice Like a Trumpet: White Clergy and the Civil Rights and Antiwar Movements, 1954–1973*. Chapel Hill: University of North Carolina Press, 1998.

Galchutt, Kathryn M. *Andrew Schulze: Lutherans and Race in the Civil Rights Era*. Macon, GA: Mercer University Press, 2005.

Garrow, David J. *Bearing the Cross: Martin Luther King, Jr., and the Southern Christian Leadership Conference*. New York: William Morrow, 1986.

Gaustad, Edwin S. *A Documentary History of Religion in America to the Civil War*. Grand Rapids, MI: Eerdmans, 1982.

Glock, Charles Y., Benjamin B. Ringer, and Earl R. Babbie, *To Comfort and to Challenge: A Dilemma of the Contemporary Church*. Berkeley: University of California Press, 1967.

Gray, Fred. *Bus Ride to Justice: Changing the System by the System*. Montgomery, AL: Black Belt, 1995.

Halberstam, David. *The Children*. New York: Random House, 1998.

Hampton, Henry, and Steve Fayer. *Voices of Freedom: An Oral History of the Civil Rights Movement from the 1950s through the 1980s*. New York: Bantam, 1991.

Harvey, Paul. *Freedom's Coming: Religious Culture and the Shaping of the South from the Civil War through the Civil Rights Era*. Chapel Hill: University of North Carolina Press, 2005.

Hawkins, Merrill M., Jr. *Will Campbell, Radical Prophet of the South*. Macon, GA: Mercer University Press, 1997.

Hill, Samuel S., Jr. *Religion and the Solid South*. Nashville, TN: Abingdon, 1972.

Hughes, Richard T. *Reviving the Ancient Faith: The Story of Churches of Christ in America*. Grand Rapids, MI: Eerdmans, 1996.

Ingram, T. Robert, ed. *Essays of Segregation*. Houston: St. Thomas Press, 1960.

Jacoway, Elizabeth, and C. Fred Williams. *Understanding the Little Rock Crisis*. Fayetteville: University of Arkansas Press, 1999.

Johnson, Jeff G. *Black Christians: The Untold Lutheran Story*. St. Louis: Concordia, 1991.

Johnston, Susan Pierce. *One Editor's Stand*. Columbia, SC: Trustees of the *South Carolina Methodist Advocate* and Friends of Rev. McKay Brabham, 1992.

Kesselus, Kenneth. *John E. Hines: Granite on Fire*. Austin, TX: Episcopal Theological Seminary of the Southwest, 1995.

Lee, Dallas. *The Cotton Patch Evidence: The Story of Clarence Jordan and the Koinonia Farm Experiment*. 1971. Reprint, Americus, GA: Koinonia Publication, 2000.

Lewis, Harold T. *Yet with a Steady Beat: The African American Struggle for Recognition in the Episcopal Church*. Valley Forge, PA: Trinity International, 1996.

Logan, Rayford W., ed. *What the Negro Wants*. Chapel Hill: University of North Carolina Press, 1944. Reprint, New York: Agathon, 1969.

Longenecker, Stephen. *Selma's Peacemaker: Ralph Smeltzer and Civil Rights Mediation*. Philadelphia: Temple University Press, 1987.

Marable, Manning. *Race, Reform, and Rebellion: The Second Reconstruction in Black America, 1945–1990*. 2nd ed. Jackson: University Press of Mississippi, 1991.

Marsh, Charles. *God's Long Summer: Stories of Faith and Civil Rights*. Princeton, NJ: Princeton University Press, 1997.

McGill, Ralph. *The South and the Southerner*. Boston: Little, Brown, 1963.

Murphy, Sara Alderman. *Breaking the Silence: Little Rock's Women's Emergency Committee to Open Our Schools, 1958–1963*. Edited by Patrick C. Murphy III. Fayetteville: University of Arkansas Press, 1997.

Murray, Peter C. *Methodists and the Crucible of Race*. Columbia: University of Missouri Press, 2004.

Newman, Mark. *Divine Agitators: The Delta Ministry and Civil Rights in Mississippi*. Athens: University of Georgia Press, 2004.

Newman, Mark. *Getting Right with God: Southern Baptists and Desegregation: 1945–1995*. Tuscaloosa: University of Alabama Press, 2001.

Norrell, Robert J. *Reaping the Whirlwind: The Civil Rights Movement in Tuskegee*. New York: Vintage, 1986.

Oates, Stephen B. *Let the Trumpet Sound: The Life of Martin Luther King, Jr*. New York: Harper & Row, 1982.

Ogden, Dunbar H., III. *My Father Said Yes: A White Pastor in Little Rock School Integration*. Nashville, TN: Vanderbilt University Press, 2008.

Polsgrove, Carol. *Divided Minds: Intellectuals and the Civil Rights Movement*. New York: Norton, 2001.

Pryor, Mark. *Faith, Grace, and Heresy: The Biography of Rev. Charles M. Jones*. New York: Writer's Showcase, 2002.

Quint, Howard. *Profile in Black and White: A Frank Portrait of South Carolina*. Washington, DC: Public Affairs Press, 1958.

Reiff, Joseph T. *Born of Conviction: White Methodists and Mississippi's Closed Society*. New York: Oxford University Press, 2015.

Schneider, William J. *American Martyr: The Jon Daniels Story*. Harrisburg, PA: Morehouse 1992.

Shattuck, Gardiner H., Jr. *Episcopalians and Race*. Lexington: University Press of Kentucky, 2000.

Shuler, Jack. *Blood and Bone: Truth and Reconciliation in a Southern Town*. Columbia: University of South Carolina Press, 2012.

Silver, James W. *Mississippi: The Closed Society*. New York: Harcourt, Brace and World, 1963.

Smylie, James H. *A Brief History of the Presbyterians*. Louisville, KY: Geneva, 1996.

Sparks, Randy J. *Religion in Mississippi*. Jackson: University Press of Mississippi for the Mississippi Historical Society, 2001.

Spears, R. Wright. *One in the Spirit: Ministry for Change in South Carolina*. Columbia, SC: R. L. Bryan, 1997.

Steensland, Brian, and Philip Goff. *The New Evangelical Social Engagement*. New York: Oxford University Press, 2014.

Stricklin, David. *A Genealogy of Dissent: Southern Baptist Protest in the Twentieth Century*. Louisville: University Press of Kentucky, 1999.

Sweet, William Warren. *Methodism in American History*. New York: Pierce and Washabaugh, 1933. Reprint, New York: Abingdon Press, 1953.

Thompson, Ernest Trice. *Presbyterians in the South*. Vol. 1. Richmond, VA: John Knox, 1963.

Thompson, Ernest Trice. *Presbyterians in the South*. Vol. 3. Richmond, VA: John Knox,1973.

Thompson, Ernest Trice. *The Spirituality of the Church: A Distinctive Doctrine of the Presbyterian Church in the United States*. Richmond, VA: John Knox, 1961.

Torbet, Robert G. *A History of the Baptists*. Valley Forge, PA: Judson, 1950.

Vaughan, Judith Bell. *A Quiet Little Civil Rights Project*. Blog.com, 2013.

Vernon, Walter N. *Methodism in Arkansas, 1816–1976*. Little Rock, AR: Joint Committee for the History of Arkansas Methodism, 1976.

Wexler, Sanford. *The Civil Rights Movement: An Eyewitness History*. New York: Facts on File, 1993.

Wilmore, Gayraud S., and James H. Cone, eds. *Black Theology: A Documentary History, 1966–1979*. New York: Orbis, 1979.

Wilson, Charles Reagan. *Baptized in Blood: The Religion of the Lost Cause, 1865–1920*. 1980. Reprint, with a new preface by the author, Athens: University of Georgia Press, 2009.

Wright, Gavin. *Sharing the Prize: The Economics of the Civil Rights Revolution in the American South*. Cambridge, MA: Harvard University Press, 2013.

Ziehr, Richard O. *The Struggle for Unity: A Personal Look at the Integration of Lutheran Churches in the South*. Milton, FL: CJH Enterprises, 1999.

Articles and Book Chapters

Adamson, June N. "Few Black Voices Heard: The Black Community and the Desegregation Crisis in Clinton, Tennessee, 1956." *Tennessee History Quarterly* 53, no. 1 (Spring 1994): 30–41.

Alvis, Joel, Jr. "Racial Turmoil and Religious Reaction: The Right Reverend John M. Allin." *Historical Magazine of the Protestant Episcopal Church*, no. 1 (March 1984): 83–96.

Ammerman, Nancy T. "The Civil Rights Movement and the Clergy in a Southern Community." *Sociological Analysis* 41, no. 4 (1981): 330–350.

"Billy's Bountiful African Harvest." *Life*, 21 March 1960, 29–30.

"Binkley Baptist's Robert Seymour." *Chapel Hill Weekly*, 21 November 1960, n.p. North Carolina Collection, Clipping File, 1976–1989, UNC Library at Chapel Hill.

"Birmingham Pastor Leads 'Concerned White Citizens' in March in Selma." *The Vanguard, Lutheran Human Relations Association of America* 12, no. 2 (March–April 1965): 1, 4.

Boles, John B. "The Discovery of Southern Religious History." In *Interpreting Southern History: Historiographical Essays in Honor of Sanford W. Higginbotham*, ed. John B. Boles and Evelyn Thomas Nolen, 510–548. Baton Rouge: Louisiana State University Press, 1987.

Braden, Anne. "David Ogden: Victim of Hate." *Southern Patriot* 18, no. 9 (November 1960): 2. Beinecke Rare Book and Manuscript Collection, Yale University.

Braden, Anne. "Little Rock Climaxes Spiritual Journey." *Southern Patriot*, no. 7 (September 1959): 3. Beinecke Rare Book and Manuscript Collection, Yale University.

Brown, Michael D. "Despite School Sentiment, Harding's Leader Said 'No' to Integration." *Arkansas Times*, 6 June 2012.

Cartwright, Colbert S. "Lessons from Little Rock." *Christian Century* 74 (October 1957): 1193–1194.

Cartwright, Colbert S. "What Can Southern Ministers Do?" *Christian Century* 73 (December 1956): 1505–1507.

"Cathedral College of Washington National Cathedral." *Christian Century* (12 July 2005): 25.

Choate, J. E. "Marshall Keeble: An Uncommon Man." *20th Century Christian*, 30, no. 10 (July 1968): 49–50.

"Clinton Minister Lives His Faith." *Christian Century* (December 1956): 1470–1471.

Cryderman, Lyn. "Do the Hard Thing." *Christianity Today* 34, no. 6 (April 1990): 12.

Cunnigen, Donald. "Black Radicals vs. White Southern Liberals." *Southern Studies* 10 (Fall–Winter 2003): 95–106.

Cunnigen, Donald. "Working for Racial Integration: The Civil Rights Activism of Bishop Duncan Montgomery Gray of Mississippi." *Anglican and Episcopal History* 67, no. 4 (December 1998): 480–501.

Dees, James P. "Should Christians Support Integration?" In *Essays on Segregation*, ed. T. Robert Ingram, 35–51. Houston: St. Thomas Press, 1960.

Donahue, Don. "Prophets of a New Social Order: Presbyterians and the Fellowship of Southern Churchmen, 1934–1963." *American Presbyterians* 701 (Fall 1996): 209–221.

Egger, Henry T. "What Meaneth This: There Is No Difference." In *Essays on Segregation*, ed. T. Robert Ingram, 27–34. Houston: St. Thomas Press, 1960.

"Eight Hundred and Ninety-Two Active Hate Groups in U.S." Publication of SPLC Southern Poverty Law Center, Montgomery, AL, 15 March 2016.

Elliot, Debbie. "Nearly Six Decades Later, Integration Remains a Work in Progress." In *Code Switch, Frontiers of Race, Culture, and Ethnicity*, 13 January 2014, online.

Finley, Jeanne Torrence, and Richard B. Faris. "'Making More Real the Church Universal': Francis Pickens Miller. *Journal of Presbyterian History* 82, no. 1 (Spring 2004): 23.

Floyd, William Kirk. "Why I Could Not Be a Career Preacher." In *Voices of Concern*, ed. Robert Meyers, 155–176. St. Louis: Mission Messenger, 1966.

Garrow, David J. "Bridge to Freedom." In introduction to chapter 6, *Eyes on the Prize Civil Rights Reader*, ed. Clayborne Carson, David J. Garrow, Gerald Gill, Vincent Harding, and Darlene Clark Hine, 204–208. New York: Penguin, 1991.

Gordon, Arthur. "Intruder in the South." *Look* 21, no. 4 (19 February 1957): 27–31.

Graveley, William B. "Christian Methodist Episcopal Church." In *Encyclopedia of Religion in the South*, ed. Samuel S. Hill, 151–153. 1984. Reprint, Macon, GA: Mercer University Press, 1997.

Huff, A. V., Jr. "The Methodist Church." In *Encyclopedia of Religion in the South*, ed. Samuel S. Hill and Charles H. Lippy, with Charles Reagan Wilson, 496–499. Macon, GA: Mercer University Press, 2005.

Jacoway, Elizabeth. "Brown and the 'Road to Reunion.'" *Journal of Southern History* 70, no. 2 (May 2004): 303–308.

Johnson, Robert E. "Editorial Introduction." *American Baptist Quarterly* 21, no. 4 (December 2002).

King, Edwin. "Bacchanal at Woolworth's." In *Freedom Is a Constant Struggle*, ed. Susie Erenrich, 27–35. Montgomery, AL: Black Belt Press.

King, Edwin. "Christianity in Mississippi, Mourners in Prison." In *To Redeem a Nation: A History and Anthology of the Civil Rights Movement*, ed. Thomas R. West and James W. Moon, 135–145. St. James, NY: Brandywine, 1993.

King, Edwin. "Growing Up in Mississippi in a Time of Change." In *Mississippi Writers: Reflections of Childhood and Youth*. Vol. 2, *Nonfiction*, ed. Dorothy Abbott, 374–385. Jackson: University Press of Mississippi, 1986.

Kirk, John A. "Arkansas, the *Brown* decision, and the 1957 Little Rock School Crisis: A Local Perspective." In *Understanding the Little Rock Crisis*, ed. Elizabeth Jacoway and C. Fred Williams, 67–82. Fayetteville: University of Arkansas Press, 1999.

Lechtreck, Elaine Allen. "'We Are Demanding $500 Million for Reparations': The Black Manifesto, Mainline Religious Denominations and Black Economic Development." *Journal of African American History* 97, nos. 1–2 (Winter–Spring 2012): 39–71.

Lewis, Harold T. "Racial Concerns in the Episcopal Church since 1973." *Anglican and Episcopal History* 67, no. 4 (December 1998): 467–479.

Litwack, Leon F. "'Fight the Power!' The Legacy of the Civil Rights Movement." *Journal of Southern History* 75 53, no. 3 (February 2009): 3–28.

Manis, Andrew Scott. "'Dying from the Neck Up': Southern Baptist Resistance to the Civil Rights Movement." *Baptist History and Heritage* 34, no. 1 (Winter 1999): 33–48.

McConnell, Tandy. "Race, Religion and the Ideology of Cooperation: A Southern Baptist Church Responds to the *Brown* Decision." *Southern Studies: An Interdisciplinary Journal of the South* (Spring 1993): 19–38.

Miles, John. "Small Increments of Justice." In *Crisis of Conscience*, ed. James T. Clemons and Kelly L. Farr, 168–169. Little Rock, AR: Butler Center for Arkansas Studies, 2007.

Morrison, Chester. "Louisville, Kentucky: The City That Integrated without Strife." *Look* 27 (13 August 1963): 41–44.

Neely, Alan. "Denominationalism, Centralization, and Baptist Principles: Observations by a Somewhat Perplexed Baptist." *American Baptist Quarterly* 21, no. 4 (December 2002): 484–498.

Overbea, Luis. "Rosa Parks Took Her Stand for Civil Rights—By Sitting Down." *Christian Science Monitor*, 29 November 1985, 1, 56.

"Presbyterians US Take Part in Selma Negro Voter Rights Demonstrations." *Presbyterian Survey* 55, no. 5 (May 1965): 40.

Randolph, Asa Philip. "March on Washington Movement Presents Program for the Negro." In *What the Negro Wants*, ed. Rayford Logan, 144–155. Chapel Hill: University of North Carolina Press, 1944.

Reese, Fred, Jr. "Dilemma and Hope Seen in Church's Race Structure." *South Carolina Methodist Advocate*, 17 March 1966, 4–9.

Reiff, Joseph T. "Born of Conviction: White Methodist Witness to Mississippi's Closed Society." In *Courage to Bear Witness: Essays in Honor of Gene L. Davenport*, ed. L. Edward Phillips and Billy Vaughan, 124–142. Eugene, OR: Pickwick Publications.

Riesman, David. Foreword. In John Ehle, *The Free Men*, vii–xi. New York: Harper & Row, 1965.

Rooke, Leon. "On the Path of Father Parker." *North Carolina Anvil*, 25 August 1967, 758–760.

Smith, Vern E., and Daniel Pedersen. "South toward Home: Facing Long Odds and Painful History, Blacks Are at Last Moving Back to the Old Confederacy." *Newsweek*, 14 July 1997, 36–37.

"Southern Baptists Adopt Vigorous Denunciation of Jim Crow Practices." *Southern Patriot* 15, no. 6 (June 1957): 3.

Stammer, Larry. "Era of Racial Separation Ending for Pentecostal Religion." *Los Angeles Times*, 17 October 1994, 1.

Stokely, James, and Wilma Dykeman. "Courage in Action in Clinton, Tennessee." *Nation* 22 (December 1956): 532–533.

Stump, Roger W. "Spatial Patterns of Growth and Decline among the Disciples of Christ, 1890–1980." In *A Case Study of Mainstream Protestantism: The Disciples' Relation to American Culture, 1880–1989*, ed. D. Newell Williams, 445–468. Grand Rapids, MI: Eerdmans, 1991.

Thomas, George O. "African Methodist Episcopal Church." In *Encyclopedia of Religion in the South*, ed. Samuel S. Hill, 3–8. 1984. Reprint, Macon, GA: Mercer University Press, 1997.

Thomas, James. "Remembering Bishop Will Herzfeld." *The Cresset* 74, no. 3 (2001): 24–27.

Thrasher, Thomas R. "Jet Propelled Gradualism." In *On the Battle Lines*, ed. Malcolm Boyd, 94–101. New York: Morehouse-Barlow, 1964.

Turner, Paul W. "The Minister's View of the Ministry." *Search* (Summer 1972): 33–39.

"What the Pew Data Tells Us." *Christian Century* 132, no. 12 (10 June 2015): 7.

Williams, D. Newell. Preface and introduction to *A Case Study of Mainstream Protestantism: The Disciples' Relation to American Culture, 1880–1989*, ed. D. Newell Williams, ix–25. Grand Rapids, MI: Eerdmans, 1991.

Zeitz, Joshua. "Convention Crisis: How These Two Men Made the Problem the Democratic Party Is Still Facing." *American Heritage* (June/July) 2004: 60–69.

Newspapers

Abilene Christian University News, 22 November 1999, 1 February 2013.

Arkansas Gazette, 30 September 1957.

Arkansas Times, 6 June 2012.

Atlanta Constitution, 20 April 1947; 7, 12, 13, 28 September 1966.

Atlanta Daily World, 7, 8, 13 September 1966.

Atlanta Journal, 1–10 January 1961; 3 October 1963.

Baptist Press, 19 June 2012.

Biblical Recorder, Journal of the Baptist State Convention of North Carolina, 6 April 1963.

Charlotte Observer, 4 July 1967.

Clarion Ledger, 9–10 January 1963.

Daily Tar Heel (University of North Carolina at Chapel Hill), 24 September 1963; 2 October 1963.

General Assembly Daily News UPCUSA, 22 May 1969.

Jackson Daily News, 4 January 1963.

Los Angeles Times, 17 October 1994; 21 June 1995; 11 July 2012.

Louisville Courier-Journal Metro, 8 December 2000.

Marianna Courier Index, 27 July 1971.

Memphis Commercial Appeal, 29 March 1968.

Milwaukee Journal Sentinel, 17 January 2004.

Nashville Banner, 17 July 1957; 5 August 1967.

Nashville Tennessean, 27 November 1959.

New York Times, 18 May 1954; 1 June–25 September 1955; 5–17 December 1956; 4–13 February 1956; 1 March 1956; 4–5 September 1957; 3 September–2 December 1958; 21 January–19 February 1959; 4 December 1960; 29 June 1962; 7 July 1962; 1 October 1962; 14 January 1963; 7 April 1963; 29 May 1963; 8–23 June 1963; 29 July 1963; 1–17 August 1963; 29–31 August–1 September 1963; 11 September 1963; 8, 13 October 1963; 4, 18–19, November 1963; 25–30 March 1964; 19 May 1964; 21–24 June 1964; 20 July 1964; 22 February 1965; 7–29 March 1965; 3, 15 August 1965; 6–8, 30 May 1966; 25 June 1966; 5–11 August 1966; 8, 11 September 1966; 6 March 1967; 12 April–31 May 1967; 12, 21 June 1967; 15–18, 27 July 1967; 2–3 August 1967; 23–24 October 1967; 26 February–15 March 1968; 5–8 April 1968; 5 May 1969; 12 June 1969; 1–4 September 1969; 20 June 1999; 25 March 2011.

North Carolina Anvil, 25 August 1967.

North Carolina News and Observer, 19 August 2001.

Selma Times-Journal, 8 March 1998.

South Carolina Methodist Advocate, 4 February 1965; 18 May 1967; 25 May 1967.

Spartanburg Herald, 20 June 1977.

Unpublished Sources and Dissertations

Branch, Ellis Ray. "Born of Conviction: Racial Conflict and Change in Mississippi Methodism, 1945–1983." PhD diss., Mississippi State University, 1984.

Coleman, Louis, Jr. *The Struggle for Freedom Continues in Kentucky*. Louisville, KY: self-published, 1987. Mimeograph.

Cooney, David Scott. "A Consistent Witness of Conscience: Methodist Nonviolent Activists, 1940–1970." PhD diss., Iliff School of Theology and University of Denver, 2000. Abstract in *Dissertation Abstracts International* 61 (2000): 04A.

Corley, Robert Gaines. "The Quest for Racial Harmony, Race Relations in Birmingham, Alabama, 1947–1963." PhD diss., University of Virginia, 1979.

Davis, Raymond Earle, Jr., "Writing About My Life." Savannah, GA, 2001. Mimeograph.

Evans, Claude. "As the Twig Is Bent, So Will the Tree Grow," sermon, Columbia, SC, 21 July 1996, audiotape in author's possession.

Haney, Eleanor Humes. "A Study of Conscience as It Is Expressed in Race Relations." PhD diss., Yale University, 1965.

Hobbie, Peter Hairston. "E. T. Thompson: Profit for a Changing South." PhD diss., Union Theological Seminary of Virginia, 1987.

King, Edwin. "Birmingham Funerals." Galloway Methodist Church, Jackson, MS, 13 September 2004. Photocopy.

Lyon, Carter Dalton. "Lifting the Color Bar from the House of God: The 1963–1964 Church Visit Campaign to Challenge Church Sanctuaries in Jackson, Mississippi." PhD diss., University of Mississippi, 2010.

Morris, John. "ESCRU, The Episcopal Society for Cultural and Racial Unity: 1959–1967." Atlanta, 1990. Photocopy.

Schroerlucke, Gilbert. Last Will and Testament of Gilbert Schroerlucke to the Louisville Conference. Louisville, KY, April 1989. Photocopy.

Sellers, Ennis G. "Tuskegee, the Methodist Church, and School Integration." Mobile, AL, 1964. Mimeograph.

Stanfield, J. Edwin. "In Memphis: Mirror to America?" Atlanta, 1968. Reel 221, XVI:246, 5–6. Southern Regional Council Papers, Auburn Research Library, Atlanta.

Stanfield, J. Edwin. "In Memphis: More Than a Garbage Strike." Atlanta, 1968. Reel 221, XVI:243, 1–4. Southern Regional Council Papers, Auburn Research Library, Atlanta.

Stanfield, J. Edwin. "In Memphis: Tragedy Unaverted." Supplement to Special Report of 22 March 1968. Reel 221, XVI:245, 1–4, Southern Regional Council Papers, Auburn Research Library, Atlanta.

Webster, Charles A., Jr. "In Explanation of My Resignation." Clemson, SC, 31 March 1963. Photocopy.

Interviews

Anderson, H. George. Interview by author. Tape recording, New Haven, CT, 25 April 2004.

Blanchard, Dallas. Interview by author. Tape recording, Pensacola, FL, 16 August 1996.

Brabham, Helen. Interview by author. Tape recording, Columbia, SC, 18 April 2002.

Brubaker, Lauren. Interview by author. Mitchellville, MD, 14 August 2004.

Bryan, G. McLeod. Interview by author. Tape recording, Winston Salem, NC, 8 August 2001.

Butts, Thomas. Interview by author. Tape recording, Monroeville, AL, 10 November 1999, 3 July 2001.

Campbell, Will D. Interview by author. Tape recording, Mt. Juliet, TN, 18 August 1995, 20 March 2001.

Davis, Rachel, and Raymond. Interview by author. Tape recording, Charleston, SC, 8 March 2003.

Edwards, George R. Interview by author. Tape recording, Louisville, KY, 8 August 2001; telephone, 23 March 2005.

Ellwanger, Joseph. Interview by author. Telephone, 29 December 2004, 5 February 2005.

Enfinger, Floyd. Interview by author. Tape recording, Fairhope, AL, 12 August 2001.

Finlator, W. W. Interview by author. Tape recording, Raleigh, NC, 12 May 1999, 16 July 2005, 19 October 2005.

Floyd, William Kirk. Interview by author. Online, 9 June 2012.

Frank, Travis. Interview by author. Online, 22 August 2015.

Garrison, Joel. Interview by author. West Memphis, AR, 9 March 1999. Online, 25 April 2012, 19 October 2017.

Gray, Duncan Montgomery. Interview by author. Jackson, MS, 21 July 2007; telephone, 9 August 2004, 16 December 2004, 17 December 2006.

Hall, Powell. Interview by author. Tape recording, Hermitage, TN, 1 June 1999.

Haugabook, C. G. Interview by author. Tape recording, Plains, GA, 17 January 2001.

Haynes, Dorise Turner. Interview by author. Telephone, 3 March 2012.

Hock, Robert L. Interview by author. Telephone, 8 June 2004.

Homrighausen, Edgar. Interview by author. Telephone, 31 January 2014.

Huffman, Edward and Normanda. Interview by author. Shelbyville, TN, 20 May 2001.

Jackson, Larry. Interview by author. Tape recording, Greenwood, SC, 20 April 2002.

Jackson, Rhett. Interview by author. Tape recording, Columbia, SC, 17 April 2002.

Jones, Dorcas. Interview by author. Chapel Hill, NC, 29 July 1999.

Keichline, Darwin. Interview by author. Telephone, 8 May 2012.

King, R. Edwin. Interview by author. Telephone, 23 November 2004; videotape, Medgar Evers College, Brooklyn, NY, 15 November 2004; telephone, 25 April 2005.

Lyles, John. Interview by author. Tape recording, Cornelius, NC, 24 April 2002.

Marmion, Doris Dissen. Interview by author. Louisville, KY, 8 August 2001.

McClain, Howard and Barbara. Interview by author. Tape recording, Chapin, SC, 14 November 1999, 17 April 2002.

McMillan, Nate. Interview by author. Tape recording, Orangeburg, SC, 10 July 2003; telephone, 30 November 2011.

McRae, Frank. Interview by author. Tape recording, Memphis, TN, 14 May 1999; telephone, 5
    November 2005, 1 May 2006.
Miller, Robert. Interview by author. Tape recording, Elizabethtown, NC, 17 July 1996.
Moffett, Thomas. Interview by author. Tape recording, Louisville, KY, 9 August 2001.
Moose, David. Interview by author. Tape recording, West Memphis, AR, 9 March 1999.
Morris, John. Interview by author. Tape recording, Augusta, GA, 15 August 2001.
Napier, Denson. Interview by author. Tape recording, Jackson, MS, 6 April 2000.
Ogden, Dunbar, III. Interview by author. Tape recording, Berkeley, CA, 25 September 1999.
Ramsey. Brooks. Interview by author. Tape recording, Memphis, TN, 10 March 1999; telephone,
    31 October 2006.
Reese, Fred. Interview by author. Tape recording, Linville Falls, NC, 15 November 1999.
Rice, Sherrard. Interview by author. Tape recording, Columbia, SC, 21 February 2000.
Sanderson, Joseph. Interview by author. Tape recording, Guntersville, AL, 16 November 1995.
Schroerlucke, Gilbert. Interview by author. Tape recording, Louisville, KY, 9 August 2001.
Selah, W. B., Jr. Interview by author. Huntsville, AL, 16 May 1999.
Sellers, Ennis G. Interview by author. Tape recording, Mobile, AL, 3 July 1997.
Seymour, Robert. Interview by author. Tape recording, Chapel Hill, NC, 14 March 2001.
Smith, Sylvia. Interview by author. Stamford, CT, 16 February 2012.
Snider, Eric, and five students from Clinton High School, TN (Sierra Cotham, Cierra Davis,
    DeMarea Whitt, J'Quan Thomas, Kristopher Morrow). Interview by author. Telephone, 11
    November 2015, 4 December 2015, 6 January 2016.
Taylor, Eben. Interview by author. Telephone, 29 January 2003.
Taylor, J. Randolph. Interview by author. Tape recording, Montreat, NC, 7 October 2001.
Tonkel, Keith. Interview by author. Tape recording, North Jackson, MS, 5 April 2000.
Tucker, Grayson. Interview by author. Telephone, 22 July 2004, 1 March 2005.
Turnipseed, S. Andrew, Sr. Interview by author. Telephone, 5 July 1995.
Turnipseed, Spencer Andrew, Jr. Interview by author. Tape recording, Montgomery, AL, 16
    January 2001.
Voigt, Arnold. Interview by author. Telephone, 11 January 2014, 1 February 2014.
Webster, Al. Interview by author. Videotape, Buford, GA, 19 May 2003.
Webster, Charles A. Interview by author. Videotape, Buford, GA, 19 May 2003.
Whiting, Marvin. Interview by author. Tape recording, Birmingham, AL, 15 August 1994.
Wiggins, James. Interview by author. Online, 6 June 2015.
Williams, Miller. Interview by author. Fayetteville, AR, 8 March 1999, 13 February 2006.
Yeuell, H. Davis. Interview by author. Richmond, VA, 10 March 2003; telephone, 18 May 2005.
Ziehr, Richard O. Interview by author. Telephone, 29 December 2013.

Oral History Programs

Campbell, Will D. *An Oral History with Will D. Campbell*. Interview by Orley B. Caudill. McCain
    Library and Archives, University of Southern Mississippi. Hattiesburg, 8 June 1976.
Cunningham, William Jefferson. Interview by Orley B. Caudill. McCain Library and Archives.
    University of Southern Mississippi. Hattiesburg, 6 August 1981.
Seymour, Robert. Interview by Bruce Kalk. Southern Oral History Collection, Manuscripts
    Department, Wilson Library, University of North Carolina, Chapel Hill, 21 May 1985.

INDEX

Abernathy, Rev. Ralph D., 55, 78, 155; arrest of, 79

Abilene Christian College (Abilene Christian University), 216; apology, 218; first African American professor, Steven Moore, 219

Adkins, Rev. Carl, Mobile, AL, 59

African Americans: church doors closed to, 94–95; cooperatives in central Mississippi, 231; families in Clinton, TN, 15; Lutheran churches in Wilcox County, AL, 219; return to the South, 246–47; students from Presbyterian mission in the Congo, 91–92

Ahmann, Matthew, March on Washington, 114

Alabama Council on Human Relations, branch of the Southern Regional Council, 56, 203

Alabama Lutheran Academy, 21

Alabama National Guard, 39

Alabama State Baptist Convention, 195

Alabama State University, Montgomery, 55

Alabama–West Florida Conference of the Methodist Church, 41; resistance to civil rights, 56, 60, 202–3

Albany, GA: mass demonstrations, 74–77; outside ministers in, 77

Aldridge, Rev. John William, apology on MLK's death, 153

Alexander v. Holmes County Board of Education, 34, 48

Alford, Billy, on Episcopal apology, 208

Ali, Muhammad, 160, 180, 275n40

all deliberate speed, 12

Allen, Mayor Ivan, Jr., Atlanta, GA, 145

Allen, Rev. Michael, St. Mark's Episcopal Church, NYC, at Selma, AL, 131

Allin, Bishop John Maury, Episcopal Church, 207, 226–27, 284n41, 288n98

Alvis, Rev. Joel, 209

American Baptist Churches, 195

American Civil Liberties Union (ACLU), goals in 1969, 280n42

American Federation of State, County, and Municipal Employees (AFSCME), 149

American Friends Service Committee, 46

American Lutheran Church (ALC), 58

American Medical Association report on Mississippi, 1963, 99

Amite County, MS, 25, 193

Ammerman, Nancy Tatom, 225, 237

Amon, Al, attacks on, Chapel Hill, NC, 124

Anderson, Rev. H. George: as bishop of the Evangelical Lutheran Church of America (ELCA), 224, 287n86; as founder of "Displaced Pastors," 223; at Lutheran Theological Seminary, Columbia, SC, 223–24

Anderson, Marion, 111, 245

Anderson, William G., Albany, GA, 74, 75

apologies for slavery and segregation: Churches of Christ, 218; Episcopal Church, 208; Methodist General Conference, 205; Southern Baptist Convention, 196

Are All White Men Israelites? (Fitch), 180

Argue, Rev. Don, National Association of Evangelicals, apology, 231

Arkansas Agricultural, Mechanical, and Normal College, 23

Arkansas Council on Human Relations, 24

Arkansas Gazette, 23

Arkansas National Guard, 20–22

Arkansas Society for Racial Unity, 189

Assemblies of God, 231

Associate Reformed Presbyterian Church (ARPC), 212

Association for the Preservation of Southern Traditions, and other white supremacist groups, 64

At the River I Stand (documentary), 165–66

Atlanta Constitution, 117

Printed in the United States
By Bookmasters